The Ultimate Algorithmic Trading System Toolbox

The Wiley Trading series features books by traders who have survived the market's ever changing temperament and have prospered—some by reinventing systems, others by getting back to basics. Whether a novice trader, professional, or somewhere in between, these books will provide the advice and strategies needed to prosper today and well into the future. For more on this series, visit our website at www.WileyTrading.com.

Founded in 1807, John Wiley & Sons is the oldest independent publishing company in the United States. With offices in North America, Europe, Australia, and Asia, Wiley is globally committed to developing and marketing print and electronic products and services for our customers' professional and personal knowledge and understanding.

The Ultimate Algorithmic Trading System Toolbox

+ Website

Using Today's Technology to Help You Become a Better Trader

George Pruitt

WILEY

Published by John Wiley & Sons, Inc., Hoboken, New Jersey.

Published simultaneously in Canada.

Library of Congress Cataloging-in-Publication Data:

Names: Pruitt, George, 1967- author.
Title: The ultimate algorithmic trading system toolbox + website : using today's technology to help you become a better trader/George Pruitt.
Description: Hoboken : Wiley, 2016. | Series: Wiley trading | Includes index.
Identifiers: LCCN 2016010889 (print) | LCCN 2016011196 (ebook) | ISBN 9781119096573 (hardback) | ISBN 9781119262961 (pdf) | ISBN 9781119262978 (epub)
Subjects: LCSH: Electronic trading of securities. | Investment analysis. | Futures. | BISAC: BUSINESS & ECONOMICS/Finance.
Classification: LCC HG4515.95 .P788 2016 (print) | LCC HG4515.95 (ebook) | DDC 332.640285/4678—dc23
LC record available at http://lccn.loc.gov/2016010889

Cover Design: Wiley
Cover Images: © agsandrew/Shutterstock

Printed in the United States of America.

10 9 8 7 6 5 4 3 2 1

CONTENTS

About the author		**ix**
Introduction to the Ultimate Algorithmic Trading Systems Toolbox		**xiii**
CHAPTER 1	**Introduction to Trading: Algorithm Development**	**1**
	What Is an Algorithm?	1
	How to Get My Trading Idea into Pseudocode	12
	Summary	23
CHAPTER 2	**Stochastics and Averages and RSI! Oh, My!**	**25**
	Oscillators	26
	Price-Based Indicators	58
	Summary	75
CHAPTER 3	**Complete Trading Algorithms**	**77**
	Trend-Trading Battle Royale	86
	Portfolio Composition	100
	Multi-Algorithm Strategy (MAS)	108
	Summary	112
CHAPTER 4	**Introduction to AmiBroker's AFL**	**113**
	Quick Start	113
	Price Bar Interface	118

AFL Array Programming 120
Syntax 129
AFL Wizard 133
AmiBroker Loop Programming 139
Summary 140

CHAPTER 5 **Using Microsoft Excel to Backtest Your Algorithm** **145**
VBA Functions and Subroutines 147
Data 148
Software Structure 149
Programming Environment 154
Summary 163

CHAPTER 6 **Using Python to Backtest Your Algorithm** **167**
Why Python? 167
Python Installation 169
PSB Installation 169
PSB Structure 171
Getting Down to Business 193
Summary 202

CHAPTER 7 **An Introduction to EasyLanguage** **203**
TradeStation IDE 204
Syntax 209
Samples of EasyLanguage 221
Summary 224

CHAPTER 8 **Genetic Optimization, Walk Forward, and Monte Carlo Start Trade Analysis** **227**
Utilizing TradeStation and AmiBroker 227
Computers, Evolution, and Problem Solving 230
Population 231
Initial Population Setup Using VBA Excel 232
Testing Fitness of Chromosomes Using VBA Excel 232
Selection 233

Reproduction 238

Mutation 240

Using Genetic Algorithms in Trading System Development 243

Preventing Over-Curve-Fitting 247

Walk-Forward Optimizer: Is It Worth the Extra Work and Time? 249

Monte Carlo Analysis 258

Start Trade Drawdown 264

Summary 269

CHAPTER 9 An Introduction to Portfolio Maestro, Money Management, and Portfolio Analysis 271

Fixed Fractional 272

Portfolio Maestro 272

Summary 290

APPENDIX A AmiBroker 293

Keywords 293

Flow Control Structures 294

Functions 295

Utilizing Exploration for Debugging 295

Position Sizing in Futures Mode 298

APPENDIX B Excel System Backtester 301

Data Arrays 301

Keywords 302

Functions and Subroutines 302

APPENDIX C Python System Backtester 309

Data Arrays or Lists 309

Keywords and Identifiers 310

Classes 310

Indicator Classes and Functions 315

Python-Specific Keywords 320

APPENDIX D **TradeStation and EasyLanguage** **323**
Importing ELD file from Book Website 323
Keywords and Functions 324
Sample Algorithm Codes 325

APPENDIX E **335**

About the Companion Website **337**

Index **339**

ABOUT THE AUTHOR

It was March of 1989 as I drove my beat-up Dodge up Hillside Rd. in Hendersonville, NC. In an attempt to pay for my last semesters of college I was answering a classified ad that was looking to hire a computer programmer. As I drove up the thin drive I passed several houses and then through a gate attached to two large stone pillars. I stopped the car and looked down at the ad again to make sure I was at the right place. I proceeded down the country lane and the view opened up into a large meadow. At the end of the lane was a circular drive and large farm house. As I circled and went back down the road I thought to myself I must have the wrong address or directions. So I followed the small road back down the main highway and then to a small convenient store. Once there I asked myself again what type of business was this Futures Truth and if I should call and get directions or just simply forget about it. Curiosity and the need for money were too much so I used the store's pay phone and called the number once again.

"Hello—Futures Truth, may I help you?" a lady's voice answered.

"Yes, this is George Pruitt and I made an appointment for an interview but I can't seem to find your office."

"Do you drive a red Dodge?" she asked.

"Yes I do. How did you know?"

"We saw you drive right by the office. When you come through the two stone pillars turn immediately to the left. Don't go all the way down the drive—that's the owner's house."

So I follow the directions and find myself in front of a small house. I knock on the door and John Fisher opens and invites me in. We go through the normal Q and A for a job interview and he finally asks if I knew FORTRAN. My first college programming class was FORTRAN so I confidently answered, "Sure!"

He then asked me if I knew anything about the Futures market. I vaguely remembered the term from one of my economics classes and of course from the Eddie Murphy movie and answer him with the question, "You mean like Trading Places with Eddie Murphy?"

John Fisher said "Sort of like that—yes."

He went on to explain how Futures Truth tried to determine market direction in the most widely traded futures contracts by using trading systems. The trading systems were programmed in FORTRAN and they needed help with the programming. In addition to trading they also published a newsletter in which they tracked publicly offered trading systems.

I asked, "Do people really buy these programs?"

John Fisher said yes and by that time an older gentlemen walked into the office and stated that he had spent thousands of dollars on these programs and was ultimately ripped off. John Hill stated this was the main reason he started Futures Truth. He wanted to bring truth to the trading system industry. Both Johns told me that most traders couldn't afford to validate the trading systems because of the cost of the computer equipment, data, and software. John Fisher pointed to the computer he was working on and asked, "How much do you think this Macintosh II cost?"

I answered him, "I am not that familiar with Macs but I know they aren't cheap."

My mouth fell open when he said "$4,000 and we have three of them." Remember this was way back in 1989 when computers were not cheap.

I was thinking to myself that they got ripped off because they could have got a much cheaper and better computer with the IBM PS/2. And what was up with using FORTRAN? Did they not know "C" was the new programming language of the 1990s? John Fisher chose the Apple Macintosh because of its easy-to-use graphical user interface (GUI) and FORTRAN because many traders and hobbyist programmers had knowledge of this language.

John Fisher also said that he and John Hill had developed what they considered the best testing platform, "Excalibur." This platform could load decades of daily and intraday data and test any trading idea that could be defined in an algorithmic form. He also said the only thing that was missing was a charting application and that was where they also needed help.

I explained that I would be wrapping up my degree after summer and both Johns agreed that I could work part time in the evening until I graduated and then we could go from there.

Well that was 27 years ago and I did work part time until I graduated with a degree in computer science from the University of North Carolina at Asheville. The "Excalibur Chart" project turned into my senior project, which blew my professors away. Over the years I have worked with many trading firms in the development of trading algorithms and testing platforms. I have seen it all and have had the great pleasure to be educated by some of the greatest minds in the industry, including John Fisher, John Hill Sr. and John Hill Jr. Even with this experience and education the ultimate trading system still eludes me. As John Hill has stated many times, "A speculator who dies rich, dies before his time!" This may be true, but I have seen traders make millions, lose millions, and make millions again. The one thing they always do when they fail is get right back up, dust themselves off, and start searching for the next great trading algorithm.

INTRODUCTION TO THE ULTIMATE ALGORITHMIC TRADING SYSTEMS TOOLBOX

If you want to learn more about high-frequency trading utilizing special order placement/replacement algorithms such as Predatory trading, Pinging, Point of Presence, or Liquidity Rebates, then this book is not for you. However, if you want to learn about trading algorithms that help make a trading decision, trade size, money management, and the software used to create these algorithms, then you're in the right place.

This book is designed to teach trading algorithm development, testing, and optimization. Another goal is to expose the reader to multiple testing platforms and programming languages. Don't worry if you don't have a background in programming; this book will provide enough instruction to get you started in developing your own trading systems. Source code and instructions will be provided for TradeStation's EasyLanguage, AmiBroker's AFL, and my own Python and Excel testing engines. I chose these platforms because they give a nice overview of different scripting languages and trading platforms. Users of different testing/trading platforms may criticize my decision to use just these platforms, but the EasyLanguage source code that will be provided can be easily ported into Multi-Charts, and AmiBroker's unique and powerful platform provides a complete trading solution. My Python and Excel software, including all source code, are included on the associated website as well as the EasyLanguage and AFL source code for the other platforms. I didn't include the use of Python's scientific libraries, NumPy or SciPy, because I wanted to keep things as simple as possible. Also I used the bare-bones IDLE (Python's own simple Integrated Development Environment) to cut down on the learning curve—I wanted to get to the bare essentials of Python without muddying the water with a sophisticated IDE. Many successful Quants utilize **R** (a GNU project for statistical computing), but again to keep things simple I stuck with the easy-to-learn Python. The majority, if not all algorithms were tested utilizing commodity and futures data only. All the testing platforms in the book can be used to test stocks and ETFs, and all the included trading algorithms can be applied to these assets as well. Stock and ETF data is very simple to acquire. Getting commodity and futures data in an easily usable format is a little more difficult. Deep histories for commodity and futures can be acquired for as little as $100 from Pinnacle Data. I have used CSI data since the late 1980s and it is the data I used for a good portion of the testing carried out in the book. I would definitely take a look at Pinnacle and CSI data, especially if you wanted your database updated daily. If you are not familiar with Quandl, then you might want to take the time to do so. Quandl is a search engine for numerical data. I was pleasantly surprised to find a free continuous futures database (Wiki Continuous Futures) on Quandl. Keep in mind this data is free and is no way as good as premium data such as CSI and Pinnalce—it is missing multiple days and data points and the continuous data is simply created by concatenating data from individual contracts. The gaps between contracts are included, which cannot be utilized on any testing platform. In real life, a futures position is "rolled-over" from one contract to another by liquidating the front-month position and initiating the same position in the next contract. This "rollover" trade eliminates the gap. I have written a Python application that takes the Wiki Futures data and creates a back-adjusted continuous contract that can be imported into the Python and Excel System Back Tester software. Since I needed the data to do testing, I have also included a 10-plus-year ASCII back-adjusted futures database for 30-plus markets on the companion website. Directions on how to use the software and download futures data from Quandl are included along with the software.

The one thing I really wanted to include in this book was the "Holy Grail" of algorithmic trading systems. I have analyzed many algorithms that claimed to be the Grail, but after rigorous testing they failed to break even. So go ahead and check this off your list. Even though the "Holy Grail" will remain hidden you will find the following:

- Twenty-seven years of experience working with non-programmers in the development of their own trading algorithms
- The tools or building blocks that are used most often in the development cycle
- The core trading models that make up the majority of publicly offered trading systems
- The most important and simplest programming techniques to transform a non-quant into a not-so-non-quant

- Simple examples and explanations of complex trading ideas such as Walk Forward and Genetic Optimization and Monte Carlo simulation
- A complete toolbox to help algorithm development from idea to a finished tradable solution

The majority of successful trading algorithms utilize quantitative analysis (QA). QA is simply the application of mathematical formulae to a financial time series. This book will solely focus on this type of analysis in the design of trading algorithms. Fundamental analysis, which is used in many trading plans, will be used, too, but it will be reduced and simplified into a pure and easily digestible data format. Fundamental data is huge and diverse and in many cases market movement reacts to it in an unpredictable manner. A good example that I have dealt with for many years is the monthly unemployment report. At the time of the writing of this book unemployment has been on a downward trend, which is usually a bullish indicator for the stock market. However, with interest rates at the time being close to 0% the market could react opposite due to the fear of the Federal Reserve doing away with quantitative easing and raising rates. This type of fundamental analysis requires many different inputs and trying to reduce it down to something testable is nearly impossible.

Quantitative analysis focuses on just the data included in a chart. Price action and price translations are easily definable and therefore can be tested. The ability to test and evaluate a trading algorithm is a tremendous tool as it shows how a model can accurately map a market's behavior. If you can interpret a market's behavior, you can take advantage of its inefficiencies. If an algorithm has been capable of exploiting a market's inefficiencies on a historic basis, then there is a possibility it will do so in the future. This hope of future performance is the only leg an algorithmic trader has to stand upon. We all know historic performance is not necessarily an indicator of future results, but what else do we have? An algorithmic trader who quickly defines and tests his system and immediately takes a leap of faith because the historic performance looks great is doomed. Doesn't this contradict what I just said about historical performance being a system trader's only gauge of quality? A good trading algorithm not only demonstrates profitability but also robustness. Robustness is an expression of how well a trading system performs on diverse markets and diverse market conditions. An algorithm can be improved to a point where the trader can feel somewhat confident putting on those first few trades as well as continuing to put trades on after a losing streak. Improving an algorithm is not simply tweaking it until the historic results look utterly fantastic (aka curve fitting); it is taking the time to learn and work with tools that are designed to make a trading algorithm fail. That's the ultimate objective—making your trading algorithm fail before any money is put on the line. Remember the absence of failure is success and if your algorithm survives the brutal gauntlet of in depth analysis, then you know you might, just *might* have a winner.

This book starts out simple in Chapter 1 with the definition and examples of algorithms. The chapter is a little longwinded but I know that the inability to put a trading idea onto paper and then into pseudocode and finally actual computer code is the biggest stumbling block for traders who want to test their own trading ideas. All trading algorithms that are reducible to a set of instructions can be properly programmed using one of two different modeling methods or paradigms. These two paradigms, Finite State Machine and Flow Chart, are fully discussed and utilized to translate written descriptions first into diagrams and then into actual pseudocode. The diagrammatic approach as well as the simple pseudocode language used to formulate trading algorithms is introduced in this chapter. It doesn't matter how sophisticated your testing software is if you can't define a testable algorithm and this chapter shows you how to do so.

Chapter 2 may be a refresher for those who are familiar with the basic building blocks of trading algorithms, indicators; however, the chapter not only explains the logic behind the indicators but shows how they can be incorporated into complete entry and exit techniques. Diagrams and pseudocode are carried on through this chapter to aid in the understanding of each indicator, its purpose, and its place in a trading algorithm. In addition, the first look at indicator-based trading algorithm performance is presented as well.

Chapter 3 introduces complete trading algorithms and their associated historical performance. Most, if not all, testing was performed on historical commodity/futures data. This data gave rise to the concept of systematic trading more than 50 years ago. Now this doesn't mean the ideas aren't transferable to the stock market. In most cases they are. However, I stuck with commodity data because that is where my expertise lies. The complete pseudocode and actual computer code of these algorithms are revealed as well. The key metrics for determining algorithm robustness are explained and utilized in the evaluation of the algorithms' results.

Chapter 4 starts the section that highlights different testing/trading software platforms that can either be purchased or leased. AmiBroker is introduced in this chapter and the most important components of a trading platform are highlighted: integrated development environment and its associated scripting/programming language, individual market and portfolio testing, and algorithm performance metrics. These components are then highlighted again in Chapter 5 with VBA for Excel, Chapter 6 with Python, and finally Chapter 7 with TradeStation.

Chapter 8 delves into the concepts of Genetic and Walk Forward Optimization, Walk Forward Analysis, and Monte Carlo simulation. A genetic optimizer is built using VBA and used to help explain the ideas of synthesizing computers with biology. The core concepts of Genetic Algorithms, fitness, selection, reproduction, and mutation are fully explained and illustrated utilizing Excel. Artificial intelligence is here to stay in the study of trading algorithms and this chapter tries to pull back the veil of mystery and show how these tools should be used, and in some cases, must be used to develop that elusive robustness. Along these lines, Machine Learning has become a very highly discussed and somewhat controversial topic in today's trading. Also "Big Data" analysis has found its way to the front as well. These topics are highly advanced and I felt beyond the scope of this book. I can state I have worked with the algorithms that were derived with machine-only input and they have stood the test of time.

A trading algorithm must work over a diverse portfolio of markets before it can be sufficiently considered useful and robust. Chapter 9 utilizes the portfolio-level testing capabilities of TradeStation and AmiBroker to demonstrate different money and portfolio management techniques. The Fixed Fractional approach, by far the most popular, will be highlighted.

The complete source code for the Python System Back Tester is included on the website. Python is the new language of many a quant and the source shows how the language can be used to develop a simple, yet powerful, back tester. Important language concepts and syntax are used to open ASCII files, and import the data into a LIST data structure, create classes and modules, and loop through the entire database while applying a trading algorithm. All the parts of building a testing platform are revealed in the source code, including Monte Carlo and Start Trade Drawdown simulation.

Most traders have Microsoft Excel on their computers and the complete source for a more simplified version of the Python back tester using VBA is included on the website as well.

This book is a toolbox and a guide and touches upon many different facets of algorithmic trading. As with any toolbox it will take time and effort to apply the tools found within to replicate the trader's ideas in a form that not only can be tested and evaluated but fully implemented.

CHAPTER 1

Introduction to Trading

Algorithm Development

What Is an Algorithm?

> *An Algorithm is an effective procedure, a way of getting something done in a finite number of discrete steps.*
>
> David Berlinski

Berlinski's definition is exactly right on the money. The word *algorithm* sounds mysterious as well as intellectual but it's really a fancy name for a recipe. It explains precisely the stuff and steps necessary to accomplish a task. Even though you can perceive an algorithm to be a simple recipe, it must, like all things dealing with computers, follow specific criteria:

1. *Input:* There are zero or more quantities that are externally supplied.
2. *Output:* At least one quantity is produced.
3. *Definiteness:* Each instruction must be clear and unambiguous.
4. *Finiteness:* If we trace out the instructions of an algorithm, then for all cases the algorithm will terminate after a finite number of steps.

5. *Effectiveness:* Every instruction must be sufficiently basic that it can in principle be carried out by a person using only pencil and paper. It is not enough that each operation be definite as in (3), but it must also be feasible. [*Fundamentals of Data Structures*: Ellis Horowitz and Sartaj Sahni 1976; Computer Science Press]

These criteria are very precise because they can be universally applied to any type of problem. Don't be turned off thinking this is going to be another computer science text, because even though the criteria of an algorithm seem to be very formal, an algorithm really is straightforward and quite eloquent. It is basically a guide that one must follow to convert a problem into something a computer can solve. Anybody can design an algorithm following these criteria with pencil and paper. The only prerequisite is that you must think like a Vulcan from *Star Trek*. In other words, think in logical terms by breaking ideas down into rudimentary building blocks. This is the first step—translation of idea into an algorithm. It takes practice to do this, and this is in part why programming can be difficult.

Another thing that makes programming difficult is understanding a computer language's syntax. Most people who have been exposed to a programming or scripting language at one time or another in their lives have probably exclaimed something like, "I forgot one stupid semicolon and the entire program crashed! Isn't the computer smart enough to know that? *Arrgh!* I will never be a computer programmer!" The question that is proffered in this temper tantrum is the question of the computer's intelligence. Computers are not smart—they only do what we tell them. It doesn't matter if you spend $500 or $5,000 on the hardware. They do things very quickly and accurately, but their intelligence is a reflection of their programmer's ability to translate idea into algorithmic form and then into proper syntax.

Algorithmic (algo) traders don't necessarily need to be programmers, but they must understand what a computer needs to know to carry out a trading signal, position sizing, and money management. If you can create an algorithm, then you are more than 50 percent there. I say more than 50 percent because most traders will utilize trading software and its associated programming or scripting language. Learning the syntax of a scripting language or a small subset of a programming dialect is much easier than learning an entire programming language like C# or C++. An algo trader only needs to be concerned with the necessary tools to carry out a trading system. The developers of EasyLanguage, AmiBroker, or TradersStudio's main objective was to provide only the necessary tools to put a trading idea into action. They accomplished this by creating a vast library of trading functions, easy access to these functions, and a simplified programming syntax. Now if you want to develop your own testing platform and want to use a full-blown programming language to do so, then you will need to know the language inside-out. If you are interested in doing this, Chapters 5 and 6 will give you a head start. In these chapters, I show how I developed testing platforms in Python and Microsoft VBA from scratch.

However, at this introductory stage, let's take a look at a very simple trading algorithm and the possible exchange between a computer and trader. Pretend a trader wants to develop and test a simple moving-average crossover system and wants to use software specifically designed for system testing. Let's call this first trader AlgoTrader1, and since he has used this particular testing platform he knows it understands a trading vernacular and provides access to the common indicator functions and data. Box 1.1 shows a possible exchange between trader and computer.

Box 1.1 Algo Testing Software

```
AlgoTrader1 - AlgoTester ON
Computer - AlgoTester ready
AlgoTrader1 - load crude oil futures data
Computer - data loaded
AlgoTrader1 - buy whenever close is above moving average
Computer - "moving average" function requires three inputs
AlgoTrader1 - help with moving average function
Computer - function calculates simple, weighted, exponential average
Computer - function syntax moving average (type, price, length)
AlgoTrader1 - buy whenever close is above moving average
  (simple,close,21)
Computer - command completed
AlgoTrader1 -short whenever close is below moving average
  (simple,close,21)
Computer - command completed
AlgoTrader1 - save algorithm as MovAvgCross
Computer - command completed
AlgoTrader1 - run MovAvgCross algorithm
Computer - run completed and results are:
  $12,040 profit, $8,500 draw down, $1,200 avg. win

AlgoTrader1 - load euro currency data
Computer - command completed
AlgoTrader2 - run MovAvgCross algorithm
Computer - run completed and results are:
  -$32,090 profit, $40,000 draw down, $400 avg. win

AlgoTrader1 - edit MovAvgCross algorithm
Computer - command completed
AlgoTrader2 - edit moving average function
Computer - command completed
AlgoTrader2 - change length input to 30
Computer - command completed
AlgoTrader2 - run MovAvgCross algorithm
Computer - run completed and blah blah blah
```

As you can see, the computer had to be somewhat spoon-fed the instructions. The software recognized many keywords such as: **load**, **buy**, **short**, **run**, **edit**, **change**, and **save**. It also recognized the moving average function and was able to provide information on how to properly use it. The trading algorithm is now stored in the computer's library and will be accessible in the future.

This simple exchange between computer and AlgoTrader1 doesn't reveal all the computations or processes going on behind the scene. Loading and understanding the data, applying the algorithm properly, keeping track of the trades, and, finally, calculating all of the performance metrics did not involve any interaction with the trader. All this programming was done ahead of time and was hidden from the trader and this allows an algo trader to be creative without being bogged down in all the minutiae of a testing platform.

Even though the computer can do all these things seamlessly it still needed to be told exactly what to do. This scenario is similar to a parent instructing a child on how to do his first long-division problem. A child attempting long division probably knows how to add, subtract, multiply, and divide. However, even with these "built-in" tools, a child needs a list of exact instructions to complete a problem. An extended vocabulary or a large library of built-in functions saves a lot of time, but it doesn't necessarily make the computer any smarter. This is an example of knowledge versus intelligence—all the knowledge in the world will not necessarily help solve a complex problem. To make a long story short, think like a computer or child when developing and describing a trading algorithm. Box 1.2 shows an algorithmic representation of the long-division process to illustrate how even a simple process can seem complicated when it is broken down into steps.

Box 1.2 Procedure for Long Division

Suppose you are dividing two large numbers in the problem $n \div m$. In this example, the dividend is n and the divisor is m.

If the divisor is not a whole number, simplify the problem by moving the decimal of the divisor until it is to the right of the last digit. Then, move the decimal of the dividend the same number of places. If you run out of digits in the dividend, add zeroes as placeholders.

When doing long division, the numbers above and below the tableau should be vertically aligned.

Now you are ready to divide. Look at the first digit of the dividend. If the divisor can go into that number at least once, write the total number of times it fits completely above the tableau. If the divisor is too big, move to the next digit of the dividend, so you are looking at a two-digit number. Do this until the divisor will go into the dividend at least once. Write the number of times the divisor can go into the dividend above the tableau. This is the first number of your quotient.

Multiply the divisor by the first number of the quotient and write the product under the dividend, lining the digits up appropriately. Subtract the product from the dividend. Then, bring the next digit from the quotient down to the right of the difference. Determine how many times the divisor can go into that number, and write it above the tableau as the next number of the quotient.

Repeat this process until there are no fully divisible numbers left. The number remaining at the bottom of the subtraction under the tableau is the remainder. To finish the problem, bring the remainder, r, to the top of the tableau and create a fraction, r/m.

A few years ago a client came to me with the following trading system description and hired me to program it. Before reading the description, see if you can see any problems the programmer (me) or a computer might encounter before the directives can be properly carried out.

> Buy when the market closes above the 200-day moving average and then starts to trend downward and the RSI bottoms out below 20 and starts moving up. The sell short side is just the opposite.

Did you see the problems with this description? Try instructing a computer to follow these directions. It doesn't matter if a computer has a vast library of trading functions; it still would not understand these instructions. The good news was, the trader did define two conditions precisely: close greater than 200-day moving average and relative strength index (RSI) below 20. The rest of the instructions were open to interpretation. What does *trending downward* or *bottoming out* mean? Humans can interpret this, but the computer has no idea what you are talking about. I was finally able, after a couple of phone calls, to discern enough information from the client to create some pseudocode. *Pseudocode* is an informal high-level description of the operating principle of a computer program or algorithm. Think of it as the bridge between a native language description and quasi-syntactically correct code that a computer can understand. Translating an idea into pseudocode is like converting a nebulous idea into something with structure. Here is the pseudocode of the client's initial trading idea:

Algorithm Pseudocode

```
if close > 200 day moving average and
close < close[1] and close [1] < close [2] and
close[2] < close[3] and yesterday's 14 day RSI < 20 and
yesterday's 14 day RSI < today's 14 day RSI then BUY
```

If this looks like Latin (and you don't know Latin), don't worry about it. The [1] in the code just represents the number of bars back. So close [2] represents the close price prior to yesterday. If you are not familiar with RSI, you will be after Chapter 2. By the time you are through with this book you will be able to translate this into English, Python, EasyLanguage, AmiBroker, or Excel VBA. Here it is in English.

> If today's close is greater than the 200-day moving average of closing prices and today's close is less than yesterday's close and yesterday's close is less than the prior day's close and the prior day's close is less than the day before that and the 14-day RSI of yesterday is less than 20 and the 14-day RSI of yesterday is less than the 14-day RSI of today, then buy at the market.

Notice how the words *downward* and *bottoming out* were removed and replaced with exact descriptions:

downward: today's close is less than yesterday's close and yesterday's close is less than the prior day's close and the prior day's close is less than the day before. The market has closed down for three straight days.

bottoming out: the 14-day RSI of yesterday is less than 20 and the 14-day RSI of yesterday is less than the 14-day RSI of today. The RSI value ticked below 20 and then ticked up.

Also notice how the new description of the trading system is much longer than the original. This is a normal occurrence of the evolution of idea into an exact trading algorithm.

And now here it is in the Python programming language:

Actual Python Code

```
if myClose[D0] < sAverage(myClose,200,D0,1) and
  myClose[D0] < myClose[D1] and myClose[D2] < myClose[D3] and
  myClose[D1] < myClose[D2] and rsiVal[D1] < 20 and rsiVal[D1]
  < rsiVal[D0]:
    buyEntryName = 'rsiBuy'
    entryPrice = myOpen
```

Don't get bogged down trying to understand exactly what is going on; just notice the similarity between pseudo and actual code. Now this is something the computer can sink its teeth into. Unfortunately, reducing a trading idea down to pseudocode is as difficult as programming it into a testing platform. The transformation from a trader to an algo trader is very difficult and in some cases cannot be accomplished. I have worked with many clients who simply could not reduce what they saw on a chart into concise step-by-step instructions. In other cases the reduction of a trading idea removes enough of the trader's nuances that it turned something that seemed plausible into something that wasn't.

It goes without saying that if you don't have an algorithm, then all the software in the world will not make you a systematic trader. Either you have to design your own or you have to purchase somebody else's. Buying another person's technology is not a bad way to go, but unless the algorithm is fully disclosed you will not learn anything. However, you will be systematic trader. I have spent 27 years evaluating trading systems and have come across good and bad and really bad technology. I can say without a doubt that one single type of algorithm does not stand head and shoulders above all the others. I can also say without a doubt there isn't a correlation between the price of a trading system and its future profitability. The description in Box 1.3 is very similar to a system that sold for over $10,000 in the 1990s.

Box 1.3 Trading Algorithm Similar to One That Sold for $10K in the 1990s Description

Entry Logic:

If the 13-day moving average of closes > the 65-day moving average of closes and the 13-day moving average is rising and the 65-day moving average is rising then buy the next day's open

If the 13-day moving average of closes < the 65-day moving average of closes and the 13-day moving average is falling and the 65-day moving average is falling then sell the next day's open

Exit Logic:

If in a long position then
    set initial stop at the lowest low of the past 13 days
If in a short position then
    set initial stop at the highest high of the past 13 days
Once profit exceeds or matches $700 pull stops to break even

If in a long position use the greater of:
    Breakeven stop—if applicable
    Initial stop
    Lowest low of a moving window of the past 23 days
If in a short position use the lesser of:
    Breakeven stop—if applicable
    Initial stop
    Highest high of the moving window of the past 23 days

That is the entire system, and it did in fact sell for more than $10K. This boils down to a simple moving-average crossover system trading in the direction of the shorter- and longer-term trend. The description also includes a complete set of trade management rules: protective, breakeven, and trailing stop. This is a complete trading system description, but as thorough as it seems there are a couple of problems. The first is easy to fix because it involves syntax but the second involves logic. There are two words that describe market direction that cannot be interpreted by a computer. Do you see them? The two words in question are: *rising* and *falling*. Again, descriptive words like these have to be precisely defined. This initial problem is easy to fix—just inform the computer the exact meaning of *rising* and *falling*. Second, it has a weakness from a logical standpoint. The algorithm uses $700 as the profit level before the stop can be moved to break even. Seven hundred dollars in the 1990s is quite a bit different than it is today. The robustness of this logic could be dramatically improved by using a market-derived parameter. One could use a volatility measure like the average range of the past N-days. If the market exhibits a high level of volatility, then the profit objective is larger and the breakeven stop will take longer to get activated. You may ask, "Why is this beneficial?" Market noise is considered the same as volatility, and the more noise, the higher likelihood of wide market swings. If trading in this environment, you want to make sure you adjust your entries and exits so you stay outside the noise bands.

This algorithm was very successful in the 1980s and through a good portion the 1990s. However, its success has been hit-and-miss since. Is this algorithm worth $10K? If you were sitting back in 1993 and looked at the historical equity curve, you might say yes. With a testing platform, we can walk forward the algorithm, and apply it to the most recent data and see how it would have performed and then answer the question. This test was done and the answer came out to be an emphatic *no!*

Had you bought this system and stuck with it through the steep drawdowns that have occurred since the 1990s, you would have eventually made back your investment (although not many people would have stuck with it). And you would have learned the secret behind the system. Once the secret was revealed and your checking account was down the $10K, you might have been a little disappointed knowing that basic tenets of the system had been around for many years and freely disseminated in books and trade journals of that era. The system may not be all that great, but the structure of the algorithm is very clean and accomplishes the tasks necessary for a complete trading system.

The most time-consuming aspect when developing a complete trading idea is coming up with the trade entry. This seems somewhat like backward thinking because it's the exit that determines the success of the entry. Nonetheless, the lion's share of focus has always been on the entry. This system provides a very succinct trade entry algorithm. If you want to develop your own trading algorithm, then you must also provide the computer with logic just as precise and easy to interpret. Getting from the nebula of a trading idea to this point is not easy, but it is absolutely necessary. On past projects, I have provided the template shown in Box 1.4 to clients to help them write their own entry rules in a more easily understood form. You can download this form and a similar exit template at this book's companion website:www.wiley.com/go/ultimatealgotoolbox.

Box 1.4 Simple Template for Entry Rules

Long / Short Entries

Calculations and/or Indicators Involved (specify lookback period). Don't use ambiguously descriptive words like *rising*, *falling*, *flattening*, *topping* or *bottoming out*.

____

____

____

Buy Condition—What must happen for a long signal to be issued? List steps in chronological order. And remember, don't use ambiguously descriptive words like *rising*, *falling*, *flattening*, *topping*, or *bottoming out*.

____

____

____

Sell Condition—What must happen for a short signal to be issued? List steps in chronological order.

____

____

____

Here is one of the templates filled out by a one-time client:

Calculations and/or Indicators Involved (specify lookback period)

Bollinger Band with a 50-day lookback

Buy Condition—What must happen for a long signal to be issued? List steps in chronological order.

1. Close of yesterday is above 50-day upper Bollinger Band
2. Today's close < yesterday's close
3. Buy next morning's open

Sell Condition—What must happen for a short signal to be issued? List steps in chronological order.

1. Close of yesterday is below 50-day lower Bollinger Band
2. Today's close > yesterday's close
3. Sell next morning's open

The simple Bollinger Band system shown in Box 1.4 is seeking to buy after the upper Bollinger Band penetration is followed by a down close. The conditions must occur within one daily bar of each other. In other words, things must happen consecutively: the close of yesterday is > upper Bollinger Band and close of today < yesterday's close. The sell side of things uses just the opposite logic. The template for exiting a trade is very similar to that of entering. Box 1.5 contains a simple template for exit rules and shows what the client from Box 1.4 had completed for his strategy.

Box 1.5 Simple Template for Exit Rules

Exits

Calculations and/or Indicators Involved (specify lookback period). Don't use ambiguously descriptive words like *rising*, *falling*, *flattening*, *topping*, or *bottoming out*.

____

____

____

Long Liquidation Condition—What must happen to get out of a long position? List steps in chronological order.

____

____

____

Short Liquidation Condition—What must happen to get out of a short position? List steps in chronological order.

____

____

____

Calculations and/or Indicators Involved (specify lookback period)

Average true range (ATR) with a 10-day lookback

Moving average with a 50-day lookback

Long Liquidation Condition—What must happen to get out of a long position? List steps in chronological order.

1. Close of yesterday is less than entry price −3 ATR—get out on next open
2. Close of yesterday is less than 50-day moving average—get out on next open
3. Close of yesterday is greater than entry price +5 ATR—get out on next open

Short Liquidation Condition—What must happen to get out of a short position? List steps in chronological order.

1. Close of yesterday is greater than entry price +3 ATR—get out on next open
2. Close of yesterday is greater than 50-day moving average—get out on next open
3. Close of yesterday is less than entry price −5 ATR—get out on next open

There are three conditions that can get you out of a long position. Unlike the entry logic, the timing or sequence of the conditions do not matter. The exit algorithm gets you out on a volatility-based loss, a moving average–based loss/win, or a profit objective. The short liquidation criteria are just the opposite of the long liquidation criteria.

This is a complete, fully self-contained trend-following trading algorithm. It has everything the computer would need to execute the entries and exits. And it could be made fully automated; the computer could analyze the data and autoexecute the trading orders. Any platform such as AmiBroker, TradeStation, Ninja Trader, and even Excel could be used to autotrade this type of system. Any trading idea, if reduced to the exact steps, can be tested, evaluated, and autotraded. Once the programming code has been optimized, verified, validated, and installed on a trading platform, the trader can just let the system run hands off. This is the true beauty of algorithmic system trading: A computer can replicate a trader's ideas and follow them without any type of human emotion.

How to Get My Trading Idea into Pseudocode

The aforementioned template is a great way to get your ideas into written instructions. However, just like with great writing, it will take many revisions before you get to the pseudocode step. Over the years, I have discovered there are two different paradigms when describing or programming a trading system. The first is the easier to program and can be used to describe a system where events occur on a consecutive bar basis. For example: *Buy when today's close is greater than yesterday's and today's high is greater than yesterday's high and today's low is less than yesterday's low.* The other paradigm can be used to describe a trading system that needs things to happen in a sequence but not necessarily on a consecutive bar-by-bar basis. Unfortunately, the latter paradigm requires a heightened level of description and is more difficult to program. Many trading systems can fit inside a cookie-cutter design, but most traders are very creative, and so are their designs. Don't fret, though, because any idea that is reducible to a sequence of steps can be described and programmed.

The Tale of Two Paradigms

I have developed names for these two different models of describing/programming trading algorithms:

1. The variable bar liberal sequence paradigm
2. The consecutive bar exact sequence paradigm

The variable bar paradigm can provide a very robust algorithm and at the same time provide a nearly limitless expression of a trader's creativity. We will begin with this one since it is the less intuitive of the two. What you learn about the variable bar sequence will make shifting to the simpler consecutive bar sequence that much easier. The consecutive bar sequence can usually be programmed by using a single if-then construct. You can see this by referring to my earlier example:

> **If** today's close is greater than yesterday's close and today's high is greater than yesterday's high and today's low is less than yesterday's low, **then** buy at the market.

This paradigm is simple to explain, program, and deploy. There is nothing wrong with this and, remember, many times a simple approach or idea to trading the markets can deliver a very robust algorithm. Both paradigms will be exemplified in different algorithms through the rest of the book. All trading algorithms fall into

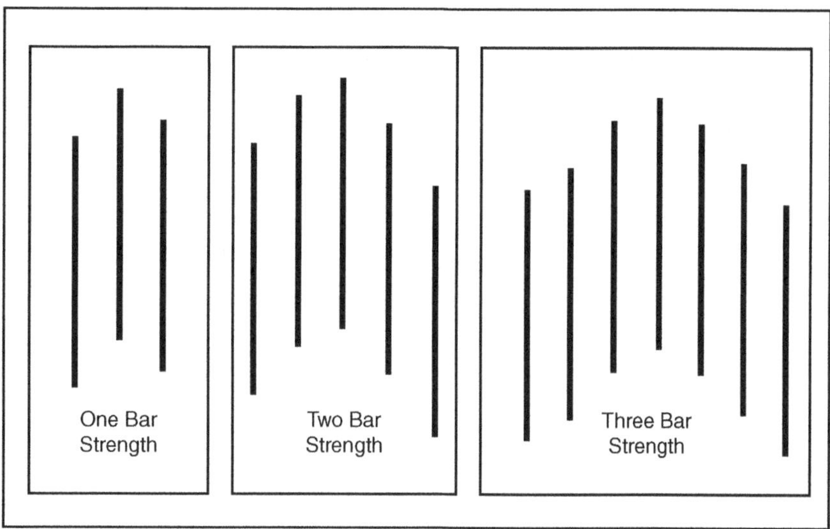

FIGURE 1.1 Examples of strength differences between pivot high points on daily bars.

either paradigm or across both, meaning that some systems require both approaches to be fully described and programmed. Most traders can easily describe and probably program a consecutive bar-type algorithm. However, traders that can't put their ideas into such a simple form and have had little or no programming experience have a more difficult time reducing their ideas into a formal description, not to mention pseudocode.

The Variable Bar Sequence Jumping headfirst into paradigm #1, the variable bar sequence, here is a somewhat creative design that incorporates pivot points and a sequence that can occur over a variable amount of days. For those of you who are not familiar with pivot points, Figure 1.1 shows different examples of pivot high points on daily bars and their differing strengths.

The strength of the pivot bar is based on the number of bars preceding and following the high bar. A two-bar pivot is simply a high bar with two bars before and after that have lower highs. The preceding/following highs do not necessarily have to be in a stairstep fashion. Here is our long entry signal description using step-by-step instructions.

Buy:

Step 1: Wait for a pivot high bar of strength 1 to appear on the chart and mark the high price.

Step 2: Wait for the first low price that is 2 percent lower than the high price marked in Step 1. If one occurs, move to Step 3. If the market moves above the high marked in Step 1, then go back to Step 1 and wait for another pivot high bar.

Step 3: Wait for another pivot high bar that exceeds the price in Step 1. Once a high bar pivot occurs that fits the criteria, mark the high price.

Step 4: Once the subsequent pivot high bar is found, then wait for another low price that is 2 percent below the high marked in Step 3. When a bar's low price fulfills the criteria buy that bar's close. If the market moves above the high marked in Step 3, then go back to Step 3 and wait for another pivot high bar. The new high that just occurred may turn out to be the pivot high bar that you are looking for in Step 3.

Additional notes: If 30 days transpire before proceeding from Step 1 to Step 4, then reset.

Figure 1.2 illustrates the sequence the above description is trying to capture. Ignore the state designations for now. They will become apparent in the following discussion.

It is easy to see the designer/trader of this entry signal is trying to buy after two pivot highs are separated and followed by a pullback of 2 percent. In addition, there are a couple of conditions that must also be met before a buy signal is triggered: (1) the second pivot high price must be higher than the first, and (2) the whole sequence must take less than 30 bars to complete. When a system allows its entry criteria to work across an unknown number of days or price levels, conditions must be used to keep the integrity of the entry signal and limit the duration of the sequence.

Since there is variability in the instruction set, the programming of this paradigm is definitely more difficult. However, as mentioned earlier, it is very doable. As a young

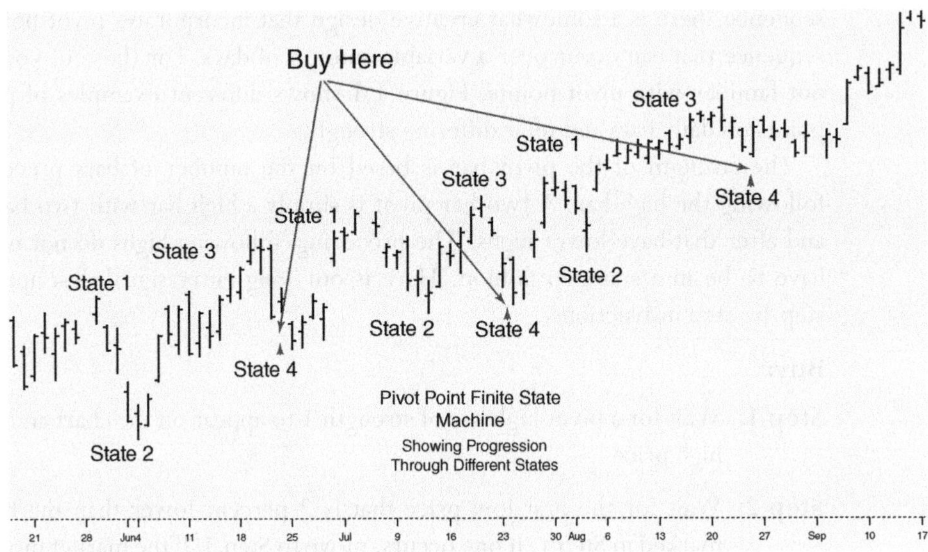

FIGURE 1.2 A depiction of the variable-bar sequence described by the long entry signal.

and inexperienced trading system programmer, I tried to program these variable sequences using a bunch of true/false Boolean flags. Box 1.6 shows an initial attempt using this method to describe the pivot point sequence. The flags are bolded so you can easily see how they are turned on and off. Comments are enclosed in brackets { }.

Box 1.6 Using Boolean Flags to Program a Trading Algorithm

```
HighPivotFound = High of yesterday > High of today and High
  of yesterday > High of two days ago
If HPivot1 = False and HighPivotFound then {first Pivot high found}
   HPivot1 = True
   HPivot1Price = high of yesterday
   HPivot1Cnt = currentBar

If HPivot1 = True and Low < HPivot1Price * 0.98 then
  {2% retracement after first Pivot high}
   LRetrace = True

If HPivot1 = True and LRetrace = False and High of today >
  HighPivot1Price then
   HPivot1Price = High of yesterday {another higher high but
     not a 2% retracement - start over}
   HPivot1Cnt = currentBar

If LRetrace = True and HighPivotFound and High of yesterday
  > HPivot1Price then
   HPivot2 = True {second Pivot high > first Pivot high and
     2% retracement between the two}
   HPivot2Price = High of yesterday

If HPivot2 = True and High of today > HPivot2Price then
   HPivot2Price = High of today {another higher high > second
     Pivot High - keep track of it}

If HPivot2 = True and Low < HPivot2Price * 0.98 then
   Buy this bar on close {Buy Order Placed - entry criteria
     has been met}
   HPivot1 = False {Start Over}
   LRetrace = False
   HPivot2 = False

HPivot1Cnt = HPivot1Cnt + 1
If HPivot1Cnt >= 30 then {reset all Boolean flags - start over}
   HPivot1 = False
   LRetrace = False
   HPivot2 = False
```

As you can see, the description using these flags is somewhat laborious and not that flexible. The flags have to have descriptive names so that the correct flag is being tested and subsequently turned on or off. In addition, all flags must eventually be turned off when either the HPivot1Cnt variable grows equal to or greater than 30 or a LONG position is established. This type of programming will work but isn't very eloquent. Good programmers don't like to use superfluous variable names and many lines of code to complete a task. And really good programmers like for others to easily read their code and comment on how clever the solution was to the problem. Eloquent code is precise and clever. So, after much trial and error as a young programmer, I finally realized that these types of trading algorithms (the paradigm #1 variety) were simply looking for an occurrence of a certain sequence or pattern in the data. When I say pattern, I don't mean a certain price pattern like a candlestick formation. As we have seen before, a trading algorithm is just a sequence of instructions. Remembering back to my compiler design class in college and how we had to write computer code to recognize certain tokens or words (patterns) in a string of characters I felt I could use the same model to program these types of systems, a universal model that could be molded to fit any trading system criteria. This model that programmers use to parse certain words from a large file of words is known as a finite state machine (FSM). The FSM concept is not as daunting as it sounds. If we translate the geek-speak, a FSM is simply a model of a system that shows the different possible states a system can reach and the transitions that move the system from one state to another. The machine starts at a START state and then moves methodically through several states by passing certain logical criteria and then arrives at an ACCEPT state.

Don't let this idea blow your mind because it is quite easy to understand and implement. Let's start off with a very simple FSM to illustrate its simplicity and eloquence. Think of a combination lock that can only be unlocked by inputting the following numbers: 6, 4, 2, 7, 5, and 1. Like most combination locks the numbers need to be inputted in the exact sequence described or the lock will not open. This lock is not very good because it lets you test to see if you have the right number before proceeding to the next input. So you plug in a number, test it, and either try again if it fails or move onto the next number if it is correct. Eventually, with time the correct combination will be inputted and the lock will open. Remember this is just a very simple example of something that can be modeled by a FSM. Without an illustration or diagram, most nonprogrammers could not design even this simple example. A picture is always worth a minimum of a thousand words and the easiest way to create an appropriate FSM is to create a diagram. The diagram in Figure 1.3 describes the FSM that models the combination lock.

The diagram is made up of circles, which represent the different **STATES** and connectors that show how the machine moves from one state to another. This FSM has a total of seven states that include a **START** and **ACCEPT** state. Pretend you are

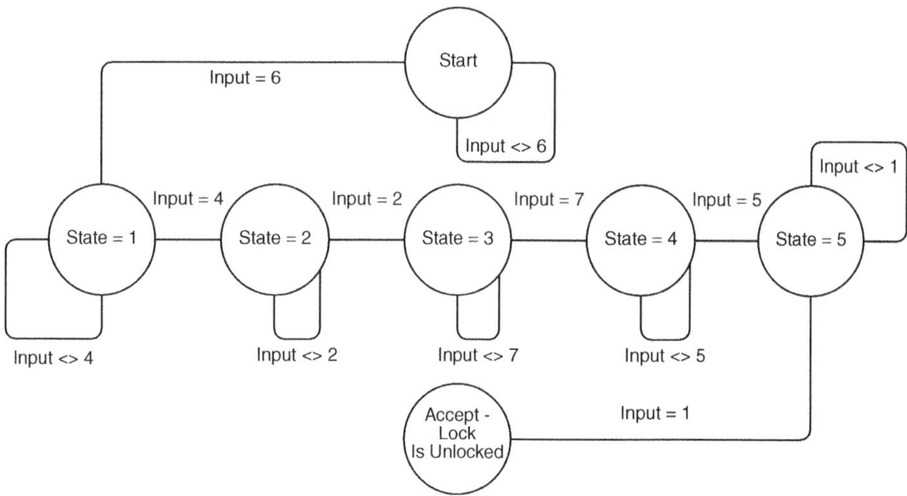

FIGURE 1.3 An FSM that models the workings of a combination lock.

sitting in front of a small screen and a numeric touchpad similar to one that is found on a cell phone, and it is prompting you to input a number from one to nine. At this point, the machine is set to the START state. If you get lucky right off the bat, you input the number six and the screen prompts you to input the second number. If you aren't lucky, it will ask you to re-input the first number in the combination. So following along with the diagram, you can see how the number six moves the machine from the START state to STATE 1. If the number six is not inputted, it moves right back to the START state. The machine moves along the paths visiting each STATE as long as the proper number is inputted. Notice you are not penalized if you don't input the proper number; the machine just sits in that particular state until the proper number is inputted.

In our pivot point example, there will also be a START and ACCEPT state. Refer back to the step-by-step instructions of the pivot point entry technique and visualize the steps as different states. The START (STEP 1) state will be assigned the value 0 and the ACCEPT (STEP 4) state will have the value 4. In between, the START and ACCEPT states will be three other states that the FSM can assume. These are intermediate states that must be achieved in sequential order. The START state tries to get the ball rolling and looks at every bar to see if a pivot high (of strength 1) has occurred. If one does, then the machine moves onto the next state, and then on to the next, and then on to the next, and then finally to the ACCEPT state. As soon as the FSM assumes the ACCEPT state, a buy order is placed at the market. The illustration in Figure 1.4 is the FSM diagram of our pivot-point long-entry algorithm.

This FSM diagram looks to be much more complicated than the combination lock, but it really isn't. There are fewer states but many more connectors. In the

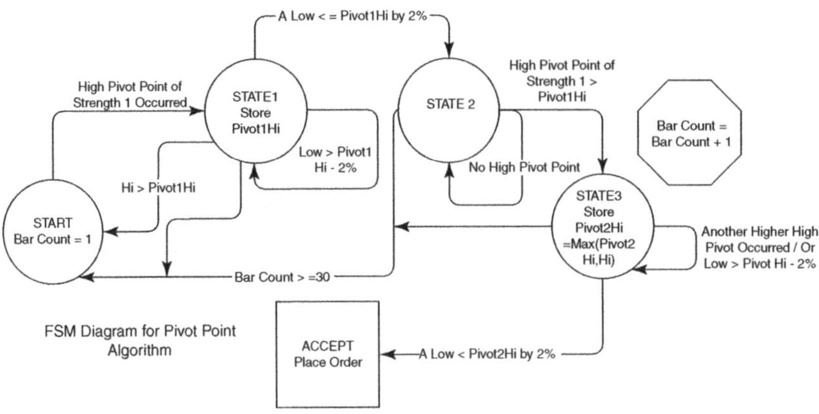

FIGURE 1.4 An FSM that models the pivot-point long-entry algorithm described in this chapter.

combination lock FSM there was only one connector connecting the different states together and the machine never went backward. Once a state was attained, the machine stayed there until the criteria were met to advance to the next state. This pivot-point FSM can move forward and backward.

Stepping through this diagram will help make it less scary. Keep in mind that all of these machines gobble up one bar at a time and then make a decision. Starting at the START state the machine looks for a pivot high of strength one. Once the machine finds this pivot point it then moves to STATE1 and starts looking for a low price that is 2 percent or less than the pivot high found in the START state. There are four paths out of STATE1: (1) a low is found that fits the criteria, (2) a low price fitting the criteria is not found, stay in STATE1, (3) 30 bars have occurred since the pivot high is found, and (4) a high exceeds the pivot high price. Only one path leads to STATE2. All other paths either return to the START state or loop back to the current state. Once the machine attains STATE2 it starts analyzing the data by gobbling each bar and searches for a higher pivot high point. Unlike STATE1 there are only three paths coming out of this state: (1) a higher pivot high is found, (2) a higher pivot high is not found, and (3) 30 bars have occurred since the pivot high was found in the START state. There is only one path to STATE3 and that is a higher pivot high. All other paths either loop or return the machine to the START state. Assuming a higher pivot high is found the machine moves to STATE3. Once in STATE3 the machine will only return to the START state if 30 bars have come and gone before the machine can attain the ACCEPT state. If new highs are found, the machine continues to stay in STATE3 and keeps track of the new highs, all the while looking for that particular low that is 2 percent or lower than the most recent pivot high. Eventually things fall into place and the machine attains the ACCEPT state and a buy order is placed. You can now refer back to Figure 1.2 and see when the machine attains the various states.

The diagram in Figure 1.4 looks clean and neat, but that's not how it started out. When I diagram a trading algorithm, I use pen/pencil and paper. A pencil is great if you don't want to waste a lot of paper. Also, you don't have to have a complete diagram to move onto the pseudocode step. Trust me when I say a diagram can help immensely. Something that seems impossible to program can be conquered by drawing a picture and providing as much detail on the picture as possible. Box 1.7 contains the pseudocode for the pivot point entry algorithm using the FSM diagram.

Box 1.7 Pivot Point Entry Algorithm for Figure 1.4

```
If initialize then
State = Start

HiPivotFound = High of yesterday > High of today and
     High of yesterday > High of prior day

If State = Start and HiPivotFound then
     State = 1
     BarCount = 1
     Pivot1Hi = High price of HiPivotFound

If State <> Start then BarCount = BarCount + 1

If State = 1 then
     If Low of today < Pivot1Hi * 0.98 then
            State = 2
     If High of today > Pivot1Hi then
            State = Start

If State = 2 then
     If HiPivotFound then
             Pivot2Hi = High Price of HiPivotFound
             If Pivot2Hi > Pivot1Hi then
                       State = 3

If State = 3 then
     If Low of today < Pivot2Hi * 0.98 then
             State = Accept
     If High of today > Pivot2Hi then
             Pivot2Hi = High of today

If State = Accept then
     Buy this market on close
     State = Start {start over}

If BarCount = 30 then
     State = Start
     BarCount = 0
```

You might understand this code or you may not. If you have never programmed or scripted, then you might have a problem with this. If you fully understand what is going on here, just bear with us a few moments. Even if you understood the diagram, this code may not be fully self-explanatory. The reason you may not understand this is because you don't know the *syntax* or the *semantics* of this particular language. Syntax was discussed earlier in this chapter, and remember, it's just the structure of the language. I tried my best to utilize a very generic pseudocode language for all the examples throughout the book and hopefully this will help with its understanding. In the pseudocode example, the language uses *ifs* and *thens* to make yes-or-no decisions. If something is true, then do something, or if something is false, then do something. These decisions divert the flow of the computer's execution. The code that is indented below the if-then structure is controlled by the decision. This structure is the syntax. Now the logic that is used to make the decision and then what is carried out after the decision is the semantics. In our example, we will eventually tell the computer that if State = 1, then do something. Syntax is the grammatical structure of a language and semantics is the meaning of the vocabulary of symbols arranged within that structure. You many notice the similarity in the pseudocode and the FSM diagram. The logic that transitions the pivot point FSM from one **state** to another is mirrored almost exactly in the code. This tells you the time you spent planning out your program diagram is time well spent. So let's start with the pseudocode and make sure the FSM diagram is fully implemented.

The START state is simply looking for a pivot point high of strength 1. When one occurs the machine then shifts gears and enters STATE1. Once we have entered the STATE1 phase, the machine stays there until one of three criteria is met: (1) the elusive low that is 2 percent or lower than the Pivot1Hi, (2) a high price that exceeds the Pivot1Hi, or (3) 30 bars transpire prior to attaining the ACCEPT state. If you look at the STATE1 block of code, you will only see the logic for the first two criteria. You may ask where is the logic that kicks the machine back to the START state once 30 bars have been completed prior to the ACCEPT state. If you look further down in the code, you will see the block of code that keeps track of the BarCount. If at any time the BarCount exceeds 30 and the machine is not in the START state, the machine is automatically reset to the START state. If a low price is observed that is lower than 2 percent of the Pivot1Hi price, then the machine transitions to STATE2. However, if a high price is observed that exceeds Pivot1Hi, then the machine reverses back to the START state and it once again starts looking for a new PivotHi. Assuming the machine does make it to STATE2, it then starts looking for another PivotHi price that is greater than Pivot1Hi. A transition from STATE2 can only occur when one of two criteria are met: (1) BarCount exceeds 30, then it's back to the START state, or (2) a higher HiPivot than Pivot1Hi is observed. If the latter criterion is fulfilled, then it is onto STATE3. STATE3 looks for a low price that is 2 percent less than the Pivot2Hi price so it can transition to the ACCEPT state. At this point the BarCount is its only enemy. It doesn't care if a high price exceeds the Pivot2Hi. If it does, then it simply replaces the Pivot2Hi with this price and continues searching for a price that is 2 percent lower than Pivot2Hi. Eventually, the machine resets itself or it finally transitions to the ACCEPT state and buys market on close (MOC).

As you can see, the description of the FSM diagram is all almost completely repeated in the description of the pseudocode. If the two descriptions agree, then it is on to the actual programming of the algorithm. Now that this more complicated paradigm has been explained, I think it is time to give it a better name. How about the *FSM paradigm*? Sounds better than *the variable bar liberal sequence paradigm*, doesn't it?

The Consecutive Bar Sequence I saved *the consecutive bar exact sequence paradigm* for the end because the FSM paradigm is much more difficult to understand and much less intuitive. Armed with our new knowledge of diagrams, it is now time to move to this simpler paradigm because it will be used a lot more in your programming/testing of trading algorithms. As I stated before, most trading algorithms will be fully describable in a step-by-step fashion. Here the logic will not be needed to be modeled by a machine; a recipe approach will do just fine. Guess what type of diagram is used to model these recipe types of instructions. If you guessed a flowchart (FC), then pat yourself on the back. A good computer programming 101 instructor introduces her students to the flowchart concept/diagram way before they even sit down in front of a keyboard. Figure 1.5 shows a very simple FC.

Can you see what is being modeled there? It's quite simple; the FC diagram starts at the top and makes one decision and, based on that decision, it carries out its objective. It starts out with you waking up and observing the time and making a decision to take the bus or the subway. This is a way oversimplified example, but it covers everything an FC is designed to do: start, make decisions, carry out the appropriate instructions based on the decisions, and then finish. Figure 1.6 shows an ever so slightly more complicated FC that deals with what this book is all about, a trading algorithm.

This diagram is a flowchart of the entry technique of a very popular mean reversion trading system. This system trades in the direction of the long-term trend after a price pullback. The trend is reflected by the relationship of the closing price and its associated 200-day moving average. If the close is greater than the average, then the trend is up. The pullback is reflected by the 14-period RSI indicator entering into oversold territory—in this case, a reading of 20 or less. The diagram illustrates two decisions or tests and, if both tests are passed, then the system enters a long position

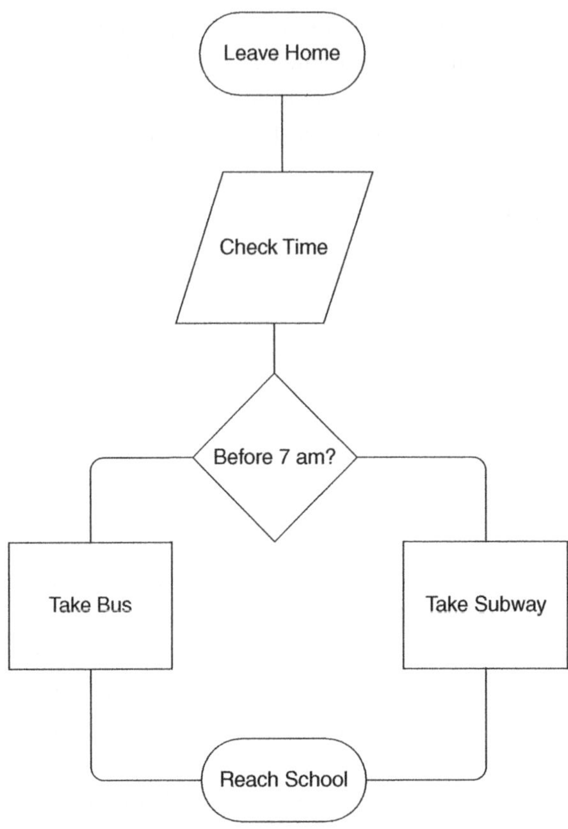

FIGURE 1.5 A very simple FC.

on an MOC order. The flow of the algorithm is linear, meaning it flows from top to bottom. The flow is diverted based on simple decisions, but it always ends at the bottom of the flowchart—either buying MOC or starting on a new bar of data. Here is the pseudocode of this mean reverting system; look quickly or you will miss it:

```
'Simple FC type trading algorithm
'An example of a mean reversion system

If Close of today > 200 day average of Close then
        If RSI(14) < 20 then
                Buy MOC
```

That's the entire entry technique, in a nutshell. Was it necessary to create a flowchart diagram? In this case, no. But as you will find out in later chapters, most trading algorithms are not this easily definable.

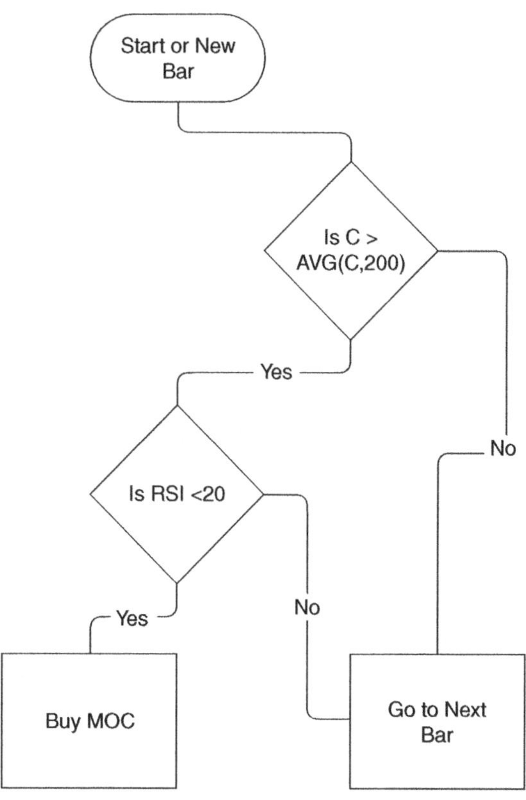

FIGURE 1.6 An FC of a trading algorithm.

Summary

In this chapter, the necessary tools for creating a trading algorithm were introduced. Describing your ideas on paper (real or virtual) is the very first step in the algorithm development process. A template was shown that can be used to help facilitate this. Just getting a trading idea on paper is not sufficient to move onto the pseudocode phase. All ideas must be translated into mathematical expressions and Boolean logic. These expressions and logic must be in a form a computer can understand. Ambiguous directions must be eliminated and replaced with pure logic. Once the idea is written down and further reduced into an extremely logical list of directives and calculations or formulae, the trader must then decide what type of paradigm to use to get the logic into something that can be eventually programmed or scripted. The FSM, as well as the FC methods, were both introduced and used to convert trading schemes into complete pseudocodes. These two paradigms have always been present, and many algorithmic traders have used them without realizing the different programming methods. With knowledge of the two different methods, hopefully an algorithmic trader can make a choice on which is best to use and get from idea to actual code in a lot less time and a lot less frustration.

Here again is a summary of the two methods:

- **Flowchart:** The "flow" of a flowchart is a process. The flowchart shows the steps and actions to achieve a certain goal. Use this method if you can define your trading logic in a step-by-step or bar-by-bar basis. A large portion of trading systems will fit into this programming paradigm.
- **Finite state machine:** The "flow" in a state diagram is always from state to state. Most FSMs have a START and ACCEPT state, similar to the beginning and end of a flowchart. Machine diagrams describe a closed system composed of multiple discrete states. The "state" in this case determines how a system behaves to stimulus or events. Use this method if criteria have to be met in a sequential manner, but the amount of time between the beginning and criteria completion is variable. Pattern-based systems will usually fall into this paradigm.

Once a potential programming method is chosen, it is time to "draw" the corresponding diagram. A diagram doesn't have to be pretty, but it must try to cover all the bases or what-if scenarios a trading system may encounter to carry out its objectives. A thoroughly thought-out diagram providing as much information as possible will definitely enable a trading algorithm to be quickly translated into pseudocode and eventually programmed into a testing platform. Over time, as your experience grows with programming trading systems, these diagrams will begin to appear in your mind's eye. However, this takes time and a lot of experience.

If you made it through this chapter, then, at least, you are now in possession of a trading algorithm that is quite similar to one that actually sold for thousands of dollars in the 1990s.

CHAPTER 2

Stochastics and Averages and RSI! Oh, My!

Indicators and price bar patterns are the most widely used building blocks of trading algorithms. Of the many trading systems I have programmed over the years, at least 90 percent utilized an indicator either straight out of the box or customized in some form or fashion. The trading community is split right down the middle when it comes to the perceived effectiveness of these price transformations. An indicator is simply a price transformation; price is transformed or changed into something that is thought to be more illustrative of the current market condition. There have already been many articles and books written about most indicators. And it is true that these indicators do not work all of the time as standalone signal generators. It is also true that there is redundancy among many of the different indicators. However, I want to discuss the mathematically simple indicators that are easily implemented into a trading algorithm and when used in concert with other ideas can produce a slight technical advantage.

Indicators fall into basically two categories, *oscillator* (usually predictive) and *price based* (lagging). Oscillators are depicted on charts that plot a value that is banded by two extremes. This information is most commonly used for short-term forecasting, but it can also reveal longer term market behavior. Price-based indicators are displayed on charts as a real price of the underlying instrument and are used to determine trend and/or volatility. These indicators are reporting back what is currently going on after the fact, hence the term *lagging*.

Oscillators

Oscillators are normalized, in most cases, to fall between two extreme levels, and are usually plotted in a subgraph. Certain indicator-based levels are then superimposed on the oscillators as benchmarks. The relationships of oscillator value and the benchmarks are then used to predict short-term market direction. The normalization process allows the oscillator family of indicators to be universally applicable to all markets. Oscillators are most often used to predict but can also be used as lagging indicators.

Average Directional Movement Index (ADX)

This oscillating indicator is one of the more popular as it measures a market's trendiness. The underlying concept of *Directional Movement* was introduced in J. Welles Wilder's 1978 book, *New Concepts in Technical Trading Systems.* As a side note, this was the book I first used to help program many of the more popular indicators into our Excalibur software in the late 1980s. Many algorithmic traders are trend followers, even though it is been proven that markets only trend a very small portion of time.

If this is the case, then why do many traders claim that "the trend is your friend"? Trend followers hope that by diversifying across many markets, they will hit upon one or two markets that sufficiently trend enough that they can negate all of the other losing markets and still make enough money to provide a profitable year. While trend followers tread water by capturing a few trends a year, they are constantly waiting and hoping they will be poised for that once-in-a-lifetime trend event. These once-in-a-lifetime trend events do happen more frequently than once in a lifetime, and most trend-following algorithms are more than capable of catching and holding on for the long haul.

The realization that commodities are limited resources and the fact that trend following has had success in the past has promoted this trading algorithm class as the most widely used in the managed futures arena. However, commodity markets over the past few years have been unkind to trend following, and if this "trend" continues, then you might see a gradual exodus of these types of traders. Stock traders, as of the writing of this book, have been riding a bull trend for several years, which has bolstered the buy-and-hold mentality. I guess the phrase about the trend could be changed to, "The trend is rarely your friend, but it's the only friend in town."

The main weakness of trend following is, of course, whipsaw trades—the ones you get into and very quickly get stopped out or, worse in some cases, reversed. Another common weakness is lack of profit retention when the ride is over. The ADX indicator is here to save the day—well, sort of. This indicator attempts to define the current market's trendiness over the past *n*-days into one simple value. The ADX value is high when the market is trending and low when it is in congestion.

The basic theory behind the ADX is based on market directional movement. This movement is either positive, negative, or neutral. In Wilder's vernacular, positive direction was described as plus directional movement (+DM) and negative as minus directional movement (−DM). Directional movement is calculated by comparing the difference between two consecutive bars' lows and the difference between their respective highs. Movement is positive (plus) when the current bar's high minus the prior bar's high is greater than the prior bar's low minus the current bar's low. This plus directional movement (+DM) then equals the current high minus the prior bar's high as long as this value is positive. If the value is negative, then the +DM would be set to zero. Negative movement or minus directional movement (−DM) does the same comparison. A −DM occurs when the prior bar's low minus the current is greater than the current bar's high minus the prior. In this case the difference between the two lows is assigned to the −DM as long as the value is positive. If the value is negative, it is assigned zero just like the +DM. Sounds a bit confusing but Figure 2.1 should help clarify things.

Figure 2.1 shows four calculation examples for directional movement. The first pairing shows a big positive difference between the highs for a strong plus directional movement (+DM). The second pairing shows an outside day with minus directional movement (−DM) getting the edge. The third pairing shows a big difference between the lows for a strong minus directional movement (−DM). The final pairing shows an inside day, which amounts to no directional movement (zero). Both plus directional movement (+DM) and minus directional movement (−DM) are negative and cancel out each other. Negative values revert to zero. Keep in mind all inside days will have zero directional movement.

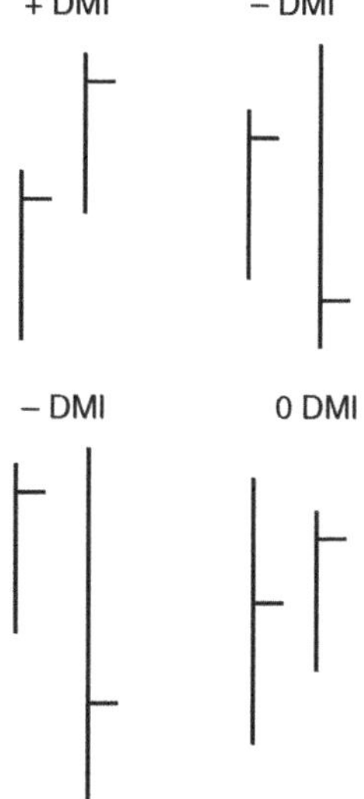

FIGURE 2.1 Examples of directional movement.

The ADX index incorporates moving averages of true range and both +DM and −DM. Data averaging is also the same as data smoothing. A moving average function cuts down the impact of abnormal data points and creates a more robust model of the data. Wilder created his indicators without the use of a computer and created a shortcut to average his data points. This Wilder's smoothing is more like an exponential calculation. Different trading/testing/charting platforms use different smoothing functions for Wilder's indicators, so be sure to check your user's manual and see which form is being utilized by your particular software. Assuming a 14-day ADX length, Wilder would sum up the first 14-day values and then divide by 14. Once these initial averages were calculated the subsequent bar values were calculated by first dividing the previous sum by 14 and subtracting it from the previous sum and then adding today's values:

$$\text{plusDM14} = \text{previous plusDM14} - \frac{\text{previous plusDM14}}{14} + \text{plusDM today}$$

This form of smoothing eliminates keeping track of the prior 14 bar values and accomplishes the desired effect (reducing the impact of outlying data points) on plus DM, minus DM, and true range. Remember, Wilder probably had the use of just a calculator, and instead of inputting 42 numbers (summing three sets of 14 numbers), he simply used the above formula and whipped out the values in a minute or less. Most of today's charting software utilizes an exponential moving average to smooth the ADX. This smoothing method creates results that can be quite different than Wilder's original method.

$$\text{Wilders:} \quad \text{ADX} = ((\text{priorADX} * 13) + \text{DX})/14$$

$$\text{Exponential:} \quad \text{ADX} = \text{priorADX} + 2/15 * (\text{DX} - \text{priorADX})$$

The smoothing factor (2/(N+1)) or in this case (2/15) can be changed to (1/N) to arrive at Wilder's calculation. This becomes more like a 27 period exponential moving average than a 14. However, this exponential method is considered accurate, but, in some cases, different charting software will offer both versions: ADX and Wilder ADX.

Calculation for a 14-day ADX:

1. Calculate the true range (TR), plus directional movement (+DM), and minus directional movement (−DM) for each bar.
2. True range (TR) = max(C[1],H) − min(C[1],L). In other words: Take the higher of yesterday's close and today's high and subtract the lower of yesterday's close and today's low. Basically, you are expanding today's range to incorporate the prior day's close if it is outside of today's range.
3. Smooth these periodic values using a 14-day moving average. You will either have to wait until 14 days have transpired or you can simply look at 14 days of prior history before commencing the ADX calculation.

4. Divide the 14-day smoothed plus directional movement (+DM) by the 14-day smoothed true range to find the 14-day plus directional indicator (+DI14). Multiply by 100 to move the decimal point two places. This +DI14 is the plus directional indicator that is plotted along with ADX.

5. Divide the 14-day smoothed minus directional movement (−DM) by the 14-day smoothed true range to find the 14-day minus directional indicator (−DI14. Multiply by 100 to move the decimal point two places. This −DI14 is the minus directional indicator that is plotted along with ADX.

6. The Directional Movement Index (DX) equals the absolute value of +DI14 less −DI14 divided by the sum of +DI14 and −DI14.

7. After all these steps, it is time to calculate the Average Directional Index (ADX). The ADX value is initially simply a 14-day average of DX.

8. Wilder went one step further and created the ADXR, which is simply the average of an *N*-day differential of the ADX. Continuing with our 14-day example, the ADXR would be calculated by applying the following formula:

$$ADXR = \frac{ADX[1] + ADX[14]}{14}$$

Figure 2.2 illustrates how the ADX can be used to help determine the trendiness of a market. A rising ADX, as shown in the early part of the price chart, demonstrates

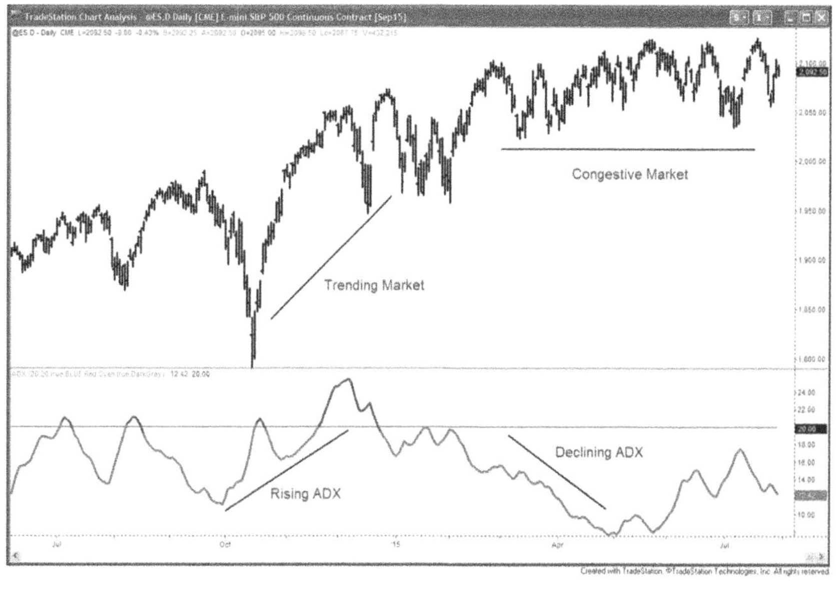

FIGURE 2.2 ADX as a trend detector.
Source: TradeStation

a trending market condition, whereas a falling ADX is saying the market has stopped trending and is entering a congestion phase. This information is very useful but very limited as well. The computer cannot determine which way the market is trending by simply looking at the ADX value. The solution to this problem can be found by comparing the +DI to the −DI. If the +DI crosses above the −DI, then the market is considered in an uptrend. When the −DI crosses above the +DI, then the market is in a downtrend.

Using this indicator in concert with a trend-following system may produce more robust entry signals. I have seen many systems incorporating the ADX in an attempt to eliminate "whipsaw" trades. Welles Wilder developed his own system around the ADX, +DI, and −DI. Box 2.1 is a description of a system that incorporates the ADX and a trailing stop for both long and short trades. The stop will get out of longs when the market closes lower than the prior three-day closings and get out of shorts when the market closes higher than the prior three days. This type of stop is not fixed as it varies based on market movement. In other words, it is a dynamic stop. If we are lucky to get in on a nice intermediate trend, the stop will follow the market in the direction of the movement and hopefully lock in some profit.

Box 2.1 Welles Wilder's Directional Movement System Description

If 14-day ADX is greater than 35 then
  If +DI > −DI, then Buy market on close
  If −DI > +DI, then SellShort market on close

If 14-day ADX is less than 35, then
  If position is long and close is less than lowest close of prior three days, then Sell market on close.
  If position is short and close is greater than highest close of prior three days, then BuyToCover market on close.

Welles Wilder's Directional Movement p–code

```
'Wilder's Directional Movement System
'Assuming Wilder's Indicator/Functions are built-in
'Also Highest and Lowest functions

myADX = ADX(14) '14 period ADX calculation
myPlusDI = PDI(14) ' 14 period Plus DI
myMinusDI = MDI(14) ' 14 period Minus DI

if myADX > 35 then
     if myPlusDI > myMinusDI then
             Buy this bar on close
     if myMinusDI > myPlusDI then
             SellShort this bar on close
```

```
if myADX < 35 then
     if MarketPosition = 1 and close < Lowest(close[1],3)
        then
             Sell this bar on close
     if MarketPosition = -1 and close > Highest(close[1],3)
        then
             BuyToCover this bar on close
```

The directional movement algorithm description is straightforward and can be modeled by a flowchart. A finite state machine is not needed because, as we discussed in Chapter 1, this system follows a certain flow that is directed by a combination of logical steps and decisions that eventually lead to termination of the process. Figure 2.3 shows the flowchart of this algorithm.

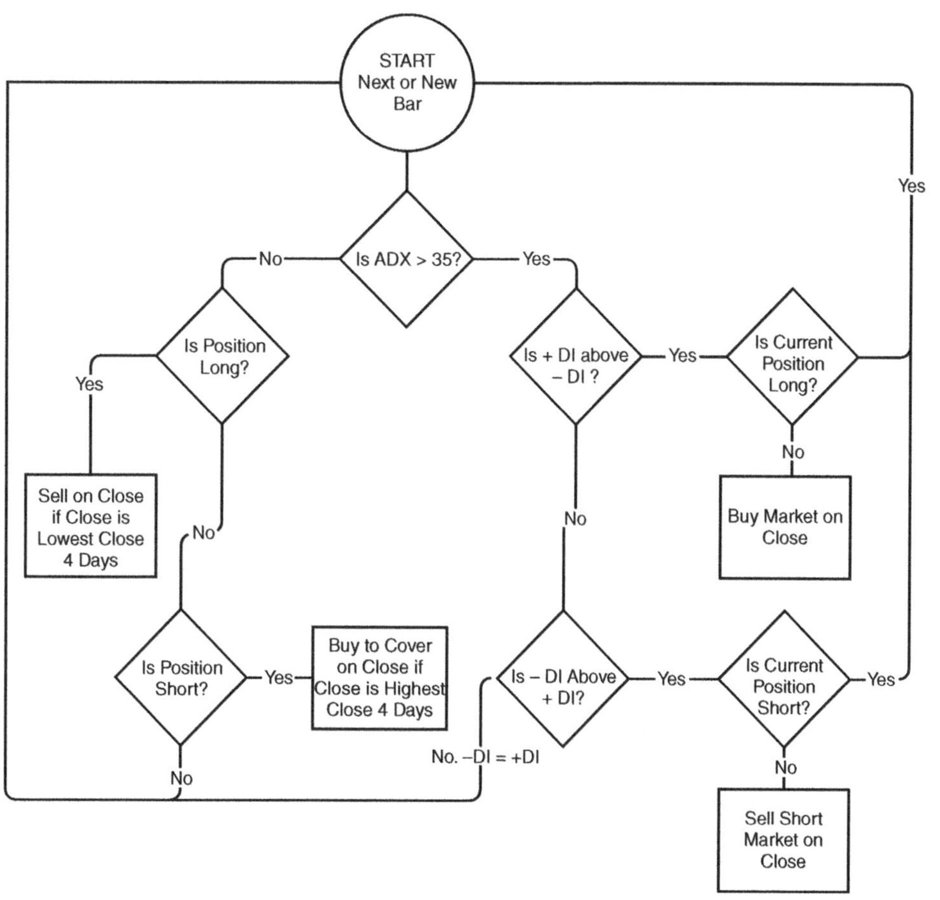

FIGURE 2.3 Wilder's directional movement algorithm.

Like the description, the diagram is straightforward as well. It might look complicated, but that is only because of the many different decisions that must be evaluated before an action is carried out. In the case of this very simple system, a flowchart diagram isn't really all that necessary. However, it is great practice, and eventually you will come across a trading scheme that will be complicated enough to merit a properly thought-out diagram.

Before proceeding to the next indicator, I must mention that the ADX along with all other indicators are just building blocks and are not to be used by themselves. Many successful trading algorithms utilize indicators but not strictly by themselves and in many cases the indicators are augmented or filtered. Many traders change some of the logic of an indicator and therefore make it their own and in doing so bring their own creativity into the process. Most trading algorithms are built on the shoulders of others. More frequently, traders will utilize a filtering process that will eliminate excessive trade signals generated by an indicator. In doing so, the trader is hoping to skip the less productive trades and target the really good ones. Table 2.1 shows the performance of the pure ADX applied to several markets.

Relative Strength Index (RSI)

Continuing on with Welles Wilder, the next indicator that we will discuss will be the Relative Strength Index (RSI). This indicator is a momentum oscillator that measures the speed and change of price movements. RSI oscillates between 0 and 100. Traditionally, and according to Wilder, RSI is considered overbought when above 70 and oversold when below 30. After moving averages, RSI might be the most popular indicator out there; every popular charting package includes it in its library.

Its popularity might be partially attributed to its simplicity. The indicator is simply measuring the momentum of the market over the past number of days. Momentum indicates the direction and strength of the market. A quickly moving uptrend will be reflected by consecutive higher-high RSI values. And consecutive lower-low RSI values will represent just the opposite, a quickly moving downtrend.

Calculation for a 14-day RSI:

1. Going back in time 14 bars compare the closing price of a bar with its prior bar. If the difference is positive, then accumulate the amount to an upSum variable. If the difference is negative, then remove the sign and accumulate the difference to a dnSum variable.

2. If C > C[1], then upSum = upSum + (C − C[1]). If C < C[1], then dnSum = dnSum + −1 × (C − C[1]).

TABLE 2.1 Performance of Directional Movement Algorithm

Ticker	Net Profit	Max. Sys DD	# Trades	Avg P/L	Avg Bars Held	% of Winners
AD0_E0B	−21140.0	−26030	43	−491.63	13.53	32.56
BP0_E0B	−5825.0	−27925	39	−149.36	12.74	38.46
C20_E0B	737.5	−10000	43	17.15	15.51	44.19
CC20_E0B	−4050.0	−13560	35	−115.71	14.86	42.86
CL20_E0B	41350.0	−26750	36	1148.61	14.67	41.67
CT20_E0B	44530.0	−20220	46	968.04	16.7	39.13
CU0_E0B	5712.5	−20925	47	121.54	15.81	40.43
DX20_E0B	150.0	−9990	51	2.94	14.51	41.18
ED0_E0B	2009.4	−1513	58	34.64	18.12	29.31
EMD0_E0B	−33400.0	−43910	31	−1077.42	13.81	29.03
ES0_E0B	−18837.5	−23050	26	−724.52	15.96	30.77
FC0_E0B	20087.5	−9588	45	446.39	17.04	35.56
FV0_E0B	8226.4	−7203	49	167.89	17.41	34.69
GC20_E0B	−32870.0	−41560	43	−764.42	12.84	27.91
HG20_E0B	300.0	−41338	34	8.82	14.5	29.41
HO20_E0B	20139.0	−40286	46	437.8	13.17	39.13
KC20_E0B	−32606.3	−42413	36	−905.73	11.61	25
KW20_E0B	9887.5	−15863	43	229.94	16.56	39.53
LB0_E0B	957.0	−17259	39	24.54	15.62	38.46
LC0_E0B	−1230.0	−9550	41	−30	17.24	26.83
LH0_E0B	1510.0	−10710	40	37.75	15.65	37.5
MP0_E0B	4775.0	−5295	33	144.7	14.42	39.39
NG20_E0B	54440.0	−69390	38	1432.63	16.11	39.47
NK0_E0B	−8425.0	−15125	28	−300.89	15.39	46.43
OJ20_E0B	−16620.0	−17790	45	−369.33	15.18	28.89
PL20_E0B	16610.0	−30895	36	461.39	16.39	33.33
RB0_E0B	−17665.2	−46813	26	−679.43	13.62	23.08
S20_E0B	−12212.5	−31463	50	−244.25	14.94	28
SB20_E0B	6563.2	−11995	61	107.59	12.95	26.23
SI20_E0B	40400.0	−51735	44	918.18	14.14	25
TF0_E0B	−24920.0	−32610	33	−755.15	12.61	24.24
TU0_E0B	12124.8	−4156	42	288.69	17.1	33.33
TY0_E0B	12109.6	−7531	48	252.28	16.69	35.42
US0_E0B	14906.4	−18031	45	331.25	16.67	37.78
W20_E0B	−19462.5	−31188	45	−432.5	14.64	26.67

3. Once these values are summed, simply divide them by the RSI period. In doing so, you will have two new values: avgUp and avgDn. In a strong upward-moving market, the upSum and corresponding avgUp will be much greater than the dnSum and avgDn.
4. Once you have arrived to the avgUp and avgDn values the relative strength (RS) is simply the quotient of the two values:

$$\text{RS} = \text{avgUp}/\text{avgDn}$$

5. The RS is the ratio of the changes in up closes to down closes. If the market is in a strong uptrend, the avgUp will be large in relation to the avgDn, thus generating a larger number. The opposite is true if the avgDn is much greater than the avgUp (an occurrence of a downward trending market).
6. The RSI is a bound indicator, meaning that it will stay within an upper and lower constraint. In the case of the RSI, as we mentioned earlier, these constraints are 0 and 100. The simple ratio of avgUp and avgDn can go from a small number to a large one. We can normalize the RS for any market and constrain it between 0 and 100 by applying the following formula:

$$\text{RSI} = 100 - \frac{100}{1 + RS}$$

Let's assume a strong upwardly trending market with an upAvg of 60 and a dnAvg of 20. Inputting this information into the formula, we arrive at the following:

$$\text{RS} = \frac{60}{20}, \quad \text{or } 3$$

$$\text{RSI} = 100 - \frac{100}{1+3}, \quad \text{or } 100 - 25 = 75$$

7. Just like the ADX, subsequent values are smoothed utilizing either an exponential moving average or Wilder's homebrew.

The default period length for the RSI is 14 so it is easy to see that this indicator was designed for a short-term approach. When using RSI in an overbought/oversold application, traders are looking for a reversion to a mean type movement—what goes up must eventually come down. Through Wilder's research he observed his indicator usually topped/bottomed out prior to an actual market top/bottom. Figure 2.4 shows a highly successful RSI trade.

Box 2.2 shows a trading system description incorporating the RSI, a volatility-based profit objective, and protective stop. The profit and stop are based off a 10-day average true range—wider profit targets and stops in high volatility. Notice how the system is trying to cut losses short and let profits run using a 3:1 ratio. I have noticed

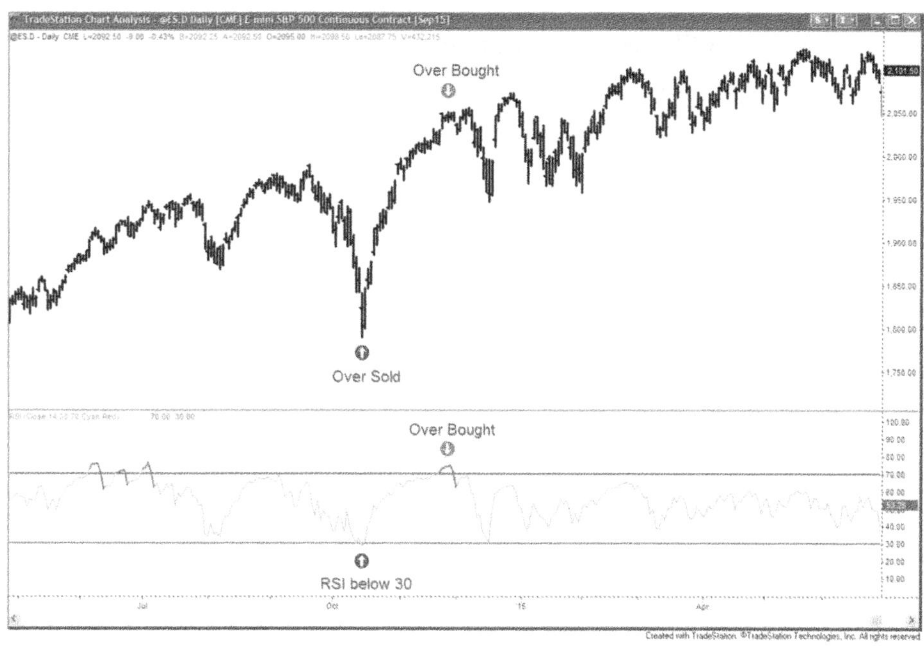

FIGURE 2.4 Example of a trade generated by RSI.

Source: TradeStation

in situations where a system is trying to trade shorter-term to intermediate-term trends a 1:3 ratio, albeit somewhat illogical, works better. Continuing along with our diagrams, Figure 2.5 shows the very simplistic flowchart.

Box 2.2 Welles Wilders RSI System Description

If 14-day RSI is less than 30, then
  Buy MOC

If 14-day RSI is greater than 70, then
  Sell Short MOC

If position is long
  Take Profit: If close > entry price + 3 ATR Sell MOC
  Protective Stop: If close < entry price − 1 ATR Sell MOC

If position is short
  Take Profit: If close < entry price − 3 ATR BuyToCover MOC
  Protective Stop: If close > entry price + 1 ATR BuyToCover MOC

Note that MOC stands for market on close.

Welles Wilders RSI System p–code

```
'Wilders Simple RSI OB/OS system
utilizing a 3 ATR profit objective
and a 1 ATR stop



If rsi(c,14) < 30 then buy this bar on close
If rsi(c,14) > 70 then sellShort this bar on close

If marketPosition = 1 then
     If c > entryPrice + 3* avgTrueRange(10) then sell this
        bar on close
     if c < entryPrice - 1* avgTrueRange(10) then sell this
        bar on close

If marketPosition = 1 then
begin
     If c < entryPrice - 3* avgTrueRange(10) then buyToCover
        this bar on close
     if c > entryPrice + 1* avgTrueRange(10) then buyToCover
        this bar on close
```

Simple enough!

Now don't get carried away, because the RSI can call an intermediate top/bottom but it can also be faked out by a strong trend move. If you simply use it as an overbought/oversold indicator, you will be disappointed. Table 2.2 shows the performance of the RSI across a portfolio of futures.

Signals can also be generated using the RSI by looking for divergences, failure swings, and centerline crossovers. Wilder suggests that divergence between an asset's price movement and the RSI oscillator can signal a potential reversal. This divergence occurs when the RSI continues in the opposite direction of the underlying asset: RSI trends down while price trends upward or RSI trends up while price trends down.

A bullish divergence forms when the underlying asset makes a lower low and RSI makes a higher low. RSI diverges from the bearish price action in that it shows strengthening momentum, indicating a potential upward reversal in price. A bearish divergence forms when the underlying asset makes a higher high and RSI forms a lower high. RSI diverges from the bullish price action in that it shows weakening momentum, indicating a potential downward reversal in price. As with overbought

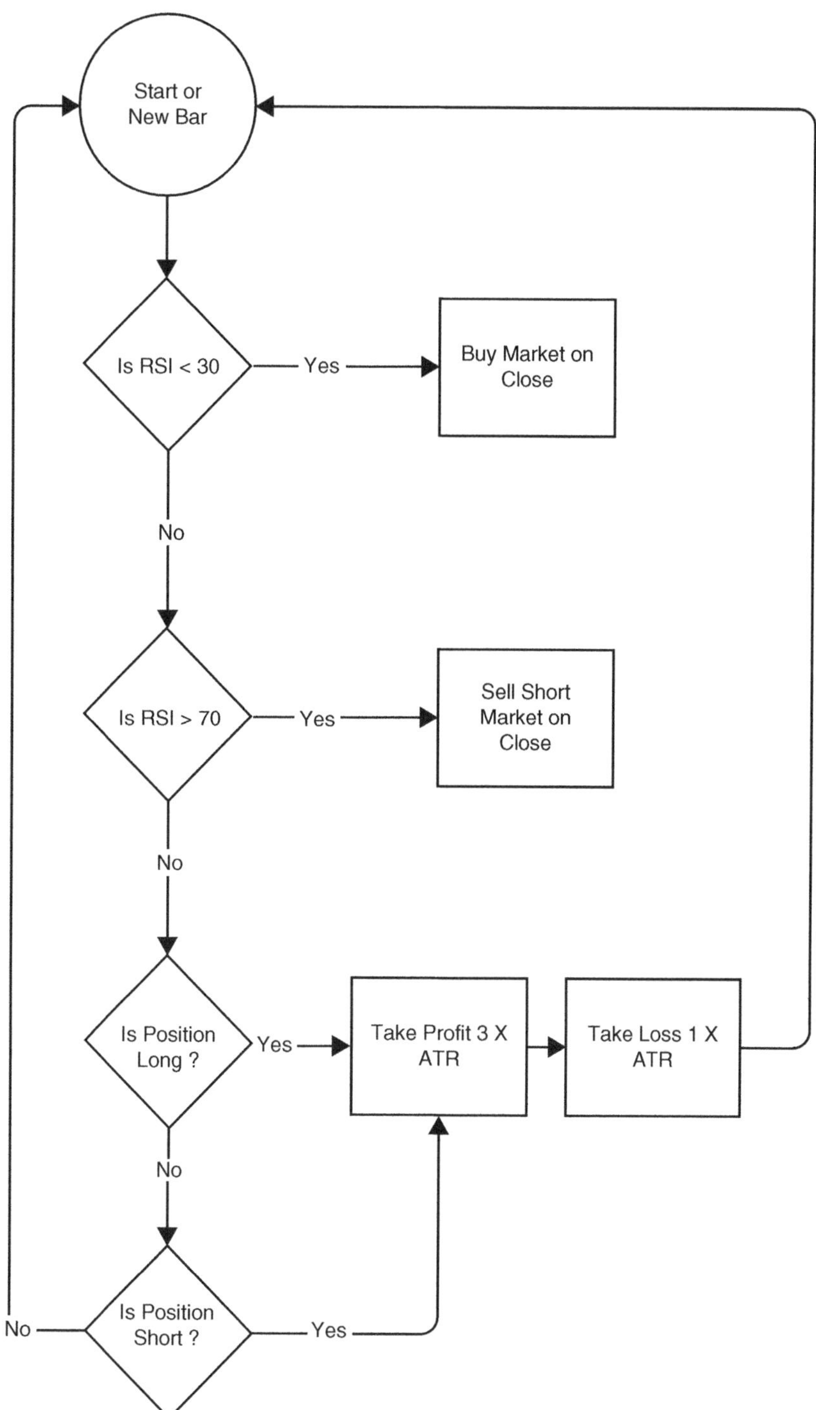

FIGURE 2.5 Flowchart diagram of RSI trading algorithm.

TABLE 2.2	Performance of RSI Algorithm					
Ticker	**Net Profit**	**Max. Sys DD**	**# Trades**	**Avg P/L**	**Avg Bars Held**	**% of Winners**
AD0_E0B	−17229.99	−19850	87	−198.05	8.4	16.09
BP0_E0B	−19812.5	−49600	68	−291.36	8.16	23.53
C20_E0B	−10550	−14250	87	−121.26	9.63	21.84
CC20_E0B	5240	−7280	87	60.23	8.07	28.74
CL20_E0B	−54340	−67120	89	−610.56	9.21	21.35
CT20_E0B	−6600	−37295	93	−70.97	7.37	22.58
CU0_E0B	−24200	−38887.5	93	−260.22	9.16	20.43
DX20_E0B	−24370	−33510	83	−293.61	8.14	13.25
ED0_E0B	−2128.13	−2137.5	136	−15.65	7.51	14.71
EMD0_E0B	−16730	−38240	79	−211.77	8.75	24.05
ES0_E0B	−16275	−29087.5	69	−235.87	7.68	17.39
FC0_E0B	−27862.5	−39787.5	105	−265.36	7.84	15.24
FV0_E0B	−9165.59	−10417	96	−95.47	8.9	21.88
GC20_E0B	5020	−42850	91	55.16	7.89	27.47
HG20_E0B	−21250	−45787.5	86	−247.09	7.92	24.42
HO20_E0B	−70366.8	−97671	92	−764.86	8.85	21.74
KC20_E0B	21693.75	−31125	74	293.16	9.41	32.43
KW20_E0B	−5025	−18762.5	99	−50.76	8.4	26.26
LB0_E0B	10010	−7667	100	100.1	8.27	28
LC0_E0B	−4850	−11780	80	−60.63	8.63	25
LH0_E0B	−2900	−11160	83	−34.94	8.13	25.3
MP0_E0B	675	−6430	90	7.5	8.31	25.56
NG20_E0B	1830.01	−42839.99	80	22.88	10.68	26.25
NK0_E0B	625	−13850	69	9.06	8.38	24.64
OJ20_E0B	5070	−7170	102	49.71	7.48	26.47
PL20_E0B	−4425	−22415	86	−51.45	9.62	26.74
RB0_E0B	−10894.8	−56884.8	92	−118.42	6.02	32.61
S20_E0B	−13237.5	−27787.5	93	−142.34	7.62	22.58
SB20_E0B	−7056	−21649.6	94	−75.06	7.5	23.4
SI20_E0B	−28240	−78915	82	−344.39	10.57	28.05
TF0_E0B	3750	−21400	66	56.82	8.42	25.76
TU0_E0B	−13703.6	−16806.2	95	−144.25	10.99	20
TY0_E0B	−500.4	−13046.8	88	−5.69	8.68	26.14
US0_E0B	11843.4	−20343.8	86	137.71	9	27.91
W20_E0B	−31037.5	−34112.5	73	−425.17	8.7	16.44

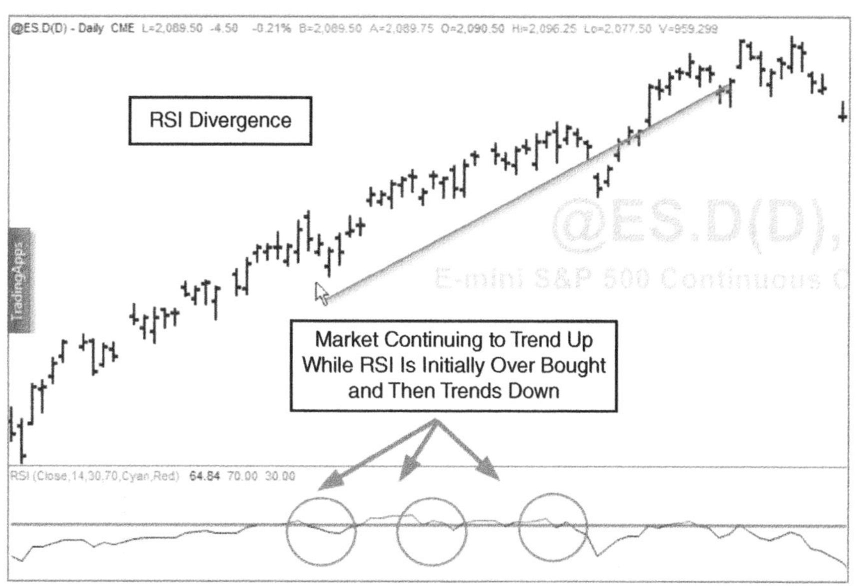

FIGURE 2.6 Example of RSI divergence.

and oversold levels, divergences are more likely to give false signals in the context of a strong trend.

A TOP failure swing occurs when the RSI forms a pivot high in overbought territory and then pulls back and forms a pivot low and then another pivot high forms that is less than the original. A sell signal is triggered at the intervening RSI pivot low level. A BOTTOM failure is the inversion of the TOP; RSI forms a pivot low below the oversold value and then moves up and forms a pivot high and then a pivot low greater than the original pivot low. Figure 2.6 illustrates these failure swings.

According to Wilder, trading the failure swings might be more profitable than simply trading the RSI overbought/oversold model. Let's see if this is the case by testing this idea. The RSI failure swing algorithm is going to be more complicated than our last RSI algorithm, but with the use of an FSM it is readily doable. Let's attack it from the short side only to start (Box 2.3).

Box 2.3 Welles Wilders RSI Failure Swing System Description

SellShort Setup: The 14-day RSI rises above 70, then pulls back below 70 and forms a low pivot. The RSI then rallies but does not take out the original pivot high level. A SellShort signal is generated once the RSI retraces to the pivot low level that was established between the two prior consecutive pivot highs. (*Note:* MOC stands for market on close.)

If position is short

Take Profit: If close < entry price − 1 ATR BuyToCover MOC

Protective Stop: If close > entry price + 3 ATR BuyToCover MOC

Welles Wilders RSI Failure Swing System p–code

```
rsiVal = RSI(C,14)

If rsiVal[1] > rsiVal and rsiVal[1] > rsiVal[2] then
     rsiPvtHiFound = true
     rsiPvtHiVal = rsiVal[1]
else
     rsiPvtHiFound = False

If rsiVal[1] < rsiVal and rsiVal[1] < rsiVal[2] then
     rsiPvtLoFound = true
     rsiPvtLoVal = rsiVal[1]
else
     rsiPvtLoFound = False

If state = 0 then
     if rsiPvtHiFound = true and rsiPvtHiVal > 70 then
               state = 1

If state = 1 then
     state1Val = rsiPvtHiVal
     if rsiVal > state1Val then state = 0
     if rsiPvtLoFound = true then
               state = 2;

If state = 2 then
     state2Val = rsiPvtLoVal
     if rsiVal > state1Val then state = 0
     if rsiPvtHiFound = true then
               if rsiPvtHiVal < 70 then state = 3

If state = 3 then
     if rsiVal < state2Val then state = 4

If state = 4 then
     sellShort this bar on close
     state = 0;

If state > 0 and rsiVal < 30 then state = 0
```

```
If marketPosition =-1 and close > entryprice +
  1* avgTrueRange(10) then
  BuyToCover this bar on close
If marketPosition =-1 and close < entryPrice -
  3* avgTrueRange(10) then
  BuyToCover this bar on close;
```

Figure 2.7 illustrates the model of the RSI failure swing algorithm. As you can see from the diagram, this isn't a flowchart. It's our old friend the FSM, so let's move through the different states of the machine. We start off gobbling one bar at a time until we come across a RSI pivot high with a value of 70 or greater. Once this occurs, the machine goes into **State 1** and starts gobbling more bars. The machine can only transition out of **State 1** if one of three events occur: an occurrence of a RSI pivot low, an RSI value > the original RSI pivot high value, or an RSI value that is less than 30. Only an occurrence of an RSI pivot low can propel the machine to **State 2**. The other two conditions will reverse the machine to the **Start** state. Once in **State 2**, the machine looks for yet another RSI pivot high. In addition to a new pivot high, another condition must be met before moving onto **State 3**, and that is the RSI pivot high must be less than the original RSI pivot high. The same conditions that reset the machine to the **Start** state exist at **State 2**. After the machine attains **State 3**, it then tries to propel itself to **State 4** by finding an RSI value less than the RSI pivot low found in **State 1**. If this occurs, an order to sell short the market is placed on an MOC basis. Again, the exact same criteria for reversing the machine back to the **Start** state are in force in **State 3**.

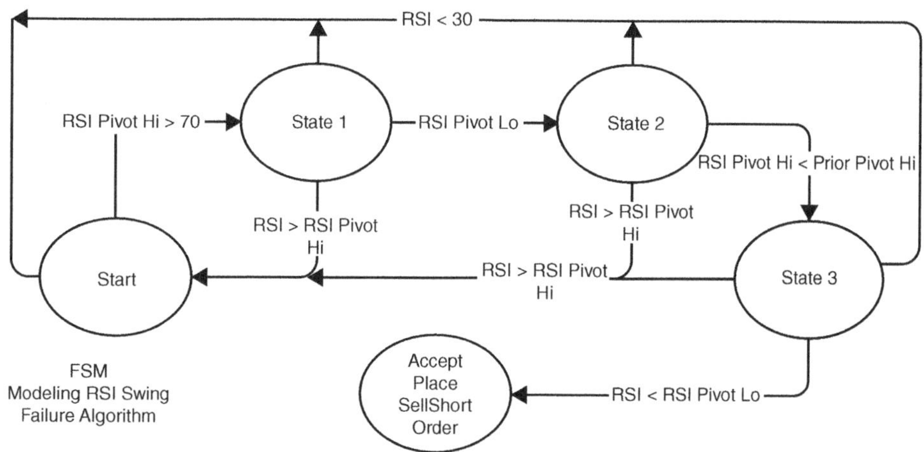

FIGURE 2.7 Example of FSM modeling RSI Swing Failure.

Table 2.3 shows the results of the RSI Failure Swing Algorithm from both the long and short side utilizing the same profit objective and stop used in the first RSI test.

George Lane's Stochastics—Fast %K: Fast %D: Slow %K: Slow %D

Developed by George C. Lane in the late 1950s, the stochastic oscillator, like the RSI, is a momentum indicator that shows the location of the close relative to the high–low range over a set number of periods. Mr. Lane stated in an interview the following concerning the oscillator: "It doesn't follow price, it doesn't follow volume or anything like that. It follows the speed or the momentum of price. As a rule, the momentum changes direction before price." The word *stochastic* is defined as a random pattern that may be analyzed statistically but may not be predicted precisely. An appropriate name, if you ask me. In similar fashion to the RSI, bullish and bearish divergences in the stochastic oscillator can be used to foreshadow reversals. In other words, if the stochastic says one thing but the market says another, then be on the lookout for a market reversal. This is very useful information from a technician's point of view but very little for the quant trader looking for a very precise entry definition. However, because the stochastic oscillator is range bound, it is also useful for identifying overbought and oversold levels.

Calculation for a 14-day stochastic [FAST]:

1. Going back in time 14 bars, calculate the highest high and lowest low prices during this period.
2. Subtract the lowest low from the current closing price and divide the difference by the range between the highest high and lowest low. Multiply this quotient by 100 and you will arrive at %K, or fast K.

$$\%K = (C - Lowest\ low)/(Highest\ high - Lowest\ low) * 100$$

3. Fast %D is a simple three-period moving average of the fast %K.

If the current close is near the lowest low, then the numerator in the %K formula will be small and will produce a low stochastic reading. If the close is near the highest high, then the numerator will be large. A strong %K indicates a strong uptrend, whereas a weak %K indicates the opposite, a strong downtrend. Both %D and %K are plotted alongside each other with the %K line acting as a signal or trigger line. The slow variation of this indicator is simply a further smoothing of the %K and %D. In the slow framework the fast %D becomes the slow %K and the slow %D

TABLE 2.3 Performance of RSI Failure Swing Algorithm

Ticker	Net Profit	# Trades	Avg P/L	Avg Bars Held
@KC	$11,381.25	45	$252.92	16.58 days
@SB	−$8,162.60	40	−$198.40	15.13 days
@ES	−$20,375.00	39	−$522.44	12.44 days
@DX	−$23,245.00	44	−$528.30	13.89 days
@C	$6,312.50	40	$157.81	13.38 days
@BP	−$1,225.00	38	−$32.24	18.66 days
@CT	−$21,485.00	47	−$456.60	13.83 days
@OJ	$7,115.00	53	$134.25	18.49 days
@CC	$18,785.00	55	$324.00	14.36 days
@HG	−$14,250.00	51	−$279.41	17.8 days
@EC	−$35,550.00	43	−$826.74	17.33 days
@HO	−$58,426.40	52	−$1,123.58	12.42 days
@TU	−$7,850.00	42	−$186.90	16.26 days
@US	−$11,568.75	42	−$275.45	17.62 days
@FV	−$4,939.06	43	−$114.86	13.86 days
@ED	$3,025.00	44	$68.75	18.18 days
@TY	−$6,540.63	43	−$152.11	14.21 days
@CL	−$45,050.00	52	−$866.35	12.25 days
@RB	−$51,377.40	45	−$1,141.72	17.24 days
@PL	$7,980.00	41	$194.63	13.83 days
@GC	$7,570.00	46	$164.57	18.26 days
@AD	−$27,980.00	44	−$635.91	14.93 days
@SI	−$9,300.00	53	−$175.47	12.34 days
@NG	$28,730.00	38	$756.05	15.76 days
@EMD	−$20,780.00	43	−$483.26	13.05 days
@TF	$16,760.00	40	$419.00	15.35 days
@S	$10,325.00	38	$271.71	14.18 days
@W	−$3,112.50	35	−$88.93	14.71 days
@LH	$15,190.00	41	$370.49	16.41 days
@LC	−$21,160.00	29	−$729.66	12.9 days
@FC	−$25,212.50	37	−$681.42	12.92 days
@KW	$8,925.00	24	$371.88	14.42 days

becomes a three-period moving average of the slow %K. The two versions can be confusing so most people simply use the slow variety. Through my obeservations the fast stochastic seems to be very erratic.

The default parameters for the slow stochastic are (14, 3, 3) where the 14 represents the raw %K calculation period, the first 3 is the initial smoothing length, and the second 3 is the secondary smoothing.

As you can see from the %K formula, the numerator will always be less than or equal to the denominator and therefore produce a reading between 0 and 100. If the close is near the lowest low, then the formula will produce a low stochastic.

Most traders utilize the stochastic (STO) as an overbought/oversold indicator with 80 and 20 as the corresponding thresholds. If the STO is high, then the momentum is very bullish, and if it's low—well, it's pretty obvious. Just like the RSI, the STO can be faked out into believing a market has become overbought/sold when in fact the market is in a very strong trend. A unique feature of the STO (and some other oscillators) is that it incorporates a *trigger*. Instead of simply buying/selling in the oversold/overbought territory a trader can wait until the slow %K crosses above/below the slow %D. Remember, these calculations are simple moving averages of the raw %K and when a shorter-term average crosses the longer term, this indicates a short-term shift in momentum.

Figure 2.8 shows trades where the slow %K crosses slow %D in overbought and oversold territories.

Entry signals for a stochastic oscillator crossover algorithm can be defined by simple if–then constructs. So a simple flowchart can be used to model this type of trading algorithm. The flowchart is shown in Figure 2.9.

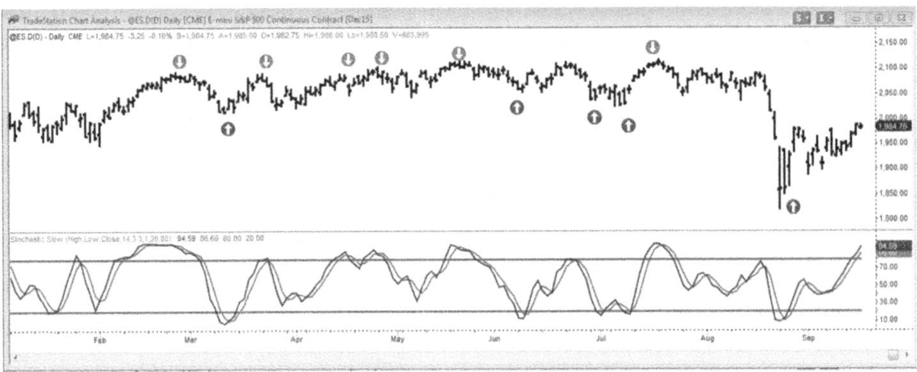

FIGURE 2.8 Chart showing trade signals from stochastic crossover algorithm.

Source: TradeStation

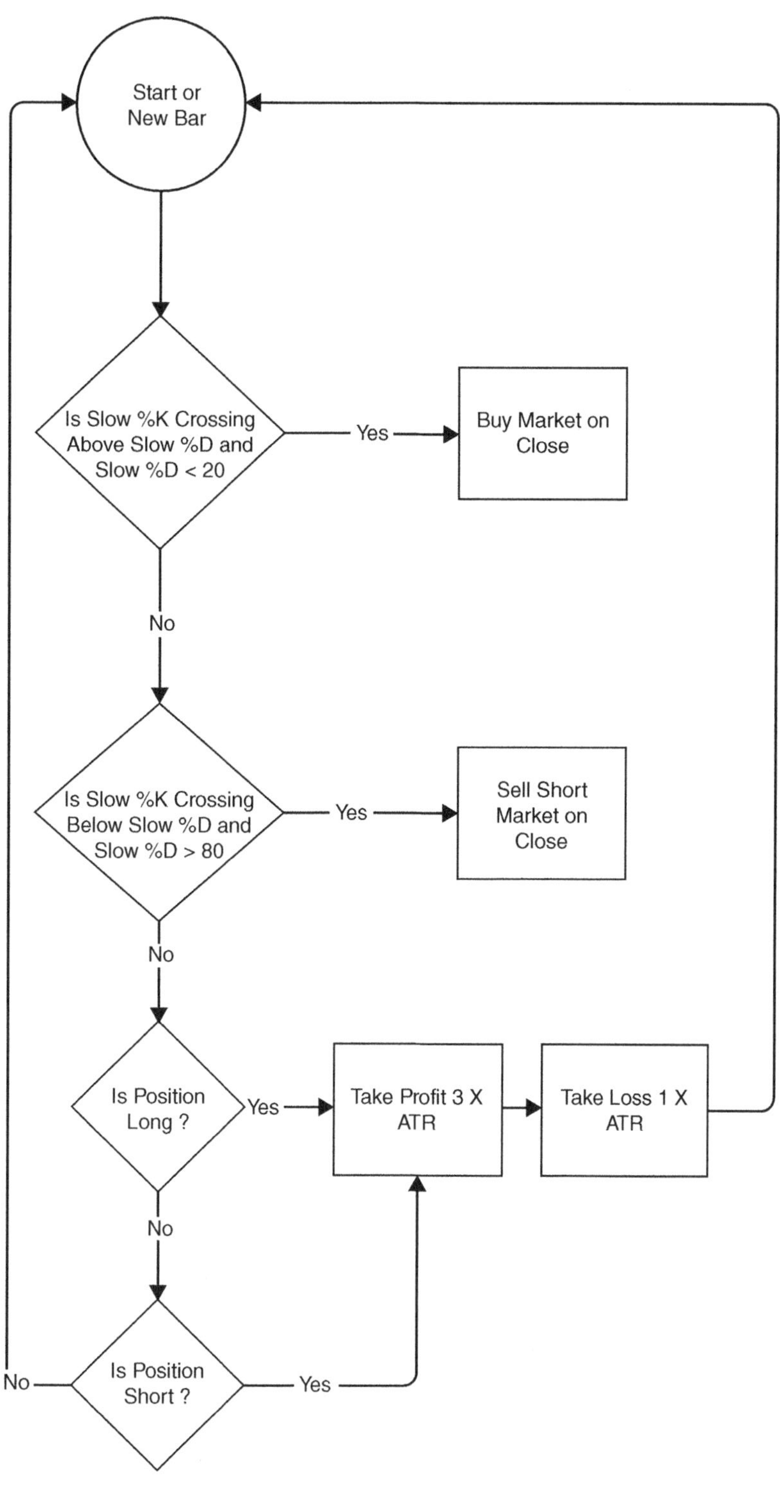

FIGURE 2.9 The flowchart for an algorithm using a stochastic oscillator crossover as an entry signal.

Box 2.4 gives a description of a simplistic version of a stochastic crossover system utilizing the same profit-and-loss objectives as the RSI algorithms. The results of this stochastic algorithm applied to several markets are shown in Table 2.4.

Box 2.4 George Lane's Slow Stochastic System Description

If 14-day slow %K crosses below slow %D and slow %D is greater than 80, then Buy MOC

If 14-day slow %K crosses above slow %D and slow %D is less than 20, then Sell Short MOC

If position is long
Take Profit: If close > entry price + 3 ATR Sell MOC
Protective Stop: If close < entry price − 1 ATR Sell MOC

If position is short
Take Profit: If close < entry price − 3 ATR BuyToCover MOC
Protective Stop: If close > entry price + 1 ATR, BuyToCover MOC

Note that MOC stands for market on close.

George Lane's Slow Stochastic System p–code

```
'Most software will provide a function that
'provides all the components of the stochastic

Value1 = stochastic(h,l,c,rawKLen,smooth1,smooth2,1,myFastK,
   myFastD,mySlowK,mySlowD)

If mySlowK crosses above mySlowD and mySlowD < 20 then buy
   this bar on close
If mySlowK crosses below mySlowD and mySlowD > 80 then
   sellShort this bar on close

If marketPosition = 1 then
      If c > entryPrice + 3* avgTrueRange(10) then sell this
   bar on close
      if c < entryPrice - 1* avgTrueRange(10) then sell this
   bar on close
If marketPosition =-1 then
      If c < entryPrice - 3* avgTrueRange(10) then buyToCover
         this bar on close
      if c > entryPrice + 1* avgTrueRange(10) then buyToCover
         this bar on close
```

TABLE 2.4 Performance of Stochastic Algorithm

Ticker	Net Profit	Max. Sys DD	# Trades	Avg P/L	Avg Bars Held	% of Winners
AD0_E0B	−34820	−50330	356	−97.81	7.6	26.69
BP0_E0B	41213	−40563	324	127.2	8.42	31.17
C20_E0B	8400	−15675	358	23.46	7.58	29.89
CC20_E0B	44010	−8170	341	129.06	8.21	35.19
CL20_E0B	−54320	−115190	346	−156.99	7.92	27.46
CT20_E0B	−5770	−51165	362	−15.94	7.81	30.11
CU0_E0B	−287	−53163	348	−0.83	8.01	27.87
DX20_E0B	4120	−20390	362	11.38	7.33	27.9
ED0_E0B	−4066	−4103	255	−15.94	8.93	21.96
EMD0_E0B	−53730	−89300	350	−153.51	7.29	24.86
ES0_E0B	−52200	−75975	359	−145.4	7.15	25.07
FC0_E0B	−17425	−32575	369	−47.22	7.41	26.83
FV0_E0B	−17699	−25463	345	−51.3	7.66	25.8
GC20_E0B	−27470	−67650	353	−77.82	7.54	29.18
HG20_E0B	−48938	−106225	343	−142.67	7.65	26.82
HO20_E0B	36343	−96319	340	106.89	8.07	30
KC20_E0B	16838	−30375	334	50.41	8.26	28.74
KW20_E0B	−188	−41688	350	−0.54	7.67	30.86
LB0_E0B	5302	−34562	418	12.68	6.53	28.95
LC0_E0B	42500	−8750	344	123.55	7.98	34.3
LH0_E0B	−14110	−17640	363	−38.87	7.2	26.17
MP0_E0B	1730	−10580	297	5.82	8.34	28.96
NG20_E0B	−193860	−199740	336	−576.96	7.95	25.3
NK0_E0B	17300	−38025	375	46.13	7.34	30.4
OJ20_E0B	34275	−8055	321	106.78	8.3	32.4
PL20_E0B	25415	−40470	341	74.53	7.91	30.5
RB0_E0B	−48266	−101884	406	−118.88	5.96	28.33
S20_E0B	−48888	−61063	367	−133.21	7.18	26.16
SB20_E0B	−7045	−33309	380	−18.54	6.9	28.68
SI20_E0B	−122305	−186355	323	−378.65	8.44	27.86
TF0_E0B	−48910	−80540	333	−146.88	7.56	26.43
TU0_E0B	−21736	−24441	309	−70.34	8.3	24.92
TY0_E0B	−37139	−54734	350	−106.11	7.52	25.71
US0_E0B	−74827	−74859	359	−208.43	7.67	25.07
W20_E0B	−27838	−43613	351	−79.31	7.98	29.06

Donald Lambert's CCI—Commodity Channel Index

Donald Lambert developed the CCI in 1980, and it was featured in *Commodities* magazine that same year. The Commodity Channel Index can be used in the same vein as RSI and stochastic: trend determination or warning of extreme conditions. Lambert originally developed CCI to identify cyclical turns in commodities, but the indicator can be successfully applied to indices, ETFs, stocks, and other securities. In general, CCI measures the current price level relative to an average price level over a given period of time. CCI is relatively high when prices are far above their average, and conversely, CCI is relatively low when prices are far below their average—hence its application as reversion to the mean tool.

The main difference between CCI and other similar oscillators is that it is not necessarily range bound. Most of the time, the CCI will oscillate between two extremes, but as you will see in its calculations, there is not a fixed boundary. The CCI introduces the concept of typical price and utilizes it in its calculations. Typical price is just the average of a bar's high, low, and close: Typical price (TP) = (High + Low + Close)/3. This calculation looks at the three most important price points on a price bar and many believe it reveals a more realistic picture of the day's action than just the close. The TP is also known as the daily pivot point. In the day, floor traders used this easily calculable price to determine current support and resistance levels.

Calculation for a 20-day CCI:

1. Going back in time, calculate the average of the past 20 days' typical prices.
2. Calculate the one standard deviation of the average found in step 1. This is where a computer/calculator comes in handy.
3. Divide the difference between today's TP and the 20-day average of TP by the product of the standard deviation times 0.015.

$$\text{CCI} = (\text{Today's TP} - \text{20-day SMA of TP})/$$
$$(\text{20-day standard deviation} * 0.015)$$

Lambert set the constant at 0.015 in the denominator to ensure that approximately 70 to 80 percent of CCI values would fall between −100 and +100. Since the numerator can be positive or negative, so can the CCI. The standard deviation is inversely proportional to sample size; the larger the sample the smaller the deviation. Since the standard deviation is in the denominator, a small lookback period will cause a more volatile CCI. A shorter CCI (10 periods) will also produce a smaller percentage of values between +100 and −100. Conversely, a longer CCI (40 periods) will have a higher percentage of values between +100 and −100.

Since this oscillator usually falls between +100 and −100 and is momentum based, most traders will use it as an overbought/oversold indicator. However, since it is boundless extended readings above +100 or below −100 can indicate very strong trend moves.

The weakness of the CCI is its variability due to the volatile nature of the underlying instrument that is being applied to. A volatile stock will cause the indicator to behave erratically and jump well above/below the standard +100 and −100. These benchmarks may have to be expanded based on the market being analyzed. Many traders also apply a smoothing function to the CCI in an attempt to eliminate knee-jerk reactions.

We will be discussing two trading algorithms based on the CCI (Box 2.5). The first will utilize the CCI in the same manner as the RSI and stochastic. The second algorithm will use the CCI in a completely opposite manner—trend confirmation.

Box 2.5 Donald Lambert's CCI OB/OS System Description

If 9-day average of the CCI 20-day crosses above −100, then
  Buy MOC

If 9-day average CCI 20-day crosses below + 100, then
  Sell Short MOC

If position is long
  Take Profit: If close > entry price + 3 ATR Sell MOC
  Protective Stop: If close < entry price − 1 ATR Sell MOC

If position is short
  Take Profit: If close < entry price − 3 ATR BuyToCover MOC
  Protective Stop: If close > entry price + 1 ATR, BuyToCover MOC

Note that MOC indicates market on close.

Donald Lambert's CCI OB/OS System p-code

```
 'Donald Lambert CCI OB/OS
'
myCCIVal = average(cci(cciLen),smooth);

If myCCIVal crosses above -100 then buy this bar on close
If myCCIVal crosses below 100 then sellShort this bar on
  close

If marketPosition = 1 then
     If c > entryPrice + 3* avgTrueRange(10) then sell this
        bar on close
     if c < entryPrice - 1* avgTrueRange(10) then sell this
        bar on close
```

```
If marketPosition =-1 then
     If c < entryPrice - 3* avgTrueRange(10) then buyToCover
        this bar on close
     if c > entryPrice + 1* avgTrueRange(10) then buyToCover
        this bar on close
```

The description of this algorithm looks very similar to the RSI and stochastic overbought/oversold, but there is one esoteric difference. Notice how the entries are initiated. Long entries require the CCI to cross above −100, meaning that the CCI has been in the oversold territory for at least one bar. Just the opposite is true for short entries; CCI must cross below +100. This is different from the other algorithms in that entries are delayed until the indicator starts moving in the same direction as the desired market direction. This delay is a double-edged sword in that you might get confirmation of market direction but at the cost of worse price.

Many of today's trading and testing platforms have the keywords CROSS ABOVE and CROSS BELOW built into the programming language. These keywords are simple shortcuts meant to make programming easier to understand and implement. Using the CCI indicator as an example, here are the equivalent computer codes to the keywords:

CROSS ABOVE −100 : CCI[1] < −100 and CCI[0] > −100

CROSS BELOW +100 : CCI[1] > +100 and CCI[0] < +100

Remember the values inside the square brackets indicate the number of bars/days in the past. In later chapters, where different platforms are discussed, you will see these keywords. Figure 2.10 shows some trades generated by this first CCI algorithm.

Since the flowchart for this algorithm is so similar to the RSI and stochastic, it will not be shown for brevity's sake. However, the all-important performance metrics are shown in Table 2.5.

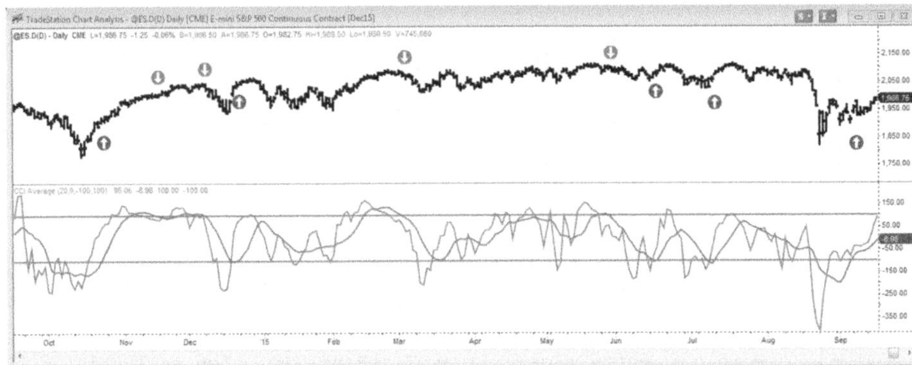

FIGURE 2.10 Trades generated by the CCI algorithm when it crosses above 100 and below −100.

Source: TradeStation

TABLE 2.5 Performance of CCI algorithm

Ticker	Net Profit	Max. Sys DD	# Trades	Avg P/L	Avg Bars Held	% of Winners
AD0_E0B	−38040.0	−47030	156	−243.85	10.9	28.85
BP0_E0B	7962.5	−59875	144	55.3	12.38	35.42
C20_E0B	−2975.0	−11538	151	−19.7	9.61	30.46
CC20_E0B	27820.0	−8400	147	189.25	11.15	38.1
CL20_E0B	−22830.0	−89180	154	−148.25	10.72	35.71
CT20_E0B	−7615.0	−44780	145	−52.52	10.82	35.86
CU0_E0B	−10900.0	−41075	147	−74.15	11.96	31.97
DX20_E0B	−37060.0	−37110	148	−250.41	10.56	27.7
ED0_E0B	−353.1	−1847	138	−2.56	14.39	34.06
EMD0_E0B	−27880.0	−47890	146	−190.96	10.93	29.45
ES0_E0B	−34525.0	−56038	152	−227.14	10.18	29.61
FC0_E0B	−1225.0	−25213	146	−8.39	10.16	32.19
FV0_E0B	−5656.1	−11047	146	−38.74	10.96	31.51
GC20_E0B	−26150.0	−49330	152	−172.04	11.16	32.24
HG20_E0B	−34350.0	−53500	129	−266.28	12.94	34.11
HO20_E0B	−53932.2	−112518	157	−343.52	10.13	31.85
KC20_E0B	−32737.5	−54263	149	−219.71	11.17	29.53
KW20_E0B	10325.0	−24513	154	67.05	10.6	38.31
LB0_E0B	21406.0	−14058	150	142.71	9.41	36.67
LC0_E0B	−31750.0	−42120	145	−218.97	10.19	24.14
LH0_E0B	−860.0	−13530	152	38.55	10.74	35.53
MP0_E0B	−565.0	−9145	146	−3.87	12.99	36.99
NG20_E0B	−46040.0	−81490	145	−317.52	10.99	29.66
NK0_E0B	−17900.0	−54000	144	−124.31	9.93	29.86
OJ20_E0B	26655.0	−9105	159	167.64	11.19	39.62
PL20_E0B	14920.0	−40290	147	101.5	9.9	34.01
RB0_E0B	−155710.8	−163069	155	−1004.59	6.61	21.29
S20_E0B	0.0	0	0	N/A	N/A	N/A
SB20_E0B	−7604.8	−25458	142	−53.55	10.7	35.92
SI20_E0B	77875.0	−39745	155	502.42	11.57	39.35
TF0_E0B	−23300.0	−47340	146	−159.59	9.36	30.14
TU0_E0B	−5704.0	−11907	143	−39.89	11	34.97
TY0_E0B	−30233.9	−34125	140	−215.96	10.73	25
US0_E0B	−63453.1	−71422	151	−420.22	10.3	25.83
W20_E0B	0.0	0	0	N/A	N/A	N/A

Now, switching gears and using the CCI as a coincident indicator, Box 2.6 provides the description of a trend-following algorithm. A coincident indicator simply means it is confirming the current market direction.

Box 2.6 Donald Lambert's CCI Trend-Following System

myCCIVal = 9-day average of the 20-day CCI

If the lowest myCCIVal for the past 3 days > 100, then
  Buy MOC

If the highest myCCIVal for the past 3 days < −100, then
  Sell Short MOC

If position is long
  Take Profit: If close > entry price + 5 ATR Sell MOC
  Protective Stop: If close < entry price − 3 ATR, Sell MOC

If position is short
  Take Profit: If close < entry price − 5 ATR, BuyToCover MOC
  Protective Stop: If close > entry price + 3 ATR, BuyToCover MOC

Note that MOC stands for market on close.

Donald Lambert's CCI Trend-Following System p − code

```
myCCIVal = average(cci(cciLen),smooth);

If lowest(myCCIVal,3) > 100 then buy this bar on close;
If highest(myCCiVal,3) < -100 then sellShort this bar on
  close;

If marketPosition = 1 then
     If c > entryPrice + 5* avgTrueRange(10) then sell this
        bar on close
     if c < entryPrice - 3* avgTrueRange(10) then sell this
        bar on close
If marketPosition =-1 then
     If c < entryPrice - 5* avgTrueRange(10) then buyToCover
        this bar on close
     if c > entryPrice + 3* avgTrueRange(10) then buyToCover
        this bar on close
```

This trading algorithm description is somewhat different from the others we have thus discussed in this chapter. Instead of repeating the words for the 9-day average of the 20-day CCI, I simply assigned it to the variable myCCIVal. This is just like you would do in an actual programming language. The words *lowest* and *highest* were also introduced and used as a shortcut to see if the myCCIVal variable was above or

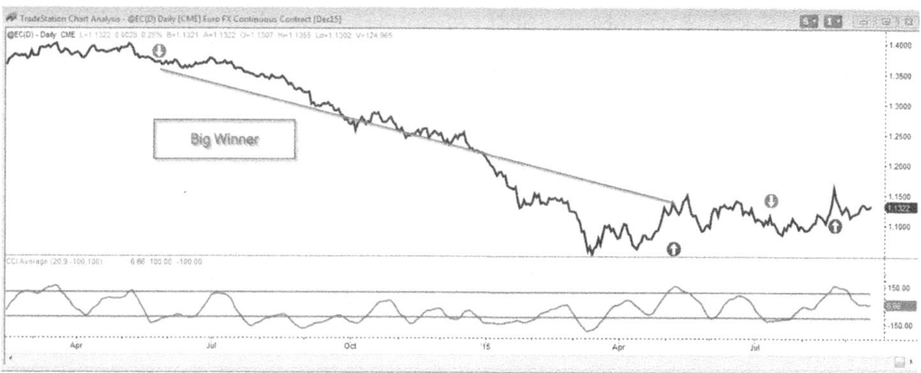

FIGURE 2.11 The CCI system detecting a downturn in the Eurocurrency.

Source: TradeStation

below a certain level for the past three days. If the lowest myCCIVal for the past three days is greater than 100, then we know that the CCI did not dip below 100 during that time period. Trend detection occurs when the CCI stays in an extreme territory for several bars. This system is triggering a buy signal when the 9-day smoothed CCI stays above 100 for three days straight. The sell signal is triggered if the indicator stays below −100 for three days straight. Since we are dealing with a trend-following approach, the profit objective as well as the stop loss has been increased to five and three times the average true range, respectively. As you can see, the instructions for entries are contained within a very precise if–then construct and therefore can be represented by a flowchart. Again, this flowchart is so similar to the RSI, stochastic, and CCI #1 flowcharts that it would be terribly redundant to show it. Figure 2.11 does show how the system is more than capable of capturing the recent downturn in the Eurocurrency.

Table 2.6 shows the performance of the CCI Trend-Follower algorithm.

Gerald Appel's MACD—Moving Average Convergence Divergence

The Moving Average Convergence Divergence (MACD) indicator was created in the late 1970s by Gerald Appel. Basically, the indicator plots the difference between a fast and slow exponential moving average. The difference line is usually plotted oscillating around a zero line. Another line representing a smoothed version of the difference line is plotted as well. The smoothed version of the difference between the two moving averages is considered the trigger. Action is usually taken when the trigger crosses the difference line. In addition, it is common to see a histogram representation of the relationship between the difference line and the trigger. The MACD is a quick snapshot summary of the relationship between two different length-moving averages.

TABLE 2.6 Performance of CCI Algorithm as Coincident Indicator

Ticker	Net Profit	Max. Sys DD	# Trades	Avg P/L	Avg Bars Held	% of Winners
AD0_E0B	36660.0	−30990	105	349.14	32.94	42.86
BP0_E0B	−35562.5	−95325	106	−335.5	32.35	34.91
C20_E0B	−12000.0	−36738	104	−115.38	31.46	35.58
CC20_E0B	−51890.0	−59700	112	−463.3	29.7	29.46
CL20_E0B	55630.0	−71870	111	501.17	31.23	39.64
CT20_E0B	−16015.0	−39350	124	−129.15	27.79	37.1
CU0_E0B	25037.5	−72988	103	243.08	32.71	41.75
DX20_E0B	40065.0	−23940	106	377.97	33.84	43.4
ED0_E0B	6471.9	−2294	95	68.13	36.76	48.42
EMD0_E0B	18790.0	−56220	101	186.04	34.5	42.57
ES0_E0B	23250.0	−38975	96	242.19	36.84	39.58
FC0_E0B	37612.5	−22688	114	329.93	28.22	45.61
FV0_E0B	26687.9	−13273	104	256.61	34.76	41.35
GC20_E0B	−18150.0	−76330	102	−177.94	35.28	39.22
HG20_E0B	105212.5	−52388	97	1084.66	35.79	47.42
HO20_E0B	15036.0	−128789	107	140.52	31.31	36.45
KC20_E0B	15881.3	−61125	103	154.19	32.87	34.95
KW20_E0B	−26350.0	−50213	116	−227.16	28.53	32.76
LB0_E0B	−7458.0	−40667	126	−59.19	25.39	39.68
LC0_E0B	−3700.0	−22240	100	−37	33.59	39
LH0_E0B	−4210.0	−24600	110	−38.27	31.46	36.36
MP0_E0B	2385.0	−12575	101	23.61	34.02	35.64
NG20_E0B	84340.0	−118220	96	878.54	34.81	44.79
NK0_E0B	29625.0	−43025	102	290.44	32	41.18
OJ20_E0B	−23430.0	−31785	111	−211.08	29.85	34.23
PL20_E0B	−19845.0	−85060	116	−171.08	28.65	37.93
RB0_E0B	78246.0	−91774	118	663.1	25.95	43.22
S20_E0B	0.0	0	0	N/A	N/A	N/A
SB20_E0B	23598.4	−16733	108	218.5	30.12	42.59
SI20_E0B	−97730.0	−186135	113	−864.87	31.5	34.51
TF0_E0B	−30550.0	−55750	92	−332.07	35.45	36.96
TU0_E0B	21468.0	−8188	93	230.84	38.05	38.71
TY0_E0B	6578.6	−22531	98	67.13	35.56	36.73
US0_E0B	40874.3	−28375	99	412.87	35.38	41.41
W20_E0B	0.0	0	0	N/A	N/A	N/A

We will discuss moving averages in the last part of this chapter, but a little knowledge of averages is necessary to fully grasp the MACD. A trend change is usually indicated when a shorter (more sensitive) average crosses above/below a longer (less sensitive) average. Unfortunately, moving average crossovers lag current market conditions, and here is where the real beauty of the MACD is revealed. The histogram component can quickly reveal when the difference between the two moving averages (MACD) and the smoothed version of MACD (trigger) is converging or diverging. Convergence means the MACD line and its associated trigger are coming together and divergence means simply the two are growing apart. As prices of an instrument increase, the short-term moving average will grow quicker than a longer-term average. The MACD histogram will reflect this momentum. As prices start to slow, the histogram will start moving in the opposite direction.

Calculation of MACD using 12-day and 26-day moving averages:

1. Calculate a 12-period EMA of price for the chosen time period.
2. Calculate a 26-period EMA of price for the chosen time period.
3. Subtract the 26-period EMA from the 12-period EMA.
4. Calculate a 9-period EMA of the result obtained from step 3.

This 9-period EMA line is overlaid on a histogram that is created by subtracting the 9-period EMA from the result in step 3, which is called the MACD line, but it is not always visibly plotted on the MACD representation on a chart.

A trading algorithm can be derived by waiting for the histogram to form a two-bar high pivot (two bars to the left and to the right are shorter than the center bar) and then entering a short position. Momentum has been positive but it is beginning to slow. A long position can be initiated when a two-bar pivot low is formed in the MACD histogram. Figure 2.12 shows how the pivot points in the histogram can initiate trade signals.

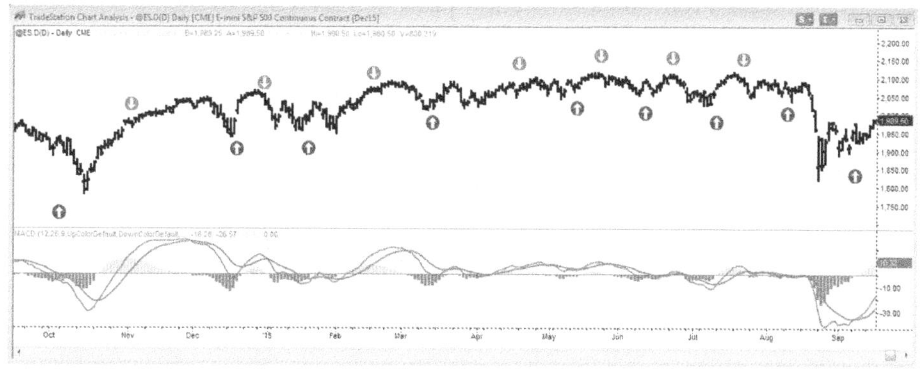

FIGURE 2.12 Histogram pivot points can initiate trade signals.

Based on our knowledge of the MACD and the chart examples, Box 2.7 shows a simple MACD histogram-trading algorithm.

Box 2.7 Gerald Appel's MACD Histogram System

Notice how the algorithm description in this example is getting closer and closer to pseudocode. As you evolve as a system tester, you will notice how the lines that separate description, pseudocode, and actual code start to blur. LeftBar2 is the second bar to the left of the pivot high/low bar and LeftBar1 is the first bar to the left of the pivot. The other variable names should be self-explanatory.

myMACD = MACD(C,12,26)

myMACDAvg = Xaverage(MACD,9)

myMACDDiff = myMACD − myMACDAvg

leftBar2 = myMACDDiff[4]

leftBar1 = myMACDDiff[3]

centerBar = myMACDiff[2]

rightBar1 = myMACDDiff[1]

rightBar2 = myMACDDiff[0]

If leftBar2 < 0 and rightBar2 < 0 and centerBar < leftBar1 and centerBar < leftBar2 and centerBar < rightBar1 and centerBar < rightBar2, then Buy MOC

If leftBar2 > 0 and rightBar2 > 0 and centerBar > leftBar1 and centerBar > leftBar2 and centerBar > rightBar1 and centerBar > rightBar2, then SellShort MOC

If position is long
Take Profit: If close > entry price + 3 ATR Sell MOC
Protective Stop: If close < entry price − 1 ATR Sell MOC

If position is short
Take Profit: If close < entry price − 3 ATR BuyToCover MOC
Protective Stop: If close > entry price + 1 ATR, BuyToCover MOC
*MOC = market on close

Gerald Appel's MACD Histogram System p – code

```
'Gerald Appels MACD histogram algorithm
'Buys - histogram forms a low 2 bar pivot with all bars below 0
'Shorts - histogram forms a high 2 bar pivot with all bars above 0
```

```
MACDAvg = XAverage( MyMACD,9)
MACDDiff = myMACD - MACDAvg

leftBar2 = MACDDiff[4]
leftBar1 = MACDDiff[3]
centerBar = MACDDiff[2]
rightBar1 = MACDDiff[1]
rightBar2 = MACDDiff[0]

If leftBar2 < 0 and rightBar2 < 0 and centerBar < leftBar1
  and centerBar < leftBar2 and
     centerBar < rightBar1 and centerBar < rightBar2 then
     Buy this bar on close

If leftBar2 > 0 and rightBar2 > 0 and centerBar > leftBar1
  and centerBar > leftBar2 and
     centerBar > rightBar1 and centerBar > rightBar2 then
     SellShort this bar on close

If marketPosition = 1 then
     If c > entryPrice + 3* avgTrueRange(10) then sell this
        bar on close
     if c < entryPrice - 1* avgTrueRange(10) then sell this
        bar on close
If marketPosition =-1 then
     If c < entryPrice - 3* avgTrueRange(10) then buyToCover
        this bar on close
     if c > entryPrice + 1* avgTrueRange(10) then buyToCover
        this bar on close
```

The MACD can be classified as an absolute price oscillator (APO), due to the fact it deals with the actual prices of moving averages rather than percentage changes. This makes the MACD different from the other indicators we have thus discussed. A percentage price oscillator (PPO) computes the difference between two moving averages of price divided by the longer moving average value.

While an APO will show greater levels for higher-priced securities and smaller levels for lower-priced securities, a PPO calculates changes relative to price. Subsequently, a PPO is preferred when comparing oscillator values between different types of trading instruments, especially those with substantially different prices, or comparing oscillator values for the same instrument at significantly different times.

The manner in which we developed the MACD algorithm does not care about absolute prices because it looks at the difference between the moving averages as either positive or negative; it does not care about the magnitude of difference.

Price-Based Indicators

Price-based indicators reflect trend and volatility. As we stated earlier, applying a moving average to an instrument's historical data will smooth out the data and soften wild market swings. In other words, a moving average eliminates a good portion of the noise associated with daily price changes.

Simple, Exponential, and Weighted Moving Averages

The most often used moving average is the simple version. Here, you sum up the closing prices over the past *N* days and then divide by *N*. The exponential moving average calculation uses a smoothing factor to place a higher weight on recent data points and is regarded as much more efficient than the linear weighted average. Having an understanding of the calculations is not generally required for most traders because most charting packages do the calculation for you. But if you are interested in the calculations, here are the steps involved in calculating the exponential and weighted moving averages:

1. Seed the exponential average initially with a simple moving average.
2. Calculate the smoothing factor: multiplier = 2 / (EMA length + 1).
3. EMA[0] = (close[0] − EMA[1]) * multiplier + EMA[1].

The key to the EMA calculation is the smoothing factor multiplier. If we were calculating a 20-day EMA, the multiplier would be equal to 2 / 21, or 0.0952. In this example, a weighting of nearly 10 percent is applied to the most recent data point. A weighted moving average is slightly more complicated to calculate. Sticking with 20 periods, here are the steps involved in the calculation:

1. Sum up the values of the length of moving average : 20 + 19 + 18 + 17 +16 +15 + 14 + 13 + 12 + 11 + 10 + 9 + 8 + 7 + 6 + 5 + 4 + 3 + 2 +1 = 210.
2. Multiply the oldest price by 1 /20 and second oldest by 2/20 and third oldest by 3/20 and so on.
3. Sum up the products and you will have a weighted moving average. As you can see, the most recent data is weighted the most.

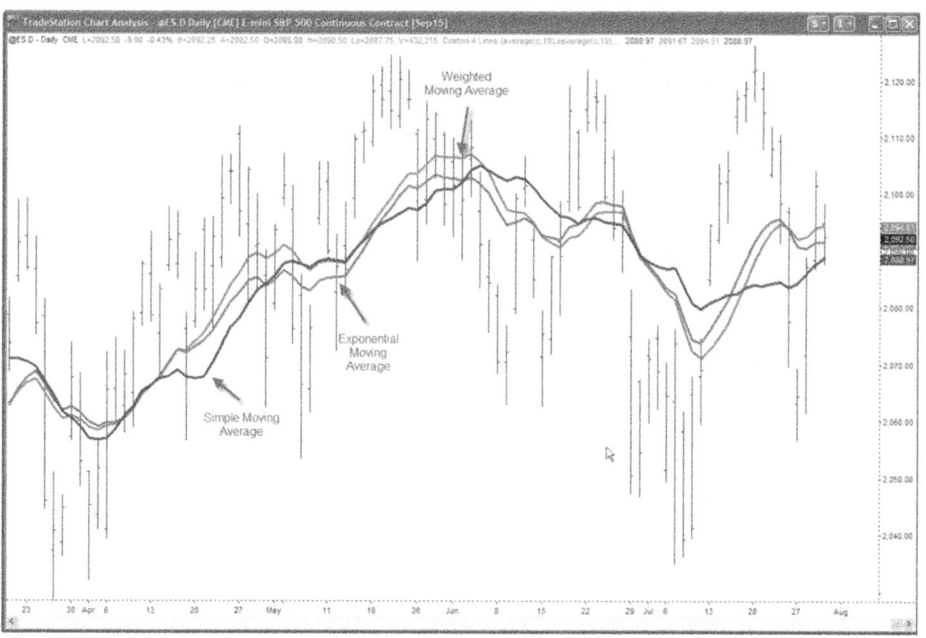

FIGURE 2.13 Three different 20-day moving averages.

Source: TradeStation

The weighted moving average addresses the problem of equal weighting. Figure 2.13 shows the three different 20-day moving averages across several days of data.

So which moving average is the best? It depends on the situation and the data that is being analyzed. As a pure price/average crossover-trading algorithm the following table might provide some insight. An 80-day period of each moving average was analyzed across 35 futures markets over a test period of 30 years and the results are shown in Table 2.7.

The performances for the three averaging methods aren't too dissimilar; they seem to make or lose money in the same sectors. However, on closer examination, at the portfolio level, notice the average trade for the weighted average is considerably lower than its siblings. This might indicate why it is the least used averaging method in technical analysis. While reviewing the performance, keep in mind that this testing did not take into consideration trade management other than allowing the algorithm to reverse its position; there weren't any protective stops or profit objectives. The fact is, trend following doesn't use a lot of trade management. Many trend algorithms will utilize a disaster stop but usually will let profits run until a reversal is signaled. If you think about this, it makes sense; a moving average is an

TABLE 2.7 Examples of Trades Generated by Stochastics

Ticker	Simple Moving Average						Exponential Moving Average						Weighted Moving Average					
	Net Profit	MAX. Sys. DD	Trds	Avg Profit/ Loss	Avg Bars Held	% of Winners	Net Profit	MAX. Sys. DD	Trds	Avg Profit/ Loss	Avg Bars Held	% of Winners	Net Profit	MAX. Sys. Draw-down	Trds	Avg Profit/ Loss	Avg Bars Held	% of Winners
AD0_E0B	−2640	−70090	404	−6.53	18.62	15.59	7700	−53380	446	17.26	16.96	16.14	−3270	−73090	493	−6.63	15.59	17.04
BP0_E0B	74113	−179000	440	168.44	18.52	15.91	58013	−183950	488	118.88	16.8	16.6	40463	−203063	566	71.49	14.62	18.2
C20_E0B	18213	−26463	378	48.18	21.41	17.72	−29388	−46100	484	−60.72	16.94	14.67	−10388	−32075	512	−20.29	16.07	17.77
CC20_E0B	−117190	−120040	487	−240.64	16.74	14.37	−108430	−111280	533	−203.43	15.38	15.38	−109730	−113060	575	−190.83	14.33	16
CL20_E0B	171330	−87180	375	456.88	21.48	19.47	126550	−85620	425	297.76	19.07	19.76	148610	−71240	519	286.34	15.8	20.81
CT20_E0B	39545	−48520	435	90.91	18.64	17.01	34695	−39435	485	71.54	16.82	16.49	1405	−68055	561	2.5	14.68	17.47
CU0_E0B	90850	−54625	401	226.56	20.23	18.95	94900	−55238	437	217.16	18.65	18.76	120775	−67600	477	253.2	17.17	20.75
DX20_E0B	16685	−49235	400	41.71	19.82	16.5	34655	−27280	431	80.41	18.46	19.26	41255	−30580	490	84.19	16.53	18.98
ED0_E0B	−17053	−19866	355	−48.04	22.72	12.68	−11034	−14566	339	−32.55	23.75	14.16	−15378	−19566	414	−37.15	19.63	14.98
EMD0_E0B	20970	−34960	293	71.57	20.91	18.43	26900	−32140	340	79.12	18.16	19.71	−88920	−89980	450	−197.6	14.14	17.56
ES0_E0B	−50000	−67588	470	−106.38	17.43	14.68	−69200	−70688	500	−138.4	16.44	15.4	−75350	−75613	578	−130.36	14.36	17.47
FC0_E0B	49313	−29350	358	137.74	22.56	18.16	83288	−18063	374	222.69	21.64	22.73	73038	−33000	480	152.16	17.08	20.21
FV0_E0B	−1805	−28908	345	−5.23	20.61	15.07	17213	−21032	381	45.18	18.76	17.32	−15784	−35951	479	−32.95	15.29	16.28
GC20_E0B	−114780	−125070	471	−243.69	17.32	12.95	−127580	−137870	565	−225.81	14.5	13.63	−126260	−137290	591	−213.64	14.01	14.89
HG20_E0B	134138	−39163	417	321.67	19.43	17.03	79013	−58988	477	165.64	17.11	17.61	61863	−74013	541	114.35	15.21	19.59
HO20_E0B	22025	−154637	457	48.19	17.8	15.54	418	−152914	507	0.82	16.15	17.16	39118	−102509	571	68.51	14.45	18.04
KC20_E0B	99019	−152544	405	244.49	19.92	17.04	45844	−167219	501	91.5	16.3	15.97	122619	−93356	517	237.17	15.82	18.76
KW20_E0B	−16163	−41075	465	−34.76	17.59	15.7	2588	−29713	495	5.23	16.59	16.77	−42938	−59900	591	−72.65	14.06	16.24
LB0_E0B	87685	−26515	392	223.69	20.69	20.92	68033	−23342	442	153.92	18.46	20.14	70031	−26345	534	131.14	15.46	21.35

LC0_E0B	−25000	−41790	398	−62.81	20.39	16.33	−33400	−49230	464	−71.98	17.64	17.03	−50560	−66380	566	−89.33	14.64	17.67
LH0_E0B	280	−29220	394	0.71	20.59	18.02	−10340	−36880	484	−21.36	16.95	18.39	−7820	−34840	520	−15.04	15.84	19.42
MP0_E0B	16770	−22620	238	70.46	22.1	18.07	5320	−26255	274	19.42	19.33	17.52	21125	−24845	307	68.81	17.62	22.15
NG20_E0B	238960	−88090	306	780.92	21.52	20.26	161390	−116370	380	424.71	17.53	18.95	209010	−121120	394	530.48	17.14	19.04
NK0_E0B	69875	−68250	306	228.35	21.24	21.57	47275	−75975	379	124.74	17.34	21.37	−62625	−72225	472	−132.68	14.29	19.07
OJ20_E0B	−8818	−39850	386	−22.84	20.87	17.1	−32283	−54738	448	−72.06	18.12	17.86	−25903	−55323	530	−48.87	15.47	18.11
PL20_E0B	33180	−60775	457	72.6	17.8	15.32	52050	−64165	507	102.66	16.15	16.57	−3540	−61390	585	−6.05	14.13	17.09
RB0_E0B	60850	−68858	410	148.41	19.58	18.78	92216	−87668	458	201.35	17.63	21.83	181639	−61591	537	338.25	15.3	21.97
S20_E0B	−55025	−67225	454	−121.2	17.99	15.42	−39125	−56238	528	−74.1	15.61	15.91	−16825	−59150	560	−30.04	14.78	17.14
SB20_E0B	6410	−33259	383	16.74	21.01	17.49	−12279	−42206	485	−25.32	16.8	14.64	5026	−36258	501	10.03	16.3	16.57
SI20_E0B	−132065	−180155	449	−294.13	18.12	14.25	−171125	−205775	523	−327.2	15.7	14.53	−101005	−146075	583	−173.25	14.18	16.64
TF0_E0B	−30230	−64260	191	−158.27	18.95	17.8	−39050	−68200	217	−179.95	16.8	18.43	−98130	−119750	262	−374.54	14.39	18.7
TF20_E0B	−30155	−63300	193	−156.24	18.74	17.62	−40420	−69560	217	−186.27	16.78	18.43	−98140	−119760	262	−374.58	14.37	18.7
TU0_E0B	22205	−19544	325	68.32	20.19	13.23	37415	−13961	311	120.3	21.06	16.08	18004	−24410	392	45.93	17.11	16.07
TY0_E0B	28377	−29506	385	73.71	21.01	17.4	38757	−22544	429	90.34	18.96	18.18	15044	−34222	488	30.83	16.78	19.88
US0_E0B	−12731	−73538	437	−29.13	18.63	18.31	−3851	−69806	501	−7.69	16.38	18.16	6405	−48757	520	12.32	15.81	20.96
W20_E0B	−40788	−57050	464	−87.9	17.63	15.3	−34238	−49750	516	−66.35	15.95	14.73	−35588	−46250	551	−64.59	15	17.06

indicator of trend and it will put you into the market in the direction it thinks the trend is going. It is self-adapting. The following is the pseudocode used in the testing of these three simplistic methodologies:

```
'Trend Following with Different Averaging Methods
'Simple Price MAV Cross Over

myAVG = SMA(C,80) 'Comment out the two you do not want to use
'myAVG = WMA(C,80)      'by placing a single quote at the
                        start of the line
'myAVG = EMA(C,80)

If close of today > myAVG then
       Buy this bar on close
If close of today < myAVG then
       SellShort this bar on close
```

Bollinger Bands

John Bollinger is the originator of this volatility-based channel indicator. It is considered a channel because the indicator consists of two lines that never intersect. The channel width is based on a standard deviation value, which is derived from an *N*-length moving average. Most Bollinger Bands are one or two standard deviations above/below the moving average. In a perfectly "normal" world, 95 percent of values from a sample will stay within two standard deviations of its mean. Theoretically speaking, would it not make sense that once price rises to the upper channel/band there exists a higher probability of price reverting to its mean? Or does it make more sense that a penetration of a band indicates strong momentum and the beginning of a trend. Like many indicators, Bollinger Bands can be used as mean reversion as well as trend following. The most successful trend-following systems use a longer-length Bollinger Band penetration algorithm for trade entry. Mean-reversion traders use a much shorter length input for this indicator.

If the market demonstrates enough momentum to carry price through two standard deviations, it seems there is a real good chance it has enough gusto to continue on in that direction. Well, this is what the trend followers of the 1990s thought, and they turned out to be right.

Figure 2.14 shows a 60-day two-standard-deviation (SD) Bollinger Band on crude oil. The Bollinger Bands are the outside lines and the centerline is the moving average. This is a perfect example of why this trend entry technique gained so much popularity in the 1990s and in the new millennium. Crude penetrated the lower band and never looked back until the trend entered into a congestive phase—a $50 move or $50,000 per contract. That's right, $50,000! And you thought I wasn't going to reveal the Holy Grail! Remember, one monster trade doesn't make a trading algorithm.

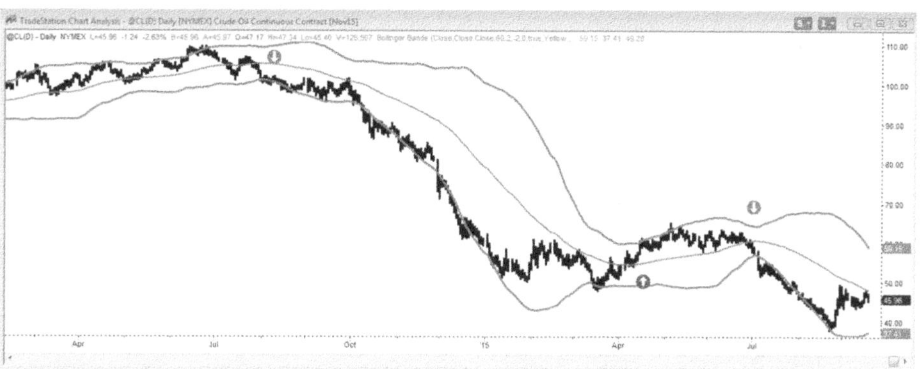

FIGURE 2.14 A 60-day, two-SD Bollinger Band on crude oil.

Source: TradeStation

Here's how you calculate Bollinger Bands:

Calculation of Bollinger Bands using 60 days and 2 standard deviations:

1. Calculate a 60-period SMA of price for the chosen time period.
2. Calculate the standard deviation of the 60-day sample (use a computer).
3. The top or upper band is the 60-period SMA + 2 standard deviations.
4. The bottom or lower band is the 60-period SMA − 2 standard deviations.

Let's put the Bollinger Band indicator to a test utilizing a common trend-following algorithm (Box 2.8).

Box 2.8 Using John Bollinger's Bands as a Trend Follower

Buy when market closes above top band.

Sell short when market closes below bottom band.

Sell when market position is long and market closes below average.

Cover when market position is short and market closes above average.

```
myAvg = Average(C,60) ' 60-day moving average calculation
myTopBand = BollingerBand(C,60,+2) ' 2 std dev above average
myBotBand = BollingerBand(C,60, −2) ' the − 2 means below average
If close crosses above myTopBand, then
    Buy MOC
```

If close crosses below myBotBand, then
    SellShort MOC

If position is long, then
    If close crosses below myAvg, then
        Sell MOC

If position is short, then
    If close crosses above myAvg, then
        BuyToCover MOC

The beauty of this algorithm is in its simplicity; we don't even need to sketch a flowchart. There is another facet of this algorithm that makes it a winner—it's self-adaptive. Meaning the bands are moving (adapting) around the average based on an intrinsic property of the underlying instrument. And that property is volatility. Volatility reveals one of the most important things we need to know about an instrument, and that is risk. Risk is directly proportional to volatility—the larger the swings, the riskier the market. I am jumping the gun here, but we will use this risk measure as a filter in version 2 of the Bollinger Band trend algorithm. Volatility also informs us of market noise. When the Bollinger Bands expand during high levels of volatility, they are indicating a chaotic situation—a situation where entry criteria should be made more difficult to trigger. The following is the pseudocode for version 1 of the trading algorithm:

```
'Trend Following with Bollinger Bands
'Utilizing 60-day average and 2 standard deviations
'Version 1
myAVG = SMA(C,60)
myTopBand = BollingerBand(C,60,+2)
myBotBand = BollingerBand(C,60,-2)

If close > myTopBand then
       Buy this bar on close
If close < myBotBand then
       SellShort this bar on close

If marketPosition = 1 and c < myAvg then sell this bar on close
If marketPosition =-1 and c > myAvg then buyToCover this bar
     on close
```

Table 2.8 shows the individual results of Bollinger Band version 1 across 35 futures markets.

In the prior paragraphs, I hinted of a version 2 of this algorithm utilizing the volatility as trading filter. Risk aversion is most often the number-one consideration in the development of a trading algorithm, and we can use the volatility as a

TABLE 2.8 **Performance of Bollinger Band Algorithm Version 1**

Bollinger Band [60 Days 2 Standard Deviations]

Ticker	Net Profit	Max DD	# Trades	Avg P/L	Avg Bars Held	% Winners
<Portfolio>	*1319369*	*−380897*	*3580*	*369*	*44*	*36*
AD0_E0B	30100	−25600	95	317	45	35
BP0_E0B	86888	−90825	107	812	41	34
C20_E0B	−1263	−23038	119	−11	42	35
CC20_E0B	−67870	−69300	123	−552	33	22
CL20_E0B	168160	−55940	101	1665	47	47
CT20_E0B	54050	−34175	112	483	40	31
CU0_E0B	167738	−27425	91	1843	50	44
DX20_E0B	84575	−13820	94	900	49	47
ED0_E0B	4997	−3363	105	48	48	31
EMD0_E0B	−18880	−38940	92	−205	39	29
ES0_E0B	−41925	−52213	120	−349	36	31
FC0_E0B	55438	−25650	101	549	49	41
FV0_E0B	23631	−15335	89	266	45	39
GC20_E0B	−19280	−59660	111	−174	39	32
HG20_E0B	76650	−42513	111	691	44	37
HO20_E0B	74941	71391	116	646	39	37
KC20_E0B	100294	−108269	99	1013	45	38
KW20_E0B	10800	−21350	109	99	41	31
LB0_E0B	37973	−24997	109	348	44	38
LC0_E0B	−11770	−30010	121	−97	39	28
LH0_E0B	10880	−25480	113	96	42	37
MP0_E0B	6755	−25070	68	99	45	37
NG20_E0B	175690	−99650	87	2019	47	45
NK0_E0B	48150	−41675	85	566	46	36
OJ20_E0B	−10130	−45408	110	−92	43	36
PL20_E0B	55340	−34340	109	508	41	31
RB0_E0B	124147	−58171	109	1139	44	39
S20_E0B	19475	−38125	115	169	41	36
SB20_E0B	31944	−13788	100	319	48	42
SI20_E0B	−25660	−113680	111	−231	39	29
TF0_E0B	−14570	−51590	49	−297	41	37
TU0_E0B	37075	−6975	78	475	50	42
TY0_E0B	42466	−19490	98	433	46	40
US0_E0B	22038	−42338	109	202	42	39
W20_E0B	−19475	−34225	114	−171	38	32

risk measure and modify version 1 to make it more risk averse. Looking back at the results you will notice a relatively high maximum drawdown at the portfolio level—greater than 30 percent. In the world of hedge funds, this is an acceptable level—I am not kidding! Some of the most successful hedge fund managers have taken their clients down more than 40 percent before rebounding. This is the main difference between hedge fund participants and the typical investor. The trade-off for higher returns is, of course, higher risk. Let's see if we can be a better hedge fund manager and reduce that 30 percent plus drawdown. Let's assume we have a million-dollar allocation (remember, we are in a dream world), we only want to risk 0.2 percent (0.002 or $2,000 per trade), and we don't want to reinvest profits (at this point). How can we use this information to reduce drawdown in version 2 of our trading algorithm?

Version 1 buys on penetration of upper Bollinger Band and gets out on the penetration of the moving average. So our initial trade risk can be defined as the distance between the upper band and the moving average. If we equate this distance to dollars, then we can filter out any trades that exceed our acceptable risk amount of $2,000. Now, will this guarantee that our largest loss will be $2,000 or less? No! Remember when I stated the bands were self-adapting? During the life of any given trade, the bands could expand and the distance between the outer bands and the moving average could grow well beyond our $2,000. This could result in an individual trade loss greater than that amount. Well, can we at least guarantee the maximum drawdown will decrease? Again, no! Maximum drawdown is a consequence of a losing streak. Even though we are filtering trades (eliminating what we consider too risky), that doesn't necessarily mean the trades involved in the losing streak will be eliminated. The filtering process might even eliminate the trades that pull the equity curve out of the drawdown. So, theoretically the risk aversion overlay might not help at all and might even make matters worse. Let's see for ourselves and use the following pseudocode on the same 35 markets:

```
 'Trend Following with Bollinger Bands
'Utilizing 60-day average and 2 standard deviations
'Version 2 - don't take any trade with risk > $2,000

myAVG = SMA(C,60)
myTopBand = BollingerBand(C,60,+2)
myBotBand = BollingerBand(C,60,-2)

filterTrade = false
'convert price range to dollars by multiplying by dollar value of points
If (myTopBand - myAvg) * BigPointValue > 2000 then
        filterTrade = true
```

```
If filterTrade = false then
    If close > myTopBand then
           Buy this bar on close
    If close < myBotBand then
           SellShort this bar on close


If marketPosition = 1 and c < myAvg then sell this bar on close
If marketPosition =-1 and c > myAvg then buyToCover this bar on close
```

Before hitting the **TEST** button, let's quickly go over the pseudocode. The only code that was added was the Boolean (true or false) typed variable **filterTrade** and its calculation. On every bar, it is initially turned off. The only way it is turned on is when the distance in terms of dollars between the upper band and the moving average exceeds $2,000. If **filterTrade** is on or true, the trade entry logic is bypassed, thereby skipping the trade. Why did we just use the top band and the moving average in our risk calculation? Shouldn't we use the bottom band and the average for short trades? One calculation is all that is needed since the distance between the top band and the average is always the same as the distance between the average and the bottom band—in this case, two standard deviations. Ready to hit the test button? Table 2.9 shows the results of version 2 of the algorithm.

Mission accomplished! Or was it? The maximum drawdown was reduced from to $381K to $103K—a whopping 73 percent. However, as we all know, reward is proportional to risk and the total profit dropped from $1.3M to less than $600K, or more than 50 percent. Was it worth it? What if we used $2,500 risk instead, or what if. . . . You can see how this stuff can become addictive. We could optimize the per-trade risk amount at the portfolio level or at the individual market level. Does it make sense to have a different risk level for crude oil than gold? If the equity curve looks better, why not? We could even eliminate all the markets that show a negative expectancy. We could work all day on different portfolios and what-if scenarios and create one great-looking equity curve. But who would we be fooling? If it was the 1980s or 1990s, the public. If we were unscrupulous and wanted to sell this miraculous algorithm, we could mislead the public with the guarantee that every number shown was generated by an exact trading algorithm. The general trading public of the latter part of the twentieth century didn't know any better and didn't understand the term "with benefit of hindsight." Nowadays, with the computer power and data at our fingertips, we would be fooling ourselves because the trading public now has the same computers and data and has been fully educated on "with benefit of hindsight." We can still fall into this same old trap, though, if we don't fully utilize the tools at our disposal.

TABLE 2.9 Performance of Bollinger Band Algorithm Version 2

Bollinger Band [60 Days 2 Standard Deviations with $2,000 Trade Filter]						
Ticker	Net Profit	Max DD	# Trades	Avg P/L	Avg Bars Held	% Winners
<Portfolio>	*513207*	*−103462*	*2224*	*231*	*43*	*34*
AD0_E0B	7360	−19900	57	129	42	35
BP0_E0B	10625	−7075	1	10625	69	100
C20_E0B	−2788	−15050	108	−26	42	34
CC20_E0B	−48940	−49270	110	−445	33	22
CL20_E0B	29460	−9970	45	655	50	51
CT20_E0B	12385	−31030	77	161	39	30
CU0_E0B	50688	−6488	4	12672	114	75
DX20_E0B	71510	−11830	56	1277	49	48
ED0_E0B	4997	−3363	105	48	48	31
EMD0_E0B	19720	−8640	37	533	44	27
ES0_E0B	−40288	−44075	80	−504	33	23
FC0_E0B	57950	−14975	75	773	51	41
FV0_E0B	25318	−12041	84	301	45	40
GC20_E0B	5840	−21110	74	79	39	32
HG20_E0B	6450	−18325	65	99	42	29
HO20_E0B	24291	−27344	50	486	38	36
KC20_E0B	51275	−35669	22	2331	39	41
KW20_E0B	7188	−23375	90	80	40	27
LB0_E0B	53134	−12761	51	1042	49	43
LC0_E0B	−12630	−30100	117	−108	39	27
LH0_E0B	12690	−20690	97	131	41	38
MP0_E0B	2770	−22135	62	45	43	34
NG20_E0B	38580	−14000	16	2411	50	50
NK0_E0B	35250	−12925	12	2938	50	33
OJ20_E0B	−16875	−49565	99	−170	41	34
PL20_E0B	−11870	−30065	72	−165	38	25
RB0_E0B	20830	−20086	40	521	43	43
S20_E0B	−10763	−34438	79	−136	37	35
SB20_E0B	17097	−12638	91	188	47	42
SI20_E0B	−4305	−42550	66	−65	40	27
TF0_E0B	18470	−6380	3	6157	78	67
TU0_E0B	28837	−7888	76	379	48	41
TY0_E0B	37841	−19212	73	518	46	41
US0_E0B	39185	−16650	38	1031	44	47
W20_E0B	−28075	−36663	92	−305	37	28

Keltner Channel

Chester Keltner brought this volatility-based indicator to public attention in 1960 through his book, *How to Make Money in Commodities*. The Keltner Channels are very similar to Bollinger Bands except the centerline is a moving average of typical price ((H + L + C) / 3) and the outer bands are calculated using average true range instead of standard deviation. Volatility can be measured in many different ways, but standard deviation and average true range are probably the two most popular.

The two key components of this indicator that set it apart from Bollinger's are the use of the typical price (TP) and the average true range. TP is simply the average of the high, low, and close prices. The TP takes into consideration the range of the day as well as the close, and as stated earlier, many feel this price is more indicative of the daily price action than simply the close. Since Bollinger and Keltner indicators are so similar, you will notice that the calculations aren't that different:

Calculation of Keltner Channels using 60 days and 2 ATR:

1. Calculate a 60-period SMA of the TP for the chosen time period.
2. Calculate the ATR of the 60-day sample (use a computer).
3. The top or upper band is the 60-period SMA + 2 ATR.
4. The bottom or lower band is the 60-period SMA − 2 ATR.

Box 2.9 shows a Keltner Channel trading algorithm that will be used throughout the rest of this chapter.

Box 2.9 Using Chester Keltner's Channels as a Trend Follower

Buy when market closes above top channel.

Sell short when market closes below bottom channel.

Sell when market position is long and market closes below average.

Cover when market position is short and market closes above average.

```
myTypicalPrice = (H + L + C);
myAvg = Average(myTypicalPrice,60) ' 60-day moving average of TP
myATR = AverageTrueRange(60)
myTopChannel = myAvg + 2 * myATR ' 2 ATR above average
myBotChannel = myAvg − 2 * myATR '− 2 ATR below average
```

If close crosses above myTopChannel, then
    Buy MOC

If close crosses below myBotChannel, then
    SellShort MOC

If position is long, then
    If close crosses below myAvg, then
        Sell MOC

If position is short, then
    If close crosses above myAvg, then
        BuyToCover MOC

Here is the pseudocode for the algorithm:

```
'Trend Following with Keltner Channels
'Utilizing Typical Price = (H + L + C)/3
'Utilizing 60-day average and 2 average true ranges

myAVG = SMA(C,60)
myTypicalPrice = (H + L + C)/3
myTopChannel = KeltnerChan(myTypicalPrice,60,+2)
myBotChannel = KeltnerChan(myTypicalPrice,60,-2)

If close > myTopChannel then
     Buy this bar on close
If close < myBotChannel then
     SellShort this bar on close

If marketPosition = 1 and c < myAvg then sell this bar on close
If marketPosition =-1 and c > myAvg then buyToCover this bar on close
```


Using the ATR instead of standard deviation creates smoother outer Bands due to how ATR reacts slower than deviation. Figure 2.15 shows a chart with both Keltner Channels (60 length and 2 ATR) and Bollinger Bands (60 length and 2 STDDEV) applied to the underlying data.

Notice how much smoother the Keltner Channels are compared to the Bollinger Bands. Does this mean they are better? Since the TP takes into consideration more data, is it a better gauge than just the close? Looking at the chart it seems like both indicators got into the short crude position at about the same time. This is a difficult question so let's use the computer tell us which is the better algorithm. This is not going to be an easy task because it is difficult to equate standard deviation to ATR. As you can tell by the chart, the Bollinger Bands encompass the Keltner Channels a majority of the time. This is a consequence of using the same settings

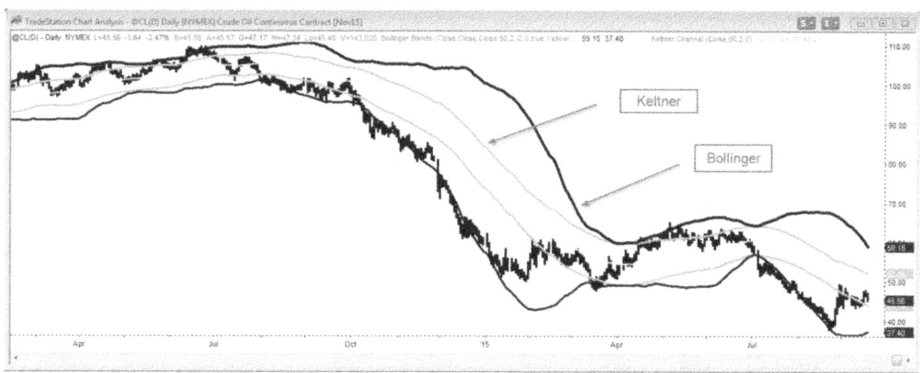

FIGURE 2.15 Keltner Channels and Bollinger Bands applied to the same data.
Source: TradeStation

for both indicators. We can plainly see that different settings need to be used if we want the indicators to behave in somewhat similar fashion. In other words, the Keltner Channel parameters need to be normalized in terms of the Bollinger Band parameters. This is the only way a fair test can be carried out. The parameters in question are the indicator length and the width of the bands/channels. We must find out the number of ATRs that are nearly equivalent to two standard deviations. Is two deviations comparable to one ATR, or is it two ATR to one standard deviation? Again, referring back to the chart, we now know that in all likelihood, two ATR does not equal two standard deviations. We know that trades are generated when price penetrates the bands/channels, and if the bands/channels are somewhat close to each other or overlapping, then a similar number of trades should be generated. Using the number of trades as the objective, a set of normalized parameters can be determined through optimization of each algorithm across different indicator lengths and channel widths. Since both standard deviation and average true range are functions of the size of the sample (length of days, in our case), both length and width will be optimized. The number of trades will be recorded for each step of the optimization. If a 60-period two-standard-deviation Bollinger Band generates 3,000 trades, then an equivalent parameter set for the Keltner algorithm would be those parameters that generated a similar number of trades. Figure 2.16 shows the number of trades generated utilizing the Bollinger algorithm by varying the length and width parameters over a basket of 36 futures markets.

This is an unusual graph, so let me explain what exactly is being plotted. The *x*-axis plots bins of varying lengths at different width values. The *y*-axis is the number of trades generated by the combination of differing lengths and widths. The length was optimized from 10 to 80 in steps of 2.0 and the width was optimized from 0.25 to 3 in steps of 0.25. The first bin holds all the results of the different-length variables while holding the width at 0.25. Like the first bin the second bin varies the lengths while holding the width to 0.50. Notice how large an impact the

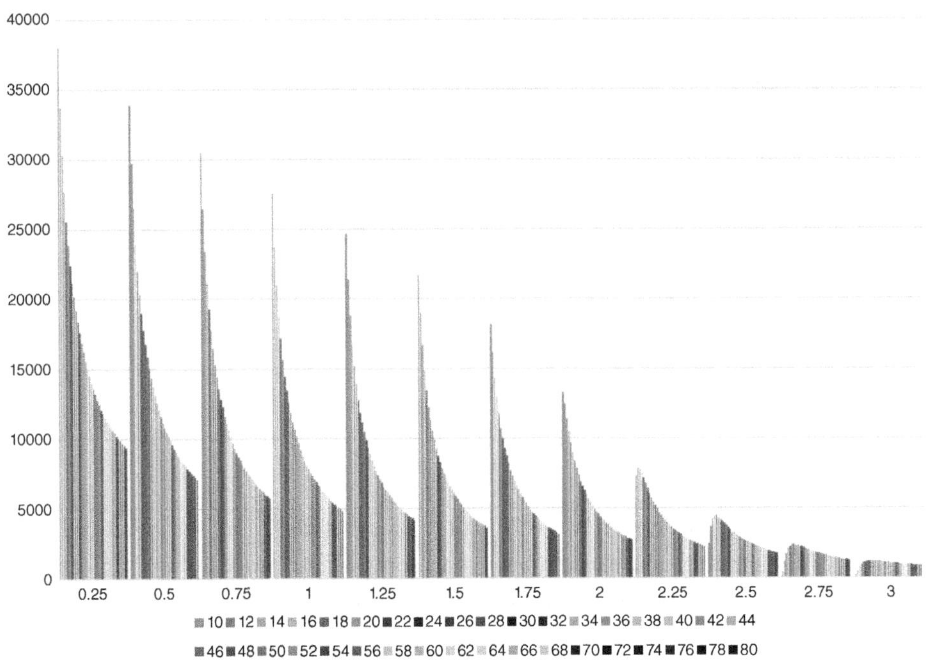

FIGURE 2.16 Bollinger Band optimization.

length parameter has on the number of generated trades in the different-width bins. Also notice initially how congruent the bars are in each bin. It seems like the drop-off of trades as we move from one bin to another occurs in a linear fashion—that is, up until bins with width values greater than 2.0. An inversion occurs in these bins (shorter lengths begin to create less trades). In addition, the number of trades start demonstrating a parabolic theme. Let's do the same exact analysis with the Keltner Channel algorithm utilizing the same data and optimization ranges. Figure 2.17 utilizes the exact same chart properties but with the newly derived results.

This graph starts out looking like the Bollinger Band graph; initially, the length parameter has a large impact in the 0.25 bin, just like the Bollinger chart. However, as we span across the different-width bins, the length parameter has less and less impact. By the time we reach the 1.50 bin, an inversion occurs, just like the Bollinger, where the lower-length parameters start to generate less trades. The two algorithms are quite similar but these graphs illustrate the difference between utilizing ATR and standard deviation.

Armed with this information, can a normalized parameter set for both the Bollinger and Keltner algorithms be derived? The 60-day two-standard-deviation algorithm generated 3,580 trades. Let's see which parameters generated nearly the same number for the Keltner algorithm. If you refer back to Figure 2.17, you will see several instances where a set of parameters generated nearly the same number

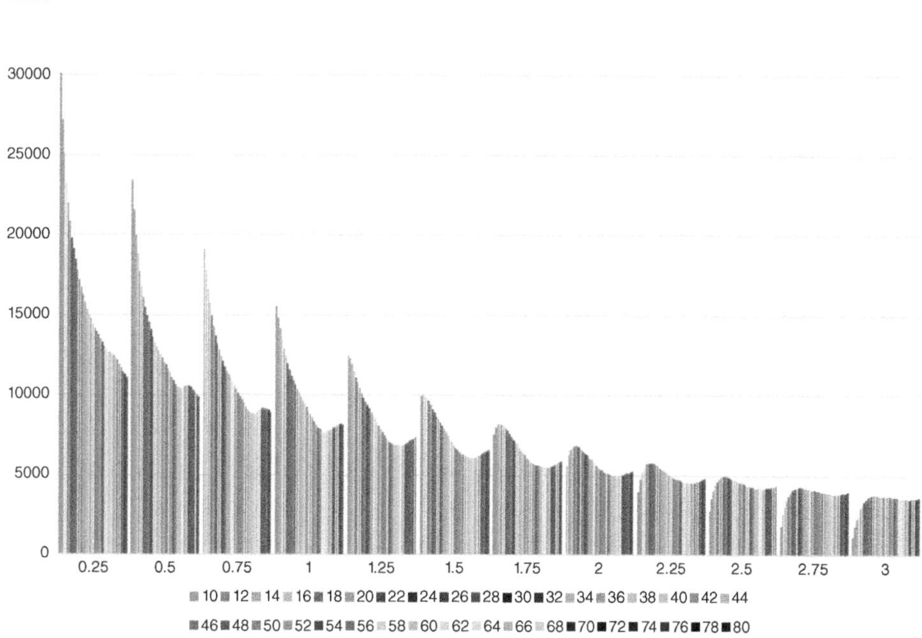

FIGURE 2.17 Keltner Channel optimization.

of trades. I scanned the Keltner Channel results and pulled out the parameter sets that generated trades within +/− 2 percent of the 3,580. Most of the selected parameter sets included the same 3.0 width. There are a couple of outliers, though. Table 2.10 shows the performance of the Bollinger Band algorithm that was derived earlier using (len = 60, stdDev = 2) and the Keltner Channel algorithm utilizing the different parameter sets that generated nearly the same number of trades.

From this information, we might be able to derive that a Bollinger Band (60, 2) is similar to a Keltner Channel (60, 3). If we accept this assumption, then the winner is easy to pick from this table. The Bollinger Band algorithm performed much better than the Keltner with these parameters. However, with such stringent criteria and utilizing the Bollinger algorithm as the benchmark, are we being fair to Keltner? We forced the Keltner to fit into criteria where a similar number of trades were generated. Let's take the gloves off and again do the same optimization and pick the top five parameter sets for both algorithms based on the average profit and net profit. In this analysis, a $50 round-turn commission will be deducted from each trade—this will take execution costs into consideration, which will in turn provide a level playing field for parameter sets that do not generate a large number of trades.

Tables 2.11 and 2.12 show the best performers for the Bollinger Band algorithm. The first set of performance metrics were derived by sorting by average profit/loss

TABLE 2.10 Bollinger Benchmark versus Keltner Challengers

Set	Net Profit	Max. Sys DD	CAR/ MDD	Profit Factor	Sharpe Ratio	# Trades	Avg P/L	Avg Bars Held	L. Avg. Bars Held
BB [60,2.00]	1677369.47	−345343	0.27	1.4	0.2	3580	469	43.59	23.72

Plateau

Set	Net Profit	Max. Sys DD	CAR/ MDD	Prft. Factor	Sharpe Ratio	# Trades	Avg P/L	Avg Bars Held	L. Avg. Bars Held
KC[56,3]	1253131.73	−443724	0.16	1.27	0.14	3612	347	44.47	24.65
KC[58,3]	1318378.23	−434112	0.17	1.29	0.15	3593	367	44.53	24.66
KC[60,3]	1338616.09	−409094	0.18	1.29	0.15	3579	374	44.56	24.6
KC[62,3]	1391495.03	−404823	0.19	1.31	0.16	3564	390	44.64	24.69
KC[64,3]	1449520.83	−410137	0.2	1.33	0.17	3535	410	44.82	24.69
KC[66,3]	1506179.43	−375805	0.23	1.35	0.17	3523	428	44.86	24.68
KC[68.3]	1520843.29	−386511	0.22	1.35	0.18	3516	433	44.81	24.61
Outliers									
KC[12,2.5]	1085527.09	−300175	0.18	1.27	0.15	3521	308	37.83	20.75
KC[26,3.0]	1299080.88	−407407	0.18	1.29	0.15	3589	362	42.1	22.21

TABLE 2.11 Best Parameter Sets of Bollinger Bands Algorithm

Ranking Based on Average Trade

No.	Net Profit	Max. Drawdown	Sharpe Ratio	# Trades	Avg Profit/Loss	Avg Bars Held	% of Winners	Len	Width
360	$1,157,014	−$302,350	0.22	1769	654.05	61.25	40.64	80	2.5
359	$1,147,202	−$308,547	0.22	1788	641.61	59.79	40.6	78	2.5
358	$1,158,434	−$358,085	0.22	1827	634.06	58.48	40.56	76	2.5
324	$1,427,825	−$323,166	0.21	2271	628.72	59.56	39.89	80	2.25
323	$1,442,568	−$379,483	0.21	2340	616.48	58.16	39.74	78	2.25

Ranking Based on Net Profit

No.	Net Profit	Max. Drawdown	Sharpe Ratio	# Trades	Avg Profit/Loss	Avg Bars Held	% of Winners	Len	Width
216	$1,792,835	−$397,785	0.19	3622	494.98	51.55	34.65	80	1.5
211	$1,789,623	−$395,046	0.18	4092	437.35	45.71	34.41	70	1.5
180	$1,788,584	−$400,129	0.18	4149	431.09	48.06	33.29	80	1.25
179	$1,765,374	−$392,321	0.17	4257	414.7	46.82	33	78	1.25
215	$1,754,942	−$408,842	0.18	3726	471	50.16	34.33	78	1.5

TABLE 2.12	Best Parameter Sets of Keltner Channel Algorithm								

Ranking Based on Average Trade

No.	Net Profit	Max. Drawdown	Sharpe Ratio	# Trades	Avg Profit/Loss	Avg Bars Held	% of Winners	Len	Width
397	$576,442	−$216,503	0.19	1193	483.19	44.77	36.88	10	3
400	$1,131,833	−$291,100	0.18	2648	427.43	42.88	36.44	16	3
431	$1,497,797	−$399,590	0.17	3568	419.79	43.92	37.3	78	3
398	$755,357	−$277,970	0.17	1804	418.71	44.11	37.03	12	3
432	$1,500,595	−$394,719	0.17	3598	417.06	43.59	37.13	80	3

Ranking Based on Net Profit

No.	Net Profit	Max. Drawdown	Sharpe Ratio	# Trades	Avg Profit/Loss	Avg Bars Held	% of Winners	Len	Width
180	$1,626,520	−$406,001	0.14	7293	223.02	29.87	29.14	80	1.25
141	$1,623,026	−$420,401	0.13	8051	201.59	28.45	27.76	74	1
140	$1,622,844	−$415,479	0.13	7974	203.52	28.83	27.77	72	1
179	$1,606,297	−$409,864	0.14	7243	221.77	30.21	29.32	78	1.25
103	$1,596,825	−$422,709	0.13	9129	174.92	26.26	25.74	70	0.75

and the second set was derived by sorting by net profit. Table 2.12 shows the same metrics for the Keltner Channel algorithm.

And the winner is? Tough call—I lean toward the Bollinger Bands because of the higher Sharpe ratios. The Sharpe ratio is just an indicator of consistency, and we will go over it and many more performance metrics in the next chapter. One thing that does stand out is the holding periods of the two systems and how different they are. The profit/loss is somewhat similar but the Bollinger algorithm holds on to trades anywhere from 20 to 50 percent longer. There might be some synergy here. Diversification is not only achieved through different markets but also through different algorithms.

Summary

Another chapter, and still no Holy Grail. However, using indicators as building blocks might get you very close to one. Several oscillators and trend indicators were discussed but these are just a few out of many. The overall purpose of this chapter was to show how to integrate these indicators into a trading algorithm. The flowcharts and FSM diagrams that were introduced in Chapter 1 were carried over and used to help explain this integration. Pseudocode was also used to demonstrate how the indicators can be programmed. Keep in mind the actual computer code will be shown in the appendices. The development of a mean reversion algorithm can be accomplished by incorporating any of the oscillators and trend detection. A trend-following algorithm is best achieved by incorporating moving averages and/or their derivatives such as Bollinger Bands and Keltner Channels. Trust me when I tell you the most successful trend-following systems incorporate either one or both.

How did we get through this chapter without talking about the Turtles, Richard Dennis, or Richard Donchian? If you are not familiar with these names, just Google them. Richard Donchian created the *N*-week breakout rule and Richard Dennis built a complete trading scheme around it. Richard Dennis was very successful and spawned Turtle trading. The *N*-week breakout is a channel indicator that uses the highest high of *N*-weeks/days as the upper channel and the lowest low of *N*-weeks/days as the lower channel. Just like a Bollinger Band algorithm, trades are initiated by the penetration of the channels. Richard Dennis and his partner Bill Eckhardt believed anybody could be trained to trade futures successfully if a trading plan was provided. So they placed classified ads in the newspaper looking for new talent. They weren't going after the prototypical Ivy Leaguer economist types. They wanted smart people who understood human behavior and who were willing to be trained. The training involved the ideas and concepts that Dennis had used to make millions. Many of the recruited traders, aka Turtles, went on to be extremely successful. Now was this a consequence of a superior algorithm or the inherent talents of the traders or being in the right spot at the right time or more simply just having a trading plan? I think it was a combination of all of the above. Don't think such a famous algorithm is going to be left out of this book. It will be introduced in the next chapter, as well as several others. Also, the Turtle money management algorithm (aka Fixed Fractional) will be discussed in Chapter 9.

CHAPTER 3

Complete Trading Algorithms

We ended the last chapter discussing one of the most famous trading algorithms of all times. Figure 3.1 is a flowchart I used to program the famous algorithm many years ago. The flowchart looks extremely complicated, but keep in mind the complete Turtle system includes two trading systems, money management, and a simulated trading module. If you break down the flowchart into its components, you will see that it is not as complicated as it seems. Most of the calculations in the Turtle system are used to determine market risk, capital allocation, market selection, and position sizing. All these components are quite important, but the meat of the diagram and the system are the two trading entry/exit algorithms and the switch that determines which system is applied. Let's go right to the heart of the Turtle by breaking just the trade entry/exit algorithms out of the complete model. The other components will be discussed a little later.

The first of the two entry/exit algorithms, let's call it System 1, is the shorter-term entry technique and is based on a very simple technique. Basically, it will buy/sell short on a 20-day Donchian breakout and exit the trade by risking whichever is closer: a 10-day Donchian breakout or a maximum of 2 percent of capital. System 1 (Box 3.1) can trade quite frequently in a choppy market. This type of start and stop can lead to a long list of losses. This choppiness can be very devastating to a trader's account and psychology. Richard Dennis tried to help alleviate this by implementing a trade filter. The Turtles were instructed to skip System 1 entries if the last trade was a winner. If the last trade was a winner, then the next trade is not "actually" executed but it is simulated. In other words, the trader would paper trade the system until a loss occurs.

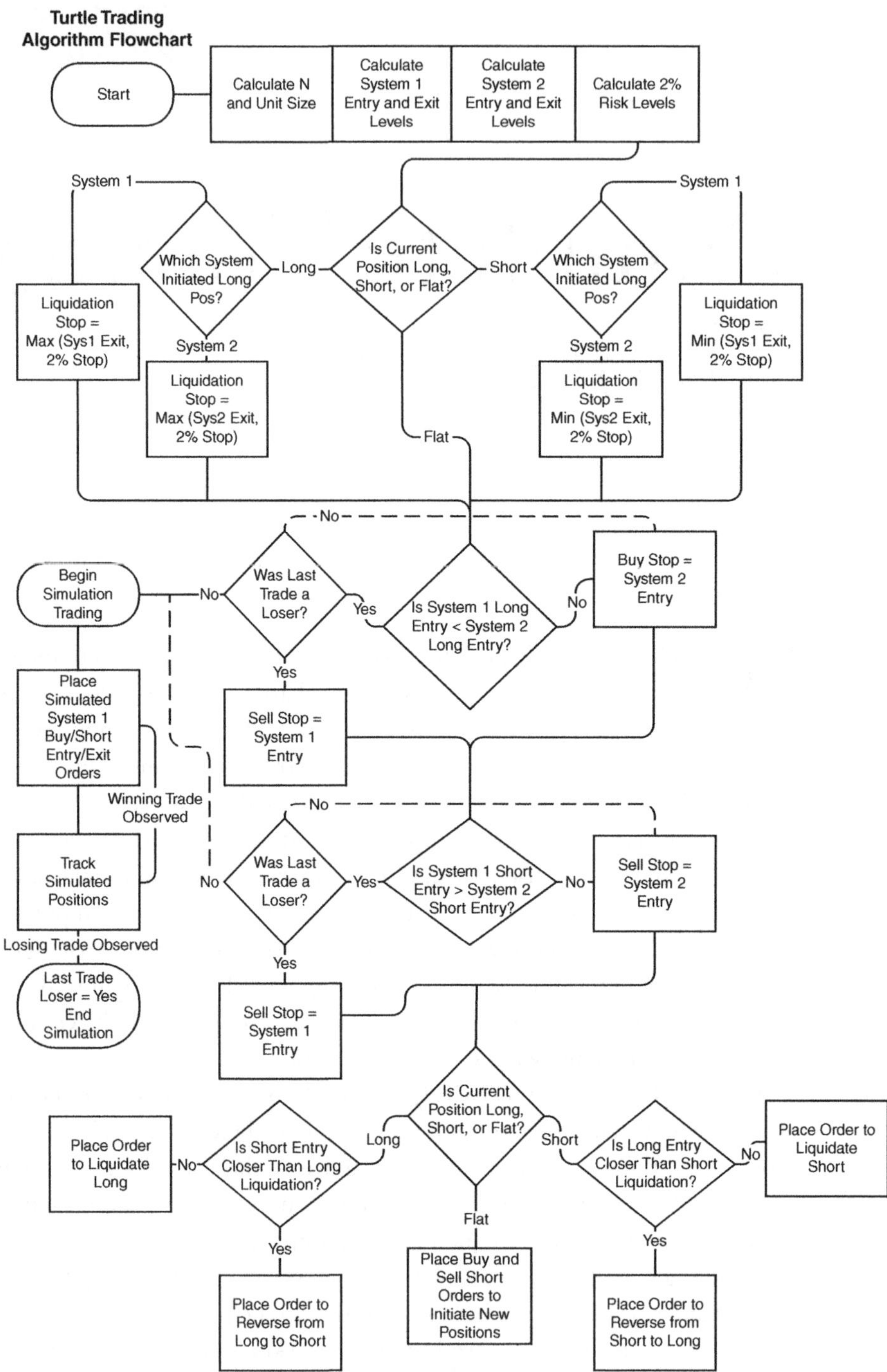

FIGURE 3.1 Turtle trading algorithm flowchart.

Box 3.1 Turtle System #1

Buy one tick above the highest high of the past 20 days stop.

Sell short one tick below the lowest low of the past 20 days stop.

If position is long, then
  Sell next bar at the maximum of:
    one tick below the lowest low of the past 10 days stop, or
    entryPrice – (0.02 * initialCapital) / bigPointValue stop

If position is short, then
  Buy next bar at the minimum of:
    one tick above the highest high of the past 10 days stop, or
    entryPrice + (0.02 * initialCapital) / bigPointValue stop

This description does not utilize the "last trade was a loser filter" (LTLF). Even with the application of the LTLF, this system is very easy to trade. A simple spreadsheet is all it takes to help keep track of actual and simulated trades. Remember a simulated trade occurs after a winning trade is realized. Real trading is turned back on once a simulated losing trade occurs.

System 2 (Box 3.2) entries are congruent with System 1, but require a much longer lookback period—55 days. Even though the Donchian Channel exit is wider, the same 2 percent maximum loss is still used.

Box 3.2 Turtle System #2

Buy one tick above the highest high of the past 55 days stop.

Sell short one tick below the lowest low of the past 55 days stop.

If position is long, then
  Sell next bar at the maximum of:
    one tick below the lowest low of the past 20 days stop or
    entryPrice – (0.02 * initialCapital) / bigPointValue stop

If position is short, then
  Buy next bar at the minimum of:
    one tick above the highest high of the past 10 days stop or
    entryPrice + (0.02 * initialCapital) / bigPointValue stop

The LTLF does not apply to these longer-term entries. If the market is making a new 55-day high/low, then the Turtle system thinks a new trend has definitely begun and the trader must be on board. This entry was considered the failsafe breakout.

This is the Turtle system in a nutshell, or should I say a turtle shell. The full-blown Turtle model involves many more calculations, pyramiding, and a totally separate position sizing and market selection algorithm. Some of these topics will be discussed in Chapter 8 and a full-blown version (except for market selection) will be provided at the end of this chapter in EasyLanguage.

Even though the complete Turtle "approach" isn't being applied here, the two systems are indeed complete trading algorithms; they both have entry and trade management techniques. System 1 was designed to capture shorter-term swings, whereas System 2 was the true trend-following component. Trading the two systems simultaneously was undoubtedly considered synergistic to the Turtles. The key to getting the benefit from both systems lies in the LTLF—it must be engaged. If it's not, then you end up just trading System 1, the 20-day breakout. A 20-day breakout will always be closer or equal to the current market price than a 55-day breakout. Here again is the idea of creating an additional level of diversification through the use of multiple systems. However, the amount of capital to allocate to the different systems was left up to the individual Turtle (trader). He or she could commit 100 percent to either system or 50 percent to one and 50 percent to the other or some other combination. How to determine how much of each system to use was obviously a very difficult question to answer, even for a Turtle. Which system would you use? If I had been a Turtle faced with this decision, I would have done the research by backtesting both systems and allocating more toward the better of the two.

As a Turtle you had three choices to make: Trade System1, trade System 2, or trade a combination of the two. Let's pretend we are a Turtle and let's see if we can make the decision. The research necessary requires each system to be tested independently and simultaneously to see if "the whole is greater than the sum of its parts." Tables 3.1 and 3.2 show the performance of each system, respectively, across the same portfolio over the same time period. Note that System 1 was initially tested without the LTLF. In these tests, the maximum loss was set to $2,000 and $100 was deducted for commission and slippage on a round-turn basis.

Table 3.1 shows the net performance along with individual market results as well. A profit of more than $430k was generated along with a hefty $220k maximum drawdown. Make a mental checkmark on the markets that showed the best results. I have a feeling you will notice a pattern among the best-performing markets throughout the rest of this chapter. Let's see how the 55-day breakout faired (Table 3.2).

Wow! The profit nearly doubled and the maximum drawdown was reduced by 10 percent. If you had traded this system in place of the 20-day breakout, you might not have received a Christmas card from your broker—less than one half the execution costs—but your banker would have been happy.

TABLE 3.1 Turtle System 1 without LTLF for the Sample Portfolio

Total Return	$439,471.42	Market	PNL
Total Realized Return	$416,450.17	@AD	($6,110.00)
Gross Profit	$5,182,686.04	@BP	($6,543.75)
Gross Loss	−$4,766,235.87	@C	($6,987.50)
Open Trade P/L	$23,021.25	@CC	($36,020.00)
		@CL	$77,690.00
Number of Trades	$5,234.00	@CT	$20,065.00
Number of Winning Trades	$1,751.00	@DX	($14,590.00)
Number of Losing Trades	$3,481.00	@EC	$84,150.00
% Profitable	33.45%	@ED	($10,800.00)
		@EMD	($70,700.00)
Average Trade	$79.57	@ES	($36,162.50)
Average Trade (%)	0.39%	@FC	$39,675.00
Standard Deviation	$3,566.48	@FV	($11,335.93)
Standard Deviation Trade %	28.39%	@GC	($19,480.00)
Largest Winning Trade	$53,275.00	@HG	$101,125.00
Largest Losing Trade	−$8,375.00	@HO	$97,287.00
		@KC	($34,106.25)
Profit Factor	1.09	@KW	($2,975.00)
Average Win/Average Loss	2.16	@LC	($32,130.00)
Sharpe Ratio	0.12	@LH	$16,570.00
K-Ratio	0.16	@NG	$28,550.00
Return Retracement Ratio	0.54	@OJ	$3,977.50
		@PL	$90,825.00
		@RB	$45,105.20
		@S	$32,693.75
		@SB	$20,252.00
		@SI	$182,700.00
		@TF	($104,090.00)
		@TU	($9,174.97)
		@TY	$16,871.88
		@US	($12,581.25)
		@W	($5,512.50)

Now let's go back and retest System 1 with the *Last Trader Was a Loser Filter* (LTLF) to see if it had any beneficial impact on the performance. Actual trades were only placed after a subsequent loss—be it from an actual loss or a simulated loss. Losses were generated by the $2,000 money management stop or a trailing 10-day stop that resulted in a loss. Table 3.3 shows the results of System 1 with the LTLF in place.

TABLE 3.2 Turtle System 2 for the Sample Portfolio

Summary	Value	Markets	PNL
Total Return	$949,937.69	@AD	$40,250.00
Total Realized Return	$889,799.88	@BP	$3,987.50
Gross Profit	$3,444,084.89	@C	$11,225.00
Gross Loss	−$2,554,285.01	@CC	($34,600.00)
Open Trade P/L	$60,137.81	@CL	$174,440.00
		@CT	$20,720.00
Number of Trades	$2,324.00	@DX	$21,150.00
Number of Winning Trades	$726.00	@EC	$83,600.00
Number of Losing Trades	$1,597.00	@ED	$1,743.75
% Profitable	31.24%	@EMD	$4,490.00
		@ES	$11,587.50
Average Trade	$382.87	@FC	$31,825.00
Average Trade (%)	0.67%	@FV	($585.93)
Standard Deviation	$5,477.96	@GC	$57,530.00
Standard Deviation Trade %	56.38%	@HG	$91,425.00
Largest Winning Trade	$90,440.00	@HO	$173,699.40
Largest Losing Trade	−$7,590.00	@KC	($19,500.00)
		@KW	$22,500.00
Profit Factor	1.35	@LC	($14,740.00)
Average Win/Average Loss	2.97	@LH	$19,660.00
Sharpe Ratio	0.16	@NG	$102,840.00
K-Ratio	0.19	@OJ	($1,155.00)
Return Retracement Ratio	1.19	@PL	$70,340.00
		@RB	$80,879.40
		@S	$70,162.50
		@SB	$28,963.20
		@SI	$134,575.00
		@TF	($13,100.00)
		@TU	$7,437.50
		@TY	($6,156.25)
		@US	$10,687.50
		@W	$3,612.50

The results agreed with my research from more than 10 years ago. In an article I wrote for *SFO* magazine in 2004, I executed the exact same analysis utilizing another testing platform, Trading Blox Builder (www.tradingblox.com), and received similar results; the profit-to-drawdown ratio increased using the LTLF. The **Trading Blox** testing platform was built around the absolute complete Turtle

TABLE 3.3 **Turtle System 1 with LTLF for the Sample Portfolio**

Summary	Value	Markets	PNL
Total Return	$667,013.78	@AD	$2,890.00
Total Realized Return	$652,511.28	@BP	($6,031.25)
Gross Profit	$3,632,117.44	@C	$5,912.50
Gross Loss	−$2,979,606.16	@CC	($19,900.00)
Open Trade P/L	$14,502.50	@CL	$107,830.00
		@CT	$7,250.00
Number of Trades	$3,301.00	@DX	$20,110.00
Number of Winning Trades	$1,125.00	@EC	$83,300.00
Number of Losing Trades	$2,175.00	@ED	($13,356.25)
% Profitable	34.08%	@EMD	($30,180.00)
		@ES	($23,475.00)
Average Trade	$197.67	@FC	$4,300.00
Average Trade (%)	0.51%	@FV	($1,917.18)
Standard Deviation	$3,963.63	@GC	$17,970.00
Standard Deviation Trade %	26.13%	@HG	$114,037.50
Largest Winning Trade	$53,275.00	@HO	$60,120.20
Largest Losing Trade	−$7,925.00	@KC	$18,531.25
		@KW	$2,450.00
Profit Factor	1.22	@LC	($18,630.00)
Average Win/Average Loss	2.36	@LH	$28,620.00
Sharpe Ratio	0.15	@NG	$64,760.00
K-Ratio	0.22	@OJ	$11,230.00
Return Retracement Ratio	1.10	@PL	$88,465.00
		@RB	$46,595.20
Compounded Annual Return	14.96%	@S	$14,581.25
Compounded Monthly Return	1.15%	@SB	$9,156.80
		@SI	$169,050.00
Average Annual Return	$44,467.59	@TF	($73,960.00)
Average Annual Return (%)	19.54%	@TU	($8,718.73)
Average Monthly Return	$3,789.85	@TY	$1,725.00
Average Monthly Return (%)	1.59%	@US	($10,581.25)
		@W	($9,400.00)
Percent Days Profitable	50.69%		
Percent Months Profitable	52.27%		
Percent Years Profitable	73.33%		
Commissions on Currencies	$165,375.00		
Commissions on Futures	$0.00		
Commissions on Equities	$0.00		
Total Commissions	$165,375.00		

algorithm (entry techniques, capital allocation, and position sizing models) by an original turtle and a very gifted programmer. As I mentioned in the Introduction, this is not one of the platforms included in this book, but it is well worth your time to investigate its capabilities. What this research is implying is that the prior trade may have an impact on the subsequent trade. In other words, it seems there does exist a higher probability of a winning trade after a losing trade has occurred at the macroscopic level on this particular algorithm. This autocorrelation could be a function of the volatility cycle. After a big run in commodity prices, it is not uncommon to see a congestive phase. In my opinion, this type of filter works better with shorter-term higher-frequency algorithms. If you think about it, this makes sense. A system that trades frequently can skip trades and still catch shorter-term trends. On the other hand, a system that trades infrequently needs every trade to add to the bottom line; skipping a single trade might keep you out of the market for a year. This is the reason the Turtles relied on the "must-take" 55-day breakout.

Let's test if there is synergy by trading both systems simultaneously. Synergy occurs when the interaction of elements, when combined, produces a total effect that is greater than the sum of the individual elements. Synergy does not occur when combining the total profits of the two systems. Addition of total P & L follows the commutative law. The synergy that does occur when combining systems is revealed in the combined maximum drawdown metric. If two systems are somewhat non-correlated, then the overall maximum drawdown will not be equal to the sum of the two individual maximum drawdowns; it may be less. So, it logically follows that the synergy of combining multiple trading strategies is reflected in the increase of the overall profit to overall maximum drawdown ratio. The overall profit is a constant (sum of all total profits) and the overall maximum drawdown is variable. If drawdown decreases, then the ratio will increase and demonstrate a somewhat synergistic effect.

This combining of systems can be accomplished by trading the two systems independently of each other in separate accounts, or in a single account. A trader can also combine the rules into one complete strategy, and trade in a single account. Many of today's testing platforms offer both methods. The backtesting method where both systems are traded independently can be simulated simply by combining the daily equity streams for both systems. This is a valid method and does reveal a reduction in max drawdown, if one occurs. The second method requires additional programming but does help with eliminating the necessity of keeping track of multiple systems. If more than one system were to be traded simultaneously in separate accounts, then capital would need to be allocated to cover all open positions margins. Even if one system is long and the other short. If the systems are combined into one account, then the net position (Long + Short = Flat) is recorded, and therefore there is no margin requirement.

Table 3.4 shows the performance of the Turtle system using both System 1 with the LTLF engaged and System 2 turned on.

TABLE 3.4 **Tandem Performance of Turtle System 1 with LTLF and Turtle System 2 for the Sample Portfolio**

Summary	Value	Markets	PNL
Total Return	$587,797.03	@AD	$14,260.00
Total Realized Return	$556,674.53	@BP	($3,718.75)
Gross Profit	$4,380,499.89	@C	($5,712.50)
Gross Loss	−$3,823,825.36	@CC	($39,040.00)
Open Trade P/L	$31,122.50	@CL	$113,720.00
		@CT	$10,195.00
Number of Trades	$4,048.00	@DX	$45.00
Number of Winning Trades	$1,334.00	@EC	$77,087.50
Number of Losing Trades	$2,711.00	@ED	($11,656.25)
% Profitable	32.95%	@EMD	($47,440.00)
		@ES	($36,700.00)
Average Trade	$137.52	@FC	$26,025.00
Average Trade (%)	−0.02%	@FV	($10,285.93)
Standard Deviation	$3,869.70	@GC	($4,420.00)
Standard Deviation Trade %	36.41%	@HG	$104,950.00
Largest Winning Trade	$53,275.00	@HO	$97,538.00
Largest Losing Trade	−$7,925.00	@KC	($4,225.00)
		@KW	($2,412.50)
Profit Factor	1.15	@LC	($14,040.00)
Average Win/Average Loss	2.33	@LH	$14,260.00
Sharpe Ratio	0.13	@NG	$36,410.00
K-Ratio	0.18	@OJ	$2,547.50
Return Retracement Ratio	0.68	@PL	$104,195.00
		@RB	$59,458.80
Compounded Annual Return	14.10%	@S	$46,856.25
Compounded Monthly Return	1.09%	@SB	$15,202.40
		@SI	$169,425.00
Average Annual Return	$39,186.47	@TF	($94,540.00)
Average Annual Return (%)	22.93%	@TU	($9,118.73)
Average Monthly Return	$3,339.76	@TY	$550.00
Average Monthly Return (%)	1.91%	@US	($11,756.25)
		@W	($6,000.00)
Percent Days Profitable	50.77%		
Percent Months Profitable	52.27%		
Percent Years Profitable	53.33%		
Commissions on Currencies	$202,825.00		
Commissions on Futures	$0.00		
Commissions on Equities	$0.00		
Total Commissions	$202,825.00		

The results are better than the simple 20-day breakout but worse than the 20-day breakout with LTLF engaged, and much worse than the simple 55-day breakout. You would think the combination of the two systems would at least beat the System 1 component. In some markets, it did. The only explanation that I can come up with is: Let's say a trade is entered on 20-day breakout, and turns out to be a winner. The next 20-day breakout is ignored, but a subsequent 55-day breakout is taken in the same direction at a worse price and with probably higher risk—a 20-day trailing stop versus a 10-day trailing stop. Following this line of thought, let's assume System 1 has a winner via a 20-day breakout, so the next 20-day breakout is skipped, but the market moves sufficiently in the same direction to trigger a System 2 trade. This trade occurs at a much worse price with an inherently higher level of risk. Still assuming, let's say the System 2 trade is stopped out for a large loss. The net between the two trades could theoretically be a loss, whereas if the trader had just traded System 1, she would have realized a winning situation. So there really isn't any synergy between the two components traded in this manner. Also due to the high correlation between the two components, combining them by trading them independently would probably still not provide any synergy. The clear winner here is the simple 55-day breakout.

Trend-Trading Battle Royale

We have reviewed a few trend-following trading algorithms and their results. Thus far, the results have shown some merit. Enough merit to continue research in this form of trading. There are many trend-following algorithms out there, but the perpetual question of which is the best has never really been *truly* answered. Perry Kaufman has come very close in his *New Trading Systems and Methods* books. Why hasn't this question ever been fully answered in an easy-to-interpret format? The main obstacle has always been the inability to compare apples to apples. However, with the tools I now have at my fingertips, maybe we can finally put this question to rest.

The following trend-following algorithms will be tested on the same data with the same commission/slippage deduction, over the same time period and on a one-contract basis and on the same testing platform, and we have plenty of capital. The trend-following algorithms that will be tested will utilize their own entry-and-exit techniques. However, a maximum loss of $3,000 will be applied to each algorithm. I figure that most of the algorithms' exits will occur prior to this stop level, and most traders would feel more comfortable knowing that at this trading level, the risk of ruin should be sufficiently small to initiate one or more of the programs.

Pause the Battle—Let's Talk Risk of Ruin Risk of ruin is a very useful tool in determining the likelihood of a trader losing his entire bankroll or reducing it to a level that trading cannot continue. Calculating this risk (RoR) is quite simple; all you need is the amount of capital to be risked on any given trade and the probability of success, also known as the algorithm's trading advantage:

$$RoR = ((1 - A) / (1 + A))^{\wedge}C$$

where A is the algorithm's trading advantage and C is the number of units in your account. To calculate A, subtract the percent chance of loss from percent chance of win. So, if you expect to win 54% of your trades, the trading advantage would be 8% (54% − 46% = 8%). To calculate C, simply divide 1 by the percent of capital you are willing to risk on each trade. So, if you are willing to risk 5% of any given trade, then you have 20 units. Plugging A and C into the formula you come up with ((1 − 0.08) / (1 + 0.08)) ^ 20. The result turns out to be around 4%. The RoR for risking 5% of your capital on each trade with an algorithm that wins 54% of time is a relatively low 4%. If the percent of wins is 50% or less, the RoR is 100%. The base number that is being raised by unit size C decreases as the trading advantage increases. As long as the percent wins are greater than 50%, the base number will always be less than one. Unit size C decreases as risk per trade increases. Raising a number less than one by higher values decreases the result or in this case the RoR. In other words, the RoR is indirectly proportional to the risk.

This simple formula only works with algorithms that win more often than they lose and each win and loss is identical. If you plug in a winning percentage of 50% or less, the RoR is guaranteed. If you applied this very simple formula to the vast majority of trend-following systems, you would never take the first trade. When determining RoR you must look beyond percent wins and risk. Most trend-following systems win less than 40% of their trades. The key performance metrics in this case are the average win and average loss in dollars. You can still win with a sub-50% winning system as long as your average trade (average win / average loss) is sufficiently high enough. The formula for RoR for when wins and losses are not identical is unfortunately much more complex. I refer you to Ralph Vince's excellent book, *Portfolio Management Formulas* (Wiley, New York, 1990) if you want to see the derivation of this formula. The formula is complicated but the algorithm is quite simple if you have the correct performance metrics of your algorithm. An Excel spreadsheet that utilizes this formula is available from this book's companion website. Here is an example of the worksheet and its computed RoR using performance metrics from a typical trend-following algorithm (see figure 3-2.).

Risk of Ruin Calculation		
Average Win $	$400	≪--Input Here
Average Loss $	$200	≪--Input Here
Percent Wins	35.0%	≪--Input Here
Initial Capital $	$35,000	≪--Input Here
Amount of Pain % (% of Capital)	50.0%	≪--Input Here
Payoff Ratio	2	
Percent Losers	65.0%	
Average Win %	1.1%	
Average Loss %	0.6%	
Sum of Possible Events (SoPE)	0.00029	
Sq.Root of Sum of Squares of (SoPE)	0.00818	
"**P**"	0.517460757	
RoR	1.39814%	

This trend-following system wins only 35% of the time but has a payoff ratio of 2 (Average Win$ / Average Loss$). If your pain threshold is 50% of your starting capital, then you run a risk of ruin of nearly 1.4%. With these algorithm performance metrics and RoR you shouldn't have a problem pulling the trigger on this system. Before you start trading be sure to check the risk of ruin and see if it fits your expectations. One more note before we resume the battle: Money management will not be utilized so that we can see the raw capabilities of each system.

Resume the Battle There will be a total of six popular trend-following algorithms tested, the Turtle system and the five shown in Box 3.3. Each test will consist of three subtests. The subtests will reflect three different parameter sets that will cause the algorithms to trade in a shorter-term, intermediate-term, and longer-term manner. For example, a simple moving average crossover algorithm will be tested utilizing moving average lengths of 19, 39, and 100. These parameters should cover the three time horizons—short, intermediate, and long. The parameter lengths were chosen without the benefit of hindsight—in other words, they were chosen based on my perceived applicability to obtain the three time horizons without looking at prior test results. This isn't really a true statement, because my experience through testing systems over the years does introduce a slight hindsight bias. All entries and exits will be executed on the closing price of the bar that generates the trade signal.

Box 3.3 Battle Royale—And the Competitors Are:

Single Simple Moving Average Crossover (SMA)

Buy when close crosses above moving average

Sell short when close crosses below moving average

Liquidate long if close < entryPrice − 3000/bigPointValue

Liquidate short if close > entryPrice + 3000/bigPointValue

Utilize moving average lengths of 19, 39, and 100

Double Simple Moving Average Crossover (DMA)

Buy when shorter moving average crosses above longer moving average

Sell short when short moving average crosses below longer moving average

Liquidate long if close < entryPrice – 3000/bigPointValue

Liquidate short if close > entryPrice + 3000/bigPointValue

Utilize moving average lengths:
  Short lengths: 9, 19, 49
  Long lengths: 19 ,49, 99

Triple Simple Moving Average Crossover (TMA)

Triple moving averages require two criteria to be met before a trade entry:

Buy:
  shortest moving average and intermediate moving average both must be greater than longer-term average
  Buy when shortest moving average crosses above intermediate moving average

Sell short:
  shortest moving average and intermediate moving average both must be less than longer-term average
  Sell short when shortest moving average crosses below intermediate moving average

Liquidate long when shortest moving average crosses below intermediate moving average or if close < entryPrice – 3000/bigPointValue

Liquidate short when shortest moving average crosses above intermediate moving average or if close > entryPrice + 3000/bigPointValue

Utilize the following moving average lengths:

Short lengths: 9, 19, 49
Intermediate lengths: 19, 49, 199
Long lengths: 49, 199, 399

Donchian Channels (DC)

Buy on penetration of highest highs for past *N* days

Sell short on penetration of lowest lows for past *N* days

Liquidate long on penetration lowest lows for past *N* / 2 days or if close < entryPrice – 3000/bigPointValue

Liquidate short on penetration of highest highs for past *N* / 2 days or if close > entryPrice + 3000/bigPointValue

Utilize the following channel lengths:
Short lengths: 20 entry, 10 exit
Intermediate lengths: 40 entry, 20 exit
Long lengths: 100 entry, 50 exit

Bollinger Bands (BB)

Buy on penetration of two standard deviations above *N*-day moving average.

Sell short on penetration of two standard deviations below *N*-day moving average.

Liquidate long on penetration of *N*-day moving average or if close < entryPrice – 3000/bigPointValue.

Liquidate short on penetration of *N*-day moving average or if close > entryPrice + 3000/bigPointValue.

Utilize the following moving average lengths of 20, 50, and 200.
The results are shown in Table 3.5.

Table 3.5 starts the battle and sets the benchmark with the results of the SMA algorithm.

Let's hope the other algorithms have better luck. Before moving on to the results of the other algorithms a clear explanation of performance metrics might be a good idea:

- **Net Profit**—summation of all profits or losses after deduction of execution costs.
- **Sys Drawdown**—the largest peak-to-valley decline experienced in the complete portfolio. This is a good metric to use in the calculation of how much capital to allocate to a trading algorithm. However, remember this is a onetime event and in many cases the **Start Trade Drawdown** analysis might be a better indicator for capitalization purposes. Start Trade Drawdown shows the different probabilities

TABLE 3.5 Single Moving Average (SMA) Crossover Algorithm

SMA	Simple Moving Average Crossover								
Length	Net Profit	CAR	Max. Sys DD	Profit Factor	Ulcer Index	# Trades	Avg Profit/ Loss	Avg Bars Held	% of Winners
19	−922061	−15.08	−986733	0.91	48.53	15814	−58.31	9.78	23.04
39	−15191	−0.1	−612726	1	16.1	11114	−1.37	13.49	19.97
100	564180	2.91	−626574	1.11	13.92	6543	86.23	21.94	16.25
200	487626	2.58	−492640	1.13	14.95	4495	108.48	30.67	12.77

of the occurrence of different magnitudes of drawdown. This analysis will be detailed in Chapter 8 along with Monte Carlo simulation.

- **Annual Return %**—compounded annual return based on a cool million-dollar investment.
- **Number of Trades:** number of trades.
- **Profit/Loss**—(Profit of winners / Loss of losers) / Number of trades. This is also known as the expectancy in terms of dollars.
- **Bars Held**—the number of bars, on average, a trade is held. You can use this as a guide to align different parameters sets across different algorithms.
- **Total Transaction Costs**—summation of execution fees.
- **Profit Factor**—profit of winners divided by loss of losers.
- **Ulcer Index**—square root of sum of squared drawdowns divided by number of bars. It measures the volatility in the downward direction.
- **Sharpe Ratio**—indicator of consistency. Average return divided by the standard deviation of returns sampled on daily, monthly, or yearly basis. The higher the better.

Armed with these performance metrics it is plain to see that the SMA as a complete trading algorithm is not that good. I hope you weren't surprised by this fact. Don't get me wrong; simple moving averages have their place in technical analysis, but not as a complete trading algorithm. Results might improve utilizing an exponential moving average, but not enough to consider it as your main trading tool. Notice how the long-term version handily outperformed its shorter and intermediate-term counterparts.

If a single moving average doesn't cut the mustard, then what about two? Table 3.6 shows the DMA utilizing three different lengths.

TABLE 3.6 Double Moving Average (DMA) Crossover Algorithm

DMA Length	Double Moving Average Net Profit	CAR	Max. Sys DD	Profit Factor	Ulcer Index	# Trades	Avg Profit/ Loss	Avg Bars Held	% of Winners
9,19	−29879	−0.19	−548958	1	20.2	8529	−3.5	17.46	35.08
19,49	61910	0.39	−743755	1.01	21.29	3997	15.49	36.11	33.1
49,99	996693	4.53	−692714	1.24	11.39	2307	432.03	61.8	34.07

TABLE 3.7 Triple Moving Average (TMA) Crossover Algorithm

TMA Length	Triple Moving Average Net Profit	CAR	Max. Sys DD	Profit Factor	Ulcer Index	# Trades	Avg Profit/ Loss	Avg Bars Held	percent of Winners
9,19,49	−71434	−0.47	−441997.88	0.99	14.68	5160	−13.84	18.21	33.93
19,49,199	527917	2.75	−374103	1.22	9.41	1850	285.36	43.49	32.7
49,199,399	711878	3.5	−211493	1.77	6.09	528	1348.25	137.61	32.01

A vast improvement. The short term and intermediate term still trail their big brother, but both improved. The DMA with lengths of 49 and 99 cranked out profits close to a million dollars. This feat was accomplished by trading just 2,307 times—less than 100 times a year across 35 markets. Could the winner already be revealed? If the double moving average stood head and shoulders above the single moving average, where do you think the triple moving average will wind up? Table 3.7 gives the details.

The trend continues. The longer-term triple crossover produced over $700K on just 528 trades. It made 70 percent of what the longer-term DMA produced but did it with a less than one-fourth the number of trades. It averaged $1,348 on every trade. Pretty impressive, but this is more like investing than trading. What if we changed the lengths of the parameters to try and match the number of trades from the longer-term DMA? Would that be curve-fitting? The parameter values that produced so few trades were initially chosen based on a preconceived notion that a certain number of trades and trade duration would be achieved. Tuning the parameters to get us into the ballpark of our objective, whatever that might be, is not over-curve-fitting. So far it looks like the longer-term versions of the DMA and TMA are producing somewhat comparable results. The next system up gets us out of the moving averages and back into Turtle mode. Table 3.8 shows the performance of three different Donchian lengths.

TABLE 3.8 Donchian Channel Breakout for Different Donchian Lengths

Donchian	Donchian Channel Breakout								
Length	Net Profit	CAR	Max. Sys DD	Profit Factor	Ulcer Index	# Trades	Avg Profit/Loss	Avg Bars Held	% of Winners
20/10	278329	1.59	−257735.79	1.05	9.61	6070	45.85	17.43	35.34
40/20	754015	3.67	−361607	1.18	8.43	2963	254.48	35.45	36.85
100/50	1114437	4.91	−367415	1.51	7.07	1366	815.84	68.65	32.01

The Turtle hit a home run! All three versions were profitable and the 100-day Donchian beat the longer-term DMA: $1.1 million on only 1366 trades. It's going to be hard to knock this system off of the podium. If any system can, it could be one based off of John Bollinger's world famous bands. Table 3.9 tells the tale of the tape.

Well that was a little bit of a disappointment. The trend did not continue as the longer-term version did not win the battle among the different Bollinger Band lengths. The intermediate-term version just barely nudged out the longer term with slightly less profit, but 10 percent less drawdown. The big news is the Bollinger Band algorithm came in third place when compared with the triple moving average and Donchian channel.

So the winner is ... Hold on! We are getting some complaints out of the Bollinger Band camp. They are saying it's not a fair test. They want a rematch! They say that we held the number of standard deviations constant at two. Just changing the lengths of the moving averages and not the width of the bands (number of standard deviations) does not reflect the true capability of such a powerful algorithm. Now the other camps are complaining, too! What to do?

Why don't we have a grudge match between the four best algorithms: DMA, TMA, DC, and BB. But this time, let's let the computer choose the best parameter sets. AmiBroker has produced the results thus far, so let's lean on it a little bit and have it help us level the playing field. Let's optimize the living daylights out of each

TABLE 3.9 Bollinger Band Breakout

Bollinger	Bollinger Band Breakout								
Length	Net Profit	CAR	Max. Sys DD	Profit Factor	Ulcer Index	# Trades	Avg Profit/Loss	Avg Bars Held	% of Winners
20-Day	−41360	−0.27	−343007	0.99	13.83	4860	−8.51	16.06	32.63
50-Day	728097	3.57	−321144	1.24	8.03	2396	303.88	32.94	32.1
100-Day	756849	3.68	−362325	1.37	8.33	1364	554.87	57.83	30.94

algorithm and see what parameter sets produce the best profit-to-drawdown ratio. Let's not stop at optimizing the lengths of the parameters but the protective stop as well. The Bollinger Band camp will be happy because not only will we optimize the parameter lengths, and the protective stop, but we will also optimize the width of the bands. Does this smell of over-curve-fitting? Sure it does, but we aren't developing a trading system here, we are just doing an analysis.

Now that we have a plan, how can we use AmiBroker to carry it out? The algorithms are already programmed (source code will be graciously provided in the appendices), but how many optimizations are we talking about? Quickly doing the math in my head—millions! Table 3.10 shows the exact number of permutations and the range that each parameter will be tested across.

The number doesn't get really large until we move to the TMA optimization—nearly seven million. This is due to the fact that we are optimizing four parameters. Well, it was a good idea. We will just have to go with what

TABLE 3.10 Comparison of Parameters for Algorithms Based on Different Strategies

Donchian	Start	Stop	Increment	# Iterations
Entry Len	9	100	1	92
Exit Len	5	100	1	96
Protective Stop	3000	6000	500	7
Total				61824
Bollinger	**Start**	**Stop**	**Increment**	**# Iterations**
Average Length	20	200	1	181
#Std. Deviations	0.25	3	0.05	56
Protective Stop	3000	6000	500	7
Total				31752
TMA	**Start**	**Stop**	**Increment**	**# Iterations**
Short Length	9	100	1	92
Intermediate Length	19	200	2	91
Long Length	49	399	3	117
Protective Stop	3000	6000	500	7
Total				6856668
DMA	**Start**	**Stop**	**Increment**	**# Iterations**
Short Length	9	100	1	92
Intermediate Length	19	200	2	91
Protective Stop	3000	6000	500	7
Total				58604

we have, because who has the time to do a multimillion-iterations optimization loop? Wait a minute—this book is about algorithms—right? This task is definitely not doable with a run-of-the-mill exhaustive search optimization engine. An exhaustive search optimization is where you use brute force and test every possible combination—no stone is left unturned. Come to think of it, AmiBroker has access to three forms of genetic optimization. With the use of genetic optimization (GO) and artificial intelligence, we can accomplish the task and do it in just a few minutes. Not all iterations are executed, only those that fit a certain fitness. Imagine millions and millions of optimizations carried out in minutes instead of days or even months. Genetic optimization is an awesome tool, and this very topic will be discussed in Chapter 8. Right now, even if you don't understand artificial intelligence, just know it is the tool that we need to accomplish this task.

All optimizations will be carried out at the portfolio level. Individual market optimizations will not be conducted. This will cut down considerably on the total number of optimizations. Each set of parameters will be applied to each market in the portfolio, and only one set will be chosen to represent each algorithm. Also, like I said earlier, we are not trying to fit a system to data in an attempt to create a trading plan. We are just trying to cover all bases in this algorithm comparison. The winning parameter sets will be used for illustration purposes only.

AmiBroker was able to complete the task in roughly 40 minutes. This time period covered all optimizations across the four algorithms. Pretty darn impressive! Table 3.11 shows the top 10 parameter sets for each algorithm and their associated profit/loss, maximum drawdown, number of trades, average trade, profit factor, Ulcer index, and percent winners.

Table 3.12 shows the best parameters sets from each optimization.

And the winner is—triple moving average! The results show a unanimous champion, the triple moving average. The Donchian algorithm came in second with the Bollinger algorithm close behind in third. The winner produced a tremendous profit-to-drawdown ratio of 7.04. Quite a bit better than the second place Donchian Channels. The TMA accomplished this feat by trading only 574 times. Before discussing the winners let's discuss the also-rans.

The DMA algorithm came in last place. It looks like using the parameter sets revolving around an ultra-short length of 9, a long length of 160, and a $5,000 money management stop shows the best results. These numbers were derived from taking an average of the top 10 parameter sets. These numbers really don't make sense; the normal 1:2 and 1:3 ratio wasn't anywhere near the top. Basically, the parameters are telling us the nine-period moving average will eventually get on the trend, after going back and forth for a while, and hold onto it tenaciously.

The Bollinger Band algorithm came in third place, but with very respectable results. The parameter sets revolving around a 100-bar moving average length and 2.25 standard deviations and a $4,000 money management stop show the best

TABLE 3.11 Top 10 Parameter Sets for Each Algorithm

Algo Name	Net Profit	CAR	Max DD	Profit Factor	Ulcer Index	# Trades	Avg Profit/Loss	Avg Bars Held	%Winners	ShortLen	InterLen	StopDollars
DMA	1338431.01	5.59	−491839.05	1.44	8.96	1991	672.24	71.42	25.62	9	162	6000
DMA	1336531.01	5.59	−492539.05	1.44	8.97	2010	664.94	70.75	25.72	9	162	5500
DMA	1333731.01	5.58	−493339.05	1.44	8.99	2038	654.43	69.79	25.66	9	162	5000
DMA	1330531.01	5.57	−494639.05	1.43	9.01	2070	642.77	68.73	25.6	9	162	4500
DMA	1325931.01	5.56	−495939.05	1.43	9.04	2116	626.62	67.26	25.14	9	162	4000
DMA	1319431.01	5.54	−498839.05	1.42	9.09	2181	604.97	65.28	25.03	9	162	3500
DMA	1310731.01	5.51	−501739.05	1.41	9.16	2268	577.92	62.82	25.04	9	162	3000
DMA	1309059.66	5.51	−515389.7	1.43	9.15	1948	672	72.98	26.49	10	156	6000
DMA	1308892.36	5.51	−522360.35	1.44	9.11	1941	674.34	73.23	25.66	9	164	6000
DMA	1308303.31	5.5	−473577.53	1.43	8.96	2004	652.85	70.96	25.45	9	160	6000
Algo Name	**Net Profit**	**CAR**	**Max DD**	**Profit Factor**	**Ulcer Index**	**# Trades**	**Avg Profit/Loss**	**Avg Bars Held**	**%Winners**	**ShortLen**	**InterLen**	**StopDollars**
TMA	1124260.22	4.94	−179037.08	2.11	4.03	574	1958.64	143.68	35.89	49	194	309
TMA	1100730.77	4.87	−167743.6	2.09	3.96	573	1921	143.33	34.73	49	194	312
TMA	1071646.95	4.78	−168698.98	2.04	3.97	576	1860.5	142.43	34.55	49	194	306
TMA	1088110.19	4.83	−181550.77	2.06	4.01	575	1892.37	143.43	35.13	48	194	309
TMA	1049097.29	4.7	−171951.93	2.02	3.91	577	1818.19	142.48	35.7	47	194	309
TMA	1069863.15	4.77	−169583.3	2.03	3.95	573	1867.13	143.02	34.38	48	194	312
TMA	1023856.17	4.62	−163224.35	2	3.93	566	1808.93	143.04	35.34	49	192	315
TMA	1005683.72	4.56	−160448.4	1.96	3.82	578	1739.94	141.37	34.95	47	194	306
TMA	1040045.32	4.67	−168261.18	1.98	3.95	577	1802.5	142.02	34.14	48	194	306
TMA	1083985.47	4.82	−195109.25	2.06	4.17	569	1905.07	144.76	36.03	49	192	309

Algo Name	Net Profit	CAR	Max DD	Profit Factor	Ulcer Index	# Trades	Avg Profit/ Loss	Avg Bars Held	%Winners	ShortLen	InterLen	StopDollars
Bollinger	1033937	4.65	−292963.4	1.63	6.09	1031	1002.85	67.16	36.28	101	2.25	3500
Bollinger	1020469	4.61	−296895	1.63	6.22	1012	1008.37	68.34	35.67	103	2.25	3500
Bollinger	885350	4.15	−238296.63	1.75	6.97	657	1347.56	87.76	38.05	129	2.5	4000
Bollinger	1024112	4.62	−296874.3	1.63	6.17	1022	1002.07	67.84	36.11	102	2.25	3500
Bollinger	1016747	4.6	−296905.3	1.61	6.3	1050	968.33	66.47	35.81	100	2.25	3500
Bollinger	877685	4.12	−249438.93	1.77	6.91	674	1302.2	82.73	36.65	123	2.5	3500
Bollinger	1182979	5.13	−384837.03	1.38	7.73	2086	567.1	51.44	31.4	89	1.25	5000
Bollinger	844532	4	−236280.73	1.77	6.95	628	1344.8	89.57	37.58	135	2.5	3500
Bollinger	1195823	5.17	−395271.98	1.39	7.71	2062	579.93	52	31.43	90	1.25	5000
Bollinger	863732	4.07	−238588.03	1.72	7.02	661	1306.71	86.3	37.52	126	2.5	4000

Algo Name	Net Profit	CAR	Max DD	Profit Factor	Ulcer Index	# Trades	Avg Profit/ Loss	Avg Bars Held	%Winners	ShortLen	InterLen	StopDollars
Donchian	972653	4.45	−183567.7	1.4	4.93	0.9	2088	465.83	31.92	35.87	92	19
Donchian	964178	4.42	−191985.6	1.39	4.98	0.89	2136	451.39	30.54	36.05	92	18
Donchian	959512	4.4	−192721.65	1.39	5.08	0.87	2147	446.91	30.52	35.96	91	18
Donchian	966614	4.43	−176310.85	1.39	4.98	0.89	2110	458.11	31.88	35.78	90	19
Donchian	963078	4.42	−193489.13	1.4	5.1	0.87	2116	455.14	30.51	36.06	94	18
Donchian	967138	4.43	−185009.95	1.39	5.03	0.88	2099	460.76	31.88	35.87	91	19
Donchian	954784	4.39	−195440.55	1.39	5.15	0.85	2129	448.47	30.48	35.93	93	18
Donchian	1038561	4.67	−214593.15	1.4	5.48	0.85	2049	506.86	37.22	34.75	81	23
Donchian	959044	4.4	−184915.55	1.38	5.08	0.87	2168	442.36	31.83	35.56	85	19
Donchian	954212	4.39	−175255.05	1.37	5.03	0.87	2183	437.11	31.8	35.41	84	19

TABLE 3.12 The Best Parameter Sets for Each Optimization

Best Parameter Sets				Money	Net	Max.	Profit to	#
Algo Name	Param1	Param2	Param3	Mngmt. Stop	P / L	Drawdown	Drawdown	Trades
DMA	9	162	–	3000	1310731	−501739	2.61	2268
TMA	49	194	309	3000	1124260	−159761	7.04	574
DC	92	19	–	3000	959512	−192721	4.98	829
BB	101	2.25	–	3500	1033937	−292963	3.53	1031

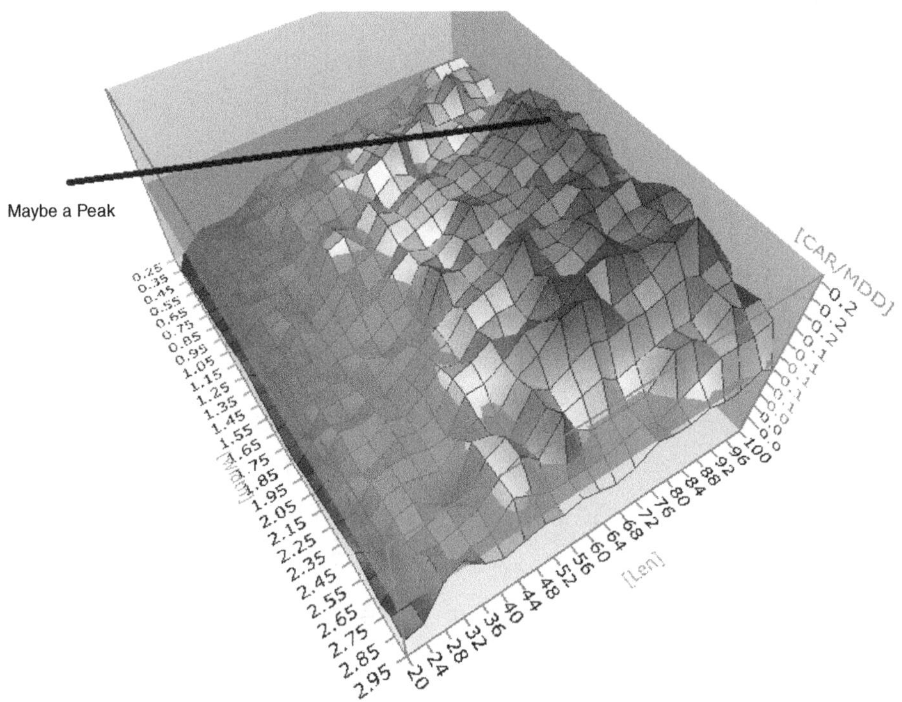

FIGURE 3.2 A three-dimensional contour chart of Bollinger performance across a subset of the parameters that were originally optimized.

Source: AmiBroker

results. One of the better parameter sets sticks out like a sore thumb (90, 1.25, 5000) due to the fact the surrounding parameters are so different, yet produce similar results. This set might be sitting on top of a peak. Figure 3.2 shows a three-dimensional contour chart of the Bollinger performance across a subset of the parameters that were originally optimized. The money management stop was held at a constant so that a three-dimensional representation could be generated. Notice where the 88 length and 1.25 width parameter lies on the chart. Almost smack-dab on a peak. This demonstrates a lack of robustness—in other words, history would have to repeat itself almost exactly for this set to be productive into the future. A parameter set on a high but somewhat level plateau is a better choice.

The TMA looks to be the best by far; it nearly kicked the rest of the competitors off of the podium. The results are very impressive, with a very high profit-to-drawdown ratio. If you look at the top 10 parameter sets, you will see the almost exact performance for each. The only parameter that varied was the long-term length. The overall effectiveness of the algorithm was not affected by variations in this parameter. It just needs to be sufficiently large. This demonstrates a high level of robustness. Also notice the ratio of the short- and intermediate-term lengths to the long-term lengths: 1 to 4 and 1 to 6, respectively. This ratio is not one that is mainly prescribed when trading the TMA.

The Donchian algorithm looks to be nearly as good nearly as the TMA. It looks like using the parameter sets revolving around an entry length of 90, an exit length of 19, and a $3,000 money management stop shows the best results. I was a little surprised by the outcome; I was looking for an entry length around 55 and an exit length around 20—the Turtle numbers. Or parameters that fit the *N* bar entry and *N* / 2 bar exit template. The mantra "Hard to get in, easy to get out" definitely fits these results. Even with such a short exit parameter, trades typically lasted 30 days. The results also demonstrated robustness among the parameter sets; results stayed somewhat constant throughout a good portion of the optimization. It's no wonder this algorithm is still being widely used.

There you have it! Four very tradable algorithms. You can't ask for much more than 60K to 70K annual return for the past 15 years, can you? On a million-dollar allocation, that works out to be 6 percent or 7 percent a year. Oh, yeah, you would have had to live through a 20 percent to 50 percent maximum drawdown. Hopefully that occurred after you had built up your equity. If it occurred right off the bat, then you would be in a heap of trouble—most traders would jump ship at that point and never look back.

Since most traders don't have a million dollars to allocate to trading, they can't afford to trade the 35-market portfolio we are currently testing. Even though this portfolio offers a tremendous amount of diversification, it is simply too large. The key to getting these systems into the realm of reality is to come up with a smaller yet diverse portfolio. Portfolio composition, especially to beginning traders, is as important as a trading algorithm. There are several steps to developing a complete algorithmic trading plan: algorithm selection, portfolio composition, proper optimization, and trade management. Position sizing is also an important component, but that will be covered later. In the next section, a smaller portfolio will be created by culling from the current large portfolio. After an algorithm has been developed and a portfolio selected, the next step is proper optimization. The final step is to develop trade management. So far, we have just used disaster stops in the development and testing of the algorithms. Are there better ways to manage a trade than waiting for a liquidation on a system-derived exit or a disaster stop? Also, is using a function of the market such as average true range better than a pure $ stop? Trade management is very important and it covers the concepts of dollar- or volatility-derived stops, profit objectives, and trailing stops. Trend-following mechanisms do not usually work with pure profit objectives unless they are sizable. You can't limit the upside, because the truly big winners don't occur all that often. Most trend-following algorithms have an inherent trailing stop mechanism built-into their logic. When the market moves up so does a moving average, a Bollinger band, and a Donchian channel. You can incorporate a more aggressive trailing stop, but again be aware that limiting the big winners will be counterproductive.

Portfolio Composition

Picking a small but diverse portfolio isn't brain surgery. The key to a good portfolio is a selection of markets that are somewhat noncorrelated and cull from different market sectors. A good portfolio should have representation from at least five sectors: currencies, financials, energies, grains, and metals. You could just randomly pick one or two markets from each sector and be done with it, but more thought should be applied to the selection process. Why not just cherry-pick the very best markets from the backtested results and use these as the future portfolio? Unfortunately, this is curve fitting even though you are wanting a portfolio with high positive expectancy.

A test on market correlation should be carried out prior to a selection of any portfolio component. Figure 3.3 shows a snapshot of a portion of the current portfolio correlation matrix. As you can see the diagonal is set to one. The diagonal represents the correlation of each market to itself.

Ticker		AD0_E0B	BP0_E0B	C20_E0B	CC20_E0B	CL20_E0B	CT20_E0B	CU0_E0B	DX20_E0B	ED0_E0B	EMD0_E0B	ES0_E0B
AD0_E0B	...	1.00	[illegible]	0.54	0.26	[illegible]	0.76	0.13	[illegible]	0.83	0.57	0.41
BP0_E0B	...	[illegible]	1.00	0.21	-0.24	0.72	-0.21	0.39	0.08	[illegible]	-0.13	0.05
C20_E0B	...	0.54	0.21	1.00	-0.15	0.28	0.58	0.30	[illegible]	0.15	0.26	0.23
CC20_E0B	...	0.26	[illegible]	-0.14	1.00	-0.14	0.01	0.39	[illegible]	0.39	0.07	-0.05
CL20_E0B	...	[illegible]	0.72	0.28	-0.14	1.00	-0.21	0.59	-0.11	[illegible]	[illegible]	[illegible]
CT20_E0B	...	0.76	[illegible]	0.58	0.01	-0.21	1.00	-0.09	[illegible]	0.59	0.65	0.54
CU0_E0B	...	0.13	0.39	0.30	0.39	0.59	-0.10	1.00	[illegible]	-0.17	[illegible]	[illegible]
DX20_E0B	...	[illegible]	0.06	[illegible]	[illegible]	-0.16	[illegible]	[illegible]	1.00	[illegible]	-0.13	0.00
ED0_E0B	...	0.83	[illegible]	0.14	0.39	[illegible]	0.59	-0.17	[illegible]	1.00	0.57	0.37
EMD0_E0B	...	0.57	-0.13	0.26	0.07	[illegible]	0.65	[illegible]	-0.16	0.57	1.00	0.97
ES0_E0B	...	0.41	0.06	0.23	-0.05	[illegible]	0.54	[illegible]	-0.01	0.37	0.97	1.00
FC0_E0B	...	-0.01	0.20	-0.09	-0.07	-0.14	0.27	[illegible]	0.35	-0.01	0.58	0.68
FV0_E0B	...	0.86	[illegible]	0.25	0.32	[illegible]	0.61	-0.17	[illegible]	0.97	0.62	0.44
GC20_E0B	...	0.93	[illegible]	0.47	0.22	[illegible]	0.68	0.08	[illegible]	0.82	0.35	0.16
HG20_E0B	...	0.46	0.31	0.47	0.17	0.32	0.41	0.50	[illegible]	0.04	0.04	0.00
HO20_E0B	...	0.18	0.53	0.65	-0.12	0.83	0.26	0.52	[illegible]	-0.25	-0.01	0.02

FIGURE 3.3 A snapshot of a portion of the current portfolio correlation matrix.

The correlation coefficients range from +1 to −1. A coefficient of +1 represents a 100 percent correlation and a coefficient of −1 also represents a 100 percent correlation, but in the opposite direction. The AD (Australian dollar) is highly correlated to GC (gold), but not very much to the CU (Euro currency), and is highly anticorrelated to DX (dollar index). If you were picking two currencies, then you would probably want to go with the AD and CU. The BP is a little too noncorrelated for my taste. So let's pick the AD and CU to represent the currencies. Moving onto energies the crude is highly correlated to both the heating oil and natural gas. Unleaded is a different story; there is very little correlation there. CL and RB (unleaded) will take care of the energies sector. The grains consist of soybeans, corn, Kansas City wheat, Chicago wheat, corn, and a few other low-volume components. According to the correlation matrix, a good mix would be the corn and KC wheat. The financials are up next and are represented by 30-year Treasury bonds, 10-year notes, 5-year notes, 2-year notes, and Eurodollars. All these markets are highly correlated to each other, so there is no advantage/diversification by trading one with another. Trading a Treasury bond with Treasury note is like trading two bonds. Bonds are very shock sensitive to news events such as Fed and employment situation reports. So the less volatile but still with some bang is the Treasury notes. The safest soft commodity is sugar (SB). It trends well and seems less sensitive to crop reports than coffee (KC) or cotton (CT). There is very little correlation among these three markets so any one of the three would probably suffice. All of the metals in the current portfolio, silver (SV), gold (GC), copper (HG), and platinum (PL), are, as you would assume, highly correlated, so like the financials only one should be chosen for this initial portfolio. Copper is the only nonprecious metal in the list and used extensively in manufacturing so let's pick it. The initial portfolio will consist of the following markets: AD, CU, CL, RB, TY, C, KW, SB, and HG. You will notice that the stock indices were left out. The indices are a totally different animal. In an interview with Richard Dennis by Arthur Collins, the King Turtle stated:

> With the exception of the S&Ps, they're all the same. You have to treat them the same, for no reason other than sample size. You can optimize each system in each market individually or you can optimize them together. It's better to optimize them together.
>
> —***Technical Analysis of Stocks and Commodities*, April 2005 Issue**

An Act of Futility?

Okay, we now have a portfolio but on which algorithm should we risk our capital? Also should we use the best-optimized parameters for each algorithm that was derived from the global optimizations? Any of the four algorithms could be used—they all showed positive expectancy. The "optimal" parameters that we previously derived were for illustration purposes only. These tests simply provided evidence that these algorithms have a technical edge. A new set of tests have to be set up with our new portfolio across the four best performing algorithms. Also, we need to come up with a set of parameters for each algorithm that will hopefully stand the test of time. The test of time can be accomplished by utilizing out-of-sample (OOS) data. OOS data is a segment of historical data that the algorithms did not see during their developmental periods. The algorithms can be optimized on in-sample data (IS) and the "optimal" parameter sets can then be applied to data that has not yet been seen. The ratio between OOS and IS is a subject of much debate. Some believe you should give the algorithm more data (IS) to be trained on in hopes that the parameters will reflect more diverse market conditions. Others feel that a longer walk-forward (OOS) test will demonstrate an algorithm's true robustness. I don't believe there is a universal answer to this conundrum, but experience has shown that a 1-to-3 ratio seems to work. The test period that we have been using is 15 years, so using this ratio we come up with roughly five years of OOS and roughly 10 years IS.

Before we carry out these tests the subject of individual market optimization needs to be brought up. I have never seen, in all my years of testing, a trading algorithm utilizing different parameters on a market-by-market basis survive the test of time. Even trading algorithms that just utilize different parameters on a sector-by-sector basis haven't been all that successful over the long run. All this optimizing simply leads to over-curve-fitting. The trading systems that have stood the test of time have one and only one parameter set for the entire portfolio. Now that that question has been answered, what about periodical portfolio reoptimization? This is the idea of optimizing an algorithm for the first five or so years and then carrying over for the next year or two. At the end of the carryforward period, the parameters are reoptimized over the new unseen data and then carried forward again. This form of optimization uses a sliding IS data window. The results from the OOS data are accurate, since the parameters were not trained on that data until after the fact. This form of optimization is discussed extensively in Chapter 8.

Starting with the Donchian algorithm and our new portfolio, let's optimize the parameters from January 2000 through December 2009. Using the best parameters set from this test, the algorithm will be tested across the remaining data, January 2010 through August 2015, to evaluate the robustness of the selection.

Table 3.13 shows the best results for the Donchian algorithm IS time period. The parameter set that I chose was 98, 25, and $4,000. This was a top echelon set that had a reasonable protective stop. In addition, the two length parameters were located on a plateau—they were surrounded by similar values.

Now the real test begins. A diversified portfolio has been chosen as well as a seemingly robust parameter set. Let's walk this algorithm forward and test it across the OOS time frame (January 2010 through August 2015). Table 3.14 exposes a seeming act of futility.

TABLE 3.13 **The Best Results for the Donchian Algorithm for In-Sample Time Period**

Name	Net Profit	CAR	Max. Sys DD	Profit Factor	Ulcer Index	# Trades	Avg P/L	Avg Bars Held	% Winners	Entry	Exit	Stop Dollars
Donchian	466438	3.9	−57391	2.21	2.27	324	1439.62	46	40.74	64	26	5000
Donchian	417508	3.55	−55451	2.33	1.72	272	1534.96	45.46	40.07	95	28	3000
Donchian	420843	3.57	−56764	2.36	1.98	262	1606.27	46.6	43.13	99	26	4500
Donchian	421760	3.58	−56764	2.31	1.94	262	1609.77	47.39	43.51	97	26	5500
Donchian	421849	3.58	−56764	2.35	1.98	263	1603.99	46.61	42.97	98	26	4500
Donchian	421762	3.58	−56764	2.34	1.92	260	1622.16	47.47	43.85	98	26	5500
Donchian	420241	3.57	−56764	2.34	1.72	261	1610.12	48.18	41.76	96	28	4000

TABLE 3.14 **Results for the Donchian Algorithm when Walked Forward across an Out-of-Sample (OOS) Time Period**

Name	Net Profit	CAR	Max. Sys DD	Profit Factor	Ulcer Index	# Trades	Avg P/L	Avg Bars Held	% Winners
<Portfolio>	25678	0.45	−166243	1.08	8.2	161	159.49	41.32	32
AD0_E0B	−16980	−0.31	−29050	0.61	1.83	20	−849	39	25
C20_E0B	−18413	−0.33	−35138	0.53	2.25	21	−876.79	39.14	33
CL20_E0B	11230	0.2	−39180	1.23	1.82	19	591.05	32	26
CU0_E0B	37713	0.66	−24450	2.99	1.14	13	2900.96	51.54	31
HG20_E0B	−16438	−0.3	−28638	0.62	1.87	19	−865.13	33.74	32
KW20_E0B	1463	0.03	−14725	1.07	0.54	19	76.97	41.95	32
RB0_E0B	−2927	−0.05	−60503	0.96	2.93	21	−139.4	29.9	14
SB20_E0B	15918	0.28	−12749	2.68	0.89	17	936.33	52.59	53
TY0_E0B	14113	0.25	−8084	2.54	0.37	12	1176.05	66.67	50

Well, at least the system made some money. However, the drawdown is just way too great. What did we do wrong? We did all our homework—picked a fairly diversified portfolio and a robust parameter set. How could we have been so far off? Out of pure sick curiosity, I optimized the algorithm across the OOS data to see how far off we missed the target. Table 3.15 has the best parameters sets for our small portfolio over the OOS timespan.

Boy, were we way off! A couple of the best parameter sets had the exit length parameter greater than the entry length—illogical, you say! In these situations, the system becomes a reversal system until it is stopped out with the money management stop. I am almost too scared to continue, but like looking at a car accident, let's

TABLE 3.15 The Best Parameters for the Portfolio over the Out-Of-Sample (OOS) Time Period

Net Profit	CAR	Max. Sys DD	Profit Factor	Ulcer Index	# Trades	Avg P/L	Avg Bars Held	% Winners	Entry	Exit	Stop Dollars
182607	3.04	−95572	1.42	3.85	253	721.77	48.67	39.53	30	30	5500
182607	3.04	−95572	1.42	3.85	253	721.77	48.67	39.53	30	30	4500
182607	3.04	−95572	1.42	3.85	253	721.77	48.67	39.53	30	30	4000
182607	3.04	−95572	1.42	3.85	253	721.77	48.67	39.53	30	30	3500
182607	3.04	−95572	1.42	3.85	253	721.77	48.67	39.53	30	30	3000
182607	3.04	−95572	1.42	3.85	253	721.77	48.67	39.53	30	30	6000
182456	3.04	−95583	1.42	3.85	253	721.17	48.67	39.53	30	42	3000
182412	3.04	−95593	1.42	3.85	253	720.99	48.67	39.53	30	84	3000
182412	3.04	−95593	1.42	3.85	253	720.99	48.67	39.53	30	100	5500

TABLE 3.16 The Optimization of the Bollinger Algorithm for the In-Sample (IS) Time Period

Name	Net Profit	CAR	Max. Sys DD	Profit Factor	Ulcer Index	# Trades	Avg P/L	Avg Bars Held	% Winners	Len	Width	Stop Dollars
Bollinger	498208	4.13	−59466	2.55	2.2	247	2017.04	66.91	37.65	103	1.5	5000
Bollinger	480108	4	−66439	2.46	2.23	256	1875.42	63.79	38.28	98	1.5	5000
Bollinger	492573	4.09	−59399	2.53	2.07	251	1962.44	65.7	38.25	102	1.5	4500
Bollinger	489796	4.07	−59466	2.49	2.15	250	1959.18	65.93	37.2	103	1.5	4500
Bollinger	516639	4.25	−63828	2.71	2.02	239	2161.67	68.67	38.49	105	1.5	6000
Bollinger	502931	4.16	−61884	2.64	2.06	240	2095.54	68.08	38.33	108	1.5	4000
Bollinger	516685	4.25	−64074	2.74	2.04	243	2126.27	66.91	37.86	105	1.5	4000
Bollinger	515383	4.24	−63828	2.7	2.06	239	2156.42	69.05	38.08	106	1.5	6000
Bollinger	511872	4.22	−63828	2.67	2.1	240	2132.8	68.34	38.33	105	1.5	5500
Bollinger	516735	4.25	−65095	2.72	2.09	231	2236.95	71.45	38.53	110	1.5	5000

continue in this same vein. Maybe the Donchian is just an inferior algorithm. Table 3.16 is the IS optimization of the Bollinger algorithm and Table 3.17 is the OOS results.

Okay, looks good. I selected the parameter set [108, 1.5, 4000]. How did it do during the OOS timespan?

I think I see a trend developing. I would show you the TMA and the DMA, but it would be just a waste of paper! I am talking reverse makeover. So what happened? Where do we place the blame? I went back and recreated a portfolio of the top nine markets based on IS performance and the OOS results were even worse than our

TABLE 3.17 Results for the Donchian Algorithm when Walked Forward across an Out-of-Sample (OOS) Time Period

Name	Net Profit	CAR	Max. Sys DD	Profit Factor	Ulcer Index	# Trades	Avg P/L	Avg Bars Held	% Winners
<Portfolio>	−31803	−0.58	−222494.3	0.91	11.93	158	−201.28	56.15	30
AD0_E0B	−2570	−0.05	−26410	0.91	1.64	16	−160.62	64.56	38
C20_E0B	−8500	−0.15	−26325	0.71	1.73	20	−425	53.85	30
CL20_E0B	−14060	−0.25	−58490	0.78	3.36	21	−669.52	40.95	29
CU0_E0B	16888	0.3	−39763	1.62	2.17	14	1206.25	67.57	36
HG20_E0B	−25763	−0.46	−38750	0.56	2.47	19	−1355.92	45.26	26
KW20_E0B	8525	0.15	−15063	1.4	0.59	17	501.47	65.71	41
RB0_E0B	−29267	−0.53	−79688	0.7	4.51	24	−1219.48	36.63	13
SB20_E0B	15185	0.27	−19315	2.07	1.28	11	1380.44	94.27	36
TY0_E0B	7760	0.14	−9334	1.46	0.49	16	484.99	65.38	38

small diversified portfolio. We did everything humanly possible to make these trend-following systems work: algorithm selection, optimization, and portfolio selection. What if we performed a more frequent periodic reoptimization? We saw the best parameter set shifting from just five years ago. This shift may be attributable to the disappearance of the pit session and the adoption of purely electronic markets. Who knows why, but the fact remains that the commodity markets have had a fundamental shift. Indicators such as the ones we have experimented with are adaptive by nature; they change based on market activity and/or volatility. Theoretically, they should be able to keep up with the evolution of the markets. In practice, this was not the case.

AmiBroker has a walk-forward backtesting capability—meaning we can periodically reoptimize parameters throughout a historic backtest. I discuss this optimization method in great detail in Chapter 8. After this chapter, if you like, you can skip to Chapter 8 to help you understand exactly what is going on here. Figure 3.4 illustrates the basic concept of walk-forward testing. Basically it involves two primary steps:

1. Backtest and derive—backtest and extract the best parameter set based on some criteria. It could be profit, drawdown, profit-to-drawdown ratio, etc.
2. Walk forward—take the parameter sets and apply them forward in time on data not used in the backtest. Do this on a periodic basis.

In this example, the Bollinger Band algorithm will be reoptimized annually based on the best-performing parameters for the prior four years. Keep in mind that we are not cheating, as only the OOS (out-of-sample) data will be used to calculate performance metrics. Let's see if this method can turn around the trend of this trend-following method. Figure 3.4 shows the process of walking forward.

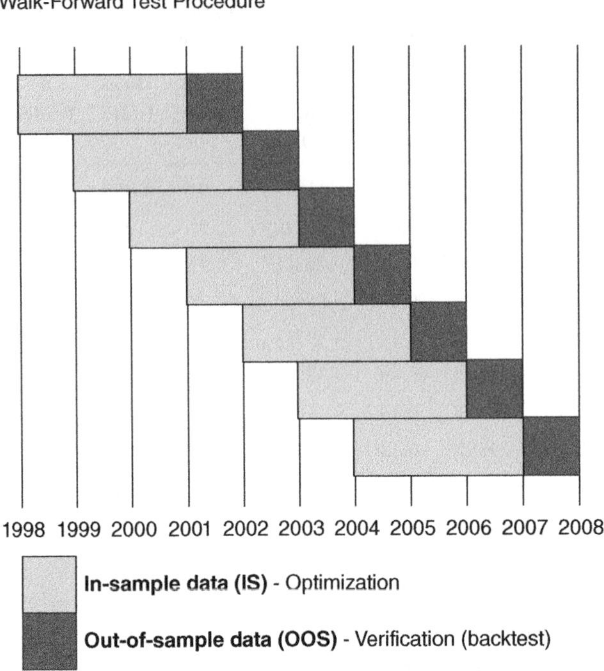

FIGURE 3.4 Walk-forward testing begins with a backtest used to derive the desired parameter. Then, it applies that parameter going forward.

Source: AmiBroker

AmiBroker's walk-forward optimizer (WFO) derived the best parameter set from January 1, 2006, to January 1, 2010, and then carried those parameters forward from January 1, 2010, to January 1, 2011. In this test, the algorithm netted $35,330 for 2010. It then included 2010 and backed up to January 1, 2007, and then carried those parameters forward through 2011. However, this time the algorithm lost a whopping −$56,532. Keep stepping through the figure and you can see how the system performed through the present. What's really interesting is the shift in the parameter sets. You would think by adding just another year to the backtest during the periodic readjustment the parameters wouldn't shift that much. Take a look at Figures 3.5 and 3.6.

The first year in our OOS window is 2010. The WFO picked the parameter set [72 day, 1.5 std. devs., 3000 stop] to apply to 2010 and the results looked great. Notice the wide shift in the parameters for 2011 [111, 0.25, 6000]. These parameters performed horribly, losing over $56,000. The parameters for 2012 shifted some more [143, 0.25, 3500]. These parameters didn't do much better. 2013 also shows a dramatic shift, [45, 3, 3500], but at least the algorithm made a little money. The parameter set stayed constant for 2014, and the algorithm really brought it home, with almost $72,000 in profit. The end result with periodic reoptimization beat the pants off of the static set with $45,000 in profit and a little

Mode	Begin	End	Net Profit	Max. Sys Dra...	Max. Trade ...	Net % Profit	Exp...	CAR	RAR	Max. Trade ...	Max. Sys ...	Recovery F...
OOS	1/1/2007	1/1/2008	15,316.70	-25,814.70	-17,883.60	1.48	1.33	1.49	111.43	-97.68	-2.46	0.59
IS	1/1/2004	1/1/2008	97,996.80	-37,397.30	-31,319.40	9.80	2.52	2.37	93.82	-99.96	-3.46	2.62
OOS	1/1/2008	1/1/2009	199,375.30	-75,565.50	-26,900.00	18.96	5.65	19.02	336.30	-99.51	-6.70	2.64
IS	1/1/2005	1/1/2009	362,383.50	-47,370.70	-22,482.60	36.24	1.98	8.05	406.63	-99.93	-3.89	7.65
OOS	1/1/2009	1/1/2010	-25,990.90	-55,114.00	(1) -9,752.40	-2.08	0.71	-2.09	-294....	-98.96	-4.32	-0.47
IS	1/1/2006	1/1/2010	448,370.10	-57,759.50	-22,812.50	44.84	4.56	9.72	213.07	-99.74	-4.85	7.76
OOS	1/1/2010	1/1/2011	35,330.30	-49,916.40	(2) -10,362.50	2.88	2.71	2.92	107.69	-99.95	-4.03	0.71
IS	1/1/2007	1/1/2011	504,694.70	-70,702.00	-24,660.00	50.47	7.37	10.76	146.01	-99.93	-5.27	7.14
OOS	1/1/2011	1/1/2012	-56,532.00	-107,505.70	(3) -17,310.00	-4.49	2.89	-4.53	-157....	-99.94	-8.31	-0.53
IS	1/1/2008	1/1/2012	364,551.40	-80,003.30	-26,665.80	36.46	7.07	8.09	114.49	-99.66	-5.78	4.56
OOS	1/1/2012	1/1/2013	-12,043.00	-47,503.00	(4) -18,970.00	-1.00	2.48	-1.01	-40.62	-99.64	-3.85	-0.25
IS	1/1/2009	1/1/2013	57,057.90	-31,338.80	-12,726.00	5.71	0.49	1.40	287.99	-99.21	-2.93	1.82
OOS	1/1/2013	1/1/2014	707.70	-13,531.60	(5) -9,504.60	0.06	0.18	0.06	33.67	-99.50	-1.12	0.05
IS	1/1/2010	1/1/2014	45,025.90	-31,338.80	-12,726.00	4.50	0.44	1.11	253.23	-99.50	-2.97	1.44
OOS	1/1/2014	1/1/2015	71,980.00	-7,490.70	(6) -4,937.50	6.04	0.67	6.07	904.36	-95.84	-0.62	9.61
IS	1/1/2011	1/1/2015	86,743.20	-31,338.80	-12,726.00	8.67	0.42	2.10	499.55	-99.50	-3.06	2.77
OOS	1/1/2015	1/1/2016	-5,309.40	-11,173.10	-4,912.50	-0.42	0.01	-0.70	-9,16...	-82.63	-0.88	-0.48
IS	1/1/2012	1/1/2016	70,532.10	-9,966.80	-7,270.00	7.05	0.23	1.91	830.04	-98.19	-0.98	7.08

Result list | Info | **Walk Forward**

Completed in 892.39 seconds. Number of rows: 764

FIGURE 3.5 AmiBroker's walk-forward optimizer in action.

OOS	1/1/2008	1/1/2009	1	190,164.40	-68,628.00	102	2.25	6,000	18.53
IS	1/1/2005	1/1/2009	3,133	362,383.50	-47,370.70	27	2	5,500	36.24
OOS	1/1/2009	1/1/2010	1	-25,990.90	-55,114.00	27	2	5,500	-2.14
IS	1/1/2006	1/1/2010	1,620	448,370.10	-57,759.50	72	1.5	3,000	44.84
OOS	1/1/2010	1/1/2011	1	35,330.30	-49,916.40	72	1.5	3,000	2.97
IS	1/1/2007	1/1/2011	500	504,694.70	-70,702.00	111	0.25	6,000	50.47
OOS	1/1/2011	1/1/2012	1	-56,532.00	-107,505.70	111	0.25	6,000	-4.61
IS	1/1/2008	1/1/2012	602	364,182.60	-79,642.10	143	0.25	3,500	36.42
OOS	1/1/2012	1/1/2013	1	-10,421.80	-45,881.80	143	0.25	3,500	-0.89
IS	1/1/2009	1/1/2013	3,088	57,057.90	-31,338.80	45	3	3,500	5.71
OOS	1/1/2013	1/1/2014	1	707.70	-13,531.60	45	3	3,500	0.06
IS	1/1/2010	1/1/2014	1,712	41,965.90	-34,398.80	45	3	3,000	4.20
OOS	1/1/2014	1/1/2015	1	71,980.00	-7,490.70	45	3	3,000	6.21
IS	1/1/2011	1/1/2015	446	86,743.20	-31,338.80	45	3	3,500	8.67

FIGURE 3.6 Parameters selected to carry forward for the following year.

more reasonable drawdown of $90,000. Figure 3.7 shows an equity curve of the walk-forward performance from 2006.

Is this the solution? Stick with your algorithm and readjust based on recent performance. That is a tough question to answer, and is best left up to what the trader truly believes when it comes to using optimization in the development of an algorithm's parameters. In today's trading environment, I think everything should be taken into consideration. Don't be afraid of new technology.

After the second coming of trend following in 2008, the only bright spot has been the second half of 2014. And things are looking a little better here in 2015. It seems, for right now, that the commodity markets are behaving a little trendier. With prices in the tank trend followers are waiting for the eventuality of their springing back to life. They are limited resources, right? But how many trend followers will still be left out there? A lot more than you might think. Due to the nature of commodity price moves, you cannot simply abandon the trend-following methods. There is just way too much potential.

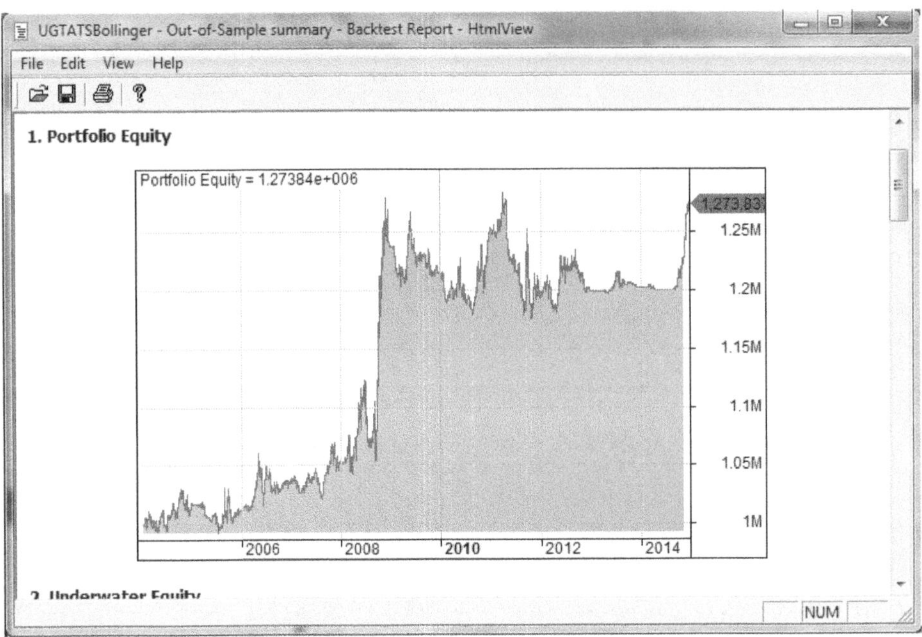

FIGURE 3.7 Performance of the WFO of the Bollinger Band system.

Source: AmiBroker

So what is the answer for a smaller account? In a similar fashion to diversifying through markets, a trader can diversify further through trading multiple algorithms. In a trader's perfect world, there would exist robust trend-following, short-term swing and day trading systems. Ones that were not closely correlated with the others. This perfect world doesn't exist due to the fact a robust short-term swing system is hard to find. The ones that seem to work on a somewhat consistent basis mostly work only on the stock indices. However, that's not a bad thing, because this is a very weak sector for trend followers. The best short-term algorithms that I have come across incorporate mean reversion or pattern recognition components. The marriage of trend following and these other types of algorithms might be one solution. This union brings together two different algorithms, as well as two noncorrelated portfolios.

Multi-Algorithm Strategy (MAS)

Mean reversion is a trading algorithm that trades in the direction of the trend but takes advantage of a temporary countertrend move.

The most recent performance of this algorithm looks very respectable. This algorithm utilizes the Bollinger B% indicator/function (Box 3.4). Basically, it trades in the direction of the 200-day moving average but waits for a pullback for longs and rallies for shorts. The Bollinger B% function returns the location of the current close in relationship to the upper and lower Bollinger bands. If the function returns a small value, then the close is close to the lower band and vice-versa for a high value. This system is programmed in EasyLanguage and the source code will be revealed in the Chapter 7.

Box 3.4 Mean Reversion (MR)

Calculate the 200-day moving average of closing prices

Calculate the 5-day Bollinger B% value

Calculate the 3-day moving average of the Bollinger B% value

If c > MAV(c,200) and MAV(BB%,3) < 0.25, then buy next bar at open

If c < MAV(c,200) and MAV(BB%,3) > 0.75, then sell short next bar at open

Liquidate long MOC when BB% > .75 or close < entryPrice - 2000/bigPointValue

Liquidate short MOC when BB% < 0.25 or close > entryPrice + 2000/bigPointValue

Take a look at the equity curve in Figure 3.8. Here is a pattern system that trades the stock indices as well.

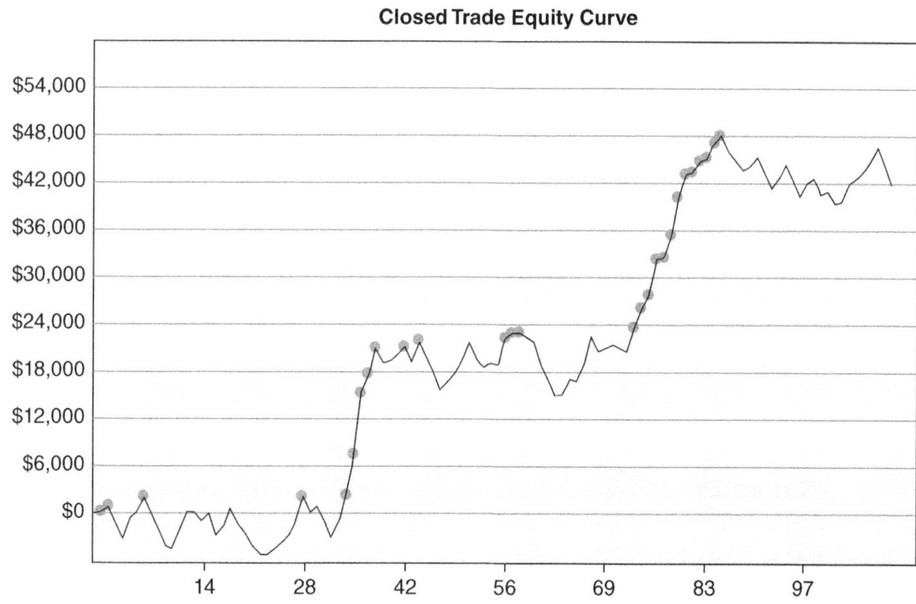

FIGURE 3.8 Equity curve that reflects a pattern system.

This system looks at the last day of the month, and if it closes down a certain amount from the prior day's close, it looks to buy if the first day of the month also closes below its open (Box 3.5). This is a reoccurring pattern, and it's based on the flip of the month.

> **Box 3.5 LastBarOfMonth Pattern (LBM)**
>
> Calculate percentage change between yesterday's close and the prior day's close:
> %Chg = (close(1) – close(2)) / close(1) * 100
>
> If today is the first trading day of the month and the %Chg < -0.2 and today's close < today's open, then buy MOC
>
> If today is the first trading day of the month and the %Chg > 0.2 and today's close > today's open, then sell short MOC
>
> Liquidate long at the open of the fifth day after entry day or on a stop @ entryPrice −2000/bigPointValue
>
> Liquidate short at the open of the fifth day after entry day or on a stop @ entryPrice + 2000/bigPointValue

Day trading is a great complement to trend following as well. The equity curve in Figure 3.9 illustrates a mini-Russell day trading system that trades after a narrow

FIGURE 3.9 Mini-Russell day trading system using a narrow range day. It initially puts on two contracts, pulling the first one off after a certain profit is reached and leaving the second to run its course.

range day and initially puts on two contracts and then pulls one off after a certain profit level and then lets the second contract run its course. It is out on the close no matter what. This algorithm incorporates trade management in the form of protective stop, breakeven stop, and trailing stop (Box 3.6).

Box 3.6 Day trading the mini Russell

```
CanTrade = False
CanBuy = False
CanShort = False
If yesterday's True Range < MAV(TR,10), then CanTrade = True
If yesterday's close >= prior day's close, then CanBuy = True
If yesterday's close < prior day's close, then CanShort = True
If CanTrade, then
   If CanBuy, then buy 2 units tomorrow at open +0.2 *MAV(TR,10) stop
   If CanShort, then sell short 2 units tomorrow at open −0.2*MAV(TR,10)
      stop
If market position = long
   If current size = 2 units, then
      If H of 5 minute bar > entryPrice + 4.00, then
         exitLong 1 unit at H of day – 4.00 on a stop
   If current size = 1 unit, then
      exitLong at entryPrice stop or MOC
If market position = short
   If current size = 2 units, then
      If L of 5 minute bar <= entryPrice – 4.00, then
         exitShort 1 unit at L of day + 4.00 on a stop
   If current size = 1 unit, then
      exitLong at entryPrice stop or MOC
```

How about a system that lets the Commitment of Traders Report (COT) guide its directional trades—one that only trades in the direction of the commercial interests? If the net commercial position is positive, then only take long positions, and vice versa. This type of trading system uses the COT as a sentiment indicator. Several trading platforms allow you to import the COT data. This system will be included on this books companion website and www.georgepruitt.com.

Summary

There are a lot of algorithms out there that are not correlated, so it might be best not to put all of your eggs in one basket. I think the best trend-following mechanism might even be a combination of a Donchian / Bollinger hybrid; use one indicator to confirm the other. I went back and redid all the testing on the four major trend-following candidates utilizing a multiple of an average true range (ATR) stop and the conclusions were exactly the same. A fixed-dollar stop is as good as an adaptive volatility stop. I will continue my search for that elusive combination of algorithms or a better trend-following mousetrap and report my findings on www.georgepruitt.com website. Chapter 4 starts the second section of this book, where different trading and testing platforms are discussed. This is where the real programming begins. Have fun!

CHAPTER 4

Introduction to AmiBroker's AFL

This chapter starts the second part of the book that covers different programming languages and trading platforms. This second part discusses AmiBroker, Visual Basic (VBA) for Excel, Python, and TradeStation. The major goal of this particular chapter is to introduce AmiBroker and illustrate some of its very powerful capabilities. However, some very important building blocks of programming languages, reserved words, data types, operators and expressions, and precedence of operators, are quickly reviewed and used throughout the next three chapters. Even if you are not interested in AmiBroker, make sure you read the first part of this chapter to get a grasp on the universal usage of some key building blocks that are included in all programming languages.

Quick Start

AmiBroker is a complete database management, charting, testing, trading, and optimizing program. So far we have covered many different trading algorithms and every one of them can be easily implemented in the AmiBroker Function Language (AFL). There are several features that make AmiBroker a serious contender as a go-to trading platform:

- *Price*. The cost of the software ranges between \$279 and \$339 and once you purchase it, it is yours. There are no lease fees. You get free upgrades for one year after purchase and it's up to the purchaser to upgrader thereafter.

- *Speed*. AmiBroker utilizes multithread processing, which means it can utilize multicore processors and carry out subprocesses or threads simultaneously. In other words, it is very fast.
- *Power*. Portfolio-level backtesting is paramount when evaluating the robustness of a trading algorithm. If an algorithm works on multiple markets, it demonstrates a high level of robustness. Robustness and positive expectancy is all you can ask from a trading algorithm. AmiBroker provides Exhaustive Search and Genetic forms of parameter optimization.
- *Data*. AmiBroker is compatible with many End Of Day(EOD) and Real-Time data feeds. It includes a very simple to use ASCII data importer.
- *Broker Integration*. Several brokers can be linked with the software for automated order execution.
- *Integrated Development Environment*. AmiBroker has two IDEs to help the user develop complete trading algorithms and technical analysis tools. The main IDE (AFL Editor) is a complete scripting tool and the AFL Code Wizard utilizes a drag-and-drop development paradigm. Both IDEs utilize the AmiBroker Function Language (AFL) as their programming/scripting language and a vast library of strategies, functions, and indicators.
- *Support*. Tomasz Janeczko, the founder and chief software architect of AmiBroker, holds PhD and MSc degrees in Computer Science and Telecommunications from Worclaw University of Technology. This developer really loves his software and stands behind it and provides much of the tech support. There is a devout, almost cultlike, following for AmiBroker, and many questions can be easily answered by searching the Internet and/or joining the user groups.

If you have purchased my prior books, you know that I use TradeStation. I love its tightly integrated components and EasyLanguage. I will discuss TradeStation in Chapter 7. However, I felt I would be amiss if I didn't show off a little bit of AmiBroker. I was first introduced to the software through Howard Bandy's excellent book, *Quantitative Trading Systems*. I have included all of his books in "George's List of Must-Own Trading Books" in the appendix. The software that was described in Bandy's book really piqued my interest, so I contacted Dr. Janeczko for a review copy, and he more than graciously provided his complete software suite. I fell in love with the AFL Wizard and the speed of his backtester. Coming from a bar-by-bar algorithm development paradigm, I was really impressed and initially confused by Dr. Janeczko's array processing. Array processing is extremely fast versus bar-by-bar and in many cases is easier to learn. What is also very cool about AmiBroker is that you can flip from array to bar processing quite easily.

Things All Programmers Need to Know

Before I go into detail about array programming, let's go over a short introduction to some key concepts that all programming languages have in common, including AmiBrokers AFL: reserved words, remarks or comments, variables and variable naming conventions, data types, expressions and operators, and precedence of operators. Here is a quick synopsis:

- *Reserved words.* Words that the computer language has set aside for a specific purpose. You can only use these words for their predefined purposes. Using these words for any other purpose may cause severe problems.
- *Remarks or comments.* Words or statements that are completely ignored by the compiler. Remarks are placed in code to help the programmer, or other people who may reuse the code, understand what the program is designed to do. Double forward slashes // inform the AFL interpreter that anything that follows is a comment. The double forward slashes can be used anywhere within a line. The forward slash asterisk combination /* and */ is used for multiline commentary. The /* opens the remarks and */ closes the remarks block. Anything inside /* --- */ is ignored by the computer.
- *Variables.* User-defined words or letters that are used to store information. AFL is not a strongly typed language. You don't have to formally declare a variable name or its type prior to its use.
- *Data types.* Different types of storage; variables are defined by their data types. AFL has three basic data types: numeric, boolean, and string. A variable that is assigned a numeric value, or stored as a number, would be of the numeric type. A variable that stores a true or false value would be of the boolean type. Finally, a variable that stores a list of characters would be of the string type.

Variables and Data Types A programmer must understand how to use variables and their associated data types before they can program anything productive. Let's take a look at a snippet of code.

```
mySum = 4 + 5 + 6;
myAvg = mySum/3;
```

The variables in this code are mySum and myAvg and they are of the numeric data type; they are storage places for numbers. AFL is liberal concerning variable names, but there are a few requirements (Table 4.1). A variable name cannot:

- Start with a number or a period (.)
- Be a number
- Include punctuation

Correct	Incorrect
myAvg	1MyAvg
mySum	.sum
sum	val+11
val1	the//sum
the.sum	my?sum
my_val	1234

Variable naming is up to the style of the individual programmer. AFL is not case sensitive (you can use upper- or lowercase letters in the variable names). (*Note:* The following is my preference—may not be everybody's.) Lowercase letters are preferred for names that only contain one syllable. For variable names that have more than one syllable, we begin the name with a lowercase letter, and then capitalize the beginning of each subsequent word in a multi-word identifier.

```
sum, avg, total, totalSum, myAvg, avgValue, totalUpSum,
  totDnAvg
```

Operators and Expressions In programming, statements are made up of expressions. An expression consists of a combination of identifiers, functions, variables, and values, which result in a specific value. Operators are a form of built-in functions and come in two forms: unary and binary. A binary operator requires two operands, whereas a unary operator requires only one. AFL can handle both. Examples of unary operators are ++ and --. Some of the more popular binary ones are: + − / * < = > >= <= <> AND OR. These binary operators can be further classified into two more categories: arithmetic and logical.

Expressions come in three forms: arithmetic, logical, and string. The type of operator used determines the type of expression. An arithmetic expression includes + − / *, whereas a logical or boolean expression includes < = > >= <= <> AND OR.

Arithmetic Expressions	Logical Expressions
myValue = myValue + 1	myCondition1 = sum > total
myValue = sum − total	myCondition1 = sum <> total
myResult = sum*total+20	cond1 = cond1 AND cond2
myCounter++	cond1 = cond2 OR cond3

Arithmetic expressions always result in a number, and logical expressions always result in true or false. True is equivalent to 1, and false is equivalent to 0. String expressions deal with a string of characters. You can assign string values to string variables and compare them.

```
myName1 = "George";
myName2 = "Pruitt";
cond1 = (myName1 <> myName2);
myName3 = myName1 + " " + myName2;
```

Concatenation occurs when two or more strings are added together. Basically, you create one new string from the two that are being added together.

Precedence of Operators It is important to understand the concept of precedence of operators. When more than one operator is in an expression, the operator with the higher precedence is evaluated first, and so on. This order of evaluation can be modified with the use of parentheses. Most programming languages' order of precedence is as follows:

1. Parentheses
2. Multiplication or division
3. Addition or subtraction
4. <, >, =, <=, >=, <>
5. AND
6. OR

Here are some expressions and their results:

```
20 - 15/5      equals 17 not 1
20 - 3         division first, then subtraction

10 + 8/2       equals 14 not 9
10 + 4         division first then addition

5 * 4/2        equals 10
20/2           division and multiplication are equal

(20 - 15)/5    equals 1
5/5            parentheses overrides order

(10 + 8)/2     equals 9
18/2           parentheses overrides order

6 + 2 > 3      true
8 > 3
```

```
2 > 1 + 10    false
2 < 11

2 + 2/2 * 6   equals 8 not 18
2 + 1 * 6     division first
2 + 6         then multiplication
8             then addition
```

These examples have all of the elements of numerical or logical expressions. They are to be evaluated, but they don't do anything. A statement informs the computer to do something. When you tell the computer to use an expression and then do something you have created a complete programming statement. When you assign the result of an expression to a variable, myVar = x + 2, then you have told the computer to do something. When you program, you create lines of statements.

Price Bar Interface

A price chart consists of bars built from historical price data. Each individual bar is a graphical representation of the range of prices over a certain period of time. A five-minute bar would have the opening, high, low, and closing prices of an instrument over a five-minute time frame. A daily bar would graph the range of prices over a daily interval. Bar charts are most often graphed in an open, high, low, and close format. Sometimes the opening price is left off. A candlestick chart represents the same data, but in a different format. It provides an easier way to see the relationship between the opening and closing prices of a bar chart. Other bar data such as the date and time of the bar's close, volume, and open interest is also available for each bar. Since AFL works hand-in-hand with the charts that are created by AmiBroker, there are many built-in reserved words to interface with the data. These reserved words were derived from commonly used verbiage in the trading industry. You can interface with the data by using the following reserved words. (*Note:* Each word has an abbreviation and can be used as a substitute.)

Reserved Word	Abbreviation	Description
Open	O	Open price of the bar.
High	H	High price of the bar.
Low	L	Low price of the bar.
Close	C	Close price of the bar.
Volume	V	Number of contracts/shares traded.
OpenInt	OI	Number of outstanding contracts.

AFL uses functions **DateNum()**, **DateTime()**, **Hour()**, **Minute()**, **Second()** to retrieve the date and time of the price bar.

Array programming or vector languages generalize operations on scalars to apply transparently to vectors, matrices (2d-array), and other higher-dimensional arrays. Sounds complicated, right? It really isn't. An array is simply a list of like data. In most testing platform scripting languages price data is held in arrays. When we code and use the word *high* we are usually referring to an array or list of *high* prices of the underlying instrument. When we use a subscript in the array, we are referring to that singular element in the list: High[6] is the *high* price six bars ago. Most of the programming discussed thus far in this book has dealt with scalar programing in a pseudocode framework. The fundamental idea behind array programming is that operations apply at once to an entire set of data. An example will help clarify. How do we calculate a 20-day moving average of price bar's midpoint in a scalar (bar-by-bar) framework?

```
sum = 0
for i = 1 to 20
          sum = sum + (high[i] + low[i]) / 2 #notice the subscript i
next i
avgMP = sum / 20
```


This programming structure is known as a *for* loop. The loop variable is the letter ***i*** and the statement that is indented will be executed 20 times before the next line of code is processed. The ***sum*** variable accumulates the high price over the past 20 bars. This moving average calculation requires five lines of code. Of course this code segment could be put into a function and in most testing languages or scripts it is. However, be it in a function module or inline, the code is executed on every given bar of data. Here's how it is done in an array-programming framework:

```
avgMP = MA((H + L)/2,20)
```

A new array labeled **avgMP** is created and completely loaded with a 20-period moving average of the price bar's midpoint. **avgMP** is not a scalar or single value—it is a full-blown array just like the **High** and **Low** arrays. Array processing eliminates the need for additional looping and this means much quicker execution. You might think a language like EasyLanguage is doing the same thing when it invokes the **average** function:

```
avgMP = average((H + L) / 2,20);
```

However, this is not the case. The code inside the **average** function consists of a loop and is called on each and every bar.

If you have a lot of experience with scalar programming (Java, C++, or EasyLanguage), then picking up AFL might require a little patience, but it will definitely be worth it. As you know, learning a new programming script/language is best performed by working through examples. If you own AmiBroker, make sure you go to this link and download Howard Bandy's book: http://introductiontoamibroker.com/book.html. This book will get you up and going very quickly. Bandy helps explain the sophisticated database management that you get with AmiBroker. Data is to a trading algorithm like gas is to an automobile.

AFL Array Programming

Here is a simple moving average crossover system in AFL:

```
PositionSize = MarginDeposit = 1;
avgLen = Optimize("Len",20,10,100,1);
avgLen = Param("Length",81,10,100,1);

Buy = C > MA(C,avgLen);
Short = C < MA(C,avgLen);

Sell = Short;
Cover = Buy;
```


For right now, ignore lines 2 and 3—the ones starting with the word **avgLen.** If you are testing futures data, then don't forget the first line must be in every trading algorithm. This tells AmiBroker's backtester to only trade one contract and sets the margin deposit to one as well. The variable avgLen is the length of the moving average indicator the algorithm will utilize. Let's set it to 100.

```
Buy = C > MA(C,avgLen);
```

This line of code tells AmiBroker to set the BUY array to true or 1 if the close is greater than the 100-day moving average of closes. If the test fails and the close is not greater than the moving average, then it is set to false or 0. Since we are array processing, this done all at one time. The BUY array is filled completely up with either 1s or 0s. The SHORT array does just the opposite—true if the close is less than the 100-day moving average and false if it's not. This system simply flips back and forth between long and short positions—it's always in the market. If you use **Buy** and **Short** arrays to initiate positions, then you must have values for the **Sell** and **Cover** arrays. If you only use **Buy,** then you only need a value for **Sell**. This applies to **Short** and **Cover** as well. If you are using a pure stop and reverse algorithm, you can set up your **Sell** and **Cover** arrays like this:

```
Sell = Short;

Cover = Buy;
```

These two lines tell the computer to cover long positions at the same price a short position is established and to cover short positions at the same price a long position is put on. Or you can do it like this:

```
Sell = 0;

Cover = 0;
```

If you don't take into consideration the arrays that get you out of a position, AmiBroker will give you a warning message, and will not execute the backtest. AmiBroker requires the **BUY** order and its corresponding **SELL** order to be defined prior to processing. The same goes for **SHORT** and **COVER**. In some platforms, you do not need to define **SELL** and **COVER** if the algorithm is always in the market long or short.

This little bit of code seems quite simple on the surface, but there is a lot going on behind the scenes. AFL has a plethora of built-in functions such as the **MA** function used in this simple program. So calculating the 100-day moving average is very simple; just call the function. The four arrays (**BUY, SHORT, SELL, COVER**) that instruct AmiBroker to establish and liquidate trades are instantly populated with 1s and 0s; it's a one-pass process. This process is extremely fast and efficient. Once this single pass is completed, the back tester is fed the necessary information to simulate the backtesting of the algorithm. As you can see, entry and exit prices are not defined, so they are defaulted to the close of the bar. This default can be changed using the settings dialog box.

Let's give this simple algorithm a run. The next instructions assume you have worked with AmiBroker and know how to plot charts, apply indicators, and work with price databases.

Go ahead and launch AmiBroker and load your database of choice. I imported an ASCII database of futures prices that I got from CSI data. The software is compatible with CSI and there are instructions in the online manual on how to create a database, and have it updated automatically. This may require an additional monthly data fee. Figure 4.1 shows how to get to the AFL editor from the main AmiBroker File menu.

Once the editor launches you will see a window like the one in Figure 4.2.

This is your tabula rasa—blank slate. Anything you can dream up can be accomplished by typing in the right code. Go ahead and type in the code from the

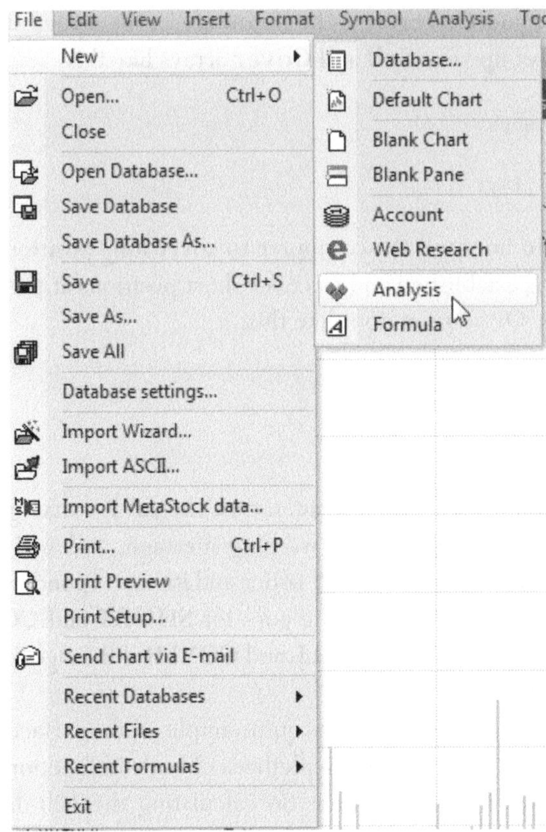

FIGURE 4.1 Launching AmiBroker's AFL editor.

moving average example. The AFL Editor is one of the most powerful editors you will find in any trading or programming platform. It features outlining, collapsible, or text folding, function tips, and auto-completion. There's just a little bit of typing, so go ahead and just do it and I will highlight some of these key features along the way. Here it is again, so you won't have to flip back to the prior page.

```
PositionSize = MarginDeposit = 1;
avgLen = Optimize("Len",20,10,100,1);
avgLen = Param("Length",81,10,100,1);

Buy = C > MA(C,avgLen);
Short = C < MA(C,avgLen);

Sell = Short;
Cover = Buy;
```

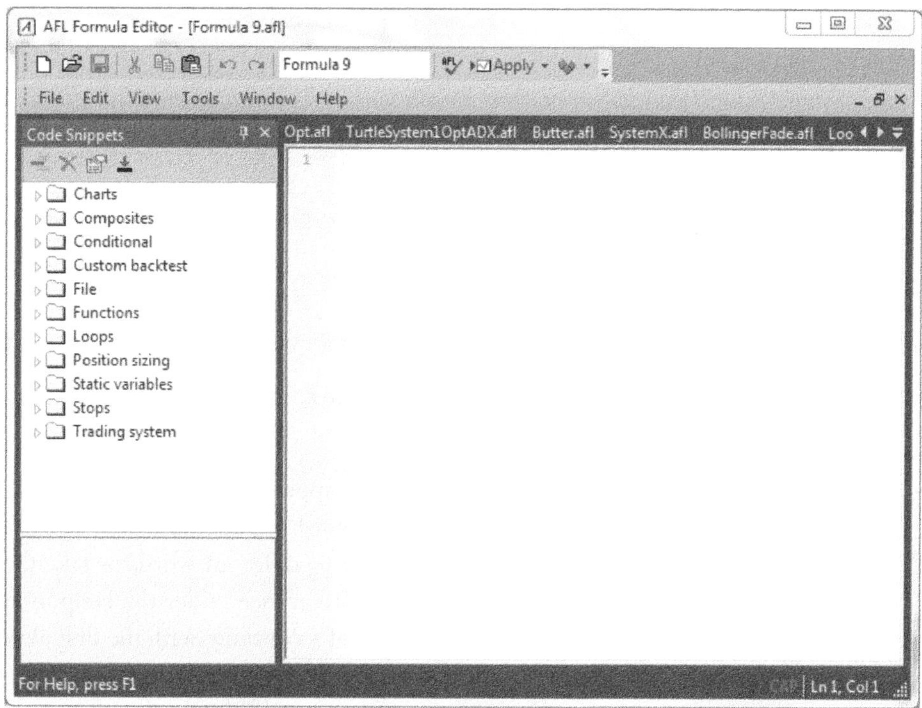

FIGURE 4.2 The AmiBroker Editor window.

As you type the first line of code you will notice the words **PositionSize** and **MarginDeposit** turn bold. If you didn't capitalize the P or the S in the word **PositionSize**, the editor will automatically do so after you type the last letter in the word and hit the space bar. The editor is letting you know these are keywords or tokens. And that you can't use these for variable names. If you are looking for a keyword or a function name, and you type what you think it is and it doesn't turn bold or change colors, then you know you have not used the correct word. The editor can help you find the proper keyword or function name through its auto-completion feature. Later we will develop an algorithm based on Bollinger Bands, but for illustration purposes let's assume you want to calculate an upper Bollinger Band now, but don't know the exact words for the function. You probably think the function name starts with the letter "b," so for now type the letter "b" after the first line and press the <Ctrl> and <spacebar>. A list of keywords and functions starting with the letter "b" will appear in your editor window (see Figure 4.3).

If you look down the list, you will see the name **BBandTop.** If you select and double-click on the name, the function call will be automatically inserted into your code. The more of the function name you type, the smaller the list of options will appear after pressing <Ctrl> and <spacebar>. If you type **BBand** and hit the

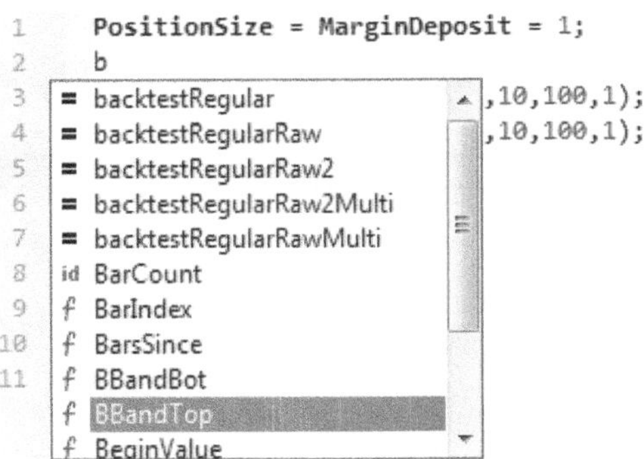

FIGURE 4.3 The AFL Editor's auto-completion tool.

keyboard sequence, only two options will appear: **BBandBot** and **BBandTop**. If you still can't find the name of the keyword or function, then you will have to use the trial-and-error method and keep typing different words or take the time and look up the keyword in the AFL Language Reference under the Help menu. Delete whatever you typed as the second line and let's continue with the first algorithm. As you type the second line of code and type the keyword **Optimize** it will turn blue and right after you type the left parentheses a small box will open up right under your cursor (Figure 4.4).

The box is helping you by providing a template of what the function **Optimize** is expecting (this is called the informal parameter list). If a word turns blue, the editor is letting you know the keyword is a built-in function. This line of code links the source code with the AmiBroker optimizer. This is how I was able to do all those cool optimizations in Chapter 3. The function Optimize wants you to provide a name inside quotes, a **default value** for the variable avgLen, a **min value**, a **max value**, and a **step value**. When you optimize the variable avgLen it will start out at the **min value** and increase each iteration by the **step value** until it reaches the **max value**. If you don't run the optimizer, the variable will assume the **default value**. The AFL editor has all these helpers or tips for all of the built-in functions. You will notice another helper window pop up as you type the keyword **Param**. The **Param** function acts similarly to the **Optimize** function. Instead of providing an interface to the optimizer, the **Param** function provides an interface

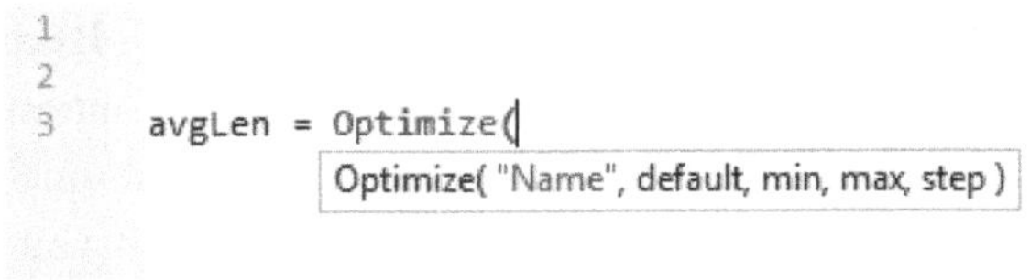

```
avgLen = Optimize(
         Optimize( "Name", default, min, max, step )
```

FIGURE 4.4 AFL Editor function helper.

to the user. Instead of having to retype different values for avgLen every time you want to test a different value, you can simply change it at the **Analysis** phase. I will show how easy this is a little later. Go ahead and finish typing in the rest of the code and go under the File menu and save it to your Desktop or a folder on the C drive as MyFirstAlgo. Now you need to check the syntax to make sure you have typed everything properly. Click on the AFL Check icon (see Figure 4.5).

If you type everything in correctly, then nothing will happen. If you mistyped a word, you might get something like Figure 4.6. If this happens, just make sure you have everything typed properly and then hit the icon again. After the syntax has been properly checked (compiled), click on the **Send To Analysis** window icon (see Figure 4.7).

This will create an Analysis tab in the AmiBroker program. I have continuous crude oil data plotted in the first chart. If you don't have crude oil data, don't worry, just create a chart of something. I inform AmiBroker to apply MyFirstAlgo to the current data by using the dropdown menu in the top-left corner (Figure 4.8). Before we click on the BackTest icon, go ahead and click on the Parameters icon. It's the icon that looks like an old equalizer (Figure 4.9).

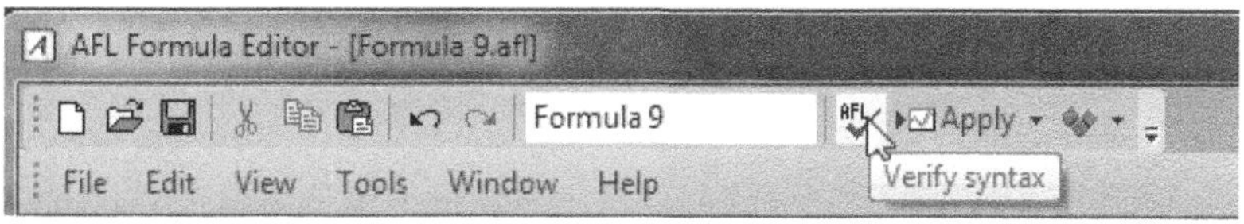

FIGURE 4.5 The AFL Check icon.

Opt.afl TurtleSystem1OptADX.afl Butter.afl SystemX.afl BollingerFade.afl Loo

3 **error(s)** and 0 **warning(s)** found in the formula. Go to error

```
PositionSize = MarginDeposit = 1;
avgLen = Optimize("Len",20,10,100,1);
avgLen = Param("Len",81,10,100,1);

Buy = C > MA(C,avgLen)
Short = C < MA(C,avgLen);
```
Error 30. Syntax error, unexpected IDENTIFIER
```
Sell = Short;
```
Error 29. Variable '**short**' used without having been initialized.
```
Cover = Buy;
```
Error 29. Variable '**buy**' used without having been initialized.

FIGURE 4.6 An error warning.

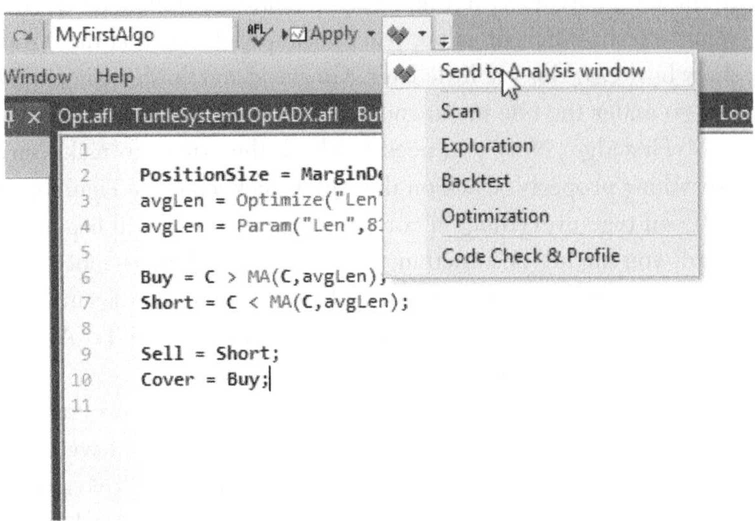

FIGURE 4.7 The "Send to Analysis" window icon.

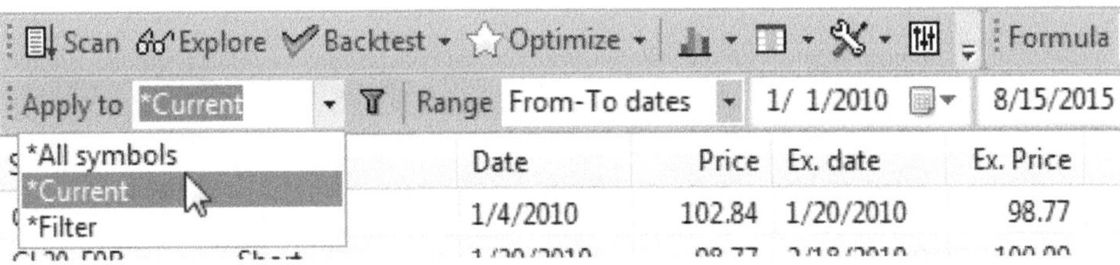

FIGURE 4.8 Apply the algorithm to the current data.

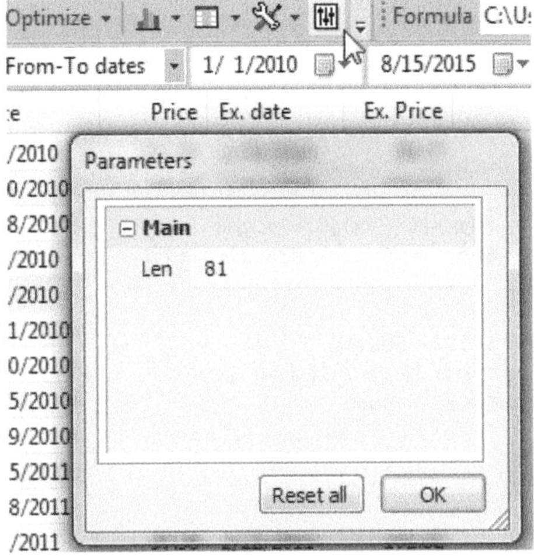

FIGURE 4.9 Set the parameters for the backtest.

This is where you can change the values of the avgLen parameter. Change it to 50 and click OK. I get the sense that AmiBroker was originally designed to trade equities only, so you have to set up the backtester to work with futures data by going into the **Settings** button in an Analysis sheet. Only do this if you are truly testing futures data. If you aren't, then just skip this paragraph. The Settings button has a small picture of wrench and screwdriver and is located directly to the left of the **Parameters** button. A dialog box like the one in Figure 4.10 should open. Click on the box beside the **Futures mode** option. It instructs AmiBroker's back-tester to use the margin deposit and point value that was set up when the database was created for its calculations.

Now click the **Backtest** button (five buttons to the left of the **Parameter** icon). This will apply the algorithm to the data and create a trade-by-trade report in the analysis window. If you have a database loaded as I do and you select the **Portfolio Backtest**, then the algorithm will be applied to all of the markets in the database. Don't be surprised if this only takes a few seconds. AmiBroker is really applying the algorithm to every single bar of data in the portfolio. Figure 4.11 and Figure 4.12

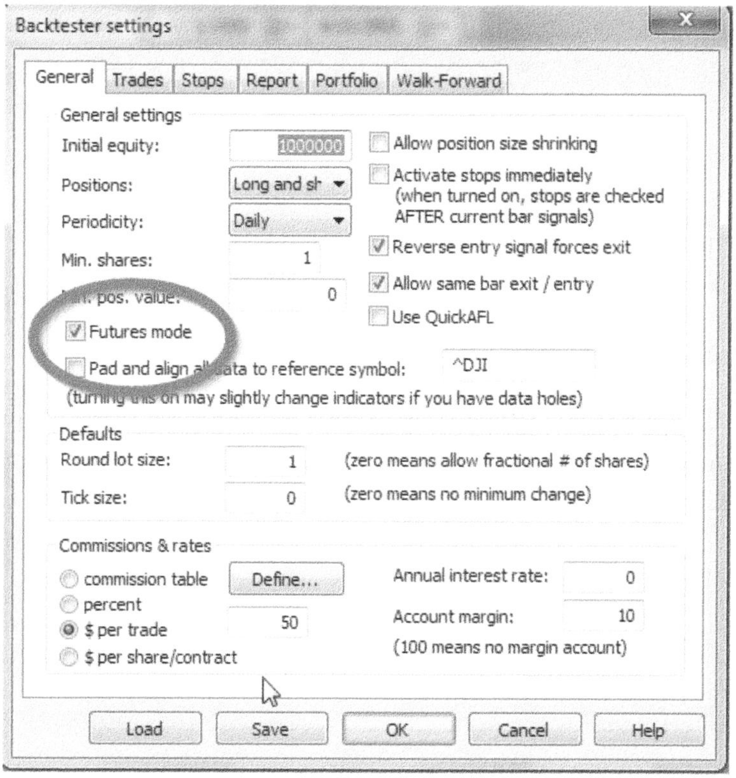

FIGURE 4.10 Set Futures mode.

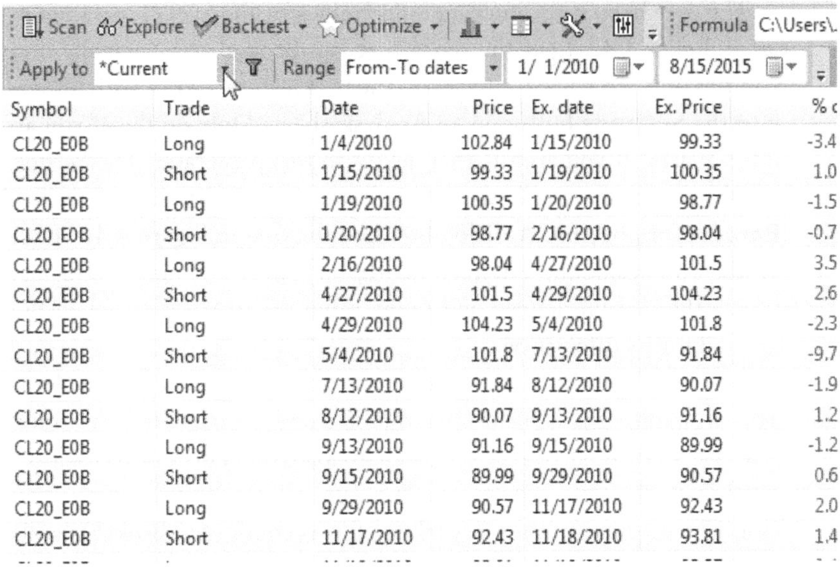

Scan | Explore | Backtest | Optimize | Formula C:\Users\.
Apply to *Current | Range From-To dates | 1/ 1/2010 | 8/15/2015

Symbol	Trade	Date	Price	Ex. date	Ex. Price	% c
CL20_E0B	Long	1/4/2010	102.84	1/15/2010	99.33	-3.4
CL20_E0B	Short	1/15/2010	99.33	1/19/2010	100.35	1.0
CL20_E0B	Long	1/19/2010	100.35	1/20/2010	98.77	-1.5
CL20_E0B	Short	1/20/2010	98.77	2/16/2010	98.04	-0.7
CL20_E0B	Long	2/16/2010	98.04	4/27/2010	101.5	3.5
CL20_E0B	Short	4/27/2010	101.5	4/29/2010	104.23	2.6
CL20_E0B	Long	4/29/2010	104.23	5/4/2010	101.8	-2.3
CL20_E0B	Short	5/4/2010	101.8	7/13/2010	91.84	-9.7
CL20_E0B	Long	7/13/2010	91.84	8/12/2010	90.07	-1.9
CL20_E0B	Short	8/12/2010	90.07	9/13/2010	91.16	1.2
CL20_E0B	Long	9/13/2010	91.16	9/15/2010	89.99	-1.2
CL20_E0B	Short	9/15/2010	89.99	9/29/2010	90.57	0.6
CL20_E0B	Long	9/29/2010	90.57	11/17/2010	92.43	2.0
CL20_E0B	Short	11/17/2010	92.43	11/18/2010	93.81	1.4

FIGURE 4.11 The trade-by trade report.

Scan | Explore | Backtest | Optimize | Formula C:\Users
Apply to *All symbols | Range From-To dates | 1/ 1/2010 | 8/15/2015

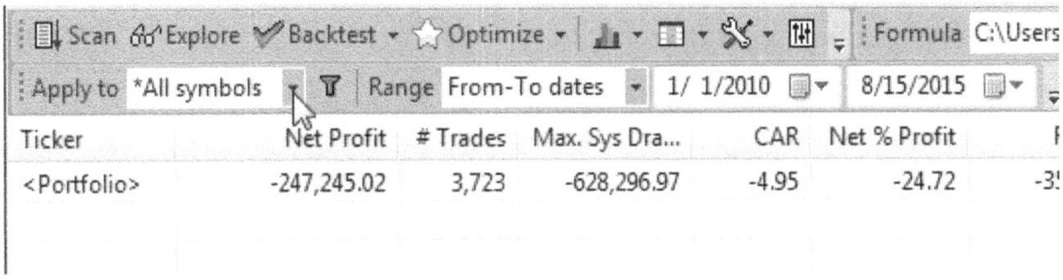

Ticker	Net Profit	# Trades	Max. Sys Dra...	CAR	Net % Profit	
<Portfolio>	-247,245.02	3,723	-628,296.97	-4.95	-24.72	-3!

FIGURE 4.12 The portfolio results.

provide a snapshot of the trade-by-trade report on the crude oil and the portfolio results on the entire database.

The results don't look that great, so let's test a double moving average crossover system. Work your way back over to the AFL Editor—it should still be open. Go under the File menu and create a new formula by clicking on New. Once a blank Editor window opens, type in the following exactly:

```
Filter = 1;
PositionSize = MarginDeposit = 1;
avgLen1 = Optimize("Len1",9,9,49,1);

avgLen2 = Optimize("Len2",19,19,99,1);
```

```
shortMav = MA(C,avgLen1);
longMav = MA(C,avgLen2);

Buy = Cross(shortMav,longMav);
Short = Cross(longMav,shortMav);

Sell = Short;
Cover = Buy;
```

To save some typing, I copied the code from MyFirstAlgo and made the necessary changes. This is the code for a double moving average system where you buy when the short (fast) moving average crosses above long (slow) moving average and you short when the fast moving average crosses below the slow moving average. The beauty of AmiBroker's AFL is it reads almost like English. After you check the AFL and send it to an **Analysis** window, go back to AmiBroker. Instead of clicking on the **Backtest** button**,** click the **Optimize** button. AmiBroker will now optimize the fast length from 9 to 49 and the slow length from 19 to 99 and report the results from each iteration. This might take a few seconds. When the optimization has completed, click on the down arrow beside the **Optimize** button and select **3D Optimization chart**. A chart like the one in Figure 4.13 will appear on your screen.

This is the result of the optimization where the *x*-axis and *y*-axis are the varying lengths of the moving averages and the *z*-axis is the net profit. You can also see the water level; this represents where the profit is equal to zero. Hopefully, most of your mountains are above this level. This 3D chart only works on a two-parameter optimization.

You may want to play around with some of the other icons and familiarize yourself with their functions. AmiBroker is very sophisticated, and it took me several hours to become somewhat comfortable with the charting, reports, and applying trading and indicator algorithms. Again, I refer you to the excellent online manual, the AmiBroker forums, and of course, Bandy's book.

Syntax

The AmiBroker Function Language is very powerful, and, once you grasp the array-processing paradigm, quite easy to use. In some programming languages you have to declare variables and sometimes their types before you can use them. This is not so for the AFL. However, when you create a variable know that it is an array or list and not just a single memory location. Because of this, you can't do this:

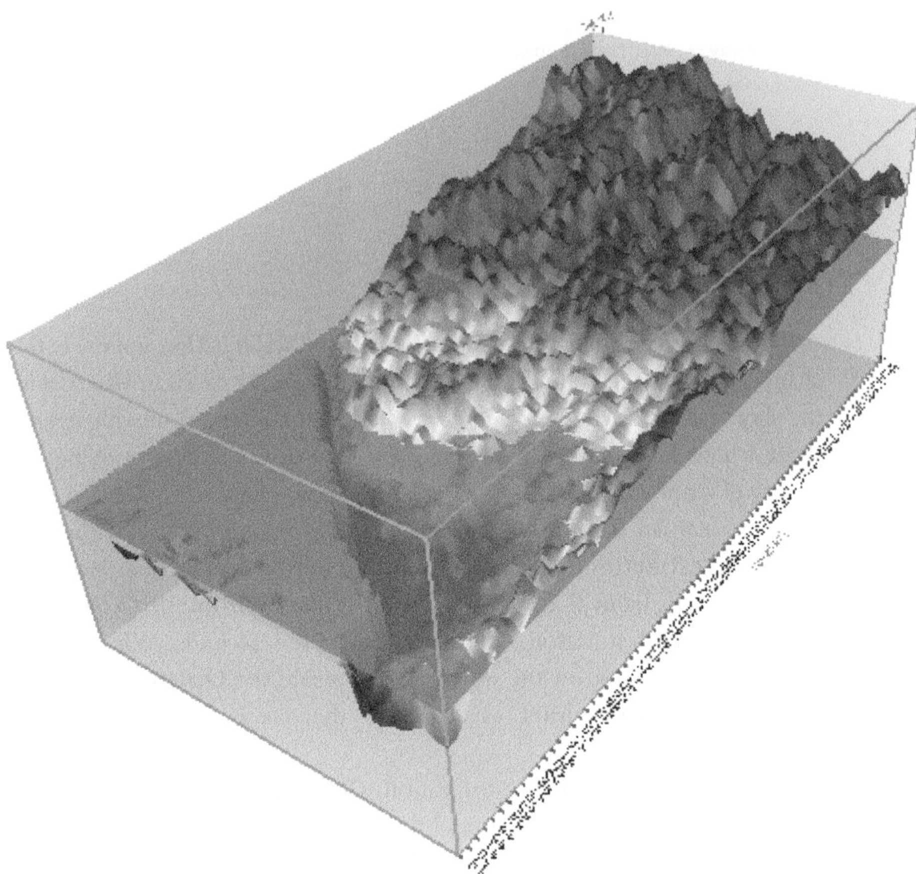

FIGURE 4.13 A 3D optimization chart.

Source: AmiBroker


```
myValue = (H + L)/2;

if (C > myValue){
        Buy = 1;
}
```

If you type this and check the syntax, you will receive the following message:

```
Condition in IF, WHILE, FOR statements has to be Numeric or
  Boolean type.
```

Basically, you are asking AmiBroker to compare the **close** array with **myValue** array. You were probably thinking you were comparing the current close price to the current value in **myValue**, but you weren't. Forget about using **if's** in your code. This is a very difficult thing to do if you are used to working in a bar-by-bar paradigm. Instead, use something like this:

```
myValue = (H + L)/2;
Buy = C > myValue;
```

Tomasz Janeczko has provided this type of array processing functionality in his software. This accomplishes the same thing as the previous **if** statement. How do you think you compare today's close with the prior day's close? You can't use an **if** statement, so could you do it like this?

```
cond1 = C > C[1];
cond2 = C < C[1];

Buy= cond1;
Short = cond2;
```

If you type this in and check the syntax, it will pass. You will also be able to send it to an **Analysis** window, and backtest it. However, it will not work. The computer doesn't come out and say, "I'm sorry, Dave, I'm afraid I can't do that." It just won't generate the correct trades. These statements are syntactically correct, but they are logically incorrect. You are comparing the first element of the close array with the close array. In other words, you are comparing an element in the list with the list. This is how you do it in AFL:

```
cond1 = C > Ref(C,-1);
cond2 = C < Ref(C,-1);

Buy= cond1;
Short = cond2;
```

The **Ref(C,-1)** function returns the prior close price in the close array. The function processes the array and allows you to compare today's closing price with yesterday's closing price. You can use any negative number to reference previous values of any array. You can do this as well:

```
myValue = (H + L)/2;
cond1 = myValue > Ref(myValue,-1);
```

And you have probably noticed that all lines end with a semicolon (;). This tells the parser that the line of code has terminated and to go onto the next line. What do you think the next bit of code does?

```
sl = Param("ShortLen",9,9,100);
il = Param("InterLen",19,19,200);
mmStop = Param("StopDollars",3000,3000,6000);

Buy = MA(C,sl) > MA(C,il) ;
Short = MA(C,sl)< MA(C,il);

Sell = short;
Cover = buy;

ApplyStop(stopTypeLoss,stopModePoint,mmStop/PointValue,0);
```

The variables **sl** and **il** are defaulted to 9 and 19, respectively. The **Param** function allows the user to change the variables to values between 9 and 100 and 19 and 200, respectively. The variable **mmStop** defaults to 3000 but can be changed to values ranging from 3000 to 6000. The array **Buy** is filled with 1s when the moving average of **sl** (shortLength) is greater than the moving average of **il** (intermediate-Length). The **Short** array is filled when the opposite happens. This is a very simple double moving average crossover system. The **ApplyStop** function tells AmiBroker to stop out on the close any time the current position reaches a loss of $3,000. The close is checked in this particular case. The **ApplyStop** function has many different ways of exiting a position: stop loss, trailing stop, or a profit objective. Here are three examples:


```
ApplyStop(stopTypeLoss, stopModePercent,2, True );
/* single-line implementation of Chandelier exit */
ApplyStop(stopTypeTrailing, stopModePoint, 3*ATR(14), True, True );
/* N-bar stop */  ApplyStop( stopTypeNBar, stopModeBars, 5 );
```

This is a very powerful function and can fulfill almost every possible criterion to exit an existing position with a stop.

Referring back to **MySecondAlgo**, you might have noticed these two lines of code:

```
Buy = Cross(shortMav,longMav);

Short = Cross(longMav,shortMav);
```

The keyword **Cross** is actually a function call. The function gives a "1" or true on the day that the **shortMav** crosses above the **longMav**. Otherwise, the result is false or zero. To find out when shortMav crosses below longMav, simply reverse the order of the arrays. I admit this took me a few minutes to understand, but like the rest the AFL functions, it makes perfect sense. The opposite of the short-term moving average crossing above the long-term average is the long-term average crossing above the short-term average.

Coding like this might not be your cup of tea—having to remember the function calls and how the **Cross** function works and all the business about arrays. If you want to test with AmiBroker, but don't want to work with the full-blown AFL editor, you can still do this. The next part of this chapter introduces the AmiBroker AFL wizard.

AFL Wizard

Imagine creating trading algorithms with point-and-click ease and minimal typing. Enter the AmiBroker AFL Wizard. Instead of typing MySecondAlgo into the AFL Editor, let's create it in the AFL Wizard. Get back to AmiBroker and click on the **AFL Wizard** button (Figure 4.14). Once you click on the button a window like the one in Figure 4.15 will pop up.

FIGURE 4.14 The AFL Code Wizard button.

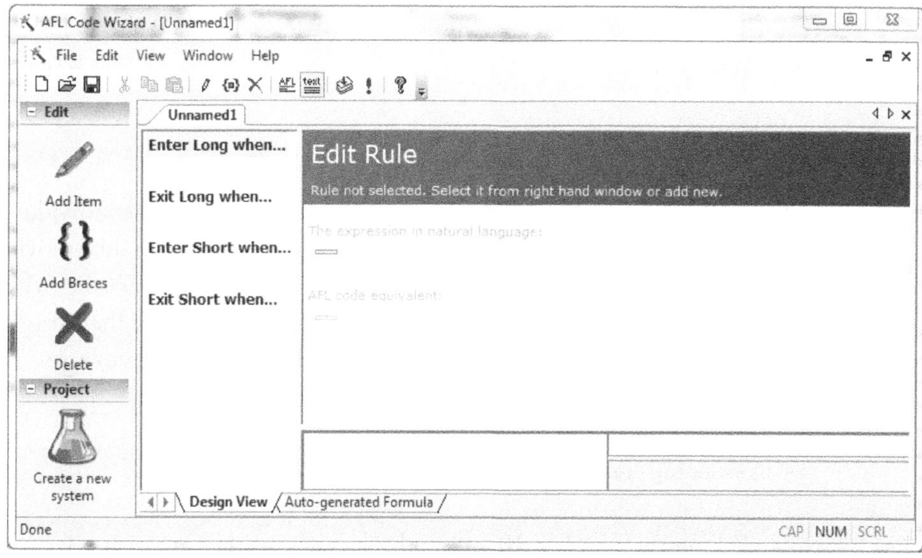

FIGURE 4.15 A new AFL Code Wizard window.

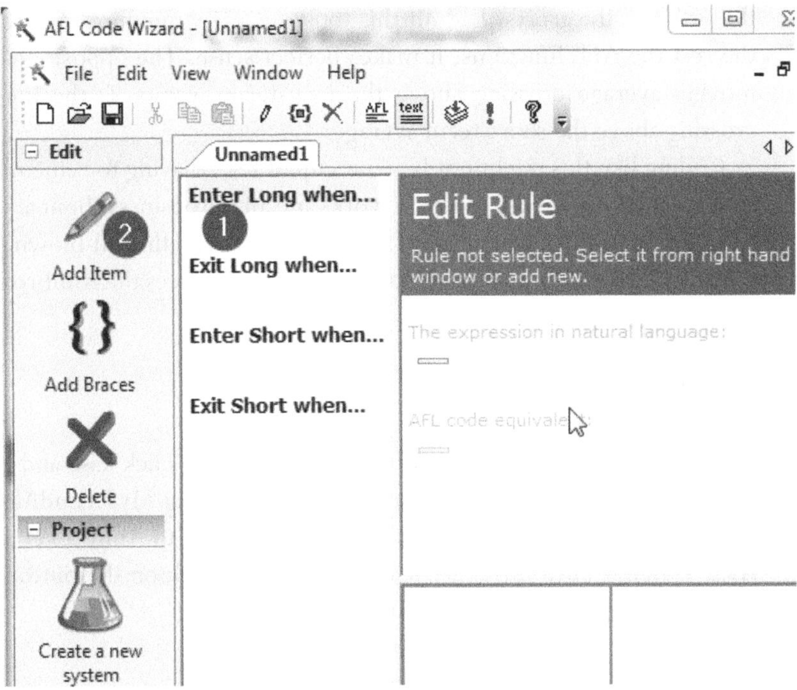

FIGURE 4.16 Add item in AFL Code Wizard.

This is the **AFL Code Wizard**, and it's a really cool way to create a trading algorithm without having to create it from scratch. The interface is really quite simple, so let's start by first adding a long entry rule. Click on the words **Enter Long when . . .** and then click on the pencil icon labeled **Add Item** (Figure 4.16). This will put the following code in the **Edit Rule** section and also below **the Enter Long When . . . .**

```
Value of Close (now) is greater than 10
```

Now this is where things get really cool. You can click on the individual words in the code and change them. Remember **MySecondAlgo** was a dual moving average crossover. Click on the words **Value of**. A list of different functions will appear in the pane below the **Edit Rule** pane. Figure 4.17 shows where the list is located.

Click in the pane and select **MA - Simple Moving Average**. The words **15-bar moving average of** will take place of **Value of.**

```
15-bar moving average of Close (now) is greater than 10
```

Now click on the number **10** and go back down to the same pane we selected the first MA and select MA again. The code will change to:

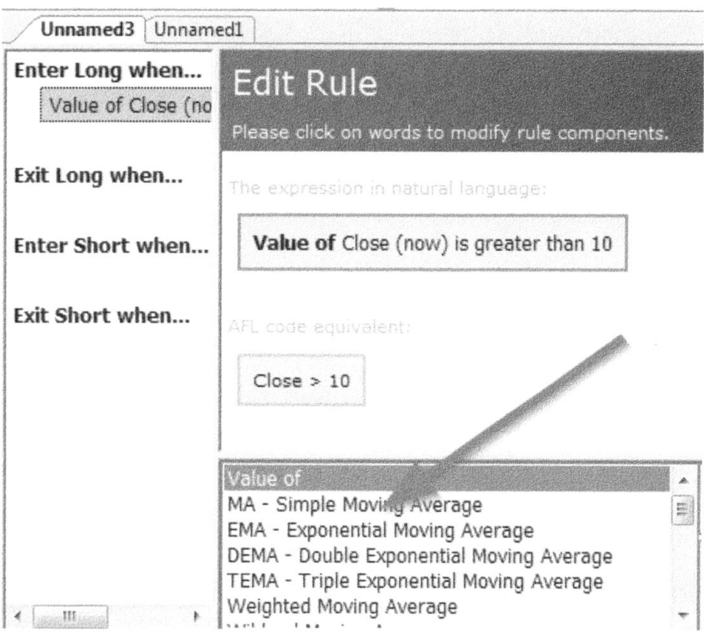

FIGURE 4.17 The AFL Code Wizard "Edit Rule" dropdown list.


```
15-bar moving average of Close (now) is greater than 15-bar
  moving average of Close now
```

Well, this won't do. The 15-bar moving average of Close will never be greater than the 15-bar moving average of Close. Click on the number 15 in the second moving average phrase and slide down to the pane right beside the pane with the list of functions (see Figure 4.18). Change the period from 15 to 30. The code in the Edit Rule should now read:

```
15 -bar moving average of Close (now) is greater than 30 -bar
  moving average of Close now
```

So the rules for entering a long position are now defined. Buy when the 15-bar moving average (fast) is greater than 30-bar moving average (slow). As you point and click the AFL code equivalent is created simultaneously. The AFL code equivalent thus far is:

```
MA( Close , 15 ) > MA( Close , 30 )
```

If you want to see what is going to be ported in the **AFL Editor**, click on the tab labeled **Auto-generated Formula.** The tab is to the right of the **Design**

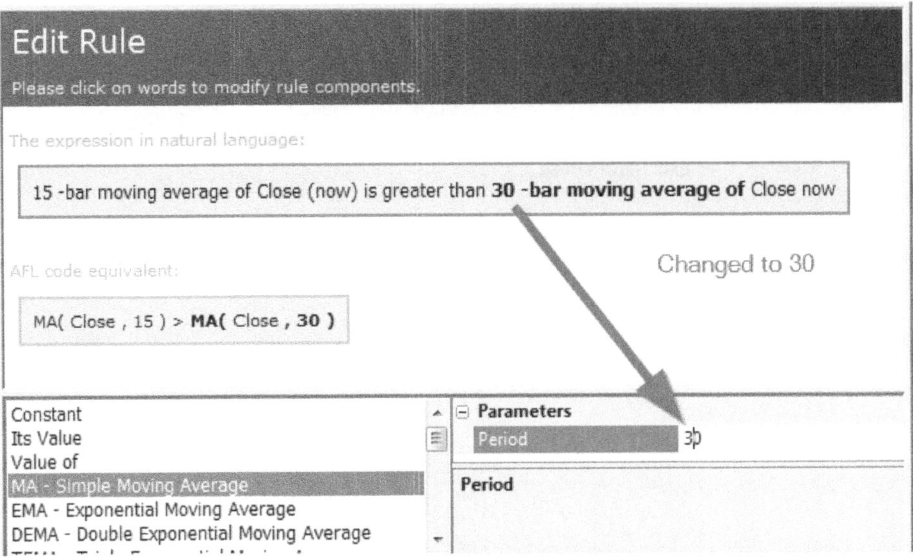

FIGURE 4.18 Changing the parameters in the "Edit Rule" pane.

View that we are currently located within. When you click on it you will see the following code.

```
Buy =  MA( Close , 15 ) > MA( Close , 30 );

Sell = 0;

Short = 0;

Cover = 0;
```

This should look familiar. The **AFL Wizard** has auto-generated the rules for the four trading arrays: **Buy**, **Sell**, **Short,** and **Cover**. The Buy array is turned on when the **MA(Close , 15)** is greater than **MA(Close , 30)**. Click back on the **Design View** tab and let's point-and-click our way to a short entry rule. Click on **Enter Short when …** and then the **Add Item (Pencil)** icon. You will once again see the following code:

```
Value of Close (now) is greater than 10
```

Following the same steps we did for the long entry rules:

- Click **Value of** and slide down to the function pane and select **MA**.

- This time click on **is greater than** and slide down to the function pane. You will notice that the list of functions has now changed to just three options:
    1. **Is greater than**
    2. **Is less than**
    3. **Is equal to**
- Select **is less than**.
- Click on the number **10** and slide down again to the function pane and select **MA—Simple Moving Average.**
- Click on **15-bar moving average of** and change the period to **30**.

If you click on the **Auto-generated Formula** tab, you should now see the following code:

```
Buy = MA( Close , 15 ) > MA( Close , 30 );
Sell = 0;
Short = MA( Close , 15 ) < MA( Close , 30 );
Cover = 0;
```

Now if you are testing a stock, you can send this directly to AmiBroker and have it **Backtest** or **Scan**. Before we test it, go ahead and save it somewhere as **MySecondAlgoWizard**. Assuming a stock database is loaded in AmiBroker, click on the **Exclamation** mark to send it to AmiBroker (see Figure 4.19).

If you switch back to AmiBroker, you will be presented the **Automatic Analysis** dialog with your newly designed formula loaded. This dialog looks like the one in Figure 4.20.

From here, you can click on **Back Test, Scan, Optimize, Explore,** etc. If you are testing a futures market, it is better to click on the icon that is right

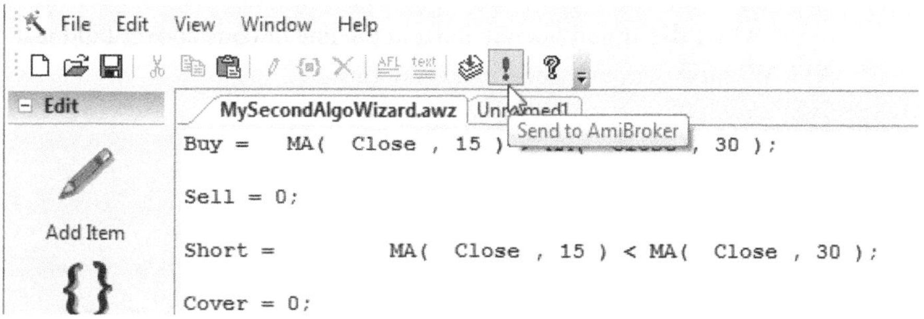

FIGURE 4.19 Click the exclamation point to send your request to AmiBroker.

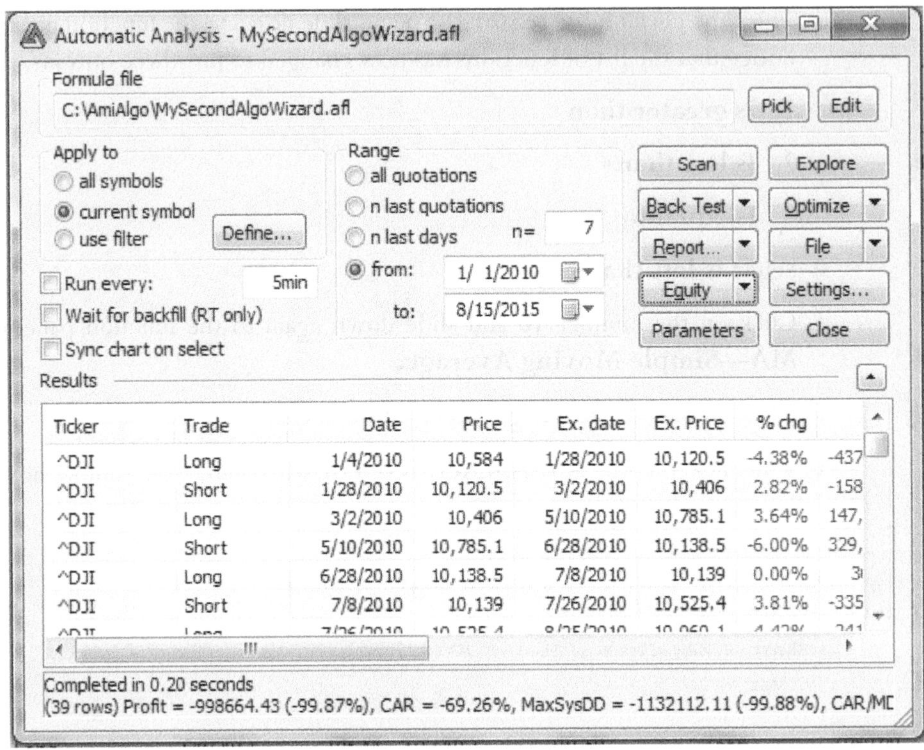

FIGURE 4.20 Automatic Analysis dialog box.

beside the **Exclamation** mark. This will build the formula and export it with a ".afl"extension. You can then open it with **AFL Editor** and add the necessary code for testing a futures contract:

```
PositionSize = MarginDeposit = 1;
```

For practice, go ahead and click on the **Build and Export a formula** icon and save it somewhere on your desktop or in a folder in your C: drive. You then can go to the **AFL Editor** and open it and add the line of code above. I did just that and my **AFL Wizard** designed code looks like this:

```
PositionSize = MarginDeposit = 1;

Buy =      MA( Close , 15 ) > MA( Close , 30 );
Sell = 0;
Short =    MA( Close , 15 ) < MA( Close , 30 );
Cover = 0;
```

This should look very similar to the code we originally typed in for **MySecondAlgo**. The AFL Wizard can get you up and running very quickly and can also be used as a learning tool. It automatically builds the AFL code so you can start your design with the **Wizard** and have it generate the framework and then move onto the **AFL Editor** and complete your coding of your algorithm there.

AmiBroker Loop Programming

As powerful as AmiBroker's array programming is, there are times when you want to program on a bar-by-bar basis. Dr. Janeczko has built this capability into his software as well. With this feature you can program with your precious **If** constructs. Here is a familiar algorithm utilizing loops:

```
PositionSize = MarginDeposit = 1;

mav = MA(C,20);

for( i = 0; i < BarCount; i++ ){
        if (C[i] >= mav[i]) {
                Buy[i] = 1;
        }
        if (C[i] <= mav[i]) {
                Sell[i] = 1;
        }
}
```


This is the simple price crossing moving average reversal algorithm. The **mav** array is set to a 20-day simple moving average of closes. This line of code is still utilizing array programming. A **for loop** is then set up so that individual elements of the different arrays can be examined. The **for loop** construct in AFL is very similar to one in the C language. The loop variables are controlled by what is inside the parentheses.

(i = 0; i < BarCount; i++)

Here the loop will start at zero and stop at **BarCount** and the loop variable **i** will increment by one each time **i++.** The **i++** is the same as **i = i + 1**; since we are not processing arrays, we can now use **if** constructs. Notice how the comparison of the **C[i]** element and the **mav[i]** element is enclosed in parentheses. If the close is greater than the 20-bar moving average, then the following code is executed: Buy[i] = 1; This sets the **ith** element in the **Buy** array to one. Also, notice how the curly brackets { } are used in the code. The curly brackets inform the computer and the

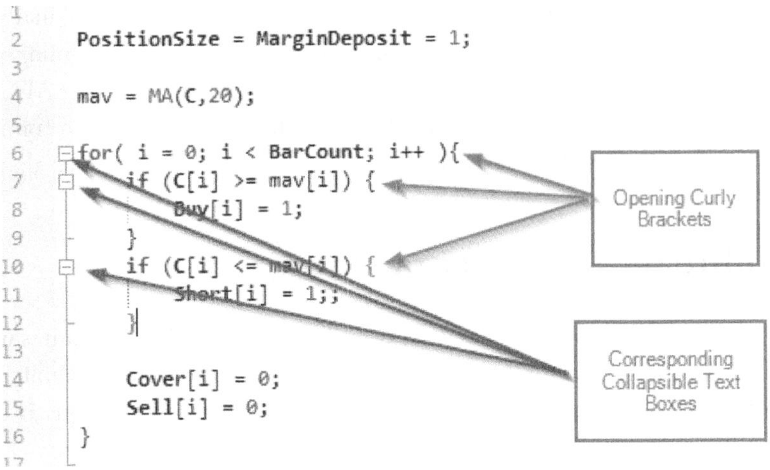

```

PositionSize = MarginDeposit = 1;

mav = MA(C,20);

for( i = 0; i < BarCount; i++ ){
    if (C[i] >= mav[i]) {
        Buy[i] = 1;
    }
    if (C[i] <= mav[i]) {
        Short[i] = 1;;
    }

    Cover[i] = 0;
    Sell[i] = 0;
}
```

Opening Curly Brackets

Corresponding Collapsible Text Boxes

FIGURE 4.21 Sample loop programming code.

programmer that certain lines are controlled by a loop or if construct. All the code involved with the **for loop** is surrounded by curly brackets. The code controlled by the **if** statement is surrounded by nested curly brackets. By matching an opening left curly bracket with a closing curly right bracket, the programmer can easily see what code goes with the **for loop** or the **if** statement. The left curly bracket right after the loop definition opens up the block of code consisting of six lines. The last-right curly bracket closes the loop and the block of code.

In addition to having to use the curly brackets to tell the computer which lines of code go inside the **loop** or the **if** construct, it's good practice to also indent the lines of code enclosed within brackets. This is not a necessity, but it makes the readability of the code so much easier. Now that we are using loops and ifs, we can highlight the collapsible or folding text feature of the editor. Look at the code in Figure 4.21.

Notice where the arrows for the opening curly brackets are pointing. Now look at the small boxes with a dash inside that correspond to the curly brackets. If you click on the first box, the code controlled by the corresponding line of code will collapse or hide. Go ahead and do it—see for yourself. If you click on the very first box, all the code disappears except the **for loop** definition. The second box collapses the code that goes with the first **if**. This is a neat feature if you want to streamline the look of your code, or if you want to hide it and send a screenshot to someone else. The combination of array and loop programming capabilities in AmiBroker should facilitate any programming needs you come across.

Summary

All programming languages are built on expressions and operators and the precedence of those operators. A solid understanding of these concepts is absolutely necessary before a single line of code is typed. We have just skimmed the surface of the capabilities of AmiBroker. It is a very powerful and easy-to-use tool. I learned AFL while writing this book, and used it for most of the testing in Chapters 2 and 3. Once you get your futures data into a database and create different portfolios, testing across the entire portfolio is as simple as clicking on a single button. The optimization capabilities of AmiBroker are simply mindblowing. You can use a genetic optimizer to optimize not only a single market but an entire portfolio—just like I did in Chapter 3. The best way to learn AFL is through examples. Also the online community is absolutely terrific! I found answers to all my questions online and I didn't have to search very far.

Here are some of the codes for the various systems I tested in Chapters 2 and 3:

Code Samples

```
// Chapter 2 Double Moving Average Cross Over
// with Dollar Stop

Filter = 1;
PositionSize = MarginDeposit = 1;


sl = Param("ShortLen",9,9,100);
il = Param("InterLen",19,19,200);
mmStop = Param("StopDollars",3000,3000,6000);
OptimizerSetEngine("cmae");

Buy = MA(C,sl) > MA(C,il) ;
Short = MA(C,sl)< MA(C,il);

Sell = short;
Cover = buy;

ApplyStop(stopTypeLoss,stopModePoint,mmStop/PointValue,1);



// Chapter 2 Bollinger Band Algorithm

PositionSize = MarginDeposit = 1;
len = Optimize("Len",60,10,80,2);

width = Optimize("Width",2,0.25,3,.25);
```

```
Buy = Cross(C,BBandTop(C,len,width));
Short = Cross(BBandBot(C,len,width),C);

Sell = Cross(MA(C,len),C);
Cover = Cross(C,MA(C,len));



//Chapter 2 Bollinger Band using
//RISK filtering


PositionSize = MarginDeposit = 1;

riskAmt = (BBandTop(C,60,2) - MA(C,60)) * pointValue;

COND1 = riskAmt <= 2000;

Buy = Cross(C,BBandTop(C,60,2)) AND COND1;
Short = Cross(BBandBot(C,60,2),C) AND COND1;

Sell = Cross(MA(C,60),C);
Cover = Cross(C,MA(C,60));



//Chapter 2 MACD utilizing AMIBROKERS
//Exploration Feature
//Refer to the AMIBROKER Appendix for
//further explanation

Filter = 1;

PositionSize = MarginDeposit = 1;

myMACD = MACD(fast=12,slow =26);
myMACDAvg = MA(myMACD,9);

myMACDDiff = myMACD - MYMACDAvg;

leftBar2 = Ref(myMACDDiff,-4);
leftBar1 = Ref(myMACDDiff,-3);
centerBar = Ref(myMACDDiff,-2);
rightBar1 = Ref(myMACDDiff,-1);
rightBar2 = Ref(myMACDDiff,0);
```

```
COND3 = C > MA(C,100);

COND1 = centerBar < 0 AND centerBar < Min(leftBar2, leftBar1)
  AND centerBar < Min(rightBar1,rightBar2);

COND2 = centerBar > 0 AND centerBar > Max(leftBar2, leftBar1)
  AND centerBar > Max(rightBar1,rightBar2);

Buy = COND1 AND COND3;
Short = COND2 AND NOT(COND3);


BuyPrice = C;
ShortPrice = C;

longEntryPrice=ValueWhen(Buy,BuyPrice,1);
shortEntryPrice = ValueWhen(Short,ShortPrice,1);

Sell = Cross(C, longEntryPrice - 3 * ATR(10));
Cover = Cross(ShortEntryPrice + 3 *ATR(10),C); ;

AddColumn(longEntryPrice,"BuyPrice");
AddColumn(longEntryPrice - 3 * ATR(10),"longStop");
AddColumn(Sell,"Sell ?");
```


This last algorithm introduces the **AddColumn** and **ValueWhen** functionality. The **AddColumn** is useful for many purposes, but is probably used more as a debugging tool. Basically, this prints information out to the spreadsheet in **Exploration** mode. The **ValueWhen** function, in this example, returns the element of the **BuyPrice** array when the first value of 1 occurs in the **BUY** array. In other words, it is the long entry price. This code is somewhat sophisticated, as it introduces methods of debugging and gathering the last entry price. This code is fully explained along with utilizing AmiBroker's Exploration feature in the AmiBroker appendix.

CHAPTER 5

Using Microsoft Excel to Backtest Your Algorithm

The majority of the testing that has been performed thus far in the book was carried out using either AmiBroker or TradeStation. These are complete trading solutions and should be able to fulfill all the needs of a trader. However, some traders would like to use software that they already have on their computer. Microsoft Excel has been a major player in the trading algorithm arena since the beginning. Spreadsheets combine data with formulas, and as we have seen these are the major ingredients to trading algorithms. Several years ago, I developed a very simple spreadsheet to help a client generate his trading signals for the next day. The system incorporated several indicators across several different markets. The Excel workbook turned out to be quite large and required the user to type in the daily data after the close each day. Excel spreadsheets are very powerful but when it comes to calculating indicators and trade signals they can become very cumbersome.

This is where VBA (Visual Basic for Applications) comes in very handy. VBA combines the power of the BASIC programming language with the power of spreadsheets. I have created a simple single-market algorithm-testing platform for those who wanted to use Excel and VBA. I call it the Excel System Backtester, ESB for short. Here is a version of the Bollinger Band algorithm that has been evaluated in the previous chapters programmed in our ESB platform.

```
'*****************************************************************
'**** This is a good place to put all of your function calls ****
'**** and system calculations.                            ****
'*****************************************************************

  Call BollingerBand(myClose, 60, 2, avg, upBand, dnBand,
    i, 1)
  simpleAvg = Average(myClose, 10, i, 1)
  rsiVal = RSI(myClose, 14, i, 1)
  Call Stochastic(3, 4, 7, stoK, stoD, slowD, i, 1)

'*****************************************************************
'****          Put All Of Your Orders Here          ****
'*****************************************************************
  prevMarketPosition = marketPosition
  If marketPosition <> 1 Then
    Call Trade(Buy, "BB-Buy", upBand, stp, i)
  End If
  If marketPosition <> -1 Then
    Call Trade(Sell, "BB-Sell", dnBand, stp, i)
  End If
  If marketPosition = -1 Then
    Call Trade(ExitShort, "ExitShortStop", entryPrice +
       2000 / myTickValue, stp, i)
    If barsShort > 10 And myClose(i) > entryPrice Then
      Call Trade(ExitShort, "10dayShOut", myClose(i), moc, i)
    End If
  End If
  If marketPosition = 1 Then
    Call Trade(ExitLong, "ExitLongStop", entryPrice -
       2000 / myTickValue, stp, i)
    If barsLong > 10 And myClose(i) < entryPrice Then
      Call Trade(ExitLong, "10dayLgOut", myClose(i), moc, i)
    End If
  End If

'*****************************************************************
'****          End of Main Traiding Loop          ****
'****        No orders allowed below this point        ****
'*****************************************************************
```

This system buys/sells short on the penetration of 60-day two-standard-deviations Bollinger Bands, then risks $2,000 per trade and exits if the trade is not profitable after 10 days. The code is Visual Basic, so it follows that syntax. In developing this testing software my overall objective was simplicity—I wanted a very easy sloping learning curve. You don't need to know VBA to invoke the indicator or trading functions. You will just need to follow the included templates.

If you are interested in learning some VBA and want to see under the hood, a discussion of the source code is included in the ESB appendix. First off, let's learn how to use the software and its indicator and trading functions. The VBA tester is based on one large loop. The software loops through each and every bar of data and allows the user to create indicators and analyze patterns and make trading decisions on each and every bar. Conceptually, it works like AmiBroker and TradeStation, but doesn't have all the bells and whistles. It can only test one market at a time, and has limited performance metrics. However, it is sufficient to get your feet wet, and since the source code is open, you can take it and do as you want.

VBA Functions and Subroutines

The heart of this algorithm is a 60-day Bollinger Band, and just like AmiBroker, you get access to this indicator by calling a function:

```
Call BollingerBand(myClose, 60, 2, avg, upBand, dnBand, i, 1)
```

Some indicators return a single value and some return several. This function call is actually a subroutine that returns three parts of the Bollinger Band indicator: the moving average, the top band, and the lower band. The subroutine needs five inputs or arguments to calculate the bands: price (myClose), length (60), number of deviations (2), the current bar we are on (i), and the offset (1). Don't worry about the difference between a subroutine and function because in this application they do the same thing, return indicator values. The only difference is in the way you call the indicator and how the indicator values are assigned. Notice the difference between a pure function call and our BollingerBand subroutine call:

```
myHH = Highest(myHigh, 20, i, 1)

Call BollingerBand(myClose, 60, 2, avg, upBand, dnBand, i, 1)
```

The function **Highest** returns a single value and that value is assigned to the variable myHH. The subroutine **BollingerBand** is invoked by preceding the name of the subroutine with the keyword **Call**. The values that are used for trading decisions are included in the list of arguments that are passed into and out of the subroutine. The information that is passed to a function is only used by the function internally and is not passed back. The variable in our function call, **myHH**, holds the output off the function. In this case, it will be the highest high of the past 20 days starting from yesterday. A neat feature of VBA is that once you define functions or subroutines, the editor will help you fill out the argument list just like AmiBroker. (see figure 5.1.)

```
Call BollingerBand(
        BollingerBand(dataList, length, numDevs, avg, upBand, dnBand, index, offset)
```

`**************************************************************`

FIGURE 5.1 Once you define the Bollinger Band routine, you can easily incorporate it into trading.

If you are trying to invoke a function or subroutine and this helper box doesn't appear, then you probably do not have the function/subroutine spelled correctly or it doesn't exist. All functions and subroutines in the ExcelSystemTester will be listed and explained in the appendix. All functions and subroutines require two bits of information: (1) the current bar and (2) how many days back to start the calculations. In the case of the **Highest** function, the current bar is **i** and the offset is **1**. An offset of two starts the calculations the day before yesterday. Remember, we are working in one big loop and each bar is examined by incrementing the variable *i*.

Data

Accessing the date, price, volume, or open interest data is accomplished by using seven different arrays: **myDate**, **myOpen**, **myHigh**, **myLow**, **myClose**, **myVol**, and **myOpInt**. Two more arrays provide access to daily range and true range: **myRange** and **myTrueRange**. Unlike AmiBroker's array processing, you must index these arrays to get the data for a particular bar. **myOpen(10)** is the tenth bar's open from the very beginning of the data. **myDate(10)** is the date of the bar with **myOpen(10)** opening price. The arrays are synchronized. All data arrays are preceded with **my**—so don't forget this. Let's say you want to see if yesterday was a high pivot of strength one. This is how you would test for this occurrence:

```
If myHigh(i-1) > myHigh(i) and myHigh(i-1) > myHigh(i-2) then
     myHighPivot = 1
End if
```

Remember, **i** is the current bar in the loop. So by subtracting 1 you get yesterday's bar and subtracting 2 gets the day before yesterday's bar. If you add 1, then you will have tomorrow's data today and you can make a killer trading system. With this information, you will finally have the Holy Grail in your grasp. On the other hand, save yourself a lot of time and heartache by not adding—just subtracting. I can't tell you how many times a client has come to me with a 90% winning trading idea and I burst their bubble once they discover they are taking advantage of *future leak*. Here is the best example of future leak: Buy tomorrow's open if the high is greater than the open. This obviously is a mistake, but other forms of future leak are more esoteric.

If high of tomorrow is greater than the buy stop, then buy price = buy stop. This one makes sense, where is the future leak; the price moved above the buy stop so the stop was filled at the specified price. If you test using this exact logic in the ESB, then you will hyperinflate your algorithm's performance. The error is hard to see, but it's there. What if the high is equal to your buy stop? Using this logic, the trade will not be executed and you will skip a trade that buys the absolute high price of the day. Skipping these trades will, without a doubt, increase your bottom line. Most system-testing platforms go out of their way to prevent future leak. TradeStation's EasyLanguage only lets you peek at the next bar's open. You can use it as a price to execute a trade or as a base price in a calculation of stop or limit orders. You can say buy next bar at open of next bar + 1/2 ATR(10) on a stop or buy next bar at open – 1/2 ATR(10) on a limit. This makes future leak impossible and that should be a good thing. In most cases, this is true. However, this safety feature can make things a lot more difficult, too. Let's say you are placing multiple orders for the next bar, and one of them is filled, and you need to know exactly which order was executed. Some platforms simply execute the trade and don't let you know which order generated the trade. You might have different trade management algorithms for each order. In the ESB, I give the user complete power and therefore unlimited creativity. However, as you know, with great power comes great responsibility. Just be careful.

Software Structure

Figure 5.2 shows a simplified structure of how the software works. There's a lot more going on behind the scenes, but this diagram gives a good overview of how the software in general works.

There are just two major components in the ESB, as you can see from the diagram. The two components are actuated by two simple buttons on the Data worksheet in the workbook. The **GetData** component forms the top of the diagram. This is where the programs asks for and then processes the data and puts the data into a digestible format. The second component, **TestSystem**, makes up the rest of the diagram and the rest of the software. Here is a breakdown of each component:

- **GetData**—this button first asks you to locate a comma-delimited file (CSV) through an Open File dialog box. Once the file is opened it is cross-referenced with the data in the DataMaster to determine the **Tick Value** and **Min Tick** properties. The first two letters of the file names are used as the search key. If the file name is CLXXX.CSV, then the CL will be used to determine what market data is being utilized. In most cases CL is crude oil. If the symbol is not located in the DataMaster, then the software assumes it is a stock and defaults the **Tick Value** to one dollar and the **Min Tick** to a penny.

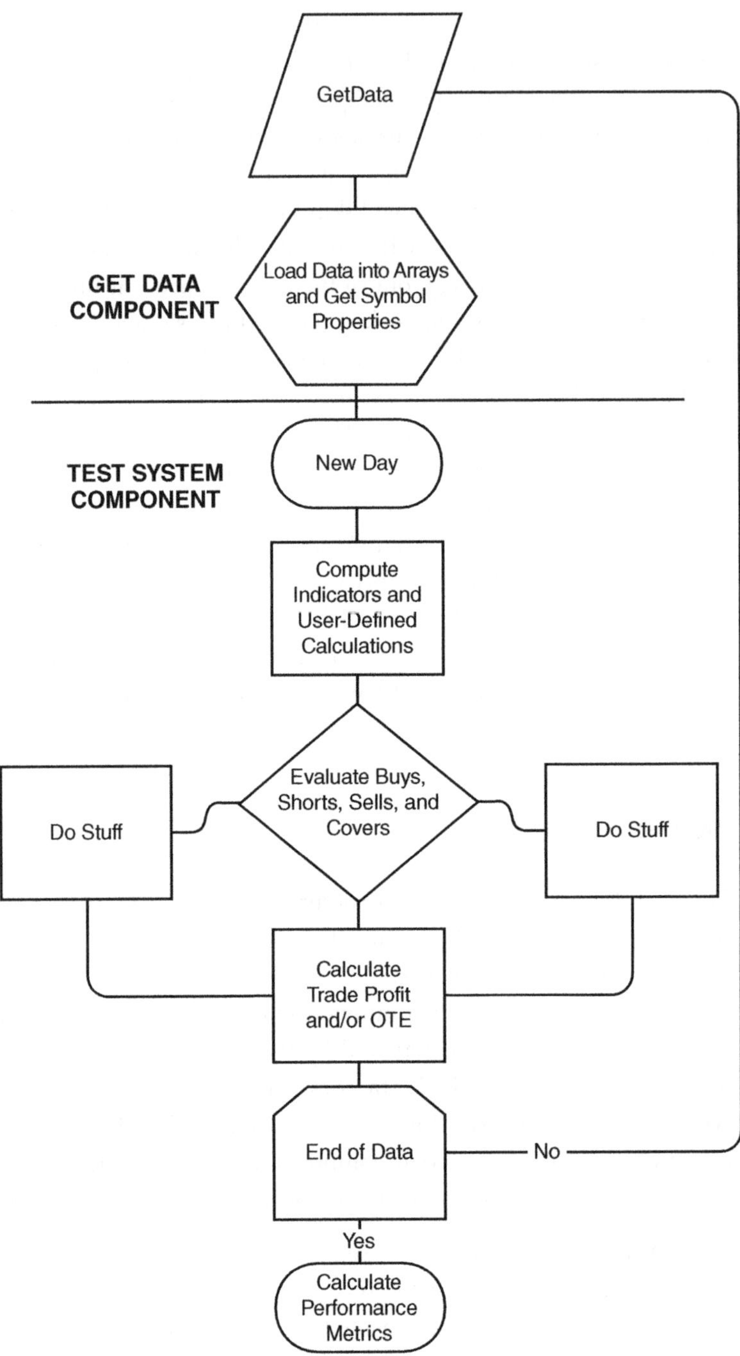

FIGURE 5.2 The structure of the backtesting software.

- **TestSystem**—this button reads the data that was dumped into the **Data** worksheet and puts it into the seven data arrays. The program then starts looping through each bar and flows through the user-defined entry and exit logic. If the consequence of the user-defined logic results in a trade entry or exit, the software makes a note and processes the order as if it was actually executed. At the termination of the data loop, all trades are processed and an equity stream of closed trade profits and open trade equity is dumped out into the **EquityStream** worksheet.

Keep in mind this is a very simple program and can only work on one market one system at a time. Figure 5.3 shows a typical layout of the Data worksheet.

The **GetData** component was previously actuated by simply clicking the button and as you can see the different cells, **open**, **high**, **low**, **close**, **volume**, and **open interest**, were then populated. Also, the **Tick Value** and **Min Tick** values were cross-referenced in the DataMaster and their respective cells were filled in as well. The DataMaster worksheet contains the symbols and their properties in the current data universe. As you can see, stocks are not listed, but that doesn't mean you can't test them. Commodities and futures contracts have different sizes and values. These values must be stored somewhere so the software can gain access to them during the testing process. Originally, the software simply asked the user to input this information, but I quickly discovered this was way too cumbersome and decided to create the DataMaster worksheet (see Figure 5.4).

These data properties were derived directly from the underlying data. If you don't get these values right, then your results will be completely wrong. Most data vendors will provide this information when you purchase their end-of-date (EOD) historic database. I use two data vendors, CSI and Pinnacle, for commodity and futures price quotes. You can buy deep historic databases from either of these vendors for a very reasonable price. If you purchase data through a reliable vendor,

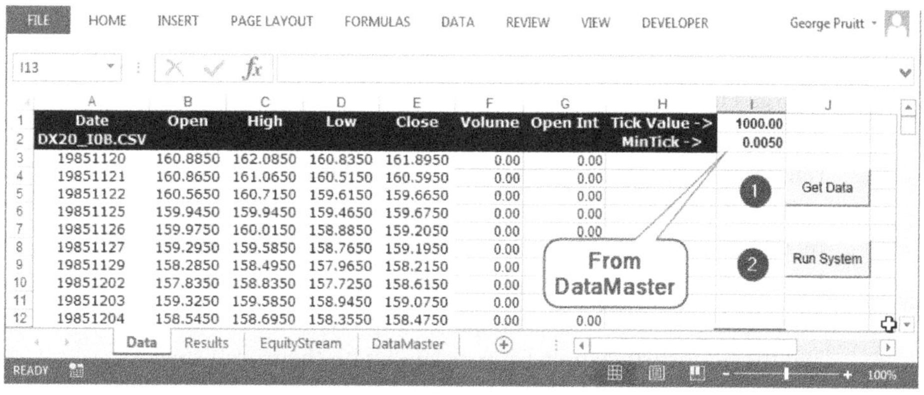

	A	B	C	D	E	F	G	H	I
1	Date	Open	High	Low	Close	Volume	Open Int	Tick Value ->	1000.00
2	DX20_I0B.CSV							MinTick ->	0.0050
3	19851120	160.8850	162.0850	160.8350	161.8950	0.00	0.00		
4	19851121	160.8650	161.0650	160.5150	160.5950	0.00	0.00		
5	19851122	160.5650	160.7150	159.6150	159.6650	0.00	0.00		
6	19851125	159.9450	159.9450	159.4650	159.6750	0.00	0.00		
7	19851126	159.9750	160.0150	158.8850	159.2050	0.00	0.00		
8	19851127	159.2950	159.5850	158.7650	159.1950	0.00			
9	19851129	158.2850	158.4950	157.9650	158.2150	0.00			
10	19851202	157.8350	158.8350	157.7250	158.6150	0.00			
11	19851203	159.3250	159.5850	158.9450	159.0750	0.00			
12	19851204	158.5450	158.6950	158.3550	158.4750	0.00	0.00		

FIGURE 5.3 A typical Excel data worksheet.

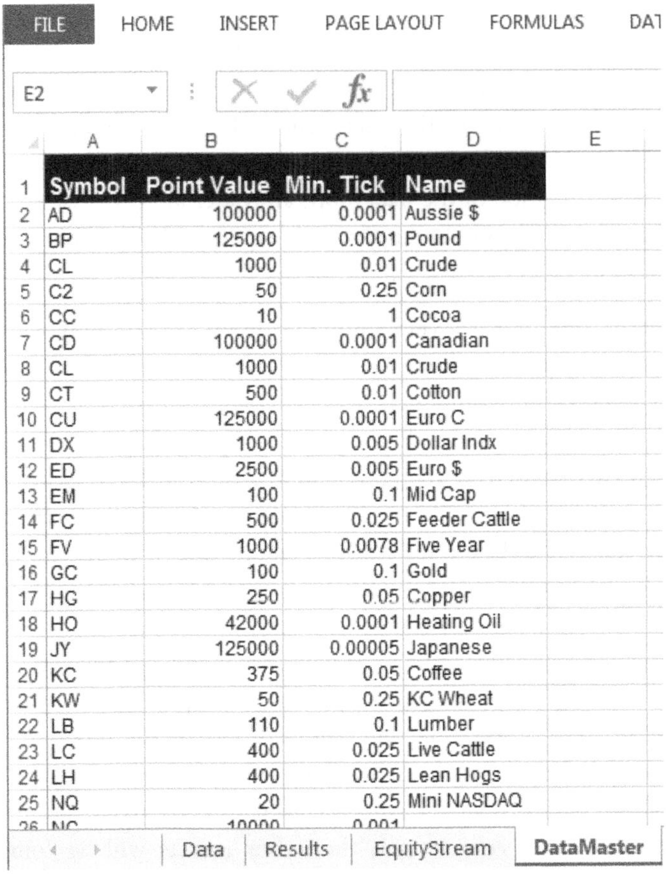

FILE HOME INSERT PAGE LAYOUT FORMULAS DAT

E2

	A	B	C	D
1	Symbol	Point Value	Min. Tick	Name
2	AD	100000	0.0001	Aussie $
3	BP	125000	0.0001	Pound
4	CL	1000	0.01	Crude
5	C2	50	0.25	Corn
6	CC	10	1	Cocoa
7	CD	100000	0.0001	Canadian
8	CL	1000	0.01	Crude
9	CT	500	0.01	Cotton
10	CU	125000	0.0001	Euro C
11	DX	1000	0.005	Dollar Indx
12	ED	2500	0.005	Euro $
13	EM	100	0.1	Mid Cap
14	FC	500	0.025	Feeder Cattle
15	FV	1000	0.0078	Five Year
16	GC	100	0.1	Gold
17	HG	250	0.05	Copper
18	HO	42000	0.0001	Heating Oil
19	JY	125000	0.00005	Japanese
20	KC	375	0.05	Coffee
21	KW	50	0.25	KC Wheat
22	LB	110	0.1	Lumber
23	LC	400	0.025	Live Cattle
24	LH	400	0.025	Lean Hogs
25	NQ	20	0.25	Mini NASDAQ
26	NG	10000	0.001	

Data | Results | EquityStream | DataMaster

FIGURE 5.4 The DataMaster worksheet can help you store the values of your commodities and futures contracts.

then you know you are getting quality data. You can cobble data together from various free services on the Internet, but remember GIGO (garbage in garbage out). For the ExcelSystemBackTester, I utilize data provided by CSI, but you can utilize any data as long as it is in ASCII and delimited by commas. The DataMaster can be used as a template and is fully editable. Some vendors use different decimal locations for the same market. If this is the case, you have got to make sure your DataMaster reflects the correct **Tick Value** and **Min Tick**.

The **Results** worksheet is the repository of all your trades and performance metrics. Every trade covers two rows, one for entry and one for exit. A profit or loss is calculated when a trade is exited and the cumulative profit or loss is updated as well. Figure 5.5 is an example of the **Results** worksheet where several trades and the performance metrics associated with them are listed.

The date, name of entry/exit signal, price of entry/exit, and the results of the trade are listed chronologically. Currently there are only four major performance metrics included in the worksheet: (1) **Total Profit**, (2) **Maximum DD**, (3) **Number of**

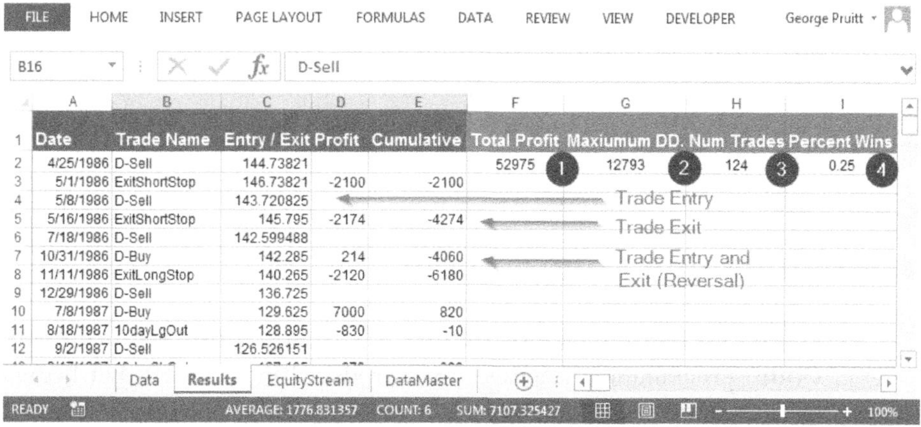

FIGURE 5.5 The Results worksheet lists multiple trades and their associated performance metrics.

Trades, and (4) **Percent Wins**. By the time this book is published, I should have a few more calculated, such as: **Average Trade**, **Average Win**, **Average Loss**, and **Profit Factor**.

The last worksheet in the ESB is labeled **EquityStream** and stores the daily equity of the trading system. There is a **Create Equity Curve** button that launches a simple macro that creates a chart (see Figure 5.6) and plots the cumulative daily equity and drawdown. This chart gives a very quick snapshot of the overall

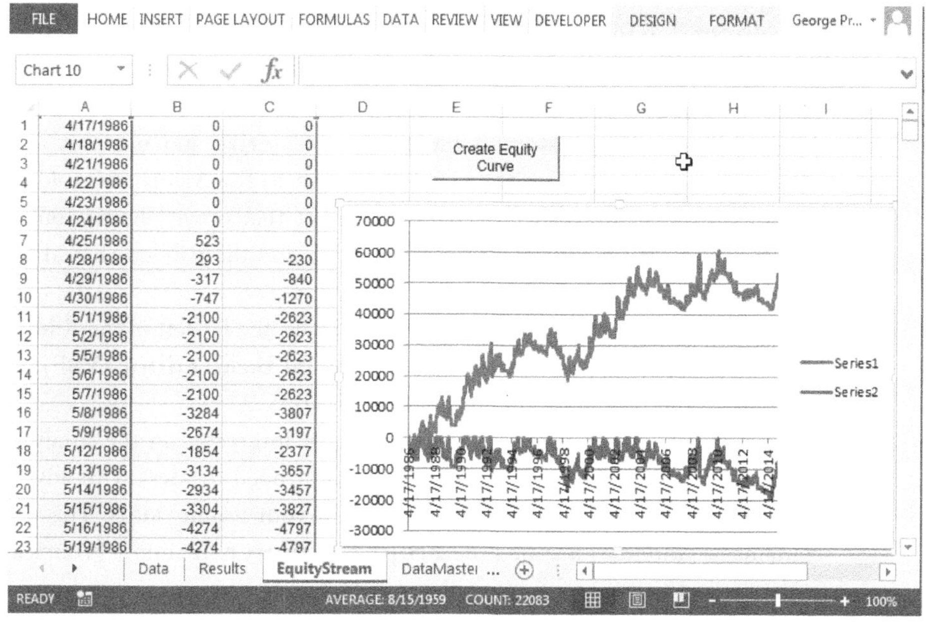

FIGURE 5.6 The EquityStream worksheet has a button that launches a macro to create a chart that plots the cumulative daily equity and drawdown.

performance of the trading system. There is enough information provided to help determine if your particular algorithm is good enough for either trading or further research. As you can see, the interface is simple enough—load data, test system, plot equity. The hard stuff is getting into the VBA and creating a trading algorithm with the tools at hand.

Programming Environment

The BASIC (an acronym for **Beginner's All-purpose Symbolic Instruction Code**) programming language was introduced in the 1960s but became popular in the mid-1970s. BASIC quickly became the most popular interpreted language for beginners. Over the years, compiler companies have extended BASIC into professional software development. Microsoft has been using BASIC derivatives for decades and it is at the heart of VBA. When you code your trading algorithm in to the ESB, you will be programming in pure BASIC. You will see a lot of lines of code (I wish I could hide them, but the VBA Editor doesn't allow for collapsible text regions) that you will not need to understand (unless you want to). There are just three major sections with which you will need to concern yourself. But before we get into all that, launch your Microsoft Excel and make sure you see the **Developer** tab in the Ribbon. If you don't see it, then you will need to turn it on. You can do this by simply clicking the **File** menu and then selecting **Options**. After Excel Options dialog opens scroll down to **Customize Ribbon** and click on it. Figure 5.7 shows the **Customize Ribbon** dialog and where to click to get the **Developer** Tab to show up in the Ribbon.

Once you return to a blank worksheet, the Developer tab should now be visible. Now go to the www.wiley.com/go/ultimatealgotoolbox and download the ExcelSystemBackTester.zip file to your C: drive and unzip it. The zip file contains two folders: Algorithms and Data. Get to the Algorithms folder and open the BollingerDX spreadsheet. The spreadsheet that opens should look similar to Figure 5.3. Now click on the **Developer** tab and the Ribbon should take on this appearance (see Figure 5.8).

The only icon that we are concerned with is to the far left of the Ribbon, **Visual Basic**. Click on the icon/button and the **Visual Basic Editor** (VBE) will launch. Make sure your VBE looks like the one in Figure 5.9.

There's a lot of stuff here. But we are just interested in the modules that are inside the red oval from Figure 5.9. You don't need to mess with anything else if you are just interested in using the ESB to test your trading ideas. The window that contains the modules is called the **Project Explorer**. It simply groups all the files in the project together for convenience.

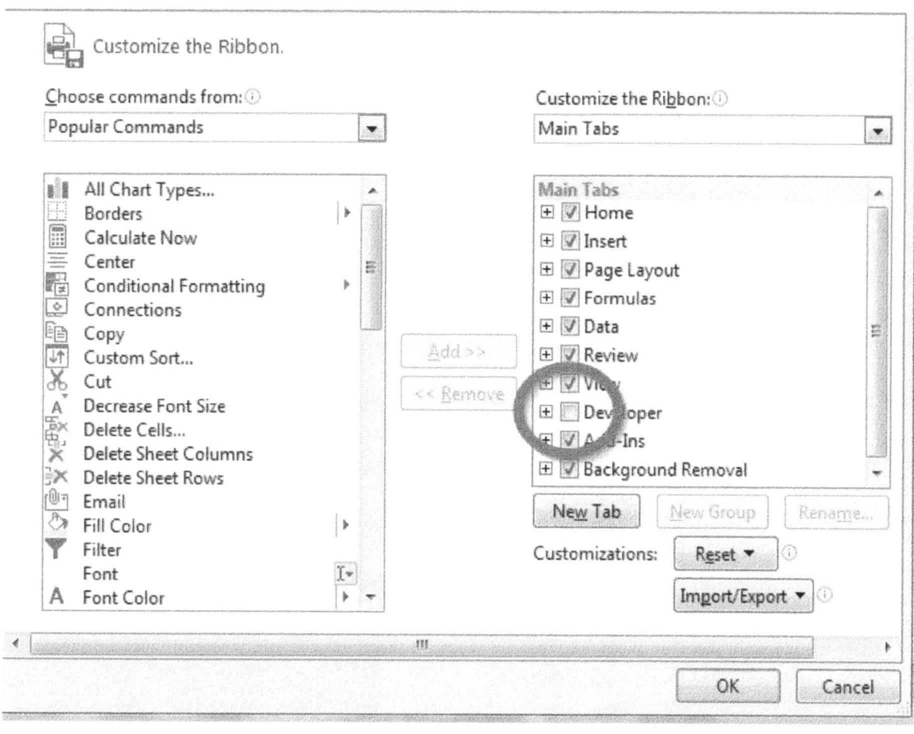

FIGURE 5.7 Customize your Excel ribbon. Make sure you check the box next to the Developer tab option.

FIGURE 5.8 The Developer tab in Microsoft Excel.

The ESB VBA Code

The modules are individual files that contain the source code to carry out the various chores necessary to test a trading system. The most import module (**Main**) is the one we will spend most of our time in. Go ahead and double-click **Main**—the source code inside the module will open in a separate window (see Figure 5.10). Inside this module are five submodules or subroutines: **declarations**, **fillTradeInfo**, **GetData**, **SystemTester**, and **main**. Most of our work will take place in the **SystemTester** module. Go ahead and scroll up and down in this window. It's going to look daunting without a doubt, but you need not concern yourself with 80 percent of the source code. Scroll to the very top of the window and you will see a lot of text

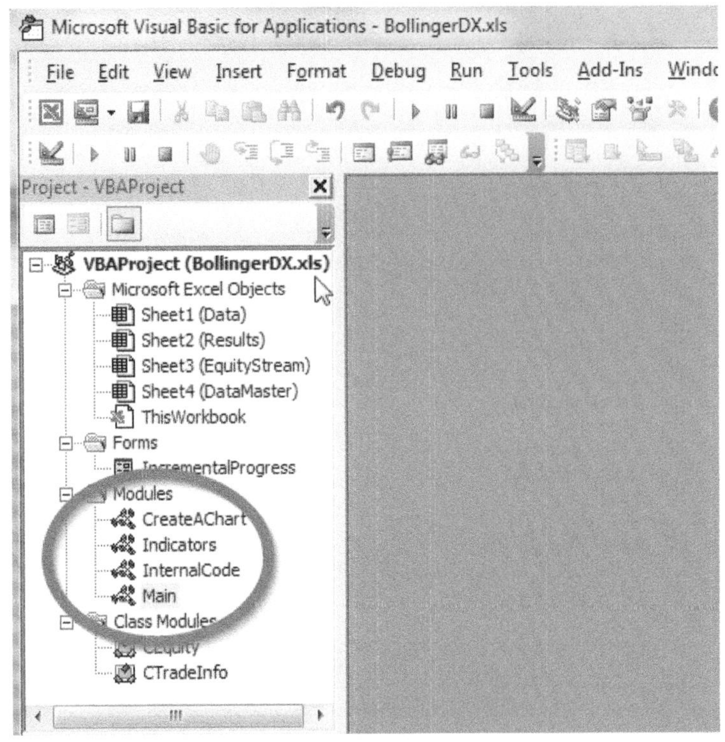

FIGURE 5.9 The Visual Basic Editor (VBE) in Microsoft Excel.

in green. In VB, everything green is considered a comment. This information is just there for the benefit of the person reading the code—it is hidden from the computer. Notice the first character in each line that is green. It is a single quote ('). A single quote at the beginning of a line of VBA code tells the computer to ignore the line. Just like the double forward slashes "//" in AmiBroker. This area of the source code lets the reader know the title, version, subversion of the software, and any notes pertaining to revisions and necessary information a user may need to know. If you scrolled through the source, you will see multiple lines of comments. I did this to modularize the code and explain what the individual sections were doing. Breaking down a large program into sections helps explain the code in block-by-block fashion. Source code read as a whole is very difficult to understand, but if you can break the code into individual blocks, it will help make things much clearer.

You will notice several banners or blocks of green text embedded in the source code. Figure 5.10 is an example of one of these blocks.

These comments, in this format, help break up the code and also explain what's happening in the next few lines of code. This commentary explains how the data contained in the cells of the Data worksheet will be imported into the individual data arrays. Column 1 holds the Dates of each individual daily bar. The first row of

```
'***************************************************************
'****  Read the data from the cells into our arrays        ****
'***************************************************************
'Read in the data
'Column 1 - Date   -- Cells(3,1)  - Cells(Row,Column)
'Column 2 - Open   -- Cells(3,2)
'Column 3 - High   -- Cells(3,3)
'Column 4 - Low    -- Cells(3,4)
'Column 5 - Close  -- Cells(3,5)
'Column 6 - Volume-- Cells(3,6)
'Column 7 - OpInt  -- Cells(3,7)
```

FIGURE 5.10 Comment text in VBA code is written in gray. It is also indicated by the single quote at the beginning of each line.

data (row 3 in our case) holds the date, open, high, low, close, volume, and open interest for one day of data. Think of the data as just in one big table consisting of rows and columns. If you want the data of the very first bar, you would access it using the following notation: Cells (3, 1). In Excel, *cells* refer to the entire table and the first index value inside the parentheses refers to the row number and the second index value is the column number. Cells (3, 2) refer to the open price of the very first bar. A newcomer to VBA might not know this nomenclature so it is included in this comment block. Since all of the data is being read into individual arrays you do not need to concern yourself with notion of cells, unless you want to.

Scroll down in the code until you find a comment block that looks like the one in Figure 5.11.

All the code that you scrolled through until you got to this point can be ignored. This area of the source code is used to set up any system-specific variables. The two lines of code following the comment block set **rampUp** to 100 and **commsn** to 100. Notice there are lines of comments to the right of each variable assignment. These are inline comments to let you know what that exact line of code is doing. You will again see the single quote (') preceding the comment. Whatever follows the single quote is ignored by the computer, be it at the beginning of a line of code or right in the middle. The **rampUp** variable informs the computer that the trading algorithm needs 100 days of data for calculation purposes before it can initiate trading. If you want to test a 100-day simple moving average algorithm, you would need to tell the ESB to skip the first 100 days of data so that the moving average


```
'***************************************************************
'****   System Specific Variables and Dims  Can Go Here     ****
'***************************************************************

RampUp = 100 ' how many days needed in calculations before trading
commsn = 100 ' commission per round turn trade
```

FIGURE 5.11 This is where the VBA comments end and the actual source code begins.

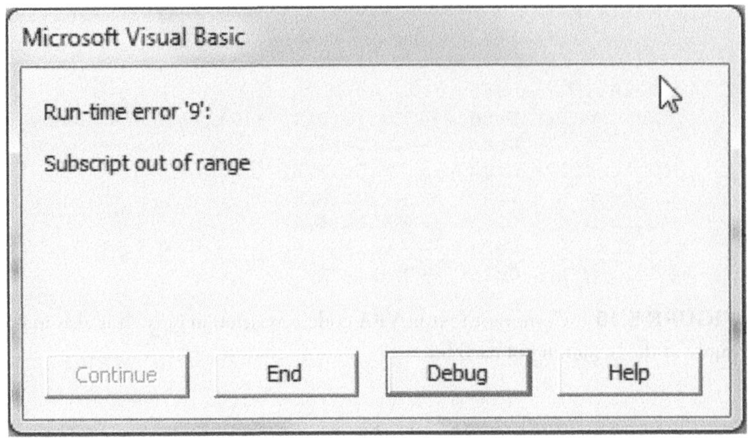

FIGURE 5.12 This error message appears if your algorithm does not have enough ramp-up data.

can be properly calculated. You must be careful and make sure you provide enough ramp-up data for your algorithm. If you don't, the computer will halt and provide an error message like the one in Figure 5.12.

This looks like a scary error message but it's simply telling you that you are trying to go back further in time than you have specified. The **commsn** variable is what the computer will deduct from each round-turn trade. In this example it is set to 100; you can change this to any value you think might be appropriate. This is also a good area to set up any user-defined variables that you might need to use later in your code. Let's say you have a special calculation that uses a constant value, like a profit objective. You could set this up by using the following code:


```
rampUp = 5 ' how many days needed in calculations before trading
commsn = 100 ' commission per round turn trade

myProfitTarg = 0.02 ' I just put this line of code in
```

Later on, in the source code you can use **myProfitTarg** to help calculate where a profit might be taken. This is a very good time to mention that VBA, in most cases, is case insensitive. This means the two variable names, **myDayCount** and **mydaycount**, are one and the same. Ignoring case can cause sloppy-looking code and difficult readability. It's good programming etiquette to use the same case throughout a program. As I have mentioned in a previous chapter, I personally like using a capital letter in a variable name where a new word begins, but not the first letter of the variable name. Here are some examples you can use as a template for your variable names: **myProfitTarg**, **longDayCount**, **myStopAmt**. You have also got to be careful not to step on one of the keywords that is used by the ESB. Unlike AmiBroker or TradeStation, VBA will not tell you ahead of time that you are reassigning a variable that is already used elsewhere in the source code. A list of keywords is provided in the appendix to help prevent this from happening.

Let's get to the heart of the ESB by scrolling down to the main trading loop. You can find it by looking for the comment block that says, "Main Trading Loop." The entire Main Trading Loop is shown below. This includes some of the code we have already discussed and some code that you can simply ignore.

```
'*****************************************************************
'****          Main Trading Loop              ****
'*****************************************************************
Do While i <= numRecords
  tradeDays = tradeDays + 1
  IncrementalProgress.Show
  i = i + 1                  'Dont touch

  sPercentage = (i / numRecords) * 100
  sStatus = "Checking " & i & " of " & numRecords &
   " paragraphs"
  IncrementalProgress.Increment sPercentage, sStatus
  intraDayTrdCnt = 0                        'Leave in.

  If barsLong <> 0 Then barsLong = barsLong + 1    'Leave in.
  If barsShort <> 0 Then barsShort = barsShort + 1  'Leave in.

'*****************************************************************
'**** This is a good place to put all of your function calls ****
'**** and system calculations.                      ****
'*****************************************************************

  Call BollingerBand(myClose, 60, 2, avg, upBand, dnBand, i, 1)
  simpleAvg = Average(myClose, 10, i, 1)
  rsiVal = RSI(myClose, 14, i, 1)
  Call Stochastic(3, 4, 7, stoK, stoD, slowD, i, 1)

'*****************************************************************
'****         Put All Of Your Orders Here         ****
'*****************************************************************
  prevMarketPosition = marketPosition
  If marketPosition <> 1 Then
    Call Trade(Buy, "BB-Buy", upBand, stp, i)
  End If
  If marketPosition <> -1 Then
    Call Trade(Sell, "BB-Short", dnBand, stp, i)
```

```
  End If
  If marketPosition = -1 Then
    Call Trade(ExitShort, "ExitShortStop", entryPrice +
     2000 / myTickValue, stp, i)
    If barsShort > 10 And myClose(i) > entryPrice Then
      Call Trade(ExitShort, "10dayShOut", myClose(i), moc, i)
    End If
  End If
  If marketPosition = 1 Then
    Call Trade(ExitLong, "ExitLongStop", entryPrice -
     2000 / myTickValue, stp, i)
    If barsLong > 10 And myClose(i) < entryPrice Then
      Call Trade(ExitLong, "10dayLgOut", myClose(i), moc, i)
    End If
  End If

'*****************************************************************
'****        End of Main Traiding Loop          ****
'****      No orders allowed below this point      ****
'*****************************************************************
```


This is the complete listing for this simple Bollinger Band system. Don't worry about any of the source code *above* the Main Trading Loop comment block:

```
'*****************************************************************
'**** This is a good place to put all of your function calls ****
'**** and system calculations.                       ****
'*****************************************************************
```

All of your programming will take place below these comments. For illustration purposes, I immediately call four indicator functions/subroutines.

```
  Call BollingerBand(myClose, 60, 2, avg, upBand, dnBand, i, 1)
  simpleAvg = Average(myClose, 10, i, 1)
  rsiVal = RSI(myClose, 14, i, 1)
  Call Stochastic(3, 4, 7, stoK, stoD, slowD, i, 1)
```

This algorithm will just use the values modified in the **BollingerBand** subroutine: **avg, upBand, dnBand**. Let's look at the other function calls in the program:

- *Average*. This function returns a moving average value for the past 10 days. Its first argument is the data array that is to be averaged, and the second argument is the length of the calculation. You will again notice the last two arguments are the same for all of the function calls: **i** and **1**. The **i** will never change but you can change the last argument. If you were to use **2**, then the indicator calculation would be offset by two days. Instead of starting yesterday and going back 10 days, it would start the day before yesterday and go back 10 days.

- *RSI.* This function returns the Relative Strength Index from the last 14 days of data. This function requires the data array and the length of the RSI calculation. As it is programmed in this example, it is utilizing the closing prices for its calculations. You can pass it high or low or volume data—it doesn't matter.
- *Stochastic.* This subroutine returns K, D, and Slow D. Here is another example of using a subroutine in place of a function. Just like the BollingerBand subroutine, this subroutine returns three values. It requires the length of the K calculation and the two additional smoothing lengths for the D and Slow D.

Examples of all the indicator functions and subroutines are included in Appendix B.

After you get your indicator values, the real fun begins. The most important code in the ESB can be found in the **Trade** subroutine. This subroutine determines if a trade takes place and then stores the information for later use. The subroutine requires five arguments (see Figure 5.13).

The first argument informs the subroutine what you are trying to do and can take on four different values: **Buy**, **Sell**, **ExitLong**, **ExitShort**. The second argument is the name of the signal that will show up in the trade listing. It is a string so it needs to be included in quotes. In this example, the signal name is "**BB-Buy**." It can be anything you want. The third argument is the price you would like to execute the order. Here we are trying to **Buy** on the penetration of the Upper Bollinger Band. The fourth argument informs the subroutine what type of order is being placed. It can take on four types of orders:

- **stp—Stop order.** The price of the order must be above the market for Buy and ExitShort or below the market for Sell and ExitLong.
- **lmt—Limit order.** The price of the order must be below the market for Buy and ExitShort or above the market for Sell and ExitLong.

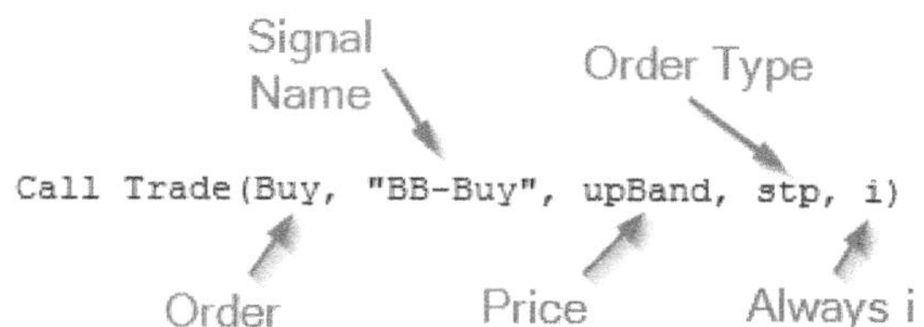

FIGURE 5.13 This tiny snippet of code contains five arguments, which are all necessary for the Trade subroutine.

- **moc—Market On Close order.** Execute the order at the closing price of the bar. Specify myClose(i) as the trade price.
- **mkt—Market order.** Executes at the opening of the bar. Specify **myOpen(i)** as the trade price.

The final argument is always the letter **i**, the current bar in the loop.

```
If marketPosition <> 1 Then
  Call Trade(Buy, "BB-Buy", upBand, stp, i)
End If
```

This order is only placed if the current **marketPosition** is not equal to 1 or long. In other words, don't place a **Buy** order if you are already long. Unfortunately, this version of the ESB doesn't allow pyramiding; however, future versions will have this capability. Entering a short position uses the same subroutine but the arguments are different:

```
If marketPosition <> -1 Then
    Call Trade(Sell, "BB-Short", dnBand, stp, i)
  End If
```


Here we are trying to **Sell** short at the lower Bollinger Band on a stop. That's it for the trade entries. Simple, thus far? Once you get into a trade, this algorithm has three different ways to exit:

- A $2,000 money management stop—any time the market moves $2,000 against the position it is exited.
- Time-based market order (MOC)—if the position is not profitable after 10 bars, the trade is exited on the close.
- Reversal if the opposite side of the Bollinger Bands is penetrated before an exit is executed.

```
If marketPosition = 1 Then
  Call Trade(ExitLong, "ExitLongStop", entryPrice -
   2000 / myTickValue, stp, i)
  If barsLong > 10 And myClose(i) < entryPrice Then
    Call Trade(ExitLong, "10dayLgOut", myClose(i),
     moc, i)
  End If
End If
```

The money management order is placed by calling the Trade subroutine with the following parameters: **ExitLong**, **"ExitLongStop," entryPrice – 2000/ myTickValue**, **stp**, **i**. Here we are informing the Trade subroutine to liquidate our long position on a stop at a price equivalent to the **entryPrice** – $2,000. The trade price can be represented by a single variable name or it can be a mathematical expression. In this case, we convert $2,000 to points by dividing 2,000 by **myTickValue**. Remember, you have got to make sure your units are compatible. If you are working with prices, then you must convert dollars to a price level. It would be a mistake in this case to forget to divide by **myTickValue**. Let's say you entered a trade in the DX at 129.050 and wanted to risk $2,000. If you didn't convert to points, then the exit price would be 129.050 – 2000. This doesn't make sense. Just remember to convert all dollar figures to points.

The time-based order is placed after the long position has been in a trade for more than 10 days and is in a losing position. The variables **barsLong** and **entryPrice** are keywords so don't use them in an assignment statement—just look, don't touch.

If barsLong > 10 tells the computer to ignore the **ExitLong** order until the trade has been on for at least 10 days and the **and myClose(i) < entryPrice** tells the computer to ignore the order if the position is in the profit. The orders to exit a short position use the keyword **barsShort**, and the logic **myClose(i) > entryPrice**.


```
If marketPosition = -1 Then
  Call Trade(ExitShort, "ExitShortStop", entryPrice +
   2000 / myTickValue, stp, i)
  If barsShort > 10 And myClose(i) > entryPrice Then
    Call Trade(ExitShort, "10dayShOut", myClose(i),
     moc, i)
  End If
End If
```

Once you type in your trading logic, simply return to Excel and go to the **Data** worksheet and click on the **Run System** button.

Summary

All the tools that you need to calculate indicators, analyze price bar relations, manage open trades, and execute them are all built into the ESB. The best way to learn how to program your trading algorithms using VBA is by following along as many examples as you can. The end of this chapter has a couple more simple examples that you should be able to build upon.

Simple Moving Average Crossover using 3 X ATR stop

```
'****************************************************************
'**** This is a good place to put all of your function calls ****
'**** and system calculations. A simple moving average   ****
'**** crossover system using a 3 ATR protective stop.    ****
'****************************************************************

  Call BollingerBand(myClose, 60, 2, avg, upBand, dnBand, i, 1)
  simpleAvg = Average(myClose, 19, i, 1)
  atr = Average(myTrueRange, 20, i, 1)
  rsiVal = RSI(myClose, 14, i, 1)
  Call Stochastic(3, 4, 7, stoK, stoD, slowD, i, 1)


'****************************************************************
'****         Put All Of Your Orders Here         ****
'****************************************************************
  prevMarketPosition = marketPosition

  If marketPosition <> 1 And myClose(i) > simpleAvg Then
    Call Trade(Buy, "CrossBuy", myClose(i), moc, i)
  End If

  If marketPosition <> -1 And myClose(i) < simpleAvg Then
    Call Trade(Sell, "CrossSell", myClose(i), moc, i)
  End If

  If marketPosition = 1 And myClose(i) < entryPrice -
   3 * atr Then
    Call Trade(ExitLong, "L-ATR Stop", myClose(i), moc, i)
  End If

  If marketPosition = -1 And myClose(i) > entryPrice +
   3 * atr Then
    Call Trade(ExitShort, "S-ATR Stop", myClose(i), moc, i)
  End If


'****************************************************************
'****         End of Main Traiding Loop         ****
'****       No orders allowed below this point       ****
'****************************************************************
```

Simple RSI system using 3 X ATR stop and 5 X ATR profit objective

```
'*****************************************************************
'**** This is a good place to put all of your function calls ****
'**** and system calculations. A simple RSI system       ****
'**** that buys when RSI < 20 and sells when RSI > 80.    ****
'**** Utilizes a 5 ATR Profit and a 3 ATR Protective Stop  ****
'*****************************************************************

  Call BollingerBand(myClose, 60, 2, avg, upBand, dnBand,
    i, 1)
  simpleAvg = Average(myClose, 19, i, 1)
  atr = Average(myTrueRange, 20, i, 1)
  rsiVal = RSI(myClose, 14, i, 0)
  Call Stochastic(3, 4, 7, stoK, stoD, slowD, i, 1)



'*****************************************************************
'****          Put All Of Your Orders Here         ****
'*****************************************************************
  prevMarketPosition = marketPosition

  If marketPosition <> 1 And rsiVal < 20 Then
    Call Trade(Buy, "RSIBuy", myClose(i), moc, i)
  End If

  If marketPosition <> -1 And rsiVal > 80 Then
    Call Trade(Sell, "RSISell", myClose(i), moc, i)
  End If

  If marketPosition = 1 Then
    If myClose(i) < entryPrice - 3 * atr Then
      Call Trade(ExitLong, "L-ATR Stop", myClose(i), moc, i)
    End If
    If myClose(i) > entryPrice + 5 * atr Then
      Call Trade(ExitLong, "L-ATR Prof", myClose(i), moc, i)
    End If
  End If

  If marketPosition = -1 Then
    If myClose(i) > entryPrice + 3 * atr Then
      Call Trade(ExitShort, "S-ATR Stop", myClose(i),
        moc, i)
    End If
    If myClose(i) < entryPrice - 5 * atr Then
```

```
     Call Trade(ExitShort, "S-ATR Prof", myClose(i),
        moc, i)
    End If
  End If


'*****************************************************************
'****        End of Main Trading Loop        ****
'****      No orders allowed below this point      ****
'*****************************************************************
```

CHAPTER 6

Using Python to Backtest Your Algorithm

Why Python?

Around the same time I started to write this book, I was teaching myself the Python programming language. If you have spent time roaming around the Internet looking for the next quant language, you have seen Python mentioned many times. The usage of this language has grown tremendously over the past few years in the quant universe. This doesn't mean Python is only found in this arena, nor does it mean it is only used by mathematicians, economists, or scientists. There are languages, such as R, that are specifically designed for mathematicians, but Python has universal usage. As I have mentioned many times in the previous chapters, most algorithmic traders do not come from a programming background. The introduction to AmiBroker and the Excel VBA–based backtester has shown that a computer science degree is not necessary to get your algorithms tested on historic data. Most algorithmic traders learn just enough of a language to get the job done. In doing so, they use a very small subset of a platforms tools—barely touching the tip of the iceberg. Imagine, though, how much more powerful their algorithm backtesting and development skills could become through learning as much as they can about programming. If I was a newbie and wanted to learn as much about programming as quickly as possible, I would learn Python. This is coming from a programmer who is deeply devoted to FORTRAN and C. The skillset that you would acquire would only enhance your abilities in other languages and testing/trading platforms.

Python has caught on for many reasons, but the biggest is ease of learning. Plus, you are exposed to the two predominant programming paradigms: object oriented and procedural. If you were formally educated in computer science in the 1970s and 1980s, you probably come from the procedural school of thought. I have a programmer friend who worked at Bell Laboratories in the 1970s, and he doesn't even want to talk about "objects." Today's programmers, or should I say constructors, can build a rich graphical user interface (GUI) in a matter of minutes—something that took me a week to do back in the 1980s. A really good programmer can use both objects and procedures.

This chapter introduces ideas from both schools of thought. However, this chapter is only a small introduction to the Python language. If you want to learn more about Python and computer science in general, I highly recommend John Zelle's *Python Programming: An Introduction to Computer Science*. This book provides a solid foundation not only in Python but also in some of the most useful topics in computer science—knowledge that can be carried over into the trading arena.

In this new world of touchscreens, the usage of typing in a command line is disappearing. Well, that is if you are not from a Unix background. Python programmers become very comfortable with the command line, because it is so powerful. In many cases, a sophisticated user interface isn't necessary and this backtesting application is one of those cases. There isn't any exposure to developing a GUI because it wasn't necessary. Time was spent on topics that provided exposure on file manipulation, simple input/output, objects, and functions. Before we start discussing the Python system backtester (PSB), here is a list of why Python was the language of choice:

- *Python is an interpreted language*. The user doesn't need to go through an additional compilation step. Once you type the program into the editor, all you need to do is run it. If there is a syntax or runtime error, the Python shell will let you know about it.
- *Python has a shell*. This interactive command line interpreter can be used for testing small bits of code, as the output window for printing out information from your programs, or as a very cool calculator. The PSB uses this window exclusively in this tutorial. This window also alerts you to syntax and runtime errors.
- *Python is dynamically typed*. A user can create a variable name on the fly without having to declare/size it before using it. This is similar to AFL and VBA. This helps the creative flow process. In other languages, when you create a variable you have to go back to the top of the code and declare it. By the time you get back to using it, you might have forgotten what you were planning on doing. Well, this is a problem I suffer; you might not. There are both advantages and

disadvantages to dynamic typing and this is a subject of much controversy in the programming arena.

- *Python is free and has a very large user's group.* The code is open source and free to use in commercial and personal applications as long as the copyright information is prominently displayed. Almost any question about how to do something in Python can be answered by simply Googling it.
- *Python is perfect for our purposes.* All the trading system tracking/bookkeeping/analysis has already been programmed. All you need to do is use Python language and the PSB tools to create the perfect mousetrap.
- *Python has no foo bar.* Most other languages use the words **foo** and **bar** as variable names in example code snippets. Their origination is from the military acronym **fubar** and was probably first used at MIT. Python uses the words **spam** and **eggs** instead. The creators of Python wanted it to be fun, so they named the language after *Monty Python*, the British comedy group. Most people wouldn't put the words "fun" and "programming" together, but some of us would. **Spam** and **eggs** come from *Monty Python's Flying Circus*.

Python Installation

You will need to install Python on your computer before we can do anything. This is another benefit of Python—it is very easy to install. Go to the website www.python .org and click on **Downloads**. You will be provided links for different operating systems. As of the writing of this chapter the latest version was 3.5. The PSB was written in 3.4 and is upwardly compatible. Download the installer and run it. Just click through the prompts—the default values will be fine. This installer should install both IDLE (Python GUI) and Python (command line). If you are using a Windows operating system, a folder with the Python programs and manuals will be installed in your **Apps** screen. I use **Classic Shell** on my Windows 8 machine and both applications flow to the Start menu. Of course, if you are using Windows 7, it goes without saying you will find Python on the Start menu.

PSB Installation

Download the PSB.zip file from this book's companion website (www.wiley.com/go/ultimatealgotoolbox). Unzip it to your C: drive or to another convenient location.

IDLE

The PSB was programmed exclusively with **IDLE**, the standard Python development environment. Its name is an acronym of "Integrated DeveLopment Environment."

It works well on both Unix and Windows platforms. It includes a Python shell window, which gives you access to the Python interactive mode. Before we can start looking at the PSB, we need to learn a little bit about IDLE. So go ahead and launch it through your Apps screen or Start menu. The Python Shell should now be in front of you. Doesn't look that special; it's barebones in fact. This is by design to keep the Python learning curve as a gradual incline.

A prompt, preceded by >>>, should now be blinking at you. Currently, the Shell is in interactive mode—meaning that it wants you to give it a command. Type **4 + 6** and hit enter. The prompt now comes back with the answer—**10**. Now type **print("Hello World")** and hit enter. The prompt comes back with **Hello World**. Now type **100 ** 0.5** and hit enter. You should get the number **10**. Now type **import this** and hit enter. Your screen should be filled with the following:

The Zen of Python, by Tim Peters

Beautiful is better than ugly.
Explicit is better than implicit.
Simple is better than complex.
Complex is better than complicated.
Flat is better than nested.
Sparse is better than dense.
Readability counts.
Special cases aren't special enough to break the rules.
Although practicality beats purity.
Errors should never pass silently.
Unless explicitly silenced.
In the face of ambiguity, refuse the temptation to guess.
There should be one—and preferably only one—obvious way to do it.
Although that way may not be obvious at first unless you're Dutch.
Now is better than never.
Although never is often better than *right* now.
If the implementation is hard to explain, it's a bad idea.
If the implementation is easy to explain, it may be a good idea.
Namespaces are one honking great idea—let's do more of those!

This is an "Easter egg" of a poem created by Python pioneer Tim Peters. Pretty cool, huh? Some people live, eat, and breathe Python. You don't need to go overboard to get the benefits of learning a programming language such as Python.

You can now see why they call it an "interactive" shell. Let's switch gears and use IDLE as an IDE. Go under the **File** menu and select **Open ...** and then navigate your way to the PSB folder and open **PSBBollinger**. The file that opens is a trading algorithm based once again on Bollinger Bands.

PSB Structure

The PSB consists of a collection of files or modules. The main module is this one—it pulls or calls all the other modules to facilitate the loading of data, looping through each and every bar, accounting for all of the trades and input/output. If you want to create another trading algorithm, you start with an existing one and simply save it as a different name. There aren't separate submodules that simply include trading logic. This is just like the VBA-based ESB. This is unlike AmiBroker and TradeStation. In these softwares, trading rules, functions, and indicators are stored in a library.

Everything you program will take place in this module or the indicators.py module. All Python source code files have the .py extension. The PSB is very simple—type in your trading logic, which hopefully you have derived from a flowchart or a finite state machine, and then **Check Module** under the **Run** menu. If it passes, then you simply **Run** it by going under the **Run** menu and selecting **Run Module**.

Let's run this PSBBollinger module by selecting **Run Module** from the **Run** menu. After you select **Run Module**, a File Browser window titled **Select Markets To Test** will open. The PSB is asking you to select a .CSV file or files that in can read into memory to which it will apply the Bollinger algorithm. Navigate to the Commodity Data folder and select the file that starts with CL (crude oil). Once you select the file and click OK, data and results generated by the algorithm will flow to the Python Shell and be displayed there. The results are presented in the following order:

- *Combined results*. The PSB will combine the results of a multimarket selection. If only one market is selected, then it will just be the results from the single market.
- *Combined monthly results*. The monthly results in $ are shown for all markets selected.
- *Individual market results*. Performance metrics for each market are displayed.
- *Trade-by-trade results*. A list of entries and exits and the $P/L derived from each trade are shown.

That's it. There aren't any fancy charts involved—everything is presented in a tabular format. If you want to see indicator values, you simply print them out to the Shell. The PSB structure, just like IDLE, was kept as simple as possible. Let's learn some Python by looking at the different PSB modules.

Indicator.py

This module contains all of the indicators that are utilized in the PSB. Go under the **File** menu in the Shell and open **indicators.py**. Keep the Python Shell open and quickly accessible. There are two types of indicators in this file. Some are just simple function modules and some are a little more sophisticated and are programmed as a class structure. I said you would be exposed to procedural (functions) and object-oriented (classes) programming. Let's start slowly with a simple indicator function.

sAverage

```
def sAverage(prices,lookBack,curBar,offset):
    result = 0.0
    for index in range((curBar - offset) - (lookBack-1),
      curBar - offset +1):
        result = result + prices[index]
    result = result/float(lookBack)
    return result
```

This looks pretty palatable! All functions or, if you like, subprograms, use the key word **def** to let the interpreter know a function is about to be defined. The function has to have a name, and in this case it is **sAverage** (simple moving average). Remember how we called functions in AFL and VBA? You do it exactly the same way in Python. The list of arguments or parameters that are included in the parentheses after the function name are known as the formal argument list. These parameters are called formal because they're included in the function definition. Since we are using Python you don't need to employ function prototyping or forward declaration. In other words, you don't need to tell the interpreter the types of the arguments before-hand. The **sAverage** function requires four parameters:

- **prices.** This is a list of price data (open, high, low, close, volume, or open interest). In this application of Python, we will be using the word *list* instead of **array**, but know they mean basically the same thing. The Python **list** structure is very powerful as you will find out.
- **lookback.** The number of days in the calculation of the indicator. This would equate to 20 in a 20-day moving average.
- **curBar.** Simply the historic bar being evaluated.
- **offset.** Just like the ESB, this number will usually be set to one. The indicator value from the prior day. You can go offset with a more positive number. If you use two, then it will return the indicator value form two days prior.

Notice the colon (:) at the end of the function definition. The colon tells the interpreter that the indented code (four spaces) below is controlled by the current line. So everything that is indented below the function definition header is included in the function. Indentation is *very important* in Python. Don't use tabs to indent; simply hit the spacebar four times. Don't forget this—spacebar four times. Things will become much clearer very quickly.

In Python variables are assigned values with the equal sign (=). Equality between two variables is verified by using a double equal sign (==). Jump over to the Python Shell really quick. I hope you still have it close at hand. There might be a bunch of stuff in the window, so just scroll down to the very bottom until you find the >>> prompt. Once there type **a** = **5** and hit enter. Type **a** and hit enter. The number 5 should appear at the prompt. You have basically assigned 5 to the variable **a**. Now type **b** = **5** and hit enter. Type **a==b** and hit enter. The prompt should return with **True**. In this case **a** equals **b**. Type **a** != **b** and hit enter. The prompt will return with **False**, because **a** does equal **b**. You are asking if **a** doesn't equal **b** and the answer is **False** because it does. Remember to use == to test for equality and **!=** for inequality.

The next line of code is very important because you will see it often.

```
for index in range((curBar - offset) - (lookBack-1), curBar - offset +1):
```

This is an example of a definite loop; the number of repetitions is known ahead of time. This **for-loop** will iterate across the number of items in the range from ((curBar – offset) – (lookBack–1) to curBar – offset +1). This only looks complicated because of the variables in the **range** function. Here is a more simplified version of the Python for loop:

```
myList = list()

myList = [1,2,3,4]

for index in range(0,3):
    print(myList[index])
```

The output of this code will print only the first three elements in the list named **myList**. The function Range(0,3) returns 0, 1, and 2. The upper bound in the **Range** function is not inclusive. So to print out **myList** in its entirety, you must use Range(0,4). Referring back to the original bounds in our **Range** function, let's simplify by substituting some numbers for the values. Assume:

curBar = 500

offset = 1

lookback = 20

So, range ((500 – 1) – (20 –1), 500 – 1 + 1) equals range (499 – 19, 500). The loop will iterate from 480 to 499 because 500 isn't included. Since 480 is inclusive, the number of iterations turns out to be 20. Count on your fingers if you want to prove this starting at 480 and going to 499. The loop will start at yesterday if the offset is one and go back 20 days and sum up whatever data is in the list that is passed to the function. Once the loop completes, the summation is divided by the number of days in the calculation—the average of lookback days. This value is then returned to the calling program. That's all there is to this function. Sum up all requested values and divide by the number of requested values. The complicated part was deciphering the values in the **Range** function. Notice how the only line that was indented was **result = result + prices[index]**. This was because the **for-loop** was only controlling this one line of code. The rest of the lines were not under the influence of the **for-loop**. They were still indented in relationship to the **def** keyword and this was because the lines were encapsulated in the function body. Can you tell what these other functions are doing?

```
def highest(prices,lookBack,curBar,offset):
    result = 0.0
    maxVal = 0.00
    for index in range((curBar - offset) - (lookBack-1),
      curBar - offset + 1):
        if prices[index] > maxVal:
            maxVal = prices[index]
    result = maxVal
    return result

def lowest(prices,lookBack,curBar,offset):
    result = 0.0
    minVal = 9999999.0
    for index in range((curBar - offset) - (lookBack-1),
      curBar - offset + 1):
        if prices[index] < minVal:
            minVal = prices[index]
    result = minVal
    return result
```


If you guessed calculate the highest high and lowest low of lookback days, then give yourself a gold star. If not, just go back over the code until you get it. Notice the indentations and the use of the colon.

rsiClass That wasn't too bad now, was it? Are you ready to attack the indicators that are defined as a **class**? Let's take a close look at the RSI indicator:

```
class rsiClass(object):
    oldDelta1 = 0
    def __init__(self):
        self.delta1 = 0
        self.delta2 = 0
        self.rsi = 0
        self.seed = 0
    def calcRsi(self,prices,lookBack,curBar,offset):
        upSum = 0.0
        dnSum = 0.0
        if self.seed == 0:
            self.seed = 1
            for i in range((curBar - offset) - (lookBack-1),
              curBar - offset):
                if prices[i] > prices[i-1]:
                    diff1 = prices[i] - prices[i-1]
                    upSum += diff1
                if prices[i] < prices[i-1]:
                    diff2 = prices[i-1] - prices[i]
                    dnSum += diff2
                self.delta1 = upSum/lookBack
                self.delta2 = dnSum/lookBack
        else:
            if prices[curBar - offset] > prices
              [curBar - 1 - offset]:
                diff1 = prices[curBar - offset] - prices
                  [curBar - 1 - offset]
                upSum += diff1
            if prices[curBar - offset] < prices
              [curBar - 1 - offset]:
                diff2 = prices[curBar - 1 - offset] -
                  prices[curBar - offset]
                dnSum += diff2
            self.delta1 = (self.delta1 * (lookBack -1) +
              upSum) / lookBack
            self.delta2 = (self.delta2 * (lookBack -1) +
              dnSum) / lookBack
        if self.delta1 + self.delta2 != 0:
            self.rsi = (100.0 * self.delta1) /
              (self.delta1 + self.delta2)
        else:
            self.rsi = 0.0
        return (self.rsi)
```

This indicator is programmed as a **class** object. We have ventured over into the land of objected-oriented programming, but don't worry; we are just going to work in an introductory mode to get the job done. You are probably asking yourself, why didn't he just program the RSI as a function module? The quick answer is I wanted to encapsulate the data and functions in one block of code so I could cut down on using global variables.

The first time an RSI indicator is called, it uses a special calculation to seed the indicator value. Subsequent calls to the indicator utilize the seed value and a different set of calculations. So I had to know, within the indicator code, if it was the first time it was being called. Also, I needed to store the seed and prior values in the class for subsequent calculations.

By preceding the name of the class object with the keyword **class**, you are informing the interpreter that a class definition is about to be defined with the name that follows the ***class*** keyword. In this example, we are defining a class named **rsiClass**. The keyword **object** within parentheses follows the name of the class. This would be a great time to explain the difference between a class and an object. A class is a template and an object is an actual thing that reflects the class template. Think of it like this: A class is blueprint and an object is the house that is instantiated or created with the use of the blueprint. One blueprint can be used to create many houses. The following snippet of code informs the interpreter about data to be stored in the class:


```
def __init__(self):
    self.delta1 = 0
    self.delta2 = 0
    self.rsi = 0
    self.seed = 0
```

The bit of code, **def __init__(self):**, is the function name the object itself calls to set the initial values of the data variables (class members) when the class is instantiated. The key word **self** refers to the class itself. The keyword **init** must be preceded by two underscores and followed by two underscores. The keyword **self** must be followed by a period to access the different data encapsulated in the class. As you can see from the code, the variables **self.delta1**, **self.delta2**, **self.rsi**, and **self.seed** are all initially set to zero.

The next line of code should look familiar—it looks like the functions we discussed earlier in the chapter.

```
def calcRsi(self,prices,lookBack,curBar,offset):
```

The only difference in this function header is the word **self** in the argument list. Basically, when the function **calcRsi** is called, the first argument or parameter is going to be the class structure itself. The other arguments are: the data to be used in the calculations, the lookback period, the current bar, and the offset.

Take a close look at the following code snippet:

```
upSum = 0.0
dnSum = 0.0
if self.seed == 0:
    self.seed = 1
    for i in range((curBar - offset) - (lookBack-1),curBar - offset):
        if prices[i] > prices[i-1]:
            diff1 = prices[i] - prices[i-1]
            upSum += diff1
        if prices[i] < prices[i-1]:
            diff2 = prices[i-1] - prices[i]
            dnSum += diff2
        self.delta1 = upSum/lookBack
        self.delta2 = dnSum/lookBack
else:
```

The function starts out by setting the variables **upSum** and **dnSum** to zero. The next line of code utilizes the keyword **self** and accesses the value of seed through the dot (.) notation. If **self.seed** is equal to zero, then all the indented code below the **if** construct will be executed. If **self.seed** is equal to zero, the very first line of code sets **self.seed** to one. In doing so, these lines of code will only be executed the very first time the function is called. Notice the variables **upSum** and **dnSum** do not use the dot notation. These variables are not members of the class and are temporary. They do not need to be remembered from one function call to the next. By using the dot notation, you are setting the data member to a value that will be remembered from one call to the next. By the way, a function inside a class is called a method. This function/method calculates the initial RSI value by looping back in time and calculating, accumulating, and averaging the up and down sums. The **upSum** and **dnSum** averages are stored in the class data members, **self.delta1** and **self.delta2**, respectively. The next time this function is called, this portion of the function will be bypassed, but the data stored in the data members will be available for future use. The second part of the function:

```
else:
    if prices[curBar - offset] > prices[curBar - 1 - offset]:
        diff1 = prices[curBar - offset] - prices
         [curBar - 1 - offset]
        upSum += diff1
```

```
    if prices[curBar - offset] < prices[curBar - 1 - offset]:
        diff2 = prices[curBar - 1 - offset] - prices[curBar - offset]
        dnSum += diff2
    self.delta1 = (self.delta1 * (lookBack -1) + upSum) / lookBack
    self.delta2 = (self.delta2 * (lookBack -1) + dnSum) / lookBack
```

will be executed every time. **Self.delta1** and **self.delta2** are used and reassigned each time the function is called. You might be able to see that the Wilder's averaging method is being used to calculate the current RSI components:

$$upSumAvg_{today} = \frac{(upSumAvg_{yesterday} \ * 13 + upSum_{today})}{14}$$

The final snippet of code is executed every time and returns the RSI calculation.

```
if self.delta1 + self.delta2 != 0:
    self.rsi = (100.0 * self.delta1) / (self.delta1 + self.delta2)
else:
    self.rsi = 0.0
return (self.rsi)
```


Since the design of this class-based indicator is a little more involved than a regular run-of-the-mill function, you would expect the call routine to be more involved as well. This is the case, but it only requires one additional line of code. In the case of this RSI indicator, all you need to do is add the line of code to your program: **rsiStudy = rsiClass()**. You can instantiate the **rsiClass** by calling it like a function. Instantiation is the creation of a shell that follows the class template/plan. In this case, the class object is assigned to the **rsiStudy** variable. Once the class is assigned to a variable, you can access the data and methods of that class by using the name of the variable (object) and dot notation. Here is how you call the **calcRsi** method through the **rsiStudy** variable name: **rsiVal = rsiStudy.calcRsi (myClose, 10, curBar, i)**. That's all there is to using the RSI indicator.

Scroll through the rest of the indicators in **indicator.py** and familiarize yourself with them. You can add you own indicators by using one of the existing functions or indicator classes as a template. Just include the code in this file and import the name of the indicator in the main trading program.

SystemTester.py The main module that calls all the other modules is **SystemTester.py**. As I explained prior, you use this as a template to develop other trading algorithms. I usually open **SystemTester.py** and *save as* immediately. If I am working on a Donchian type of algorithm, I will use a name like **DonchianSys1.py**. Instead of listing the program in its entirety, let's break it up section by section.

Import Section

```
#--------------------------------------------------------------
#Import section - inlcude functions, classes, variabels
#form externam modules
#--------------------------------------------------------------
import csv
import tkinter as tk
import os.path
from getData import getData
from dataLists import myDate,myTime,myOpen,myHigh,myLow,
   myClose
from tradeClass import tradeInfo
from equityDataClass import equityClass
from trade import trade
from systemMarket import systemMarketClass
from portfolio import portfolioClass
from indicators import highest,lowest,rsiClass,stochClass,
   sAverage,bollingerBands
from systemAnalytics import calcSystemResults
from tkinter.filedialog import askopenfilenames
```

The hash sign (#) at the beginning of any text informs the interpreter to ignore whatever follows up to the end of the line. Use this symbol for comments in your Python code—just like we did with the single quote (') in VBA. You can also use it to temporarily hide a line of code from the interpreter. All of the external files and functions/classes are pulled into the main program by using the keywords **from** and **import**. This is similar to C's **include** statement—on the surface, anyway. For all intents and purposes, we will use it simply to import external code. The name of the external module follows **from** and the function/class name follows the **import** keyword. Look at the line that starts, **from indicators import ...** You will see a good portion of the indicator functions and classes that were defined in **indicator.py**.

Some of the imports are strictly Python related:

```
import csv
import tkinter as tk
import os.path
from tkinter.filedialog import askopenfilenames
```

All these files deal with opening and reading a comma-delimited file. The rest of the imported files all deal with the PSB.

Helper Functions for the PSB These functions help parse the **.csv** file into the individual **myDate**, **myHigh**, **myLow**, **myClose**, **myVol**, and **myOpInt** lists. The attributes of each data file, symbol, **pointValue**, and **minMove** are collected here as well. A function that calculates the results of exiting a trade is also located here. I won't bore you with the details of these functions right now, but I want to bring to your attention another really cool thing about Python. A Python function can return multiple values. The **exitPos** function returns three values: **profit**, **trades**, and **curShares**. When you call a multiple return function, make sure you have the correct number of variables on the left side of the assignment:

```
myProfit, myTrades, myCurShares = exitPos(price,myDate[i],
   "RevLongLiq",curShares)
```

The larger **exitPos** function was put here because it uses several global variables. These variables are shared among most of the functions in this file module. I didn't want to have to pass these variables back and forth within different function calls. I was slightly lazy in doing this, but it does help improve readability by reducing the number of different parameters included in the argument list.

```
#------------------------------------------------------------
  #Helper Functions local to this module
#------------------------------------------------------------
def getDataAtribs(dClass):
   return(dClass.bigPtVal,dClass.symbol,dClass.minMove)
def getDataLists(dClass):
   return(dClass.date,dClass.open,dClass.high,dClass.low,dClass.close)

def calcTodaysOTE(mp,myClose,entryPrice,entryQuant,myBPV):
    todaysOTE = 0
    for entries in range(0,len(entryPrice)):
        if mp >= 1:
            todaysOTE += (myClose - entryPrice[entries])
             *myBPV*entryQuant[entries]
        if mp <= -1:
           todaysOTE += (entryPrice[entries] - myClose)
             *myBPV*entryQuant[entries]
    return(todaysOTE)
```

```
def exitPos(myExitPrice,myExitDate,tempName,myCurShares):
    global mp,commission
    global tradeName,entryPrice,entryQuant,exitPrice,
      numShares,myBPV,cumuProfit
    if mp < 0:
        trades = tradeInfo('liqShort',myExitDate,tempName,
         myExitPrice,myCurShares,0)
        profit = trades.calcTradeProfit('liqShort',mp,
        entryPrice,myExitPrice,entryQuant,myCurShares) * myBPV
        profit = profit - myCurShares *commission
        trades.tradeProfit = profit
        cumuProfit += profit
        trades.cumuProfit = cumuProfit
    if mp > 0:
        trades = tradeInfo('liqLong',myExitDate,tempName,
         myExitPrice,myCurShares,0)
        profit = trades.calcTradeProfit('liqLong',mp,
        entryPrice,myExitPrice,entryQuant,myCurShares) * myBPV
        trades.tradeProfit = profit
        profit = profit - myCurShares * commission
        cumuProfit += profit
        trades.cumuProfit = cumuProfit
    curShares = 0
    for remShares in range(0,len(entryQuant)):
       curShares += entryQuant[remShares]
    return (profit,trades,curShares)
#----------------------------------------------------------------
  #End of functions
#----------------------------------------------------------------
```


Lists and Variables Initiation You can use this section to initialize your own lists and variables. These lines of code are pretty cool.

```
#----------------------------------------------------------------
 #Lists and variables are defined and initialized here
#----------------------------------------------------------------
alist, blist, clist, dlist, elist = ([] for i in range(5))
marketPosition,listOfTrades,trueRanges,ranges =
   ([] for i in range(4))
dataClassList,systemMarketList,equityDataList =
   ([] for i in range(3))
```

```
entryPrice,fileList,entryPrice,entryQuant,exitQuant =
   ([] for i in range(5))
#exitPrice = list()
currentPrice,totComms,barsSinceEntry = 0
numRuns,myBPV,allowPyra,curShares = 0
#--------------------------------------------------------------
 #End of Lists and Variables
#--------------------------------------------------------------
```

```
alist, blist, clist, dlist, elist = ([] for i in range(5))
```

The first line of code creates five different lists using an implicit **for loop**, a one-liner **for loop**. You are probably starting to see the magic of Python.

Data Import and Configuration and Portfolio Setup The list of data class objects are assigned whatever is returned by the function **getData()**. When the PSB is launched, one of the first things it asks the user is to pick some data (commodity, equities, or index prices). The **getData** function handles the creation of an **Open File** dialog, the selection of data files, and determining the market specifications for each file selected. The following is the complete listing of the function's source broken down into easily explainable components.


```
#--------------------------------------------------------------
  #Get the raw data and its associated attributes
    [pointvalue,symbol,tickvalue]
  #Read a csv file that has at least D,O,H,L,C - V and OpInt
    are optional
  #Set up a portfolio of multiple markets
#--------------------------------------------------------------

dataClassList = getData()
numMarkets = len(dataClassList)
portfolio = portfolioClass()


import csv
import tkinter as tk
import os.path
from marketDataClass import marketDataClass
from dataMasterLists import commName, bigPtVal, minMove
from tkinter.filedialog import askopenfilenames
from equityDataClass import equityClassdataClassList = list()

fileName = "c:\PBS\dataMaster.csv"
```

```
def getData():
    totComms = 0
    with open(fileName) as f:
        f_csv = csv.reader(f)
        for row in f_csv:
            commName.append(row[0])
            bigPtVal.append(float(row[1]))
            minMove.append(float(row[2]))
            totComms = totComms + 1
    f.close
```

The function starts out by opening the file C:\PBS\dataMaster.csv and reading its contents into three different lists: **commName**, **bigPtVal**, and **minMove**. Here is a quick snapshot of the contents of this file:

```
"AD",100000,0.0001
"BP",125000,0.0001
"CL",1000,0.01
"C2",50,0.25
"CC",10,1
"CD",100000,0.0001
"CL",1000,0.01
"CT",500,0.01
"CU",125000,0.0001
"DX",1000,0.005
"ED",2500,0.005
"EM",100,0.1
"FC",500,0.025
"FV",1000,0.0078
"GC",100,0.1
"HG",250,0.05
"HO",42000,0.0001
"JY",125000,0.00005
```

As you can see, the data are separated by commas, and there are three data values per line. The first data value is the string (enclosed in quotes) that will be assigned to **commName**. The second is the value of a big point move (a single increment of the number right before the decimal point (British pound is quoted as 1.5631, so a move from 1.5631 to 2.5631 would equate to $125,000), and the third is the minimum move of the market. The minimum move in stocks is 0.01 or one penny. In the British pound, it is 0.0001. Just like the ESB, the PSB needs to know this information ahead of time so it can properly calculate price-based values and perform accurate trade accounting. This file is easily editable and you can customize it to fit your own data and its format.

Python has a ton of reusable code and helper modules. This little bit of code relies on the built-in **csv.Reader**. If you noticed the dot notation, then you realize that **csv** is class and **.Reader** is a method from that class. Before using the csv class, it had to be imported. If you look back at the source code, you will see it is the first module to be imported. After the file is opened using `with open(fileName) as f:` , the file pointer (f) is passed to the **csv.Reader** method. The **f_csv** is then utilized to read each row of data in the file. The columns in each row are demarked by using a subscript. So row[0] is the commName, row[1] is the big point value, and row[2] is the minimum move. Since we are inside a definite **for loop**, the loops ends when the last row of data is read. Once the loop has terminated, the file is closed. These six or seven lines of code open the file, loop through each row of data, read the data into predefined lists, and then close the file. Pretty simple and concise!

This next snippet of code does a lot and is a little more sophisticated, so only the most important parts will be discussed.

```
root = tk.Tk()
root.withdraw()
cnt = 0
files = askopenfilenames(filetypes=(('CSV files', '*.txt'),
                                    ('All files', '*.*')),
                                    title='Select Markets To Test')
fileList = root.tk.splitlist(files)
fileListLen = len(fileList)
for marketCnt in range(0,fileListLen):
    head,tail = os.path.split(fileList[marketCnt])
    tempStr = tail[0:2]
    for i in range(totComms):
        if tempStr == commName[i]:
            commIndex = i
    newDataClass = marketDataClass()
    newDataClass.setDataAttributes(commName[commIndex],
        bigPtVal[commIndex],minMove[commIndex])
    with open(fileList[marketCnt]) as f:
        f_csv = csv.reader(f)
        for row in f_csv:
            newDataClass.readData(int(row[0]),float(row[1]),
            float(row[2]),float(row[3]), float(row[4]),
             0.0,0.0)
            cnt = cnt + 1
    dataClassList.append(newDataClass)
    f.close
return(dataClassList)
```

The single line of code:

```
files = askopenfilenames(filetypes=(('CSV files', '*.txt'),
                                    ('All files', '*.*')),
                                    title='Select Markets To Test')
```

opens an OS-independent **File Open Dialog** labeled **Select Markets To Test** and asks the operating system to list all files with a .CSV extension in that particular location. Once the user selects one or more files, the selection is passed back and stored in the variable **files**.

```
fileList = root.tk.splitlist(files)
```

The files are then listed separately and stored in a list named **fileList**. This is all handled with the built-in method **root.tk.splitlist(files)**. This method takes all of the files the user selected and then splits them apart and stores the individual file names in a list.

```
head,tail = os.path.split(fileList[marketCnt])
tempStr = tail[0:2]
for i in range(totComms):
    if tempStr == commName[i]:
        commIndex = i
```

Another OS method **os.path.split** takes the name of each individual file and splits the path name (**C:\myPath\Data**) and the actual filename apart (**BP.CSV**). The **head** variable is assigned the pathname and the **tail** variable the filename. Once the filename is separated the first two letters in the filename can be accessed by simply indexing into the string: **tempStr = tail[0:2]**. The first two characters in the filename represent the **symbol** that was selected. From this the **symbol** can be cross-referenced in the **DataMaster** and the market name, big point value, and minimum move can be attached to the symbol.

```
newDataClass = marketDataClass()
newDataClass.setDataAttributes(commName[commIndex],
   bigPtVal[commIndex],minMove[commIndex])
```

As soon as the filename is cross referenced with **DataMaster**, a **marketDataClass** object with the variable name **newDataClass** is instantiated by calling the **marketDataClass()** method. The **marketDataClass** class looks like this:

```
class marketDataClass(object):
    def __init__(self):
        self.symbol = ""
        self.minMove = 0
        self.bigPtVal = 0
        self.seed = 0
        self.date = list()
        self.open = list()
        self.high = list()
        self.low = list()
        self.close = list()
        self.volume = list()
        self.opInt = list()
        self.dataPoints = 0
    def setDataAttributes(self,symbol,bigPtVal,minMove):
        self.symbol = symbol
        self.minMove = minMove
        self.bigPtVal = bigPtVal
    def readData(self,date,open,high,low,close,volume,opInt):
        self.date.append(date)
        self.open.append(open)
        self.high.append(high)
        self.low.append(low)
        self.close.append(close)
        self.volume.append(volume)
        self.opInt.append(opInt)
        self.dataPoints += 1
```


This class acts like a container that holds all of the price data and market attributes for each file selected by the user. It also contains the methods for gathering that data. The **init** method creates all of the storage needed to handle years and years of data. Other than the single variables **self.symbol**, **self.minMove**, **self.bigPtVal**, the rest of the data holders are lists. Each list is capable of holding tremendous amounts of data. The other two methods, **setDataAttributes** and **readData**, are used to set the market specifications and fill up the lists with price data. Notice Python uses the **.append** method to add values to an existing list. Lists act like arrays, but are much more powerful due to their associated methods. If I want to know the number of elements in a list, all I have to do is: **listLen = len(myList)**. **Len()** is simply a method of the **list** class.

Now keep in mind all of this code is inside a **for loop**. The number of loops is determined by the number of markets selected by the user. If the user selected five files, then this loop would be performed five times. You would have five instantiations of the **marketDataClass** objects, and each would be used to set the market specifications for the five markets and read in the different price data from the five different files. A total of five different objects would be spawned to handle all of the data. The best way to keep these classe objects together would be to put them in a **list**. I bet you knew a **list** can contain primitive data types like numbers, strings, letters, and Booleans. But, I bet you didn't know a list can contain complex data structures like our **marketDataClass**. Jump over the Python Shell and type the following:

```
>>> a = list()
>>> a = ["apple","banana","strawberry"]
>>> a
```

When you hit enter after the last line, the Shell will display:

['apple', 'banana', 'strawberry']

No surprise here, it basically repeated what we put into the list. Now type this:

```
>>>b = list()
>>> b = ["pineapple","coconut","mango"]
c = list()
>>> c.append(a)
>>> c.append(b)
>>> c
```

and hit return. The Shell shows:

[['apple', 'banana', 'strawberry'], ['pineapple', 'coconut', 'mango']]

You have a list that contains two other lists. Notice the grouping? ['apple', 'banana', 'strawberry'] is the **a** list and ['pineapple', 'coconut', 'mango'] is the **b** list.

This line of code, `dataClassList.append(newDataClass)` inserts the individual **marketDataClasse object** in the **dataClassList list**. This list will be accessible to the rest of the program later on.

Getting back to:

```
dataClassList = getData()
numMarkets = len(dataClassList)
portfolio = portfolioClass()
```

The first simple line of code does quite a bit. The next line starting with numMarkets gets the length of the list that contains all the **marketDataClass** objects. In other words, it returns the number of **marketDataClass** objects, which is the number of markets selected by the user. The next line of code instantiates a **portfolioClass** objectd labeled **portfolio**. The **portfolioClass** is quite large, so I won't regurgitate it here. I will in the appendices. There are some very important and cool things going on in this class, so I want to highlight those very quickly. But before we do, that there are two important class structures that are a prerequisite to the

portfolioClass. These classes are named **equityClass** and **marketSystemClass**. The **equityClass** is used to store the daily equity for each individual market. A new **equityClass** object is instantiated for each different market in the market list. Here's what the data containers in the **equityClass** class look like:

```
def __init__(self):
    self.equityDate = list()
    self.equityItm = list()
    self.clsTrdEquity = list()
    self.openTrdEquity = list()
    self.cumuClsEquity = 0
    self.dailyEquityVal = list()
    self.peakEquity = 0
    self.minEquity = 0
    self.maxDD = 0
```

After you open a trading account and start trading something happens every day to your account. It either stays flat, goes up, or goes down. These daily fluctuations are caused by the P/L from a closed trade or the change in market value of an open trade. Cumulative equity reflects the growth of your account. This **equityClass** keeps track of P/L from closed trades, change in daily open trade equity, and the cumulative equity for any given time period. If you buy Apple today at $100 a share and buy just one share, then today's equity simply reflects the difference between the closing price and $100. Let's pretend Apple closed at $105, so your closed trade equity is equal to zero, but your open trade equity (OTE) is $5. Today's equity in your account is $5. Let's pretend a little further and say Apple moves up to $110, and you decide to cover your long position. Today's equity is derived from a closed trade profit of $10. Since there is no open position, then there is no OTE. Tracking your two-day performance, you show daily equity of $5 for yesterday and $10 for today. Your cumulative equity stands at $10. Feeling a little more bullish, you buy Apple again on the third day at $112, but unfortunately, some bad news comes out of China and the stock drops back to $105. So today's equity reflects the cumulative closed out equity $10 and today's OTE that stands at −$7. Your cumulative equity drops by $7 and now stands at $3. The next day Apple drops further and you start feeling bearish so you sell short at $100. Unfortunately, China states their GDP is growing a little faster than the analysts predicted and Apple rebounds and closes at $110. What is your cumulative equity now?

$$\text{Day } 1 : \text{Cum.E } (\$5) = \text{Cum.Cls.TE } (0) + \text{OpenTE } (5)$$

$$\text{Day } 2 : \text{Cum.E } (\$10) = \text{Cum.Cls.TE } (10) + \text{OpenTE } (0)$$

$$\text{Day } 3 : \text{Cum.E } (\$3) = \text{Cum.Cls.TE}(10) + \text{OpenTE}(-7)$$

$$\text{Day } 4 : \text{Cum.E } (-\$12) = \text{Cum.Cls.TE}(-2) + \text{OpenTE}(-10)$$

The one trade that you took on Day 4 was a disaster. First off, you closed out a $12 loser ($112 − $100), and to add insult to injury your OTE is −$10 ($100 − $110). You real cumulative losses stand at −$2 and your paper loss stands at −$10. All these values are needed to calculate a daily equity stream and that is why we have: **self.cls TrdEquity**, **self.openTrdEquity**, **self.cumuClsEquity**. The rest of the module keeps track of the daily equity stream as well as the maximum equity peak, and the subsequent equity valley. From these values the worst-case drawdown can be derived.

```
def setEquityInfo(self,equityDate,equityItm,clsTrdEquity,
    openTrdEquity):
      self.equityDate.append(equityDate)
      self.equityItm.append(equityItm)
      self.cumuClsEquity += clsTrdEquity
      tempEqu =self.cumuClsEquity+openTrdEquity
      self.dailyEquityVal.append(tempEqu)
      self.peakEquity = max(self.peakEquity,tempEqu)
      maxEqu = self.peakEquity
      self.minEquity = min(self.minEquity,tempEqu)
      minEqu = self.minEquity
      self.maxDD = max(self.maxDD,maxEqu-tempEqu)
      maxDD = self.maxDD
      maxDD = maxDD
```

The next class, **systemMarketClass**, is used to keep track of each system on each individual market. I did this in case a future version of PSB might combine multiple markets on multiple systems. You could have a bunch of these **systemMarketClass** objects reflecting the performance on several system/markets; you then could combine certain ones to produce a very efficient equity curve. For right now, though, these class objects contain the following data:

```
def __init__(self):
      self.systemName = ""
      self.symbol = ""
      self.tradesList =list()
      self.equity = equityClass
      self.avgWin = 0
      self.avgLoss = 0
      self.avgTrade = 0
      self.profitLoss = 0
      self.numTrades = 0
      self.maxxDD = 0
      self.perWins = 0
```

Each **systemMarketClass** contains the name of the system and the symbol. In addition, it stores a list of trades, the equity stream, the average win, loss, and trade, percent wins, number of trades, and maximum drawdown. The methods in this class set the pertinent data, such as system name and symbol, and calculate all the performance metrics.

```
def setSysMarkInfo(self,sysName,symbol,trades,equity):
    self.systemName = sysName
    self.symbol = symbol
    self.tradesList = list(trades)
    self.equity = equity
    temp1 = 0
    temp2 = 0
    temp3 = 0
    temp4 = 0
    temp5 = 0
    temp6 = 0
    temp7 = 0
    numTrades = 0
    for i in range(0,len(self.equity.dailyEquityVal)):
        temp5 = self.equity.dailyEquityVal[i]
        temp6 = max(temp6,temp5)
        temp7 = max(temp7,temp6-temp5)
        self.maxxDD = temp7
    for i in range(0,len(self.tradesList)):
        if self.tradesList[i].entryOrExit == 1:
            numTrades += 1
        if self.tradesList[i].tradeProfit > 0:
            temp1 += self.tradesList[i].tradeProfit
            temp2 += 1
        if self.tradesList[i].tradeProfit < 0:
            temp3 += self.tradesList[i].tradeProfit
            temp4 += 1
    if temp2 != 0: self.avgWin = temp1/temp2
    if temp4 != 0: self.avgLoss = temp3/temp4
    if numTrades != 0: self.avgTrade = temp5/numTrades
    self.numTrades = numTrades
    self.profitLoss = temp5
    if numTrades != 0: self.perWins = temp2 / numTrades
```

The **setSysMarkInfo** method is the only method in this class, but it does a bunch of work. Notice about halfway through the variables with **temp** in their name; these are temporary holders for data that is not stored in the class. They are born when the method is called and die when the method exits. They are not members of the class. The **portfolio** class is similar to the **systemMarketClass**, but is much more macroscopic in nature. Basically, it sits on top of **systemMarketClass** and stores aggregate information concerning the multiple markets in the portfolio.

```
class portfolioClass(object):
    def __init__(self):
        self.portfolioName = ""
        self.systemMarkets = list()
        self.portEquityDate = list()
        self.portEquityVal = list()
        self.portclsTrdEquity = list()
        self.portDailyEquityVal = list()
        self.portPeakEquity = 0
        self.portMinEquity = 0
        self.portMaxDD = 0
        tempEqu = 0
        cumEqu = 0
        maxEqu = -999999999
        minEqu = 999999999
        maxDD = 0
```

As you know, a portfolio is simply a collection of different markets. A portfolio has to have a name, a list of the different **systemMarkets** or just markets, and lists that make up **equityDate**, **equityVal**, **clsTrdEquity**, and **dailyEquity** at the portfolio level. The methods involved with this class are rather long and for brevity's sake will not be displayed here. All classes including their methods will be listed in the appendix. There are a couple of Pythonesque list features I would like to discuss, because they are so cool. If you have traded commodities or futures, you know some days one market is open and another closed. Creating a master date list to contain the daily portfolio equity had to take this into consideration. The use of Python's lists made creating a master date list that included all the dates of the entire portfolio very easy. I simply concatenated (added together) all of the different date, not data, streams from each **systemMarket**.


```
for i in range(0,len(self.systemMarkets)):
    masterDateList += self.systemMarkets[i].equity.equityDate
```

This loop starts at 0 and loops through all the **systemMarkets**. If you have five markets in your portfolio, then the loop would start at 0 and end at 4. You will notice the **+=** operand after **masterDateList** in the code. This is a shortcut like **a = a + 1**. Using this operand eliminates repeating the variable name after the equal sign. If you want to see how this works, jump over to the Python Shell and type this:

```
>>> a = list()
>>> a = [1,2,3,4,6,7,8,9]
>>> b = list()
>>> b = [1,2,3,4,5,6,7,8,10]
```

```
>>> c = a + b
>>> c
```

After you hit enter following the last c you will be presented with this:

[1, 2, 3, 4, 6, 7, 8, 9, 1, 2, 3, 4, 5, 6, 7, 8, 10]

This is simply a concatenation of the two lists. It includes all values from both lists. Now type this:

```
>>> c.sort()
>>> c
```

Hit enter after the last c, and the list is now sorted and stored back in the original list.

[1, 1, 2, 2, 3, 3, 4, 4, 5, 6, 6, 7, 7, 8, 8, 9, 10]

This is how I created a master data list that included all the dates in the different equity streams from each market. I then used a **removeDuplicates** function to remove the duplicate list entries. The other cool thing in this class is this snippet of code:

```
def createMonthList(li):
    myMonthList = list()
    for i in range(0,len(li)):
        if i != 0:
            tempa = int(li[i]/100)
            pMonth = int(li[i-1]/100) % 100
            month = int(li[i]/100) % 100
            if pMonth != month:
                myMonthList.append(li[i-1])
            if i == len(li)-1:
                myMonthList.append(li[i])
    return myMonthList
```

This code takes a large list of dates and extracts the beginning date of each month in that list, and then creates a list with just the different months. This is how I was able to create a monthly breakdown of the time period used in the testing of the system.

```
20110930      2249      2249
20111031     -2545      -296
20111130         0      -296
20111230      -913     -1209
20120131         0     -1209
20120229         0     -1209
20120330         0     -1209
20120430      -120     -1329
```

```
20120531          921        -408
20120629        -1735       -2143
20120731          955       -1188
```

One last bit of code that shows off the power of Python follows. After this, I will demonstrate how to pull all this together and test a trading algorithm.

```
for i in range(0,len(masterDateList)):
    cumuVal = 0
    for j in range(0,len(self.systemMarkets)):
        skipDay = 0
        try:
            idx = self.systemMarkets[j].equity.equityDate.
              index(masterDateList[i])
        except ValueError:
            skipDay = 1
        if skipDay == 0:
            cumuVal += self.systemMarkets[j].equity.
              dailyEquityVal[idx]
        combinedEquity.append(cumuVal)
```


This snippet of code is important because two very important concepts are covered. If you review the code, you will see the keyword **try**: The code controlled by **try** is simply finding if and where the last day of a month is located in a **systemMarket's equityDate** stream. Let's say we are trying to see if July 31, 2012, is in an **equityDate** list. If it is, then the variable **idx** returns the location in the list. If it's not located in the list, then an error is returned. This is where **except** comes into play. The code controlled by **except** is only executed if the method **index** returns an error. Back to the Python Shell!

Type the following and hit enter after the last line:

```
>>> a = list()
>>> a = [100,300,200,800]
>>> a.index(300)
1
```

This example returns the location of the number 300 in the **a** list. Remember Python is zero based. The first element is number 0.

Getting Down to Business

Okay, we now have somewhat of an understanding of how the PSB works. I designed it to be like one of those calculators or watches that is encased in see-through plastic. Everything is there if you just look for it. However, just like the watch or calculator, you don't need to know exactly how one works to use it. This software allows the users to do whatever they want, including looking into the future, so be careful. Our first test is going to be the ol' Bollinger Band algorithm.

```
    for i in range(len(myDate) - numBarsToGoBack,len(myDate)):
        equItm += 1
        tempDate = myDate[i]
        todaysCTE = todaysOTE = todaysEquity = 0
        marketPosition[i] = marketPosition[i-1]
        mp = marketPosition[i]
        buyLevel,shortLevel,exitLevel = bollingerBands
         (myDate,myClose,60,2,i,1)
        print(tempDate," avg ",exitLevel," ",buyLevel - exitLevel)
        atrVal = sAverage(trueRanges,10,i,0)
        rsiVal = rsiStudy.calcRsi(myClose,10,i,0)
        stopAmt = 3000/myBPV
#        print(myDate[i],"rsi ",rsiVal," atrVal ",
          atrVal*myBPV," ",myBPV)
#        fastKVal,fastDVal,slowDVal = stochStudy.
#                                     calcStochastic(3,9,9,myHigh,
                                      myLow,myClose,i,1)

#        if (mp > 0 and maxPositionL < 3) : maxPositionL = mp
#        if (mp < 0 and maxPositionS < 3) : maxPositionS = mp


 #Long Entry Logic - Bolloinger
        if (mp == 0 or mp == -1)  and myHigh[i] >= buyLevel:
            profit = 0
            price = max(myOpen[i],buyLevel)
            if mp <= -1:
                profit,trades,curShares = exitPos(price,
                 myDate[i],"RevShrtLiq",curShares)
                listOfTrades.append(trades)
                mp = 0
                todaysCTE = profit
            tradeName = "Boll Buy"
            mp += 1
            marketPosition[i] = mp
            numShares = 1
            entryPrice.append(price)
            entryQuant.append(numShares)
            curShares = curShares + numShares
```

```
            trades = tradeInfo('buy',myDate[i],tradeName,
              entryPrice[-1],numShares,1)
            barsSinceEntry = 1
            totProfit += profit
            listOfTrades.append(trades)
#Long Exit - Loss
        if mp >= 1 and myLow[i] <= entryPrice[-1] - stopAmt
          and barsSinceEntry > 1:
            price = min(myOpen[i],entryPrice[-1] - stopAmt)
            tradeName = "L-MMLoss"
            exitDate =myDate[i]
            numShares = curShares
            exitQuant.append(numShares)
            profit,trades,curShares = exitPos(price,
              myDate[i],tradeName,numShares)
            if curShares == 0 : mp = marketPosition[i] = 0
            totProfit += profit
            todaysCTE = profit
            listOfTrades.append(trades)
            maxPositionL = maxPositionL - 1
# Long Exit - Bollinger Based
        if mp >= 1 and myLow[i] <= exitLevel:
            price = min(myOpen[i],exitLevel)
            tradeName = "L-BollExit"
            numShares = curShares
            exitQuant.append(numShares)
            profit,trades,curShares = exitPos(price,
              myDate[i],tradeName,numShares)
            if curShares == 0 : mp = marketPosition[i] = 0
            totProfit += profit
            todaysCTE = profit
            listOfTrades.append(trades)
            maxPositionL = maxPositionL -1
```


This is just the code for long entries and exits, and I must admit it looks a little bit ugly. Like I mentioned earlier, everything is exposed and the user has to do a little more of the programming that is taken care of behind the scenes with software such as AmiBroker and TradeStation. However, if you can program in the PSB, you can program anywhere.

The first thing we need to calculate is the Bollinger Bands. We are going to buy on a stop when the high of the day exceeds a 60-day two-deviation upper band.

Shorting occurs when the low of the day exceeds a 60-day two-deviation lower band. This line of code provides exactly what we need.

```
buyLevel,shortLevel,exitLevel = bollingerBands(myDate,
   myClose,60,2,i,1)
```

Prior to actually programming your algorithm, it is important to know how your algorithm enters trades: on a stop, market, or on a limit. Unlike AmiBroker, the ESB, or TradeStation, it is up to the user to program the different **if** constructs that pertain to the different types of orders. Don't worry; it's not nearly as complicated as it sounds. The **buyLevel**, **shortLevel**, and **exitLevel** are all calculated by the **BollingerBands** function. This algorithm also utilizes a $3,000 protective stop. Prepared with this information we are now ready to enter battle. With the PSB you must determine if the daily market action met the requirements for trade entry and/or exit. In other words, you have to test the bar's extreme prices to see if an entry or exit level was exceeded. You might want to follow along in the code box as you read the following instructions. First, I have to make sure I am not already in a long position (**mp**—market position not equal to 1), and then I look at today's high; I am peeking into the future here, to see if the market would have exceeded or equaled the **buyLevel**. If it did, then I know I should have entered a long position. With this method of backtesting, you tell the computer a trade has taken place. In other platforms, the computer tells you a trade has taken place. Once you determine a trade should have been executed, you only need to change a little bit of code in the Long Entry Logic. The code that needs to be changed is bolded in the following code listing.

```
if (mp != 1) and myHigh[i] >= buyLevel:
    profit = 0
    price = max(myOpen[i],buyLevel)
    if mp <= -1:
        profit,trades,curShares = exitPos(price,myDate[i],
         "RevShrtLiq",curShares)
        listOfTrades.append(trades)
        mp = 0
        todaysCTE = profit
    tradeName = "Boll Buy"
    mp += 1
    marketPosition[i] = mp
    numShares = 1
    entryPrice.append(price)
    entryQuant.append(numShares)
    curShares = curShares + numShares
```

```
trades = tradeInfo('buy',myDate[i],tradeName,
  entryPrice[-1],numShares,1)
barsSinceEntry = 1
totProfit += profit
listOfTrades.append(trades)
```

That's all the code you have to concern yourself with. There is a lot of code, but most off it stays the same from one algorithm to the next.

In the case of this system, all entries and exits are executed as stop orders. Since we are dealing with stops, we must test the **myHigh[i] (today's high)** against the **buyLevel**. If the high of the day is greater than or equal to our buy stop, then we can safely assume the order was filled. Did the market gap above our buyLevel—you must test for this as well. The code is already in place: **price = max(myOpen[i], buyLevel)**. If the market did indeed gap above our **buyLevel**, then the fill price is moved to the open of the day. This line of code is only necessary if a gap open could impact the fill price on a stop order. The only other thing you need to change is the **tradeName** variable. In this case, we change the name inside the quotes to **Boll Buy**. That's all you have to change in the code. The rest of the code is for internal use only. If IDLE had a collapsible text feature, I would just collapse this down so you wouldn't have to see it. You can edit your Python code in a more sophisticated text editor such as NotePad ++ (https://notepad-plus-plus.org/). Figure 6.1 demonstrates the collapsible text feature.

We would all agree this is a much cleaner interface. NotePad ++ is available for download for a small donation. The reason I didn't use NotePad++ in this book is because it is not exactly easy to integrate into IDLE and I wanted to keep things as simple as possible.

```
#Long Entry Logic
        if (mp == 0 or mp == -1)  and myHigh[i] >= buyLevel:
            price = max(myOpen[i],buyLevel)
            tradeName = "Boll Buy"
#Long Exit - Loss
        if mp >= 1 and myLow[i] < entryPrice[-1] - stopAmt and barsSinceEntry > 1:
            price = min(myOpen[i],entryPrice[-1] - stopAmt)
            tradeName = "L-MMLoss"
#Long Exit - Time Based
        if mp >= 1 and myClose[i] < entryPrice[-1] and barsSinceEntry >= 10:
            price = myClose[i]
            tradeName = "L-TimeExit"
```

FIGURE 6.1 NotePad++'s collapsible text feature.

That was the long entry logic only and now we must program the two exits associated with this algorithm: a money management stop and a moving average stop. Here is the money management stop logic:

```
if mp >= 1 and myLow[i] <= entryPrice[-1] - stopAmt and
  barsSinceEntry > 1:
    price = min(myOpen[i],entryPrice[-1] - stopAmt)
    tradeName = "L-MMLoss"
    exitDate =myDate[i]
    numShares = curShares
    exitQuant.append(numShares)
    profit,trades,curShares = exitPos(price,myDate[i],
      tradeName,numShares)
    if curShares == 0 : mp = marketPosition[i] = 0
    totProfit += profit
    todaysCTE = profit
    listOfTrades.append(trades)
    maxPositionL = maxPositionL - 1
```

If **mp** >= 1, then the algorithm's current position is long. You could state **if mp ==** 1, but this software has the capability of pyramiding and scaling in and out. So just always use >= to test for a long or short position. Since we are exiting on stops, the low of the day is tested against the **entryPrice - stopAmt** ($3,000). In Python the last element in a **list** can be easily accessed by using a **-1** inside the brackets. **EntryPrice[-1]** simply refers to the last price in the **entryPrice** list, which turns out to be the price at which the algorithm assumed a long position. I have put a small **i** in the **entryPrice** list more times than I would like to admit, and this definitely will throw a monkey wrench into the works. So don't do it. If the low of the day is less than or equal to **entryPrice - stopAmt**, then an exit has taken place and all you need to do is set the **price** and the **tradeName**. The rest of the code in the block runs in the background. **BarsSinceEntry** is an internal variable that keeps track of the number of bars since the last entry, and is used in this logic to make sure an entry and an exit doesn't occur on the same bar. This version of the PSB doesn't allow more than one entry per bar. Getting out on a stop at the midpoint between the upper and lower bands is handled in the same manner. The only difference is the **price** and the **tradeName** variables.

```
if mp >= 1 and myLow[i] <= exitLevel:
    price = min(myOpen[i], exitLevel)
    tradeName = "L-BollExit"
    numShares = curShares
```

```
exitQuant.append(numShares)
profit,trades,curShares = exitPos(price,myDate[i],
  tradeName,numShares)
if curShares == 0 : mp = marketPosition[i] = 0
totProfit += profit
todaysCTE = profit
listOfTrades.append(trades)
maxPositionL = maxPositionL -1
```

Unless you are adding a new indicator to the indicator.py file, this is the only file you will ever need to modify. Once you make your changes, all you need to do to run your algorithm is go under the **Run** menu and select **Check Module**. If everything checks out, then you go under the **Run** menu once again and select **Run Module**.

I guarantee that you will get some type of syntax error or run-time error every time you create a new trading algorithm module. This is a good learning experience, as IDLE will point out the offending line of code. Figure 6.2 is an example of a syntax error message dialog and Figure 6.3 shows the offending line. You will see this until you stop forgetting the difference between the assignment operator (=) and the comparison operator (==).

Another easy thing to forget is using parentheses ( ) when you really want to use square brackets [ ]. If you do make this mistake you will see the error message shown in Figure 6.4.

This is a run-time error because it will pass the **Check Module**. However, when you run the module, it will pop this error message into the Python Shell. The

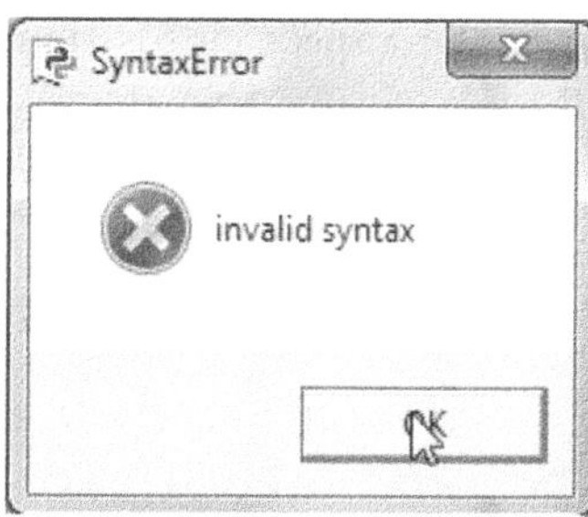

FIGURE 6.2 A Python syntax error message.

```
#Long Entry Logic
        if (mp = 0 or mp = -1)  and myHigh[i] >= buyLevel:
            profit = 0
```

FIGURE 6.3 In this case, the syntax error was the result of confusion between the assignment operator (=) and the comparison operator (==). Python highlights the problematic code.

```
Traceback (most recent call last):
  File "C:\PythonBackTester\Bollinger60.py", line 173, in <module>
    if (mp == 0 or mp == -1)  and myHigh(i) >= buyLevel:
TypeError: 'list' object is not callable
>>>
```

FIGURE 6.4 A Python run-time error resulting from using parentheses instead of square brackets.

good thing is it tells the offending module and line number. Unfortunately, Python doesn't use line numbers, but if you go up under the **Edit** menu in the offending module and select **Go To Line**, a small dialog will open and you can plug in the line number and it will take you to the offending line.

Similar to any testing platform or programming language, the more you use it, the better you will become. Here are a couple more algorithms in the PSB that utilize market and limit orders.

If you are entering on the close, then you do not need to use a 1 offset in your indicator calculations. Basically, you are calculating the indicator at the close and executing at the close—in real time this is somewhat difficult, but if you want to test it, you can. Here is a dual moving average crossover algorithm in the PSB. For brevity's sake, only the important code snippets were included.


```
        avg1 = sAverage(myClose,19,i,0)
        avg2 = sAverage(myClose,39,i,0)
        print(myDate[i],"avg1 ",avg1," avg2 ",avg2)
```

Notice how a 0 is used as the offset—I want to use today's data in the calculation. Since we don't have graphing capabilities, you can print right out to the Python Shell using the keyword print. Basically, put everything you want printed out in a list separated by a string or a space enclosed in quotation marks and a comma. This print statement will print out the date, the word avg1, the value of avg1, the word avg2, and the value of valu2. Here's what the printout looks like.

```
20150429 avg1  57.15842105263158  avg2  54.38384615384615
```

```
#Long Entry Logic
if (mp != 1) and avg1 > avg2:
    profit = 0
    price = myClose[i]
----------------
----------------
#Long Exit - Loss
```

```
if mp >= 1 and myClose[i] < entryPrice[-1] - stopAmt and
   barsSinceEntry > 1:
              price = myClose[i]


# Short Logic
if (mp !=-1) and avg1 < avg2:
    profit = 0
    price = myClose[i]
----------------
----------------
# Short Exit Loss
        if mp <= -1 and myClose[i] >= entryPrice[-1] +
          stopAmt and barsSinceEntry > 1:
              price = myClose[i]
```

The only problem with this logic is that the system gets right back in the next bar after a money management exit if the moving averages are still aligned. Other testing software might get right back in at the same price it exits if the software allows multiple entries on a single bar. If you want to force a new crossover, then just add these lines:

```
prevAvg1 = sAverage(myClose,19,i,1)
prevAvg2 = sAverage(myClose,39,i,1)
avg1 = sAverage(myClose,19,i,0)
avg2 = sAverage(myClose,39,i,0)
```

You create two new variables and assign them the moving average values using an offset of 1. **PrevAvg1** and **prevAvg2** are the moving averages from yesterday. Your long and short entries should look something like this:

```
#Long Entry
if (mp != 1) and avg1 > avg2 and prevAvg1 < prevAvg2:
    price = myClose[i]

#Short Entry
if (mp !=-1)  and avg1 < avg2 and prevAvg1 > prevAvg2:
    price = myClose[i]
```

Notice how the comparison of the prior day's moving average values is incorporated in the logic. Yesterday's **prevAvg1** must be less than yesterday's

prevAvg2 and today's **avg1** must be greater than today's **avg2**—a crossover. There are a few different ways you could accomplish this, but until you become more comfortable with Python, the PSB, and lists, I would suggest simply offsetting the indicators to get the values you need. This is highly inefficient, but I don't think, unless you are doing it a lot, you will see a degradation in performance.

If you are using limit orders, just make sure you test the worst-case scenario. Most limit orders are not executed unless the price penetrates and trades one tick through the limit price. So you know how it important it is to use >= and <= in your price comparisons for stop orders. In limit orders forget the = sign. Like this:

```
#Long Exit - Profit
if mp >= 1 and myHigh[i] > entryPrice + profAmt and
   barsSinceEntry > 1:
     price = max(myOpen[i],entryPrice + profAmt)
     tradeName = "L-Prof"
```

Using just the > sign informs the PSB to make sure the market action penetrates the **entryPrice + profAmt**. In reality, there is a chance that a limit order will be filled if the order is touched. But we always want worst-case scenario when developing a trading algorithm. There is a bunch more Python code in the appendix and a few tutorials on the website. This version of the PSB is really in its infancy. I will continue to enhance it into the future by including some basic graphing utilities and loading it into a more sophisticated IDE.

Summary

I love Python, and it really is a great language for quants and quant wannabes. It is the language to learn if you are new to programming. You will hear things out there about how it is inferior to C# and other faster languages. Unless you are an HFT trader, don't take these criticisms seriously. Others may complain that Python is not a purely objective language due to its deviations from the philosophy of "OO." I look at Python as means of getting something done quickly and accurately. Traders need to concern themselves with trading concepts more so than programming theory.

CHAPTER 7

An Introduction to EasyLanguage

TradeStation has come a long ways from its early days, when it was known as SystemWriter. TradeStation, just like AmiBroker, is a complete testing and trading platform. The main difference between the two is you must use TradeStation's data servers and TradeStation's clearing services if you want to automate your trading algorithm. TradeStation is one of the most used trading platforms currently. You will find it in large hedge funds and CTAs as well as on the computers of smaller retail traders. Most system vendors have a TradeStation-compatible version of their software, because of its far reach. You don't have to trade through TradeStation's clearing services to use TradeStation. Many TradeStation users lease the software and data and then execute through their own broker. The beauty of trading through TradeStation is you can get the platform for free if you trade enough to meet a certain threshold. Else you will need to lease the TradeStation software for $249 per month. The supplementary products **RadarScreen** and **Portfolio Maestro** require additional fees.

I have used TradeStation for the last 25 years and have written a book on using it to develop trading systems (*Building Winning Trading Systems with TradeStation*). The latest version is 9.5, the culmination of three decades of hard work. The online community, just like AmiBroker's, is extremely large and many programming questions can usually be found with a quick Google search. In this chapter I will discuss TradeStation's development environment (TDE) and **EasyLanguage**.

TradeStation IDE

TradeStation has beautiful charts and a huge library of indicators and drawing tools. Technicians love this interface. Chart creation is very simple and since TradeStation uses its own data servers, database management is not an issue. You log on, log in, and the data is but a few keystrokes away. This tight integration is one of the things that make TradeStation so popular. The other thing that makes TradeStation so good is EasyLanguage (EL). EL is similar in concept to AmiBroker's AFL and the code that makes up the Exel and Python backtesters that we have discussed.

The **TradeStation Development Environment** (TDE) can run independent of TradeStation 9.5 and you can launch it by finding it under the start menu or double-clicking its icon. This is helpful sometimes when you simply want to modify some code or start a new strategy or analysis technique and don't need to see the results of your work. However, if you do want to see the results of your coding instantaneously, then you should have both running. If you have TradeStation, you can follow along with this tutorial. If not, you can still follow along to see if TradeStation and EasyLanguage might fit your testing/trading needs. Let's launch TradeStation 9.5. For this exercise, let's go ahead and log on by typing in your UserName and Password. Your screen should look somewhat similar to Figure 7.1.

Inside this figure you should see a small tab labeled **TradingApps**. Click on the tab and another window like the one in Figure 7.2 will open up.

This window shows all the additional trading tools that have been turned on in your TradeStation platform. The one we are interested in right now is the button labeled **EasyLanguage**. Click it and you should be transferred over to the TDE. Check to make sure your screen looks like Figure 7.3.

With version 8.8, TradeStation finally developed a powerful IDE. It is now similar in capabilities to other professional program authoring tools. If you went

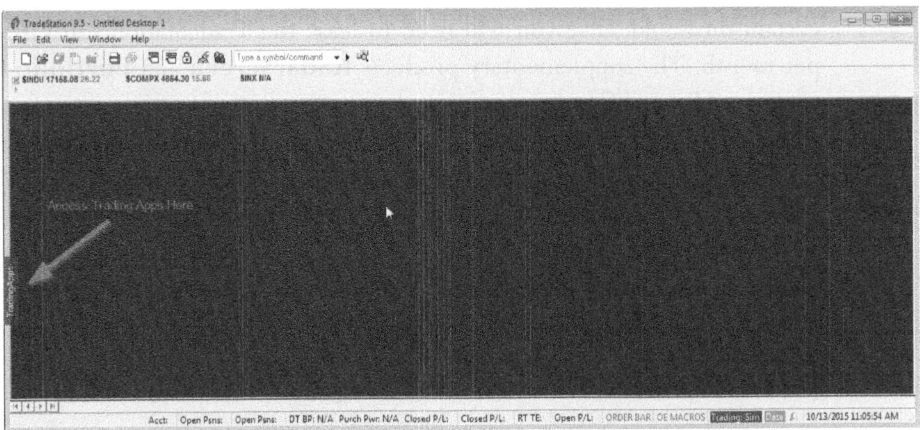

FIGURE 7.1 The TradeStation home screen.

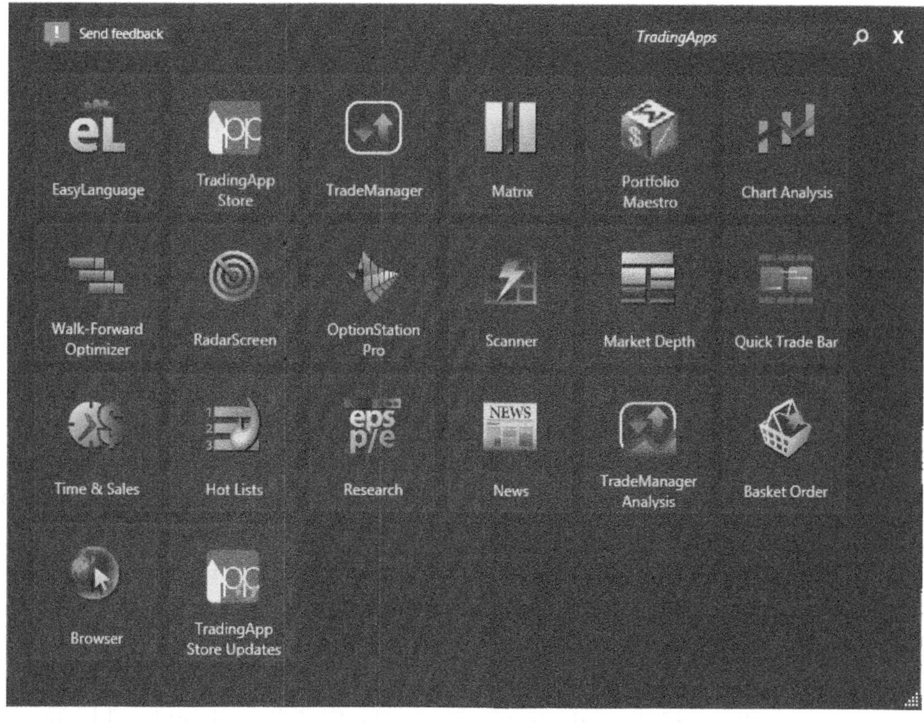

FIGURE 7.2 TradeStation's trading apps.

Source: TradeStation

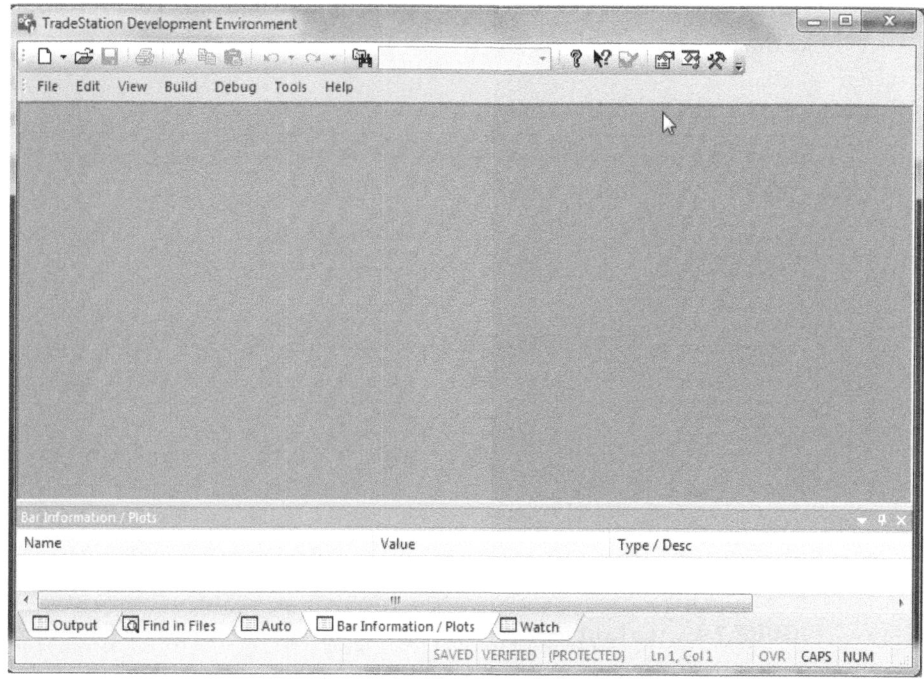

FIGURE 7.3 The initial screen of the TradeStation Development Environment.

through Chapter 4, you will also notice a very close similarity to the AFL editor. Here is a quick tutorial on the editor.

An impressive feature of this editor is the ability to quickly and easily move from the source code of one program to another. When you open to edit more than one analysis technique, each program or file is opened underneath its own tab very similar to the way Microsoft Excel uses tabs for different worksheets. This is a nice feature because it makes copying existing code from one **Strategy**, **Function**, **Indicator**, or **Paintbar** to another very easy. As you have seen thus far in the book, building trading algorithms is done by extending existing code. After programming for a while, you will develop a library of ideas that you use and reuse again and again. So it's nice to be able to program a new idea with bits and pieces of old ideas. The multiple-tab concept makes this much simpler.

The TDE also incorporates the idea of **Outlining**. We touched on this in Chapter 4 on AmiBroker very briefly when we switched to **loop programming** mode. If you skipped that chapter or want a refresher, just follow along. **Outlining** is a feature where blocks of source code can be grouped together to make readability much easier. This also helps make programs much more modular. Let's play around with the EL Editor a bit. If you haven't downloaded the companion EL code for this book, it would be advisable to do so now. If you need help, go to the TradeStation appendix and follow the instructions. The EL Editor should still be open from our previous exercise. If not, then go ahead and launch it. From the **File** menu, select **Open** and when the **Open Easy Language Document** dialog box appears select **Strategy** in the **Select Analysis Type** drop-down menu. Your screen should look like the one in Figure 7.4.

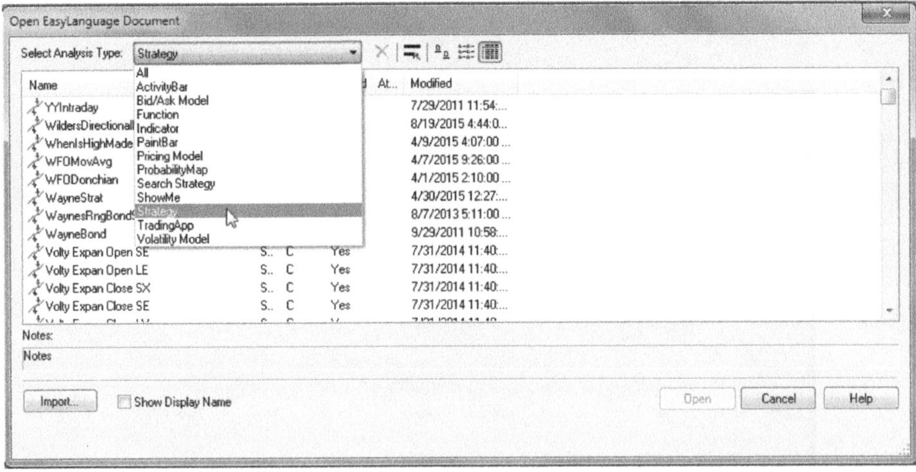

FIGURE 7.4 The EasyLanguage editor in the TradeStation Development Environment.

If you have imported the companion code properly, select **MyMeanReversion1** strategy and click **OK**. The following code listing should now be on your screen.

```
{This algorithm trades in the direction of
 the longer term trend but buys/shorts on dips
 and rallies.  The indicator BollingerB returns
 the location of the current bars close in relation
 to the 5-bar Bollinger Band.  If the trend
 is up and the current close is near the bottom
 BBand it will buy.  If the trend is down and the
 close is near the upper BBand it will Short.}

Inputs:Length(5),mmStop(2000),triggerVal(0.25),triggerSmooth(3);
Vars: myBollingerB(0);

myBollingerB = BollingerB(c,5,1,-1);

If MarketPosition = 0 and  close > average (close,200) and
        average(myBollingerB,triggerSmooth) < triggerVal then
          buy("LongReversion") next bar at market;
If MarketPosition = 0 and  close < average (close,200) and
        average(myBollingerB,triggerSmooth) > 1 - triggerVal
          then sellShort("ShortReversion") next bar at market;
If marketposition = 1 then
begin
        If myBollingerB > 1 - triggerVal then sell("L-Exit")
             next bar at market;
        If c <= entryPrice - mmStop/BigPointValue then
             sell("MML-Exit") next bar at market;
end;
If marketposition = -1 then
begin
        if myBollingerB < triggerVal then
             buyToCover("S-Exit") next bar at market;
        if c >= entryPrice + mmStop/BigPointValue then
             buyToCover("MMS-Exit") next bar at market;
end;
```

A portion of the strategy or algorithm is shown in Figure 7.5.

You can easily see how the blocks of code are outlined. There's a small box with a "-" symbol and a vertical line connecting the related block of code together. Outlining also allows you to hide the blocks of code if you wish to do so, again adding to the readability of the code. You can hide the block of code that is being

```
If marketposition = 1 then
begin            <-- Start
    If myBollingerB > 1 - triggerVal then sell next bar at market;
    If c <= entryPrice - mmStop/BigPointValue then sell next bar at market;
end;             <-- End
If marketposition = -1 then
begin
    if myBollingerB < triggerVal then buy to cover next bar at market;
    if c >= entryPrice + mmStop/BigPointValue then buyToCover next bar at market;
end;
```

FIGURE 7.5 The algorithm with a single, complete portion of the strategy marked.

outlined by simply clicking on the small box with the dash in it. This is a feature I would love to have in VBA and Python's IDLE.

EL has a huge library of reserved words, and it is very difficult if not impossible to remember them all. The EL Editor has a really cool feature called *autocompleting*. Let's say you want to code an idea that incorporates an average true range calculation and you can't remember the name of the function that does the calculation. You could, of course, stop what you are doing and go to HELP and look up the function. However, this is time consuming, so the EL Editor monitors what you are typing and provides all the possible reserved words that might match what has thus been typed. In the case of our example, all you need to do is type what you might think is the name of the function and the list appears. By typing "av" the list pops up and places you at the word *average*. You can simply scroll down to find the function **AvgTrueRange**. Let's practice this. Go to the EL Editor and new line of code at the very bottom of the **MyMeanReversion1** strategy. Start typing "av" and see what happens. You should see something very similar to what is in Figure 7.6.

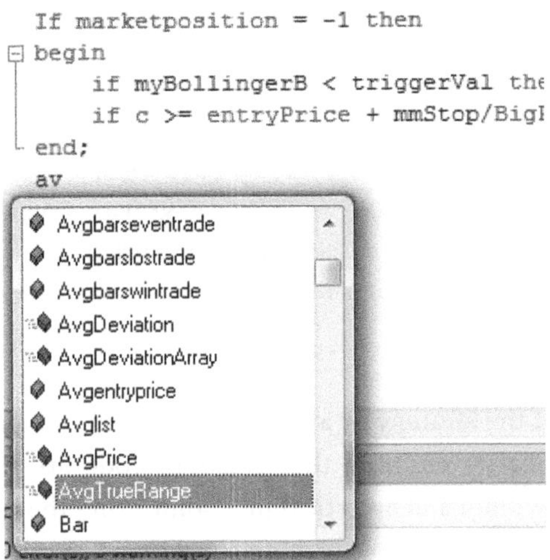

FIGURE 7.6 The EasyLanguage editor monitors what you are typing and provides likely functions.

Scroll down and select **AvgTrueRange** and it will be inserted into your code. Now go back and delete it. Keep the EL Editor open; we will be back with it shortly.

Syntax

The syntax of EasyLanguage is very similar to other programming languages, but there are a couple of differences in how remarks are demarked and the use of SKIP words:

- *Remarks or comments.* Words or statements that are completely ignored by the compiler. Remarks are placed in code to help the programmer, or other people who may reuse the code, understand what the program is designed to do. Double forward slashes // informs the EasyLanguage compiler that anything that follows is a comment. The double forward slashes can be used anywhere within a line. The curly left bracket { and curly right bracket } are used for multiline commentary. The { opens the remarks and } closes the remarks block. Anything inside { --- } is ignored by the computer.
- *SKIP words.* Words used to help EasyLanguage look more like English than a programming language. Here is a list: **an**, **at**, **by**, **does**, **is**, **of**, **on**, **than**, **the**, and **was**.

EasyLanguage is the medium used by traders to convert a trading idea into a form that a computer can understand. Fortunately for nonprogrammers, EasyLanguage is an extremely high-level language; it looks like the written English language. It is a compiled language; programs are converted to computer code when the programmer deems necessary. This is different from VBA and Python. The compiler then checks for syntactical correctness and translates your source code into a program that the computer can understand. If there is a problem, the compiler alerts the programmer and sometimes offers advice on how to fix it. This is different from a translated language, which evaluates every line as it is typed.

Unlike AmiBroker's AFL, VBA, and Python, EL requires all variables names to be declared/defined prior to use. The declaration statement defines the initial value and data type of the variable. In a compiled language, the compiler needs to know how much space to reserve in memory for all variables. The following code is a complete EasyLanguage program.

```
Vars:  mySum(0),myAvg(0);
mySum  = High  + Low + Close;
myAvg  = mySum/3 ;
```

The **Vars**: (or **Variables**:) statement tells the computer what variables are being declared and initialized. We declare the variables by simply listing them in the **Vars** statement and initialize them by placing an initial value in parentheses following the variable name. In this case, **mySum** and **myAvg** are to be equal to zero. EasyLanguage is smart enough to realize that these variables should be of the numeric data type, since we initialized them with numbers. Variable names should be self-descriptive and long enough to be meaningful. Which of the following is more self-explanatory?

```
mySum  = High+Low+Close;    or   k  = High  + Low + Close;
myAvg  = mySum/3;           or   j = k/3;
BuyPt  = Close   + myAvg;   or   l = Close+j;
```

Variables of Boolean and string types are declared in a similar fashion.

```
Vars: myCondition(false),myString("abcdefgh");
```

The variable **myCondition** was initialized to **false**. The word *false* is a reserved word that has the value of zero. This word cannot be used for any other purpose. The variable **myString** was initialized to "abcdefgh." Sometimes you will need to use a variable for temporary purposes, and it is difficult to declare and initialize all of your variables ahead of time. In the case of a temporary variable (one that holds a value for a short period of time), EasyLanguage has already declared and initialized several variables for your use; **value0** through **value99** have been predefined and initialized to zero and are ready for usage in your programs. The following is a complete EasyLanguage program as well:


```
value1 = High  + Low + Close;
value2 = (High  + Low)/2.0;
```

Notice that there isn't a **Vars** statement. Since **value1** and **value2** are predefined, the statement isn't needed. You have probably noticed the semicolon (;) at the end of each line of code. The semicolon tells the compiler that we are done with this particular instruction. Another similarity with **AFL**. In programming jargon, instructions are known as statements. Statements are made up of expressions, which are made up of constants, variables, operators, functions, and parentheses. Some languages need a termination symbol and others do not. **EL** and **AFL** need the statement termination symbol. Remember to put a semicolon at the end of each line to prevent a syntax error.

Inputs are similar to variables. They follow the same naming protocol and are declared and initialized, too. However, an input variable remains constant throughout an analysis technique—it cannot be changed. An input cannot start a statement (a line of instruction) and cannot be modified within the body of the code. One of the main reasons for using inputs is that you can change input values of applied analysis techniques without having to edit the actual EasyLanguage code. Input variables are the interface between the algorithm and user. Inputs would be perfect for a moving average indicator. When you plot this indicator on a chart, you simply type in the length of the moving average into the input box of the dialog. You don't want to have to go back to the moving average source code and change it and then verify it. **Inputs** are the same as **Param** in AFL, by the way. Also, when used in trading strategies, inputs allow you to optimize your strategies. Optimization was touched upon in the AmiBroker chapter and will be thoroughly discussed in Chapter 8. EL inputs serve two purposes: user and optimization interface.

Notice how inputs and variables are declared in similar style.

```
Inputs: length1(10),length2(20),flag(false);
Vars:   myLength1(10),myAvgVal(30);
```

However, notice how they are used differently in coding.

```
Variables

myLength1   = myAvgVal + myLength1;      {Correct}

Inputs

length1 = myAvgVal + length1;     {Incorrect}
myLength1   = length1*2;     {Correct}
```

Variables can start a statement and can be assigned another value. Since inputs are constants and cannot be assigned new values, they cannot start a statement.

In a strongly typed language, such as C, Pascal, or C++, if you assign a real value such as 3.1456 to an integer typed variable, the decimal portion is truncated and you end up with the number 3. As we all know, precision is important when it comes to trading, so EasyLanguage includes only one Numeric type. All numbers are stored with a whole and a fractional part. In the old days when CPUs were slow, noninteger arithmetic took too much time and it was advised to use integer variables whenever possible.

Like AFL, the overall purpose of EasyLanguage is to translate an idea and perform an analysis on a price data series over a specific time period. You can access the different data elements by using the keywords shown in Table 7.1.

If you wanted to determine that the closing price of a particular instrument was greater than its opening price, you would simply type: **Close > Open**, or **C > O**. The beauty of any trading platform's scripting languages is their ability to have all of the data of an instrument at your fingertips. The reserved words that we use to access the different prices of the current bar are also used to access historical data.

TABLE 7.1 EasyLanguage Keywords and Abbreviations

Reserved Word	Abbreviation	Description
Date	D	Date of the close of the bar.
Time	T	Time as of the close of the bar.
Open	O	Open price of the bar.
High	H	High price of the bar.
Low	L	Low price of the bar.
Close	C	Close price of the bar.
Volume	V	Number of contracts/shares traded.
OpenInt	OI	Number of outstanding contracts.

You do this by adding an index to the reserved word. The closing price of yesterday would be: **Close** [1]. The closing price two days ago would be: **Close** [2], and so on. The number inside the bracket determines the number of bars to look back. The larger the number, the further you go back in history. If you wanted to compare today's closing price with the closing price 10 days prior, you would type: **Close** > **Close**[10].

Before we move on, we should discuss how TradeStation stores dates and times. January 1, 2001, is stored as 1010101 instead of 20010101 or 010101. When the millennium changed, instead of incorporating the century into the date, TradeStation simply added a single digit to the year. The day after 991231 was 1000101 according to TradeStation. Time is stored as military time. For example, one o'clock in the afternoon is 1300 and one o'clock in the morning is 100.

After that brief introduction to the EasyLanguage, let's return to the EL Editor and take a look at **myMeanRev1** algorithm.

Start off by reading the first few lines of code. You will notice that these lines are comments because the comments are preceded and followed by the left and right curly brackets, {}. This is your typical mean reversion system and is designed to trade those markets that demonstrate a mean reversion propensity. All markets demonstrate mean reversion characteristics at some time or another, but the stock indices seem to revert to the mean more frequently than the others.

The next lines are the **Inputs** and **Variables** used in the algorithm. The user can change the input values through the **Format Analysis Techniques and Strategies** dialog window. This window is brought up once you have applied the **Strategy** to a chart. If you like, go ahead and create a **Chart Analysis** of daily **ES** (emini-S&P) going back 10 years. Once the chart has been populated with data, go up under the **Insert** menu and select **Strategy** (see Figure 7.7).

After selecting **MyMeanReversion1** from the list of **Strategies**, your chart window should contain some trades like the ones shown in Figure 7.8. Now we

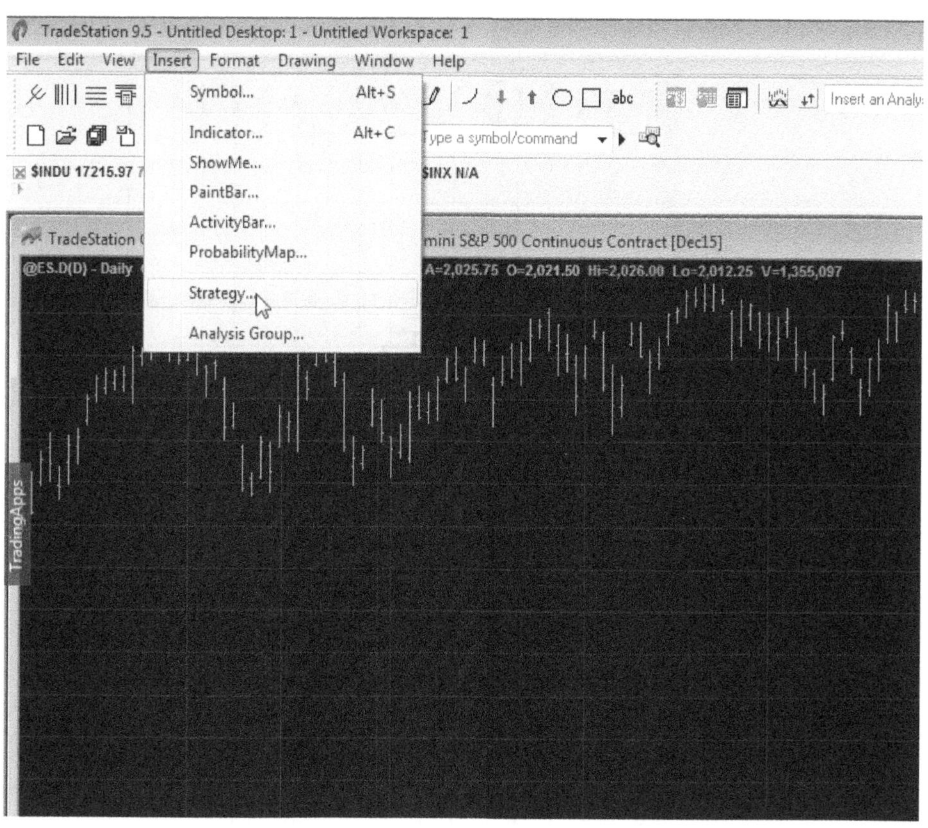

FIGURE 7.7 How to apply a strategy to your chart.

Source: TradeStation

can access the **Inputs** and change them if we like by right-clicking the chart and selecting **Format Strategies**. A dialog similar to Figure 7.9 will open.

Another dialog will follow once you select **Format** (Figure 7.10.). Here you can select any of the four **input** variables. Go ahead and select **mmStop** and change it to 3000. Then click **OK** and then **Close**. That's all there is to changing the **inputs** from the user's interface. You can always change them programmatically from the EL Editor. The next line is where you must define any variables you may use later in your code. If you have properly converted your trading idea into either a FC or FSM diagram and then into pseudocode, then you will know ahead of time the number and names of your variables. It doesn't matter how well thought out your pseudocode is; you will almost always come across the need for additional variables. Don't worry; you can always go back to the **Vars** or **Inputs** and add more variable names. Here the only variable name that will be used is **myBollingerB**, and it will be initially set to zero.

FIGURE 7.8 A reversion analysis strategy shown on a chart.

Source: TradeStation

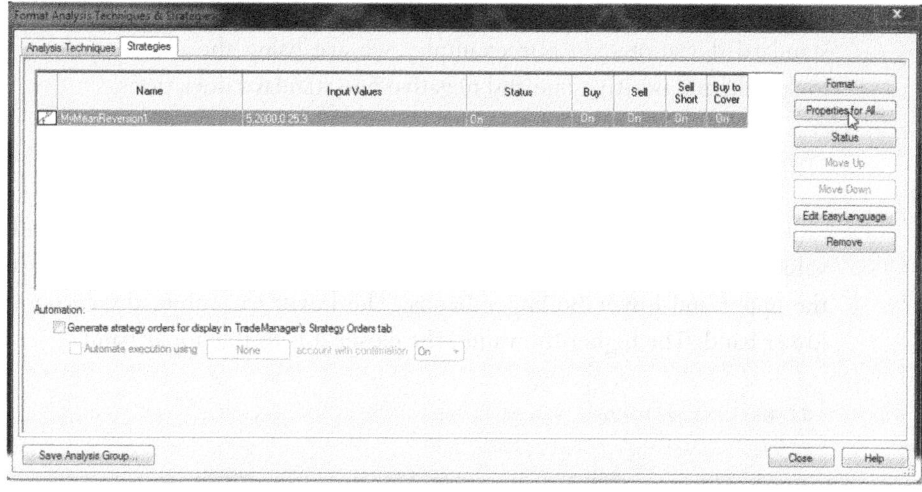

FIGURE 7.9 How to change the inputs and adjust your strategy.

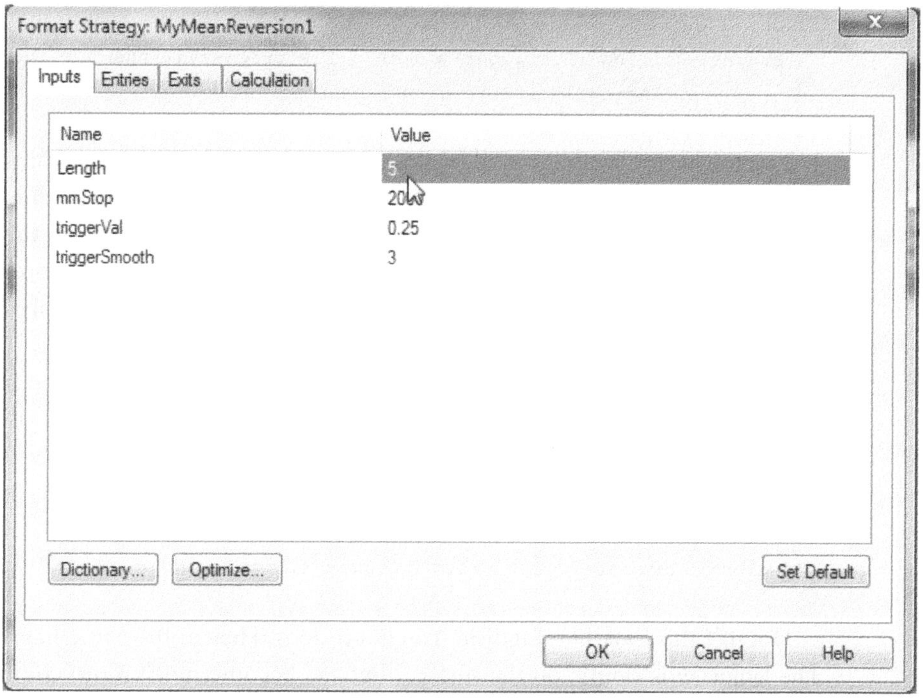

FIGURE 7.10 The four input variables to adjust the mean reversion strategy.

Continuing on through the code, the first order of business is the assignment of **myBollingerB**. **myBollingerB** is assigned the output of the function **BollingerB**. This function requires four parameters or arguments: price data array, lookback period, the number of + standard deviations, and the number of negative standard deviations. In our example, we are using the closing prices, a five-bar lookback, and positive one and negative one standard deviations.

```
myBollingerB = BollingerB(c,5,1,-1);
```

The **BollingerB** function returns a value between a negative value and a positive value and 1.00 which indicates the location of the current bar's close in relation to the upper and lower Bollinger Bands. The lower the value, the closer it is to the lower band. The higher the value, the closer it is to the upper band.

```
If MarketPosition = 0 and
close > average (close,200) and
average(myBollingerB,triggerSmooth) < triggerVal then
        buy("LongReversion") next bar at market;

If MarketPosition = 0 and
close < average (close,200) and
average(myBollingerB,triggerSmooth) > 1 - triggerVal then
        sellShort("ShortReversion") next bar at market;
```


You might not be able to tell by this code snippet, but EL follows the bar-by-bar programming paradigm. The keyword **If** might have given you a hint, though. If you have read the chapter on AmiBroker, you know you usually don't use the keyword **If** when dealing with array programming. When you use the data arrays (open, high, low, close, volume, or opInt) without an index variable you are simply looking at the very last day of data up to that point in the master loop.

C is the same as **C[0]**. The **[0]** is optional. Since there is an implied index, you can be assured you are not dealing with array programming. The lack of the index for the last value in the arrays makes EL look more like English. Take a look at the following line of code:

```
If close > average(c,200) then buy next bar at open;
```

Doesn't this look like English? You bet it does. Hence, the name EasyLanguage. The language is simple on the surface, but can become much more complicated as the complexity of the algorithm increases. This is a good thing—EasyLanguage isn't necessarily easy, but it's not weak by any stretch of the imagination. And it's getting more powerful every year.

These lines of code direct TradeStation to check the current market position, and if it is flat, to check if today's **close** > the 200-bar **moving average** and the 3-bar **moving average** of **myBollingerB** is less than the **triggerVal**. In this example, the **triggerVal** is set to **0.2**. If the criteria are met, then a market order to buy is placed for the next bar's open. A similar criterion is used to initiate a short position on the next bar's open. The only difference is the **close** must be below the 200-bar **moving average** and the 3-bar **moving average** of the **myBollingerB** variable must be greater than 1 - **triggerVal**.

There is a lot going on with this code. Any time you use the keyword **if** it must be eventually followed by the keyword **then**. Initiating long positions requires the keyword **buy** and short position requires the keywords **sellShort**. You can give names to your entry and exit signals by following the keywords **Buy/SellShort/Sell/BuyToCover** with the name of the signal enclosed within quotes and parentheses. The buy signal is this example is "**LongReversion**" and the short signal is named "**ShortReversion**." This isn't necessary but it does help when you have multiple entry and exit signals. EL requires you to use the words **next bar** or **this bar on/at close** whenever you direct TradeStation to initiate or liquidate an existing position. When programming in EL, think of yourself sitting in front of the computer screen right at the close of a bar. You can place a market order immediately and get filled at the current close, you can place a market order and get filled at the next bar's open price, or you can place a limit or stop order for the next bar. By limiting you from seeing the next bar (other than the open price), TradeStation eliminates all risks of "Future Leak." In other words, you cannot peek into the future by looking at the next bar and make a trading decision on the current bar. Both the VBA and Python back testers allow you to do this, not in order to cheat, but to allow complete testing flexibility.

Take a look at the next section of code and see if you can tell what is going on.

```
If marketposition = 1 then
begin
        If myBollingerB > 1 - triggerVal then sell("L-Exit")
             next bar at market;
        If c <= entryPrice - mmStop/BigPointValue then
             sell("MML-Exit") next bar at market;
end;
If marketposition = -1 then
begin
        if myBollingerB < triggerVal then buyToCover("S-Exit")
             next bar at market;
        if c >= entryPrice + mmStop/BigPointValue then
             buyToCover("MMS-Exit") next bar at market;
end;
```

In Python, the keyword **then** would be replaced by the colon (**:**). Since the code controlled by the **if** consists of more than one line of code, the keywords **begin** and **end** must be used to encapsulate the code. For every **begin** there must be an **end**. The **begin** and **end** informs the compiler that the code is related and must flow through all the lines in the block. If the current market position is 1 or long, then TradeStation in instructed to exit the long position if one of two criteria are met:

1. If myBollingerB > (1 – triggerVal) or 0.8, then the long is liquidated on the next bar's open.
2. If the difference between the current close price is less than the entryPrice – 2000/bigPointValue, then the long is liquidated on the next bar's open.

The short liquidation occurs in a similar manner. If myBollingerB < 0.2 or the close is greater than the entryPrice + 2000/bigPointvalue. That's the entire mean reversion system that we introduced in Chapter 3.

Another key and cool feature of EL is that all variables are special arrays. When you declare the variable myBollingerBand in the **vars:** section, you are informing the compiler to create an array with the name **myBollingerBand**. This is a special array because you don't need to worry about keeping track of the values in the array. The value is carried over from one bar to another until it is changed. Because myBollingerBand is an array, you can access the prior bar's value by indexing the variable name. The prior bar's **myBollingerBand** value is accessed by **myBollingerBand**[1]. These variables can be referred to as bar arrays.

Once you type your code in and want to see if it **Verifies** or compiles, all you need to do is go up under the **Build** menu and select **Verify**. If all goes well, you will see this dialog (Figure 7.11).

If not, then you might see what's in Figure 7.12. TradeStation is politely informing you that you have made a syntax error. If you double-click on the error, the EL Editor will take you directly to the offending line with the error. The error message also informs you of the line number. If you want the EL Editor to show line numbers, go under the **Tools** menu and select **Options**. A dialog window like the one in Figure 7.13 will open.

Click on **Line Numbers**. The EL Editor has added the capability of grouping strategies, indicators, and functions together in a neat package known as a **Project**. If you build a strategy that calls in a lot of external functions, then putting the strategy

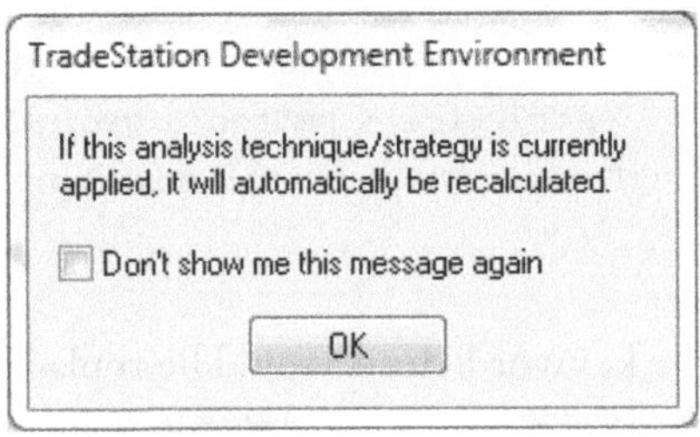

FIGURE 7.11 A message confirming that your code was verified and will be recalculated based on the new inputs.

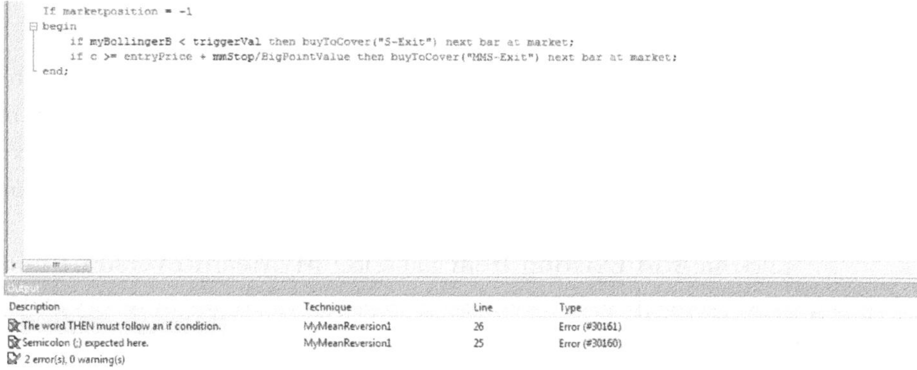
If marketposition = -1
begin
if myBollingerB < triggerVal then buyToCover("S-Exit") next bar at market;
if c >= entryPrice + mmStop/BigPointValue then buyToCover("MMS-Exit") next bar at market;
end;
Description
Technique
Line
Type
The word THEN must follow an if condition.
MyMeanReversion1
26
Error (#30161)
Semicolon (;) expected here.
MyMeanReversion1
25
Error (#30160)
2 error(s), 0 warning(s)

FIGURE 7.12 TradeStation lists any syntax errors it finds during verification in the bottom pane of the screen. The line number of the error is provided so you can easily find it in your code.

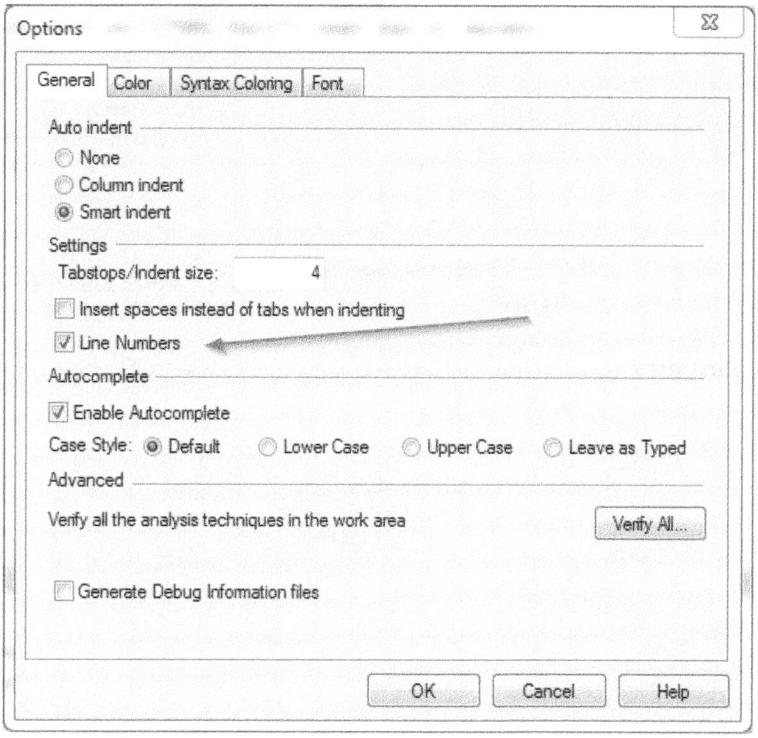

Options
General | Color | Syntax Coloring | Font
Auto indent
None
Column indent
Smart indent
Settings
Tabstops/Indent size: 4
Insert spaces instead of tabs when indenting
Line Numbers
Autocomplete
Enable Autocomplete
Case Style: Default Lower Case Upper Case Leave as Typed
Advanced
Verify all the analysis techniques in the work area
Verify All...
Generate Debug Information files
OK Cancel Help

FIGURE 7.13 The EasyLanguage editor can display line numbers to make it easy to navigate your code.

into a project makes it easier to access all the different code. Let's create a **Project**. Go under the **File** menu and go to the **Project** menu item and a hierarchical menu will open (see Figure 7.14).

The EL Editor will ask you for a name and where you would like to save the project. Select a location on your desktop or the C:\ drive and give your project the name **MeanReversion**. Once the project is created, a small dialog box will open with your new project name inside it. Right-click on the project name and a menu will open like the one in Figure 7.15.

Click on **Add Existing Item** and select **MyMeanReversion1** from **Strategies**. Close the box out and then go under the **File** menu to **Project** and select **Open Project** and select the project you just created, **MeanReversion.elx**. Click on the + beside the name **MyMeanReversion1**, and it will expand and

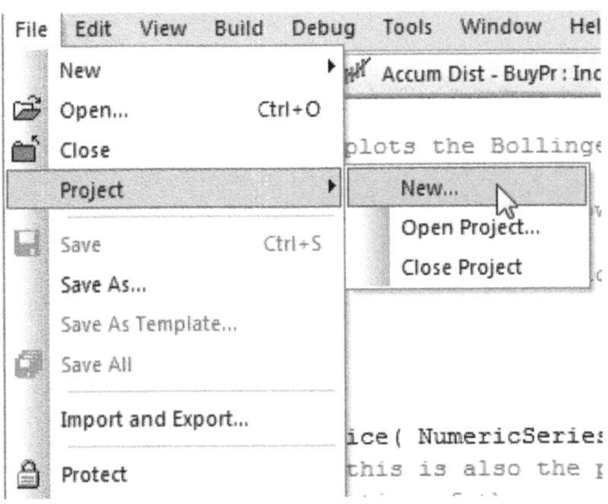

FIGURE 7.14 To create a new project using your strategy, select Project from the File menu.

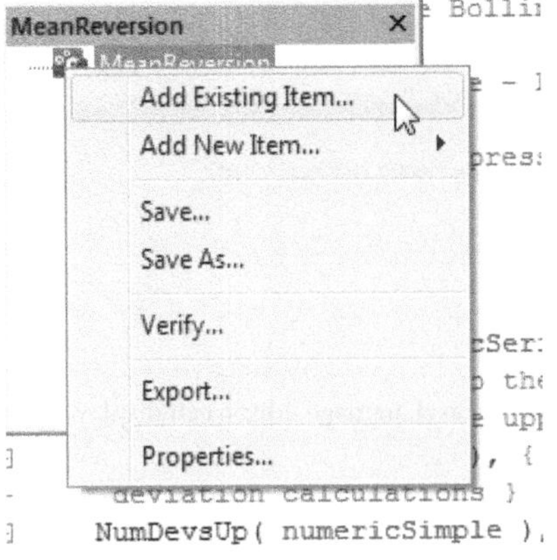

FIGURE 7.15 How to add an existing strategy to a new project.

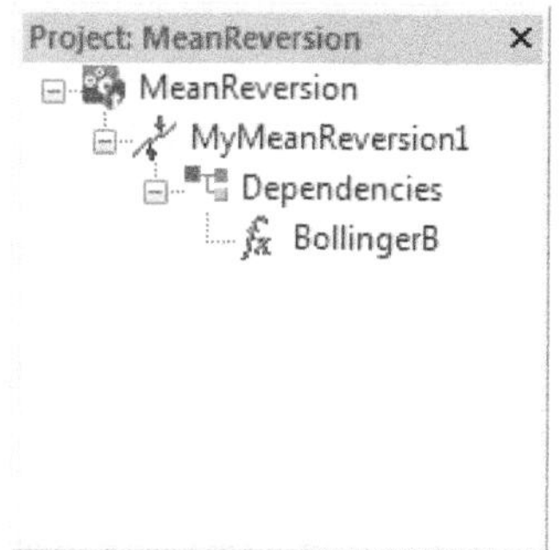

FIGURE 7.16 All dependencies and functions are nested inside their strategy algorithm.

show all the functions or dependencies included in the **Strategy** algorithm (see Figure 7.16).

This is just neat way to keep track of all the code connected to a particular project and is a relatively new feature of the EL Editor.

Samples of EasyLanguage

Here is a simple Commodity Channel Index (CCI) algorithm:

```
{CCI system utilizing 3 ATR Profit
 And  a 1 ATR Stop}

inputs: cciLen(20),smooth(9);

vars: myCCIVal(0);

myCCIVal = average(cci(cciLen),smooth);

If myCCIVal crosses above -100  then buy this bar on close;
If myCCIVal crosses below 100 then sellShort this bar on close;

If marketPosition = 1 then
begin
       If c > entryPrice + 3* avgTrueRange(10) then sell
            this bar on close;
       if c < entryPrice - 1* avgTrueRange(10) then sell
            this bar on close;
end;
```

```
If marketPosition =-1 then
begin
        If c < entryPrice - 3* avgTrueRange(10) then
             buyToCover this bar on close;
        if c > entryPrice + 1* avgTrueRange(10) then
             buyToCover this bar on close;
end;
```

This algorithm covers long positions whenever the market closes above the **entryPrice** plus 3 ATRs, or when it closes below the **entryPrice** minus 1 ATR. The same technique is programmed for short trades as well. This algorithm risks one ATR to achieve three.

The following algorithm is a simple 20-day Donchian breakout that only takes trades in the direction of the 14-day slope of closing prices. The interesting part of the algorithm is found in the trade management.

```
Inputs: linearSlopeLength(14),channelLength(20);
Inputs: atrLen(10),numAtrStop(3),numAtrProfThreshold(5),
         numAtrTrail(2);
vars: buyLevel(0),shortLevel(0),maxContractPoints(0);

buyLevel = Highest(High[1],channelLength);
shortLevel = Lowest(Low[1],channelLength);

if marketPosition <> 1 and linearRegSlope(c,linearSlopeLength)
     > 0 then
   Buy("BuyLevelEntry") tomorrow at buyLevel stop;

maxContractPoints = maxContractProfit / bigPointValue;

If marketPosition = 1 then
begin
   sell("L-ATR-Stop") next bar at entryPrice-numAtrStop *
     avgTrueRange(atrLen) stop;
   if maxContractPoints >= numAtrProfThreshold *
     avgTrueRange(atrLen) then
   begin
      value1=entryPrice + (maxContractPoints-numAtrTrail *
        avgTrueRange(atrLen));
      sell("L-Trail-Stop") next bar at value1 stop;
   end;
end;
```

```
if marketPosition <>-1 and linearRegSlope(c,linearSlopeLength)
    < 0 then
   Sellshort("ShortEntryLevel") tomorrow at shortLevel stop;

If marketPosition =-1 then
begin
   buyToCover("S-ATR-Stop") next bar at entryPrice+numAtrStop
     *avgTrueRange(atrLen)
   stop;
   if maxContractPoints >= numAtrProfThreshold *
     avgTrueRange(atrLen) then
   begin
      value1 = entryPrice - (maxContractPoints-numAtrTrail *
        avgTrueRange(atrLen));
      buyToCover("S-Trail-Stop") next bar at value1 stop;
   end;
end;
```

This algorithm incorporates a volatility-based protective and trailing stop. EL keeps track of the maximum profit a position achieved during the duration of a trade, and stores it in the keyword **maxContractProfit**. The profit is expressed in terms of dollars, and to get it in terms of points you have to divide by the **bigPointValue** of the underlying instrument. If the **maxContractProfit** achieves a level equal to, in this case, five ATRs, then a trailing stop is engaged to trail the highest point in the trade by two ATRs. If you don't want to use volatility in the stop calculations, you can use dollars. Here is the snippet of the code that engages the trailing stop:

```
if maxContractPoints >= numAtrProfThreshold*
     avgTrueRange(atrLen) then
begin
   value1=entryPrice + (maxContractPoints-numAtrTrail *
     avgTrueRange(atrLen));
   sell("L-Trail-Stop") next bar at value1 stop;
end;
```

If the **maxContractPoints** is greater than the threshold profit level, then the trailing stop level is calculated using the following formula:

value1 = entryPrice + (Highest level during trade – 2*ATR)

As the market continues to climb, so does value1 staying 2 ATR below the highest point achieved. Once the market stops climbing, value1 locks into place and waits for the market to take out the trailing stop.

Once you master just the fundamentals of programming and a few concepts that are intrinsic to a particular language, you then have most of the tools to test or program any trading idea. Practice makes perfect, so don't just stop after you have programmed your initial trading idea—keep going because I guarantee your creativity won't stop.

Summary

The objective of this chapter was to introduce the fundamentals necessary to take a trading idea and program it in EasyLanguage. Along the way we discussed data types, expressions, and statements. EL requires all variables to be declared before use and we reviewed how this is done. The use of inputs, built-in function calls, and how to verify your code was explained as well. The EL Editor is a very powerful tool and is the center of your creativity. TradeStation and its programming language, EasyLanguage, provides a very tightly integrated trading environment that can facilitate the programming of any trading idea. Learning this powerful language is best accomplished by examining as much code as you can. I have used EL for 25 years and I am still learning.

I will leave you with the finite state machine (FSM) code from Chapter 1.

```
{Finite State Machine
 Pivot Point Example from Chapter 1.
 The switch case structure is used in place of
 if-then constructs.  This increases the readability
 considerably.}

vars:state(0),maxRsi(0),state1BarCount(0),state1Price(0),
       state3Price(0),state1BarNumber(0);
vars: isHiPivot(false);

isHiPivot = h[1] > h and h[1] > h[2];

Switch(state)
begin
       case(0):
       begin
              if isHiPivot then
              begin
                     state = 1;
                     state1Price = h[1];
                     state1BarNumber = barNumber;
                     print(date," State 1 : ",state1Price,
                       " ",state1BarNumber);
                     value1 = text_new(date[2],time,h+20,"S1");;
              end;
       end;
```

```
        case(1):
        begin
                if h > state1Price then state1Price = h;
                if low < state1Price * .98 then
                begin
                        state = 2;
                        print(date," State 2 :",low);
                        value1 = text_new(date[1],time,
                          l-10,"S2");
                        text_setColor(value1,red);
                end;
        end;

        case(2):
        begin
                if isHiPivot and h[1] > state1Price then
                begin
                        state = 3;
                        state3Price = h;
                        print(date," State 3 :", state3Price);
                        value1 = text_new(date[2],time,
                          h+20,"S3");;
                        text_setColor(value1,yellow);
                end;
        end;

        case(3):
        begin
                if h > state3Price then state3Price = h;
                if l < state3Price * .98 then
                begin
                        buy this bar on close;
                        print(date," accept state : ",l);
                        value1 = text_new(date[1],time,
                          l-10,"S4");;
                        text_setColor(value1,GREEN);
                        state = 0;
                end;
        end;
end;

If barNumber - state1BarNumber > 30 then state = 0;
Sell next bar at lowest(l,60) stop;
```

CHAPTER 8

Genetic Optimization, Walk Forward, and Monte Carlo Start Trade Analysis

Utilizing TradeStation and AmiBroker

Both TradeStation and AmiBroker software includes two very powerful tools that can be utilized to help create robust trading algorithms. If you have used TradeStation or AmiBroker to develop trading algorithms but have not taken advantage of genetic or walk-forward optimization, this chapter will hopefully provide enough information to help enhance your research and unlock the potential of these powerful tools. These tools have been a part of both platforms for several years, but through my observations of other users they have been either ignored or underutilized. Users often note these stumbling blocks:

- They are hard to understand.
- They are hard to implement.
- They lead to over-curve-fitting.

The objective of this chapter is to explain that a computer science degree is not necessary to understand these tools; in some scenarios their use is absolutely necessary, they are very simple to use, and with proper application a user can make sure over-curve-fitting does not take place. Since I am somewhat of a newbie to AmiBroker and in an attempt to cut down on redundancy, a good portion of the concepts in this chapter will be illustrated with TradeStation's tools. An understanding of TradeStation, some EasyLanguage, and input optimization is assumed. As you will see in the latter part of the chapter, the ideas and algorithms will be translatable to AmiBroker and AFL.

The first part of this chapter explains the concept of a genetic algorithm, proceeds to build one, and then shows how they can be used to optimize a trading algorithm. The genetic algorithm development part is a little longer and requires a close examination. Much of this discussion, including examples and processes, was taken directly from Denny Hermawanto's excellent paper titled, "Genetic Algorithm for Solving Simple Mathematical Equality Problem." Out of all the research used in the writing of this chapter, Hermawanto's description of genetic algorithms was considered one of the easier to understand and implement. Understanding what makes up a genetic algorithm is not necessary to use one. However, even a slight understanding of how one works will eliminate the hesitation of using it and eliminate its "voodoo" factor.

The second part of the chapter describes how a trading algorithm can be automatically reoptimized periodically using the walk-forward optimizer (WFO) in concert with genetic optimization. In addition to changing parameters periodically based on algorithm performance going forward in time, the WFO also creates a report that indicates the degree of the trading algorithm's robustness. In other words, what is the probability of the algorithm continuing to work?

Genetic Algorithms: What Are They?

The first question that needs to be answered is, Why use genetic algorithms (GA) in the first place? The same question concerning walk-forward optimization (WFO) will be answered in the second part of this chapter. TradeStation and AmiBroker already have exhaustive search (ES) optimization engines built into their platforms. In this chapter, the words *searching* and *optimizing* will be used interchangeably. The ES optimization engine doesn't use any sophistication in its search process, just brute force. Why not just use this brute force approach if it looks at every possible combination of variables and no stone is left unturned? It is true that this feature is very powerful and can fulfill a good portion of a user's optimization needs. However, unlike genetic algorithms, there is a limit to the number of variables (inputs) and their respective iterations that can be optimized in a sequential manner.

GA has limitations as well, but they are very large—large in the sense that a super-large amount of data would be necessary to limit their effectiveness. The major limitation to a brute force approach is, of course, time. Even with today's superfast processors, searching a large search space is extremely time sensitive. Imagine a trading algorithm (TA1) that has five different parameters that can be optimized across 50 different values. Assuming a brute force optimization and three seconds to complete each iteration, it would take the computer almost 30 years to complete or span the entire search space (*search space* and *optimization range* are also interchangeable terms). Here is the math behind the time needed to complete this task:

$$P1(50) \times P2(50) \times P3(50) \times P4(50) \times P5(50) \times 3 \text{ seconds} = 937{,}500{,}500 \text{ seconds}$$

$$\frac{937{,}500{,}500 \text{ seconds}}{86{,}400 \text{ seconds/day}} = 10{,}850 \text{ days, or } 29 \text{ years}$$

This example is an exaggeration, but it shows multiple parameter optimizations can be very time consuming. Figure 8.1 shows how quickly the search space grows as the number of iterations increase for each of the five parameters. This is where artificial intelligence (AI) comes into play; AI uses brains over brawn. In the above example, AI can shrink the overall search space by eliminating some values of each parameter that do not lead to a favorable outcome. In doing so, it cuts down the number of total iterations, and less iteration means less time.

The first step in the process of incorporating these tools into a trader's algorithm development is to understand the basic foundations of GA. Don't let the words *genetic* or *algorithms* scare you away. They are simply terms to explain how a solution to a problem can be quickly and solidly uncovered. As we already know, probably too well, an algorithm is just a set of rules one follows to find a solution to a problem. Genetic refers to the biological process of evolution through reproduction, mutation, and survival of the fittest. Remember time is of the essence but so is a good answer and this type of algorithm provides quick yet robust solutions. Computer software and biology may seem like strange bedfellows but their synthesis makes up a large portion in the study of AI.

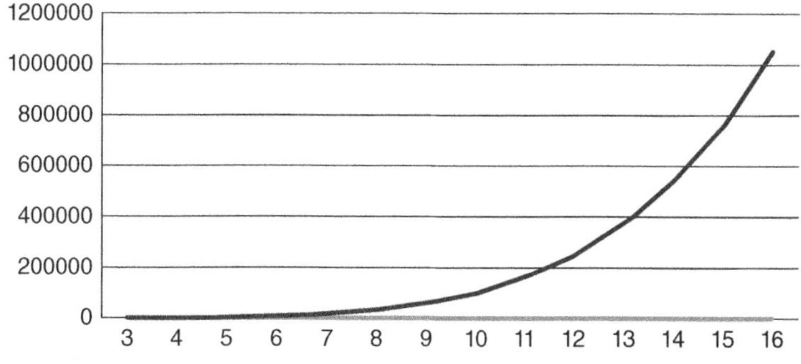

FIGURE 8.1 Iteration growth rate of five parameters.

John Holland's 1975 book titled *Adaptation in Natural and Artificial Systems* is the bible on GA and his work has paved the way for a majority of researchers in this field. Holland has stated,[1] "Living organisms are consummate problem solvers. They exhibit a versatility that puts the best computer programs to shame."

Computer speed and power has come a long way since 1975 and you may think these biologically based optimization/search algorithms have become obsolete. The exponential growth rate of multiple variable optimizations proves that this is not the case. Also humans are constantly creating more and more complex problems that continually exceed our technology. The relationship between GA and computers is as close as it has ever been.

The principles that make up GA, if taken one concept at a time, are easy to understand. The combining of these concepts into a complete algorithm can be daunting if each piece is not broken down. I programmed these concepts in a modular manner using VBA for Excel in a very small amount of time. This same software was used to illustrate the concepts and solve the initial problem in this first part of the chapter. Snippets of VBA code will be sprinkled throughout the first part of the chapter to help explain the most important components of genetic algorithms.

Computers, Evolution, and Problem Solving

Genetic algorithms borrow the following concepts from biology:

- Population and generations
- Selection of the fittest
- Reproduction
- Mutation

All these terms are easily understood in a biological framework but may not seem initially translatable into a computer/software/math paradigm. The application of these concepts to solve a complex problem can be difficult but we need not worry ourselves with this because we know our objective with TradeStation, AmiBroker, or Excel—building the world's best trading algorithms! However, a simple problem needs to be solved so we can demonstrate the eloquence of GA. The ideas and processes that will be discussed for applying a GA to finding a solution to a simple equation were derived directly from Denny Hermawanto's paper titled "Genetic Algorithm for Solving Simple Mathematical Equality Problem." The problem that we will be solving utilizes this very simple equation:

$$a + 2b + 3c + d = 40$$

[1] John H. Holland. Genetic algorithms. *Scientific American*, 267(1):44–50, 1992.

This equation involves four unknowns and multiple solutions and can be easily solved by trial and error. We could simply set *a*, *c*, and *d* equal to zero and set *b* equal to 20 and be done with it. Remember, this is an oversimplified problem to demonstrate the four core concepts of GA.

Population

There are four variables in our equation so continuing to borrow from biology let's create six chromosomes consisting of four values or genes that will be substituted into the variables *a*, *b*, *c*, and *d*. Unlike real chromosomes, these will simply be placeholders for the four different values of the variables (genes). Figure 8.2 illustrates our six amoeba-looking genes.

So the population will consist of six chromosomes that have four different genes that can be swapped or mutated. Why six chromosomes instead of four, you may ask? Just be patient; we will get to that. The initial population of chromosomes will be generated using a random number generator (RNG). Each chromosome will be defined by its genetic value, and these are the values that will be randomized. Values between 0 and 30 for each gene will be initially generated in a random fashion. You will soon discover that GA relies heavily on random numbers. This is yet another similarity with nature—randomness. Here is the initial population generated by the VBA software and its RNG:

			Genes
Generation 1:	*Chromosome(0)*	=	*[10,11,20,19]*
	Chromosome(1)	=	*[13,08,15,20]*
	Chromosome(2)	=	*[00,20,05,09]*
	Chromosome(3)	=	*[07,27,05,14]*
	Chromosome(4)	=	*[10,30,30,04]*
	Chromosome(5)	=	*[16,05,13,28]*

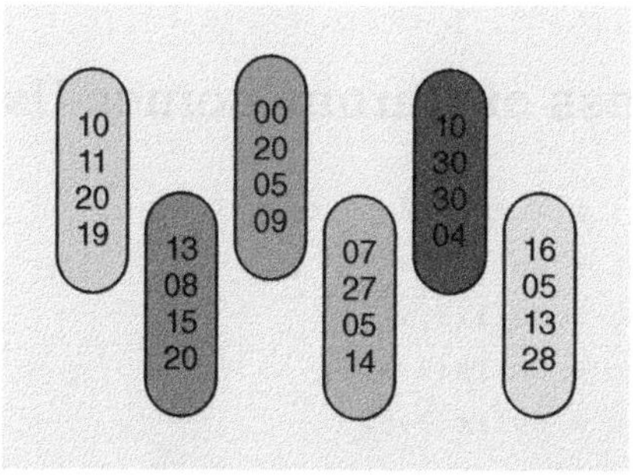

FIGURE 8.2 An illustration of our chromosomes with different genetic values.

Initial Population Setup Using VBA Excel

```
'All Lines starting with single quote is a comment
'Random variables into each chromosome's genes
'Numbers range between 0 and 30
'Chromos will be represented by a table/matrix
'The first index in the chromo table will be row #
'The second index in the chromo table will be column #
'Excel's RNG is invoked by using the Rnd function call
'Int ((upperbound - lowerbound + 1) * Rnd + lowerbound)

Randomize '<- must use this to get different numbers
For i = 0 To 5 ' Six Chromos
    For j = 0 To 3 ' Four Genes
        chromo(i, j) = Int((30 - 0 + 1) * Rnd + 0)
    Next j
Next i
```

How good or fit is this population? Fitness is determined by how close each chromosome comes to providing a solution to our equation. Remember, this is a very simple problem, but these ideas are easily scalable to problems involving extreme complexity. Calculating fitness is quite easy; simply plug in the chromosomes' genes (values) for a, b, c and d. In chromosome (0) its fitness is determined by: $a(10) + 2b(2 * 11) + 3c(3 * 20) + d(19) = 111$. The solution we are seeking is 40 so this fitness doesn't seem to be that good. However, each chromosome's fitness is relative to all the other chromosomes.

Fitness 1:	*Chromosome(0)*	=	*111*
	Chromosome(1)	=	*94*
	Chromosome(2)	=	*64*
	Chromosome(3)	=	*90*
	Chromosome(4)	=	*164*
	Chromosome(5)	=	*93*

Testing Fitness of Chromosomes Using VBA Excel

```
'Equation is : a + 2b + 3c + d = 40
'a coefficient = Cell(3,3)
'b coefficient = Cell(3,4)
'c coefficient = Cells(3,5)
'd coefficient = Cells(3,6)
'the summation of the equation is in Cells(3,7)
```

```
For generation = 1 To 100 ' total generations
    For i = 0 To 5 'Six Chromos
        FObj(i) = 0
        For j = 0 To 3 ' Four Genes
            'Calculate each expression in equation and accumulate
            If j = 0 Then FObj(i) = Cells(3, 3) * chromo(i, j)
            If j = 1 Then FObj(i) = FObj(i) + Cells(3, 4)
                      * chromo(i, j)
            If j = 2 Then FObj(i) = FObj(i) + Cells(3, 5)
                      * chromo(i, j)
            If j = 3 Then ' Test the summation against 40
                FObj(i)=Abs((FObj(i)+Cells(3, 6)*chromo(i,j))
                          -Cells(3,7))
                'if summation = 40 then solution found
                If (FObj(i) = 0) Then foundSolution = i
            End If
        Next j
    Next i
```

If we rank the chromosomes in order of fitness, then we would have the following:

Chromosome(2)	=	*64—closest to the solution (24 away)*
Chromosome(3)	=	*90—second closest (50 away)*
Chromosome(5)	=	*93*
Chromosome(1)	=	*94*
Chromosome(0)	=	*111*
Chromosome(4)	=	*164*

Selection

Now that we have our initial population and the respective chromosome fitness, we can select the chromosomes that should be carried forward and used for reproduction and mutation. It's easy to see that the top four ranking chromosomes should be selected because they are closer to our solution than the last two (the absolute difference between the chromosome fit score and 40, our solution, is smaller). However, the computer makes the decisions and it makes its selection based on probabilities. This task is accomplished by converting each chromosome's fitness in terms of probability. We can't make the selection decision for the computer, but we can make sure the computer understands that some chromosomes are more fit than others. If you remember probabilities from an old math or stat class, you know the basic premise: Rolling a dice once results in one out of six potential outcomes.

With this in mind you have a one-in-six chance of rolling a six or a probability of 16.6666667 percent.

P = Possible favorable outcomes / Potential outcomes

P = 1/6, or 16.6666667%

Keep in mind probabilities are the cornerstone of GA as well as trading algorithms.

Okay, now on to our selection process. Remember, we need to nudge the computer into making the right decision. The computer will, in effect, roll the dice to choose which chromosome will be carried into the next step for reproduction. If this is a random event, then how do we nudge the computer's decision? Think of a dartboard that has six slices and the slices are the same size. Now assume you train a monkey to throw darts while blindfolded at the dartboard. Also, it is important to assume he always hits the dartboard. The monkey has a one-in-six chance of hitting a particular slice. What if the slices were not the same size? Then he would have a higher probability of hitting the larger slices. This is the concept that will be used to nudge the computer's selection; the more fit chromosomes will get the bigger slices. Here again, we must let the computer decide the sizes of the slices but we can feed it a formula that will give priority to the more fit chromosomes. The first step is to calculate the fitness of each chromosome in terms of the size of the slice. This is a very simple formula as well:

Chromosome[slice size] = 1 / (1 + **ABS**(Chromosome[fitness] – 40))

Notice how we use the **ABS** (absolute value) function in our formula. This function simply removes a negative sign from the difference between a chromosome's fitness and our objective of 40; we don't want to have a negative-sized slice. We subtract 40 from each chromosome's fitness because we need to put the fitness in terms of our objective; the closer we are the smaller the fitness value. Since we want to allocate a bigger slice to chromosomes that are closer to our solution we divide one by our fitness score. In doing so, we are making the size of each slice inversely proportional to the fitness score; a lower fitness value (or closer value to 40) will increase size. The number 1 is also added in the denominator to prevent division by zero; computers hate division by zero. Utilizing the above formula we come up with:

Fitness 1 in terms of slice size:

Chromosome (0) = 1 / (1 + 71) = 0.01389

Chromosome (1) = 1 / (1 + 54) = 0.01812

Chromosome (2) = 1 / (1 + 24) = 0.04000

Chromosome (3) = 1 / (1 + 50) = 0.01961

Chromosome (4) = 1 / (1 +124) = 0.00800

Chromosome (5) = 1 / (1 + 53) = 0.01852

Converting Fitness in Terms of Slice Size—Using VBA Excel

```
'fitness in terms slice size
For l = 0 To 5 'calculate for each of the six chromos
    Fitness(l) = 1 / (1 + FObj(l))
Next l
```

Now that fitness has been redefined in terms of the size of the slice on the dartboard, we can now calculate the probability of each slice being hit. First off, let's calculate the total size of all slices:

$$0.01389 + 0.01812 + 0.04000 + 0.01961 + 0.00800 + 0.01852 = 0.11814$$

The dartboard has a total size of 0.11814 units. Don't worry about the units because they are not important. Now that we know the size of the chromosomes' respective slices and we know the total size of the dartboard, we can easily calculate the probability of a dart hitting the individual slices. This is accomplished by dividing the size of each chromosome slice by the total size. The probability of each chromosome slice being hit with a blindfolded monkey are:

$$\text{Chromosome } (0) = 0.0139/0.1182 = 0.1175$$
$$\text{Chromosome } (1) = 0.0182/0.1182 = 0.1538$$
$$\text{Chromosome } (2) = 0.0400/0.1182 = 0.3384$$
$$\text{Chromosome } (3) = 0.0196/0.1182 = 0.1659$$
$$\text{Chromosome } (4) = 0.0080/0.1182 = 0.0677$$
$$\text{Chromosome } (5) = 0.0185/0.1182 = 0.1567$$

Calculate Probability of Being Hit by Dart—Using VBA Excel

```
'calculate chromo probability of being hit by dart
 'accumulate probabilities and store in bins
 cumProb = 0#
 For l = 0 To 5  'this is a lower case l not a 1
     chromoProb(l) = Fitness(l) / totalFitness
     cumProb = cumProb + chromoProb(l)
     chromoProbBin(l) = cumProb
 Next l
```

Notice how the chromosome that was closest to our solution has a higher probability of being hit by a dart. Chromosome (2) covers nearly 34 percent of the dartboard.

The next thing the computer needs to do is construct the dartboard. The pie chart in Figure 8.3 is a graphical representation of how the computer would internally construct a dartboard with varying slice or sector sizes.

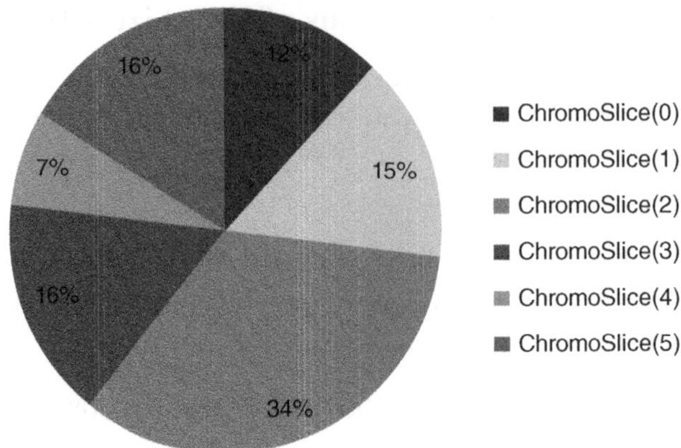

FIGURE 8.3 Chromosome dartboard.

Creating Chromosome Dartboard—Using VBA Excel

```
For l = 0 To 5
     chromoProb(l) = Fitness(l) / totalFitness
     cumProb = cumProb + chromoProb(l)
     'starting at 0 degrees in the pie/circle
     'work clockwise defining the slices
     'until the pie/circle is coverd by slices
     chromoProbBin(l) = cumProb
     'bin size = slize size
 Next l
```

Once the dartboard is constructed, the next step is to start randomly throwing six darts. Since blindfolded monkeys are hard to come by nowadays, the computer can easily replicate one by using our handy RNG. So let's proceed with the simulation and see where the six darts land.

Dart(0) hits Slice(5)

Dart(1) hits Slice(1)

Dart(2) hits Slice(2)

Dart(3) hits Slice(5)

Dart(4) hits Slice(4)

Dart(5) hits Slice(2)

Simulating a Dart-Throwing Blindfolded Monkey Using VBA Excel

```
'Generate 6 random numbers between 0 and 1
'These numbers represent the locations where
```

```
'the 6 darts landed
Randomize
For l = 0 To 5
    roulette(l) = Rnd(1#)
Next l
For i = 0 To 5
    whichBin = -1
    'which slice did the dart land in?
    For k = 0 To 4
        '6 slices but only 5 bin boundaries ?
         'if dart doesn't hit slices 1-5 then it must have
               hit slice 0
         If roulette(i) > chromoProbBin(k) And roulette(i) <=
             chromoProbBin (k + 1) Then
             whichBin = k + 1
         End If
     Next k
     If whichBin = -1 Then whichBin = 0 'dart hit slice 0
Next i
```

After the six darts are thrown, the selection process is completed. Each dart represents a chromosome, and where it lands is the chromosome that will replace it. Here is the end result:

Chromosome(0) is discarded and is cloned to be Chromosome(5)

Chromosome(1) stays the same

Chromosome(2) stays the same

Chromosome(3) is discarded and is cloned to be Chromosome(5)

Chromosome(4) stays the same

Chromosome(5) is discarded and is cloned to be Chromosome(2)

Chromosome Replacement Function—Using VBA Excel

```
'Chromosome switching function
'Pass both chromosome tables/matrices into function
'inform the function which chromosome is replaced by which
    chromosome
Public Sub switchChromo(tempChromoTable As Variant,
   chromoTable As Variant, destArrNum, srcArrNum)

For i = 0 To 3
    tempChromoTable(destArrNum, i) = chromoTable(srcArrNum, i)
Next i
```

The new population after selection is:

Chromosome(0) = [16,05,13,28] = 93–40 = 53

Chromosome(1) = [13,08,15,20] = 94–40 = 54

Chromosome(2) = [00,20,05,09] = 64–40 = 24

Chromosome(3) = [16,05,13,28] = 93–40 = 53

Chromosome(4) = [10,30,30,04] = 164–40 = 124

Chromosome(5) = [00,20,05,09] = 64–40 = 24

The somewhat fit chromosome (3) was discarded and the worst chromosome (4) was carried over. The fifth worst chromosome (0) was discarded and cloned by the third best chromosome (5). Chromosome (3) was cloned with the third best chromosome (5). Chromosome (5) was then discarded and cloned with the best chromosome (2). The formula tried its best to nudge the computer into making the right decision, but due to the random component the worst candidate was kept. The other chromosomes were somewhat upgraded.

Reproduction

Now that we have our parent pool, we can start the reproduction process. Some of the parents are from the original population and some are clones, and that is okay. The next step is to pick the parents that will produce offspring. The computer will allow you to input the cross rate (partner matching probability), and in this example, 40 percent was used. The computer will randomly generate six numbers between 0 and 100, and every time a number less than or equal to 40 is generated, it designates a crossing of two parents. In this example, the computer generated a random number for each chromosome. Out of the six random numbers, only two were less than or equal to 40. The random numbers were generated sequentially, and random number (2) and random number (4) met our criteria and were less than or equal to 40. With this information, the computer chose chromosome (2) and chromosome (4) to cross/reproduce.

Crossing Chromosomes/Finding Moms and Pops—Using VBA Excel

```
'Determine which chromosomes will cross
'using a .4 or 40% cross rate
crossRate = 0.4

For i = 0 To 5
    crossArr(i) = 0
    Randomize
```

```
        roulette(i) = Rnd(1#)
        If roulette(i) <= crossRate Then
            crossArr(i) = 1
        End If
    Next i

    crossCnt = 0
    For i = 0 To 5
        'parentsList is a simple class
        'similar to a point class with 2 coordinates
        'total of six possible matchings
        parentsList(i).mom = 999
        parentsList(i).dad = 999
        If crossArr(i) <> 0 Then
            crossCnt = crossCnt + 1
            'found mom but not dad - yet
            'store mom in parentsList(i)
            parentsList(i).mom = i
            foundMate = False
            cindex = i
            Do While Not (foundMate)
                cindex = cindex + 1
                If cindex > 5 Then cindex = 0
                If crossArr(cindex) <> 0 Then
                'found dad - store dad in parentsList(i)
                    parentsList(i).dad = cindex
                    foundMate = True
                End If
           Loop
        End If
    Next i
```

In nature, a child will receive genetic material or traits from both parents. Some children will receive more traits from the father than the mother, and vice versa. How is this determined? In nature, who knows, but inside a computer, we can discriminate how much the father and mother will contribute to the offspring. Here again, an RNG saves the day. Each chromosome holds four different genes (numbers), so we need to know how many of the four numbers will be passed on by the father and mother to the new offspring. This is accomplished by randomly calculating the split point where the numbers will be taken from both parents. In other words, if the split equals two, then the mother chromosome will contribute her first two numbers and the father chromosome will contribute his last two numbers. There are four genes in each chromosome, so the random number generator will generate a number between one and four. Figure 8.4 shows how the sharing of genetic material is accomplished when the split point is one.

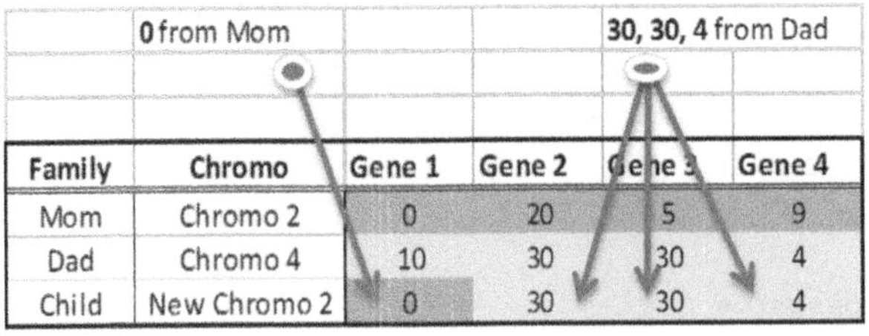

	0 from Mom			30, 30, 4 from Dad	
Family	**Chromo**	**Gene 1**	**Gene 2**	**Gene 3**	**Gene 4**
Mom	Chromo 2	0	20	5	9
Dad	Chromo 4	10	30	30	4
Child	New Chromo 2	0	30	30	4

FIGURE 8.4 At split 1 the genes that will be passed onto the offspring by the father and the mother.

In this example, chromosome (2) is the mother and chromosome (4) is the father. The crossover point was randomly generated at one, so the offspring received one gene or number from the mother and three from the father.

$$Offspring = [00,30,30,04]$$

$$Chromosome\,(2)\;crosses\;chromosome\,(4)\;at\;point\;one = New\;chromosome\;(2)$$

How to Allocate Genes to Junior—Using VBA Excel

```
'make sure mom and dad are not one in the same
'we are not dealing with earthworms - right?
If parentsList(i).dad <> parentsList(i).mom Then
    Randomize
    'how do we split mom and pop's genes?
    crossPt = Int((3 - 0 + 1) * Rnd + 0)
   'mom is replaced by combination of old mom and dad
    For k = crossPt To 3
        chromo(parentsList(i).mom,k)=
            chromo(parentsList(i).dad,k)
    Next k
```

After the creation of the offspring, it was then used to replace the old chromosome (2), just like a child taking over his parents' business. This example chose only one crossing but in later generations (after total simulation was completed) more chromosomes were crossed, and they were crossed at different points. The computer is hoping to create a better offspring than the parents but as in real life this doesn't always happen. Just ask your neighbors whose 35-year-old son still lives in their basement.

Mutation

In nature, a mutation is change in a genetic sequence. A mutation can be good or bad, but no matter—it does add diversity. In GA, a mutation occurs infrequently but can tremendously help find a solution to a complex problem. Without mutation, selection and reproduction may eventually converge and produce a nondiverse population. Mutation can randomly change a genetic element and then like a chain reaction create different selections and reproductions.

Before we mutate the initial population, let's review our chromosome population as it stood after our first selection and reproduction phase:

Chromosome (0) = *[16,05,13,28]*
Chromosome(1) = *[13,08,15,20]*
Chromosome(2) = *[00,20,05,09]*
Chromosome(3) = *[16,05,13,28]*
Chromosome(4) = *[10,30,30,04]*
Chromosome(5) = *[00,20,05,09]*

The rate of mutation should be low because you do want a convergence to occur. In other words, you want a solution, and a high mutation rate could potentially spin the population off into too many different directions. But at the same time, you don't want your population growing stale, either, and a sufficiently high mutation rate prevents this. In this example, a mutation rate of 10 percent was used. With six chromosomes, there are 24 genes or numbers total, so if the mutation rate of 10 percent is applied, then 2.4 genes will be mutated. Since we can't have a partial gene, the number is rounded down to two. So out of the 24 numbers above, 2 of them will be randomly selected and replaced with two random numbers between 0 and 30 (the same range that we initially used to seed the population).

Each gene is assigned a number between 1 and 24 in order. So chromosome (0) will have genes labeled 1 through 4. Chromosome (1) will have genes 5 through 8, and so on. Relying on the random number generator yet again (range between 1 and 24), it generates two numbers: 7 and 24. Don't put the random number generator away yet; we still need to randomize two more numbers between 0 and 30 to use in our mutation. After pushing the button on the RNG, two numbers, 22 and 15, were generated. If we map 7 and 24 across the matrix of chromosomes, then the following highlighted genes will be mutated with the numbers 22 and 15:

Chromosome (0): 16^{1} 05^{2} 13^{3} 28^{4}
Chromosome (1): 13^{5} 08^{6} $\underline{\underline{22^{7}}}$ 20^{8}
Chromosome (2): 00^{9} 30^{10} 30^{11} 04^{12}
Chromosome (3): 16^{13} 05^{14} 13^{15} 28^{16}
Chromosome (4): 10^{17} 30^{18} 30^{19} 04^{20}
Chromosome (5): 00^{21} 20^{22} 05^{23} $\underline{\underline{15^{24}}}$

Mutating Chromosomes—Using VBA Excel

```
mutRate = 0.1 ' rate of mutation
numMutations = Int(mutRate * 24) ' 24 genes available for
                mutation
Call printDivider(lineCount, 4)
lineCount = lineCount + 1
Randomize
For i = 0 To numMutations - 1 'loop for 2 mutations
    chromoMut(i) = Int((24 - 0 + 1) * Rnd + 0) 'which
                genes to mutate
    genLocRow = Int(chromoMut(i) / 4) 'locate the gene
                in the matrix
    If genLocRow = 0 Then genLocRow = 1
    genLocCol = 4 - chromoMut(i) Mod 4
    chromoMutCoOrds(i, 0) = genLocRow - 1 'found gene row
    chromoMutCoOrds(i, 1) = genLocCol + 1 'found gene
                column
    Randomize
    rndVal = Int((24 - 0 + 1)*Rnd + 0) 'randomize the new gene value
    chromo(genLocRow - 1, genLocCol - 1) = rndVal
Next i
```


After selection, reproduction, and mutation a new generation has been created. Here are the second generation's chromosomes and respective fitness values after subtracting 40:

$$\begin{aligned}
\textit{Chromosome (0)} &= [16,05,13,28] = 53\\
\textit{Chromosome (1)} &= [13,08,22,20] = 75\\
\textit{Chromosome (2)} &= [00,30,30,04] = 114\\
\textit{Chromosome (3)} &= [16,05,13,28] = 53\\
\textit{Chromosome (4)} &= [10,30,30,04] = 124\\
\textit{Chromosome (5)} &= [00,20,05,15] = 30
\end{aligned}$$

It seems redundant to state this again, but here is another example of how genetic algorithms mimic nature by not only creating inferior offspring but also creating an inferior generation. However, since these generations live inside of a computer, they are short-lived and the computer moves quickly onto the next generation until a solution is found. This GA solved the problem in 13 generations after a mutation occurred. Eventually, chromosome (2) with genes [13,0,4,15] was chosen as the solution. Test it!

$$\text{Test}: \quad 13 + 2 \times (0) + 3 \times (4) + 15 = 40$$

This is just one possible solution. You can keep propagating and create a whole slew of solutions, which is what we are after when we use genetic optimization on trading algorithms.

Go through the steps until you understand the processes involved. Each step is logical and nonmath intensive and should give you confidence to utilize this technology in your own research. Even if you don't utilize it in research you can impress your friends at your next cocktail party by explaining what a genetic algorithm is and the impact of a higher mutation rate on subsequent generations.

Using Genetic Algorithms in Trading System Development

"The same principles which at first view lead to skepticism, pursued to a certain point, bring men back to common sense."

George Berkely

Now armed with a little knowledge the veil of skepticism can be pulled back. This knowledge can now be applied to a real-life trading problem. Earlier in this chapter, a trading algorithm was mentioned that consisted of five optimizable parameters. The system (TA1) utilizes an indicator to determine the market condition so it can either apply a trend-following or choppy-market algorithm. The switch that determines condition measures the actual distance a market travels versus the entire distance a market travels over a certain time period. Imagine a subdivision with a lot of cul-de-sacs. If you leave your house and go in and out of each cul-de-sac prior to exiting the subdivision, you will have traveled a long route to go a very short distance. This indicator is based on momentum and has been around for years. It is known as the Choppy Market Indicator (CMI). Here is the formula to the indicator:

$$\text{CMI} = (\text{ABS}(\text{close}(\text{xBars}) - \text{close}))/(\text{highest}(\text{high}, \text{xBars}) - \text{lowest}(\text{low}, \text{xBars}))$$

If the difference between the today's close and the close xBars back is small and the highest high and lowest low xBars back is large, then the CMI will be a small value (Numerator small / Denominator large). A low CMI indicates the market has traveled a relatively large distance but hasn't gone anywhere. In other words, the market is chopping around with no evidence of a trend.

There are two ways we can approach a choppy market condition: We can (1) avoid it; or (2) implement a swing trading algorithm. TA1 attempts the latter by using volatility breakout from the prior day's close as an entry point. If the CMI is less than xLevel, then long entries are placed at today's close plus xPercent times xAR (Exponential Average Range) of the past 20 days. The sellshort signal uses the same algorithm, except instead of adding the volatility level, it subtracts it. Here are the choppy market long and short entries:

Buy Next Bar at Close + xPercent * xAverage(Range, 20) stop

Sell Short Next Bar at Close − xPercent * xAverage(Range, 20) stop

Now if the CMI indicates a trending market by exhibiting a higher value, then the system switches to the trend-following mechanism. Here, the system falls back on the old Donchian breakout algorithm. Longs are put on at the Highest High of xTrendBars and shorts are put on at the Lowest Low of xTrendBars. The entry rules for trending markets are:

Buy Next Bar at Highest(High, xTrendBars) stop

Sell Short Next Bar at Lowest(Low, xTrendBars) stop

Looking at our entry rules, we can see there are three optimizable parameters: xLevel, xPercent, and xTrendBars. The last two parameters can be further optimized for long entries and short entries. If we allow these two parameters to be different for longs versus shorts, then instead of two parameters we have four. So all in all, there will be a total of five optimizable parameters:

1. xLevel—Choppy Market value
2. xPercentBuys—Percent of 20-day exponential moving average of Range
3. xPercentSells—Percent of 20-day exponential moving average of Range
4. xTrendBarsBuys—Number of Highest high/Lowest low lookback bars
5. xTrendBarsSells—Number of Highest high/Lowest low lookback bars

We could simply pull out of thin air some values for these parameters or we could use TradeStation's tools to help zero in on a robust solution. We now have a trading system and a set of five optimizable parameters, so the next step is to come up with a range of values that we want to optimize the parameters across. These different ranges can also be called our search space. Here are the ranges and iterations for each of the parameters for our system, TA1:

1. xLevel { 25 to 75 by 5 increments } [11 iterations]
2. xPercentBuys { 0.25 to 0.75 by 0.05 increments } [11 iterations]
3. xPercentSells { 0.25 to 0.75 by 0.05 increments } [11 iterations]
4. xTrendBarsBuy { 8 to 20 by 4 } [4 iterations]
5. xTrendBarsSell { 8 to 20 by 4 } [4 iterations]

If we do the math (11 * 11 * 11 * 4 * 4), we come up with a total of 21,296 iterations. It will take this many iterations to search the entire space if we apply an exhaustive search algorithm. So the computer will need to run 21,296 tests on the history of each market. This test was performed on 10 years of Euro currency data and it took my "typical" computer 13 minutes. The search space could have been expanded but for brevity sake it was limited to 21,296. If just one increment was added to each of the parameters' range, the total number of iterations would have nearly doubled. The results of the exhaustive search are shown in Table 8.1. (*Note*: Results are shown without a commission/slippage charge.)

Now let's do the same thing, but instead of using the Exhaustive method let's go with the genetic option. In less than one minute the results in Table 8.2 were computed.

TABLE 8.1 Results from the Exhaustive Search Algorithm's Five Parameters

xLevel	xPercent Buy	xPercent Sell	xTrendBars Buy	xTrendBars Sell	Total Profit	Max Intra. Drawdown
25	0.3	0.75	8	20	103615	−15235
25	0.4	0.75	8	20	102435	−16080
25	0.4	0.7	8	20	101005	−15760
25	0.7	0.75	8	20	96050	−17805
25	0.75	0.7	8	20	96680	−18343
25	0.45	0.75	8	20	97435	−17255
25	0.75	0.75	8	20	94020	−18480
25	0.7	0.7	8	20	96015	−7668
25	0.5	0.75	8	20	93805	−16660
25	0.4	0.65	8	20	98763	−15485

TABLE 8.2 Results from the Genetic Search Algorithm's Five Parameters

xLevel	xPercent Buy	xPercent Sell	xTrendBars Buy	xTrendBars Sell	Total Profit	Max Intra. Drawdown
25	0.3	0.75	8	20	103615	−15235
25	0.4	0.75	8	20	102435	−16080
25	0.4	0.7	8	20	101005	−15760
25	0.7	0.75	8	20	96050	−17805
25	0.45	0.75	8	20	97435	−17255
25	0.5	0.75	8	20	93805	−16660
25	0.55	0.75	8	20	91650	−15063
25	0.45	0.7	8	20	95655	−16110
25	0.35	0.75	8	16	91575	−18843
25	0.6	0.75	8	20	86850	−15913

The results from the two tests are quite similar; results only start deviating after the top six parameter sets. This example is not perfect for demonstrating the power of GA, as the brute force approach only took 13 minutes, but the implications of its power is more than evident. In many cases, a brute force optimization scheme will be too time intensive, and the only alternative is a GA.

TradeStation makes using the Genetic form of optimization very simple. All it requires is selecting it over the Exhaustive mode. This simple switch makes implementation simple, but you do have the ability to override the Genetic optimizer's default settings. If you select Genetic as the optimization method and then click Advanced Settings, a dialog box will open that will allow you to override the default settings. Before changing these, you want to make sure you fully understand what you are doing. Here is explanation of each of the Genetic Optimization Settings.

Generations

This setting indicates the total number of generations each test will iterate to come up with a solution chromosome. In our very first example, the number of generations concluded after a single chromosome fulfilled the requirements to solve the simple equation. The computer program and process could continue until multiple solutions were uncovered. Trading algorithms don't have a black-or-white solution so you can specify to only go so far in the process. This number should increase with larger search spaces. This setting should be "Suggested" by clicking the **Suggest** button.

Mutation Rate

Remember how a gene in our example chromosomes could be randomly changed? This rate defaults to 0.1 or 10 percent, and this is probably the best value for this setting. Higher mutation rates increase the probability of searching more areas in the search space and may prevent the population from converging on an optimal solution. Searching a larger space takes more time and a mutation could randomly change the gene of a good solution after selection and reproduction and turn it into a nonoptimal solution, thus preventing convergence.

Population Size

Referring to our initial example of a simple GA, we used six different chromosomes to solve our problem. So its population size was six. Population size grows with the size of the search space. A small population on a large search space could lead to less robust solutions. Initial population sizing is very important and is very difficult to gauge. Again, let the **Suggest** button help here.

Crossover Rate

The rate that determines how many parents will mate. If the default value is set to 0.4, or 40 percent, then each chromosome has a probability of 2 out of 5 of being mated with another chromosome and being replaced. If this rate is set to 1.0, or 100 percent, then a new generation is always created—no survivors are allowed. As in life, sometimes it's good to have a member or two from the old generation to help guide us. The **Suggest** button usually changes this value to 0.9, or 90 percent probability of chromosome matching.

Preventing Over-Curve-Fitting

If optimization is a form of curve fitting, then why do it at all? Curve fitting is a necessary tool in the development of trading algorithms. If a trading system is based on a sound market principle, then modifying it by adjusting its parameters to increase productivity is a good thing. However, this can be overdone. If you "tweak" an algorithm's parameters to catch a large portion of every substantial market move and create an absolutely beautiful equity curve, then you have gone too far. The system might work well in the near future due to curve fit overhang, but the likelihood of it continuing is less probable. The future is unknown but a robust trading algorithm that does not have overly curved fit parameters has a higher probability of success. Take a look at the 3D contour chart in Figure 8.5. The *y*-axis

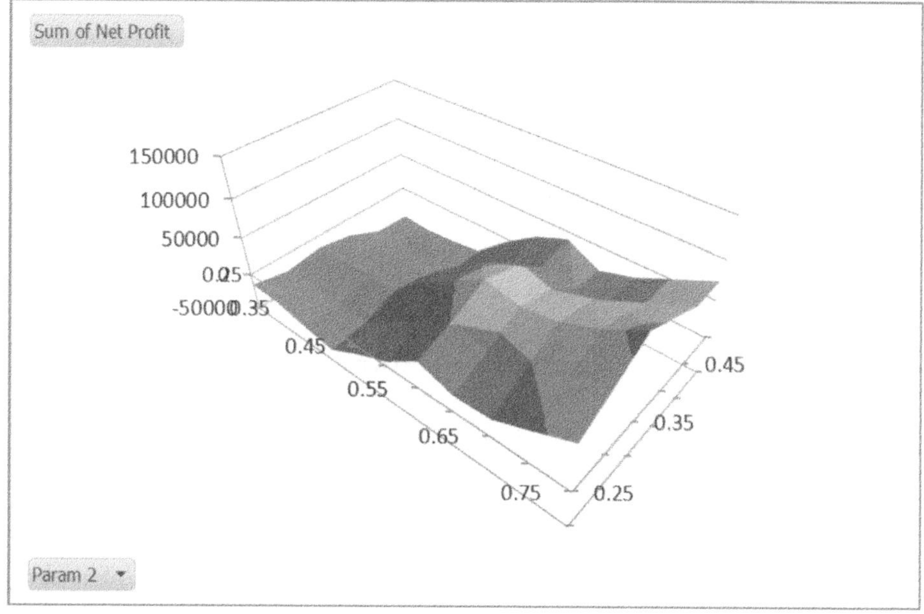

FIGURE 8.5 Robust parameter sets are found on a level plateau.

is profit, *x*-axis is one parameter, and the *z*-axis is another parameter. The curve is the different profit levels across the different values of the two parameters. If you are looking to maximize profit, then the best parameter set, historically speaking, would be at the peak (0.75, 0.35). If you are looking for robustness, then you don't want the peak; you want a parameter set located on a high plateau. Robustness is the same as parameter stability. If a parameter is stable, then changing it up or down will not have a huge impact on overall performance. If it does, then the parameter is not considered stable. TradeStation includes, with its genetic optimization method, a parameter stress test. This test includes two inputs, number of stress tests and percentage of parameter change.

If three is chosen as the number of stress tests and 10 percent as the stress increment, then the total number of tests will triple. For example, 7,250 iterations were generated by a simple algorithm optimized using the genetic method and a stress test of one. When the algorithm was reoptimized with a stress test number set to three and the stress increment to 10 percent, the number of increments increased to 21,750. What the genetic optimizer did was test each parameter set and then increased/decreased each parameter by 10 percent and then retested, thus creating three different sets of tests. A simple standard deviation algorithm example should help illustrate what the computer is doing:

Test 1: Normal

Moving Average Length = 50
Up Band = 2
Dn Band = 3

Test 2: Parameters are stressed upwardly by 10%

Moving Average Length = 50 + (10% of 50) = 55
Up Band = 2 + (10% of 2) = 2.2
Dn Band = 3 + (10% of 3) = 3.3

Test 3: Parameters are stressed downwardly by 10%

Moving Average Length = 50 – (10% of 50) = 45
Up Band = 2 + (10% of 2) = 1.8
Dn Band = 3 + (10% of 3) = 2.7

Stress testing eliminates parameter sets that fall on top of peaks, therefore theoretically revealing a more robust set. If a certain parameter is profitable, and its neighbors are nearly as profitable, then the parameter is deemed robust.

TradeStation's and AmiBroker's genetic optimization tool is a very important tool in the development of robust trading algorithms. Hopefully, this first part has demystified genetic algorithms and provided sufficient evidence that it can help a trader develop a better mousetrap—one that catches the mouse more often than not.

Walk-Forward Optimizer: Is It Worth the Extra Work and Time?

The idea of periodic reoptimization of a trading system's parameters is the one concept that divides the algorithmic trading community more so than any other. You are either pro or con; there is very little middle ground. Walk-forward optimization (WFO) has been around since the beginning of trading algorithms but until lately it has been extremely difficult to implement. TradeStation has done a wonderful job in providing the TS walk-forward optimizer. It does all the work for you.

Before describing the potential benefits of WFO, the concept and process needs to be explained. In a nutshell, it is a technique in which a system's parameters are optimized on a segment of historical data (in-sample), then tested and verified by using those parameters on a walk-forward basis (out-of-sample). Results from in-sample testing will usually be very good due to the benefit of hindsight. It's the results from testing on unseen data that provides a true reflection of a system's validity. This process is done periodically in hopes the trading algorithm will be using the most optimal parameters available at any given time.

WFO Example 1

Another example will definitely help explain the concept. Take a Turtle-like system that buys at the highest high of the past 40 days and sells at the lowest low of the past 40 days. Throughout history, there have been times when a longer (greater than 40-day) breakout or a shorter (less than 40-day) worked better. The magic questions are, of course, when to change the length of the breakouts, and by how much? These questions are easily answered with the use of a time machine.

Assume a trader trades this Turtle-like system for two years and it is somewhat profitable. Being an inquisitive trader he asks, "Was a 40-day break the best option?" An optimization run is set up and the 40-day parameter is optimized over the past two years of data, and lo and behold, the trader finds out that a 30-day breakout produced twice as much profit with much less drawdown. With this knowledge, he changes the trading algorithm to utilize a 30-day breakout in place of the 40-day. Another two profitable years go by, and he again asks the same question. This time, the best parameter turned out be the exact one he had implemented; 30 turned out to be the optimal parameter. He then carries the parameter forward another two years, but this time he suffers a large loss and a severe drawdown.

This trade, optimize, implement, and trade cycle is easy to see. Testing using this process on a long stream of historical data would be very difficult if tools such as the TS WFO were not available. A test would have to be started, stopped, results recorded, backed up, and optimized on in-sample data, started, stopped, results recorded, backed up, and optimized on in-sample data, started, stopped . . . . You get the picture.

Before proceeding, please refer to the TradeStation WFO **Help** menu to learn how to set up an optimization and then load that information into the software. The TS WFO **Help** system will also show how to perform an individual walk-forward analysis (WFA), or a cluster WFA.

Here is an individual WFA of a Turtle-like system selectively changing its parameters every two years. The first results shown are with the benefit of hindsight. The best parameters for each time period were utilized to construct the continuous track record. All the reports shown were produced using the TS WFO. The system labeled TA2 will enter and exit the market utilizing the following criteria:

```
//EasyLanguage Code for Turtle-like Algo

Buy Next Bar at Highest (H[1],xLongEntryLen) stop;

Sell Short Next Bar at Lowest (L[1],xShortEntryLen) stop;

If MarketPosition = 1 Then
Sell Next Bar at Lowest (L[1],xLongExitLen) stop;

If MarketPosition =-1 Then
BuyToCover Next Bar at Highest(H[1],xShortExitLen) stop;
```

In-Sample Testing You will notice four optimizable parameters:

1. xLongEntryLen
2. xLongExitLen
3. xShortEntryLen
4. xShortExitLen

Since the long entry parameter may not be the same as the short this system is not symmetric. This also applies to the long and short exits. Different parameters for long and short entries were used to increase the search space sufficiently to enable a genetic optimization. You will notice if the exhaustive search space is less than 10,000, then the genetic method is disabled. Table 8.3 shows the in-sample testing results of TA2 over the past 14 years on 30-year bonds.

TABLE 8.3	In-Sample Testing TA2						
Le	**Se**	**Lx**	**Sx**	**Begin Date End Date**	**Bars**	**Profit**	**Max DD**
20	20	12	10	2001/09/18–2005/06/15	975	24, 843.75	−9, 187.50
20	20	12	10	2002/10/11–2006/07/07	975	28, 375.00	−9, 187.50
20	20	16	10	2003/09/05–2007/06/27	975	23, 687.50	−8, 093.75
20	24	12	12	2004/10/04–2008/06/26	975	6, 437.50	−8, 343.75
20	20	12	14	2005/08/16–2009/04/07	975	18, 531.25	−11, 906.25
20	36	10	14	2006/08/15–2010/06/04	975	11, 843.75	−13, 843.75
20	20	12	14	2007/09/20–2011/04/18	975	21, 531.25	−13, 187.50
20	24	12	14	2008/07/17–2012/04/06	975	22, 375.00	−17, 656.25
20	56	10	14	2009/06/23–2013/03/27	975	8, 250.00	−15, 375.00
24	24	12	14	2010/09/03–2014/04/04	975	18, 187.50	−17, 656.25
						184, 062.50	

Table 8.3 shows the best parameter sets over a four-year period carried one year forward sequentially. Row 1 starts with September 2001 and ends on June 15, 2005. The best-performing parameters were selected over that time period and displayed. Row 2 starts a year later in October 2002 and ends in July 2006, and the best parameters are also shown. The process is continued through April 2014. The results are spectacular, but beware of the benefit of hindsight. Notice how the **Le, Lx, and Sx** parameters stayed somewhat consistent; this does demonstrate parameter stability. The **Se** parameter was all over the map, and you can see that the system did not want to sell short between June 2009 and March 2013; the sell entry utilized a whopping 56 days in its calculation. Figure 8.6 is a graphic representation of how the analysis rolls forward.

Out-Of-Sample Testing When you run a WFO, the software builds a database of these "best" parameter sets and then informs the algorithm when to adopt and when to abandon them. TradeStation's WFO keeps track of all parameter switching and performance metrics on the trading algorithm as it progresses through the history of whatever you are testing.

The whole purpose of this software and this type of testing is based on the belief of optimization overhang or carryover; if a parameter has done well for the past four

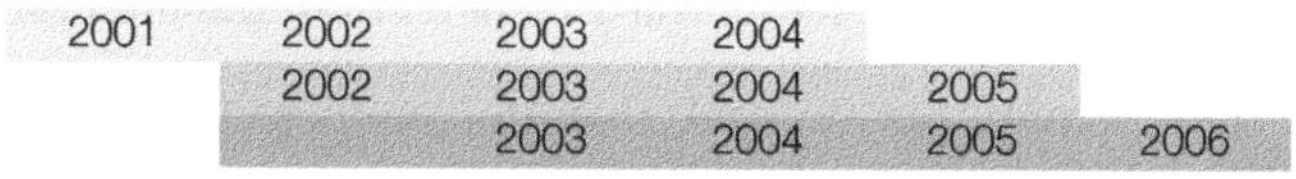

2001	2002	2003	2004		
	2002	2003	2004	2005	
		2003	2004	2005	2006

FIGURE 8.6 A graphic representation of how the walk-forward analysis (WFA) rolls forward.

TABLE 8.4 Out-of-Sample Testing

Le	Se	Lx	Sx	Begin Date End Date	Bars	Profit	Max DD
20	20	12	10	2005/06/15–2006/07/07	244	4,031.25	−2,562.50
20	20	12	10	2006/07/07–2007/06/27	244	4,437.50	−3,093.75
20	20	16	10	2007/06/27–2008/06/25	244	−3,437.50	−10,343.75
20	24	12	12	2008/06/26–2009/04/07	244	8,968.75	−7,343.75
20	20	12	14	2009/04/07–2010/04/16	244	−6,437.50	−13,187.50
20	36	10	14	2010/06/04–2011/03/29	244	8,250.00	−2,093.75
20	20	12	14	2011/04/18–2012/04/06	244	−2,500.00	−17,562.50
20	24	12	14	2012/04/06–2013/03/27	244	−1,937.50	−11,562.50
20	56	10	14	2013/03/27–2014/04/04	244	−4,062.50	−13,187.50
24	24	12	14	2014/04/04–2015/03/18	244	1,718.75	−5,156.25
						9,031.25	

years, it should overhang or carry over into the subsequent year. A practitioner of this school of thought also believes the market is changing and a trading algorithm must change or adapt as well. Table 8.4 shows the WFO of this system on the 30-year bond going back to 2001. Notice how the results start in 2005. The system backed up to 2001 and derived the best parameter set for those four years and then traded that set starting in June 2005 and ending in July 2006.

When July 2006 arrived, the system then switched to the second parameter set. These parameters were derived using data from 2002 through 2005 (refer back to table 3—second row). The WFO swapped parameters on an annual basis. Overall, the system was profitable, but the walk-forward efficiency was only 19.03 percent, and it lost 5 out of 10 years. Why did this happen? The only answer is the lack of optimization overhang in the out-of-sample periods.

System TA2 used the default WFO settings:

- Walk-forward runs = 10; in this test, the computer switched parameters 10 times over the history of the test. This works out to be about once a year. If the test period had been 20 years, then the WFO would have switched every 2 years.
- OOS% = 20%; this percentage informs the computer to utilize 80 percent of each interval's data (in-sample) to determine the best parameter set and then carry that parameter set forward 20 percent of the interval (out-of-sample).

If these settings are changed, then the number of bars used for optimization and the number of bars those optimizations are carried forward will change as well.

Here are the various calculations that are used to determine the total number of bars per run, in-sample number of bars, and out-of-sample number of bars.

TotalBarsPerRun—Total number of bars / (Walk-forward runs * Out-of-sample % + In-sample %). In our example test, there were a total of 3415 bars, 10 walk-forward runs, 20 OOS%, and 80 percent in-sample. WFO uses bars in place of days to calculate the walk-forward window lengths.
TotalBarsPerRun = 3415 / (10 * 0.2 + 0.8) = 1219

InSampleBarsPerRun – TotalBarsPerRun * In-sample%
InSampleBarsPerRun = 1219 * 0.8 = 975

OutOfSampleBarsPerRun – TotalBarsPerRun * Out-of-sample%
OutOfSampleBarsPerRun = 3414 * 0.2 = 244

The first interval analyzes the first 975 bars of data and determines the best parameter set and then carries that set on unseen data for 244 bars. The second test starts on bar 976 and ends on 1950 (976 + 974) and then walks forward 244 more days. Figure 8.7 illustrates this process by showing how four years are used to decide the best parameters using hindsight and then how those parameters are applied to unseen data the following year.

The WFO produces a WFA report that determines the usefulness of applying this type of optimization to this particular trading algorithm. Before showing the contents of this report let's create a benchmark parameter set and compare those results with those produced by the WFO. A benchmark can be created by using a fixed parameter set throughout the entire test time period. This is easily accomplished by setting the four parameters to the following values:

xLongEntryLen = 40, xLongExitLen = 20, xShortEntryLen = 40,
xShortExitLen = 20

In addition to making the parameters static notice that the system was also made symmetrical; the buy-side parameters are the same as the sell-side parameters. This particular parameter set did perform better over the walk-forward optimization as it produced almost $17,000, whereas the WFO produced nearly $10,000 in profit.

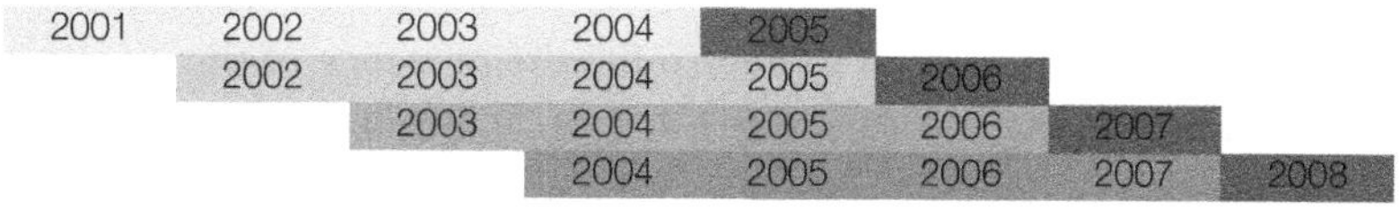

2001 2002 2003 2004 2005
2002 2003 2004 2005 2006
2003 2004 2005 2006 2007
2004 2005 2006 2007 2008

FIGURE 8.7 How four years of hindsight are used to predict unseen data for the following year.

TABLE 8.5 **WFA Report on TA2**

	Test Criteria	Result	Comment
1	Overall Profitability	Pass	Total Profit > 0. System likely to perform profitably on unseen data.
2	Walk-Forward Efficiency	Failed	< 50%. System likely to perform in future at a rate of less than 50% of those achieved during optimization.
3	Consistency of Profits	Pass	50% of walk-forward runs were profitable.
4	Distribution of Profits	Failed	Run #6 contributed more than 50% of Total Net Profit.
5	Maximum Drawdown	Pass	No individual run had a drawdown of more than 40% of init. capital.
	Overall Result	**FAILED**	

The WFO process did not outperform the static parameters on this particular algorithm. The WFA report is shown in Table 8.5.

The WFA agrees with our benchmark analysis that a WFO does not complement this type of trading algorithm. Of the five test criteria, this system failed two. The most important failed test was the walk forward efficiency (WFE). This value compares the in-sample average profit versus the out of-sample average profit. This algorithm failed with a 19.03 percent efficiency, meaning that the average OOS profit was one fifth the size of the in-sample profit. Now, does this mean TA2 is not a good trading algorithm? The robustness of the system logic and results of the static parameter analysis answers this question with an emphatic "No!" Just because a WFO didn't work well with this particular algorithm in the 30-year bonds doesn't mean it is not a good system. Other markets need to be tested and evaluated, as well as different WFO settings.

WFO Example 2

Another example of a WFO on a different type of algorithm may be a beneficial demonstration. This time, the WFO will be applied to a short-term ES (emini SP) system that produces more trades than TA2. This system, TA3, will trade in the direction of the long-term trend and buy pullbacks and sell rallies. The trend will be defined by a long-term moving average and pivot points will determine pullbacks and rallies; pivots involving the highs will determine rallies and pivots using the lows will determine pullbacks. Different protective stops and profit objectives will be used for long and short positions. The strength of the pivot points and the number of days that will be used to determine the presence of the pivot points may also be different for long and short entries. Two additional parameters will be used to limit the number of days the system is in the market. That makes a total of 11 optimizable parameters:

1.	movAvgLen	{ 50 to 150 by 10 increments } [11 iterations]
2.	pivotHiLookBack	{3 to 5 by 1 increment} [3 iterations]
3.	pivotHiStrength	{1 to 3 by 1 increment} [3 iterations]
4.	pivotLowLookBack	{3 to 5 by 1 increment} [3 iterations]
5.	pivotLowStrength	{1 to 3 by 1 increment} [3 iterations]
6.	LprofitObjective	{500 to 1500 by 50 increment} [21 iterations]
7.	LstopLoss	{250 to 750 by 50 increment} [11 iterations]
8.	SprofitObjective	{500 to 1500 by 50 increment} [21 iterations]
9.	SstopLoss	{250 to 750 by 50 increment} [11 iterations]
10.	longExitDays	{5 to 15 by 1} [11 iterations]
11.	shortExitDays	{5 to 15 by 1} [11 iterations]

$$\text{The total search space} = 11 * 3 * 3 * 3 * 3 * 21 * 11 * 21 * 11 * 11 * 11$$
$$= 5{,}752{,}902{,}771$$

That is nearly 6 billion iterations. Fortunately, the genetic method of optimization is available.

Here is the code for entries and exits:

```
Value1 = SwingHiBar(1,H,pivotHiStrength,pivotHiLookBack);
Value2 = SwingLowBar(1,L,pivotLowStrength,pivotLowLookBack);

If C > Average(C,avgLen) then
Begin
If Value1 <> -1 then Buy this Bar on Close;
End;
If C < Average(C,avgLen) then
Begin
If Value2 <> -1 then SellShort this Bar on Close;
End;

If MarketPosition = 1 Then
Begin
Sell Next Bar at EntryPrice + LprofitObjective/bigPointValue limit;
Sell Next Bar at EntryPrice - longStopLoss/bigPointValue stop;
End;

If MarketPosition = -1 Then
Begin
BuyToCover Next Bar at EntryPrice - SprofitObjective/
   bigPointValue limit;
BuyToCover Next Bar at EntryPrice + shortStopLoss/
   bigPointValue stop;
End;
```

OOS% \ Runs	5	10	15	20	25	30
10	FAILED	PASS	FAILED	PASS	FAILED	PASS
15	FAILED	FAILED	PASS	PASS	PASS	PASS
20	FAILED	FAILED	PASS	FAILED	PASS	FAILED
25	FAILED	PASS	FAILED	FAILED	FAILED	FAILED
30	PASS	FAILED	FAILED	FAILED	FAILED	FAILED

FIGURE 8.8 The Cluster WFO results matrix.

WFO Cluster Analysis The optimization using the genetic method took only a few moments. This time, instead of running a single WFO, the cluster WFO option was chosen. In this example, the cluster analysis ran 30 different walk-forward optimizations. Each optimization changed the values for OOS% and walk-forward runs. In the first single WFA, 10 runs utilizing 20 percent OOS% were evaluated to determine WFO fitness. Figure 8.8 shows the different values of WF runs and OOS% levels in a matrix format.

Similar to the single WFA on the Turtle-like system, this system failed as well, using the 10 WFA runs with 20 percent as the OOS%. However, this system passed the test on several different OOS% / Runs values. Please note that in an attempt to increase the likelihood of a passing grade, the criterion for the walk-forward efficiency was lowered from 50 to 30 percent in the test criteria setup. This criterion seems to be the one that rejects a larger portion of optimizations. To expect a 50 percent WFE is perhaps setting the bar a bit too high. The TS WFO selected a WFO using 15 percent for OOS% and 25 runs. It is the dark gray selection from Figure 8.8. This value is the center cell where a majority of its neighboring cells showed promise. This translates to using only 15 percent out-of-sample data and changing the parameters 25 times during the test period. The optimization produced over $52K in profits with a WFE of 49.9 percent. Table 8.6 shows the OOS report.

Table 8.7 provides the report card on this system using the optimal optimization values.

The cluster WFA is a very powerful tool because it allows the user to quickly look at different WFOs utilizing different OOS% values and walk-forward periods. A good trading algorithm may be rejected by simply using a single WFA. The e-mini SP system failed on the default 20 OOS% with 10 runs but passed on several different values.

The TS WFO software provides all the detailed information given in the cluster optimization matrix. A user can select any of the different optimizations and see a plethora of details. The ultimate question is then answered as to what parameter set should be used and how many days that set should be carried forward. If the

TABLE 8.6 The Out-of-Sample (OOS) Report

p1 p2 p3 p4 p5 p6 p7 p8 p9 p10 p11	Begin Date End Date	Bars	Profit	Max DD
90 5 2 5 2 900 650 13 600 400 9	2007/08/16–2007/12/11	117	−5, 512.	−7, 037
100 5 1 5 2 1450 350 14 1050 750 12	2007/12/11–2008/04/01	112	8, 325.	−4, 862
70 4 1 4 2 900 550 13 1150 750 8	2008/04/01–2008/07/16	106	4, 862.	−2, 962
100 5 1 5 2 1450 350 14 1050 750 12	2008/07/16–2008/11/10	117	21, 150	−4, 425
90 5 1 5 3 1500 350 13 1050 750 5	2008/11/10–2009/03/03	113	10, 475	−5, 150
90 5 1 5 3 1500 350 13 1050 750 5	2009/03/03–2009/05/29	87	−7, 362	−10, 400
90 5 1 5 3 1500 350 13 1050 750 5	2009/05/29–2009/10/02	126	2, 025	−1, 925
90 5 1 5 1 1400 300 13 1050 750 11	2009/10/08–2010/02/02	117	−2, 675	−4, 025
90 5 1 5 1 1450 350 8 1050 750 8	2010/02/02–2010/05/21	108	2, 050	−3, 425
90 5 1 5 1 1400 650 9 1100 650 11	2010/05/21–2010/09/03	105	−2, 200	−5, 862
90 5 1 5 1 1450 350 8 1100 750 13	2010/09/08–2010/12/27	110	4, 687	−2, 612
70 5 1 5 1 1400 450 8 1500 700 8	2010/12/30–2011/04/19	110	−2, 137	−4, 775
70 5 1 5 1 1450 350 8 1200 700 9	2011/04/19–2011/08/08	111	−1, 475	−6, 875.
100 5 1 3 1 1400 500 11 1100 700 6	2011/08/08–2011/11/23	107	662	−4, 937
100 5 1 3 1 1200 350 9 1200 700 13	2011/11/23–2012/03/22	120	3, 500	−1, 675
100 3 1 5 1 1450 350 9 1050 750 15	2012/03/22–2012/07/06	106	−1, 937	−3, 200
100 5 1 3 1 1200 350 9 1200 700 13	2012/07/12–2012/10/17	97	1, 512	−3, 337
90 4 1 3 1 1200 350 6 1200 700 9	2012/10/17–2013/02/19	125	−1, 070	−4, 932
80 4 1 3 2 1050 550 14 800 300 7	2013/02/21–2013/06/12	111	3, 800	−1, 650
90 4 1 4 1 1500 650 6 600 700 9	2013/06/12–2013/09/30	111	−750	−5, 300
90 4 1 4 1 1500 650 6 600 700 9	2013/09/30–2014/01/21	113	0	−1, 662
100 5 3 3 1 1200 700 13 1100 700 6	2014/01/21–2014/05/13	112	−2, 125	−4, 950
150 4 1 5 1 1150 350 13 950 500 14	2014/05/13–2014/08/28	108	3, 212	−3, 600
150 4 1 5 1 1150 350 13 950 500 14	2014/08/28–2014/12/18	112	2, 112	−4, 737
150 4 1 5 1 1150 350 13 950 500 14	2014/12/18–2015/04/07	110	11, 075.	−4, 087

TABLE 8.7 WFO Report Card TA3

	Test Criteria	Result	Comment
1	Overall Profitability	Pass	Total Profit > 0. System likely to perform profitably on unseen data.
2	Walk-Forward Efficiency	Pass	>= 30%. System likely to perform in future at a rate between 30–100% of those achieved during optimization.
3	Consistency of Profits	Pass	50%+ of walk-forward runs were profitable.
4	Distribution of Profits	Pass	No individual time period contributed more than 50% of Tot. Profit.
5	Maximum Drawdown	Pass	No individual run had a drawdown of more than 40% of init. capital.
	Overall Result	PASSED	

software-derived optimal set is selected (15 OOS% with 25 runs), then the following parameters are suggested to be used for next 111 days.

1.	movAvgLen	150
2.	pivotHiLookBack	4
3.	pivotHiStrength	1
4.	pivotLowLookBack	5
5.	pivotLowStrength	1
6.	LprofitObjective	1150
7.	LstopLoss	350
8.	SprofitObjective	950
9.	SstopLoss	500
10.	longExitDays	13
11.	shortExitDays	14

Now the question that started this part of the chapter can be answered. The WFO is an incredible tool that can help determine if a trading algorithm needs to be retrained periodically and also if the algorithm demonstrates sufficient robustness to match to some degree the results that were derived during its training.

Monte Carlo Analysis

As we have seen, walk-forward analysis can tell us much about an algorithm's robustness. Another tool that can reveal algorithm robustness is Monte Carlo simulation. The key to this form of simulation can be found in random numbers. Once you develop what you consider a good trading algorithm and test it against historical data, you then can really put it to the test by using random numbers and the historical trade history.

This trade history that is generated by testing your algorithm represents just one path your system traveled. What if you could create many paths by jumbling the order of the trades that your algorithm generated. These different paths could represent alternate universes. Let's say that your algorithm got lucky and had a bunch of winning trades in a row. This streak might be the portion of the equity curve that pulled the system out of mediocre status. If these trades didn't exist or hadn't fallen in place like they did, then the equity curve might look quite a bit different. A robust trading system should still produce robust performance metrics even when the trades are jumbled, some eliminated and some duplicated. If the majority of the alternate paths of an algorithm fail to produce good metrics, then the algorithm should be considered suspect.

Creating alternate paths or parallel universes is a very simple process when you have access to a random number generator and a computer. As you saw earlier in this chapter an RNG is a very special tool. Imagine all of the trades generated by your algorithm are each written on a separate piece of paper and all the pieces are then placed in a bag. You create an alternative trade history by reaching into the bag and randomly selecting trades and writing them down in a trade log in sequential manner. You do this routine until you have recorded the same number of trades that were initially generated by the backtest. One very important thing to remember is to always return the piece of paper to the bag after you record the trade. This process would be very time consuming and you might ask what's the use. Don't worry about the time involved because the computer can do it very quickly and recreating hundreds of alternative paths is well worth the effort. Will it help create a better algorithm? Probably not but it will help you make a decision to allocate real funds to an algorithm or not. Like I stated earlier, the robustness of a trading algorithm will reveal itself through Monte Carlo simulation.

Implementation of Monte Carlo Simulation Using Python The concept of this form of simulation is easy enough. And putting it into computer language is as easy. The hardest part is getting the initial trade list. Once you have that the rest falls into place relatively easily. Understanding how a computer implementation of a concept works usually helps the understanding of how the concept works in general and how it might be beneficial.

Imagine all the trades generated by a backtest are stored in a list. The list is simply an ordered collection of the trade dates and trade profits. The list might look something like this:

TradeList[0] = (20011015,−150)

TradeList[1] = (20011105,+200)

TradeList[2] = (20011202,−300)

TradeList[3] = (20011222,+500)

You could call this the source list. Now imagine you have another blank list that's called AlternateList1. The objective of the Monte Carlo simulation is to fill the AlternateList1 with trades from the source list. If there are only four elements in the list, you would need an RNG to generate random numbers from 0 to 3. Let's push the RNG button and start the process of filling up AlternateList1:

The RNG generates the number 3
AlternateList1[0] = TradeList[3]

RNG generates the number 0
AlternateList[1] = TradeList[0]

RNG generates the number 1
AlternateList[2] = TradeList[1]

RNG generates the number 3
AlternateList[3] = TradeList[3]

Our new alternate list of trades would look like this:

AlternateList[0] = (20011222,+500)

AlternateList[1] = (20011015,−150)

AlternateList[2] = (20011105,+200)

AlternateList[3] = (20011222,+500)

Simple, right? All we are doing is jumbling the order of the original list to create an alternate path the trading system might have followed. Did you notice that the RNG generated the number 3 twice? So AlternateList[3] is the same as AlternateList[0]. Does this seem right? This is correct and exactly what we want our RNG to do. This is called sampling with replacement. Remember how the piece of paper was to be put back into the bag after recording it? This method almost guarantees that we never recreate the original trade listing. This is important because we want to create as many unique alternative paths as we can.

Python provides, to its programmers, some very useful data structures. However, it does not provide the array structure like other languages (you can use arrays in Python if you import them with the NumPy library). Arrays are very powerful and can be multidimensional and this is the structure I would have used if I had used a different language. But Python has this really cool structure called a tuple. A tuple is simply a collection or a list of like data. Here are examples of a classic car tuple:

antiqueCarTuple[0] = (1967, 'Ford' , 'Mustang' , 289)

antiqueCarTuple[1] = (1971, "Chevy', 'Chevelle', 402)

As you can see each tuple element holds the various properties of a classic car. If I need to know the model of the second antique car, I can access it by using the following notation: modelName = antiqueCarTuple[1][2]

The first bracket following the name of the tuple selects which tuple you are wanting to access from the tuple list. Since Python is 0 based the [1] in this example tells the computer to select the second tuple or car. The next bracket is used to determine which element in the tuple to access. I wanted the model, or third element, of the antique car so I used the number 2 to access it.

In our Monte Carlo example each tuple will hold the date of the trade exit and the associated profit or loss. Here is the very lengthy and elaborate code for creating 1000 alternate paths of our trading algorithm:

```
mcTradeTuple = list()
for x in range(0,1000): # number of alternate histories
    for y in range(0,len(tradeTuple)):
        randomTradeNum = random.randint(0,len(tradeTuple)-1)
        tradeDate = tradeTuple[randomTradeNum][0]
        tradePL = tradeTuple[randomTradeNum][1]
        mcTradeTuple += ((x,y,tradeDate,tradePL),)
```

That's it! These seven lines of code is all it took to create 1000 different and mostly unique alternate trade histories. I won't bore you with all of the details, but I will step through the code quickly to demonstrate how easy this was to do with Python. Initially I stored all of the trade dates and trade P/L in a tuple named **tradeTuple**. From this list I culled all of the trades to fill up the 1000 alternate lists. Basically I started with the source list and for each trade in the list I created a random number between 0 and the number of trades:

```
randomTradeNum = random.randint(0,len(tradeTuple)-1)
```

Python generates random numbers through its module: **random.randint**. I then used the **randomTradeNum** as an index into the tradeTuple to extract the **tradeDate** and **tradePL**:

```
tradeDate = tradeTuple[randomTradeNum][0]
tradePL = tradeTuple[randomTradeNum][1]
```

Remember the first bracketed number following the tuple selects which tuple. The second bracketed number selects the element in that particular tuple. In the **tradeTuple**, [0] is the trade date and [1] is the trade P/L. While stepping through the alternate histories sequentially, trades were randomly selected from the original trade history and inserted. All of the alternate histories were then stored in a list of tuples named **mcTradeTuple**. The **+=** operand simply appends the current alternate trade history to the list. In the end, you have one huge list that includes all of the alternate histories.

AmiBroker's Monte Carlo Simulation The Python Monte Carlo simulation is included in the Python System Backtester. I programmed the simulation because I wanted to fully understand the mechanism. Fortunately, you don't need to program these types of tools because they are usually included in your favorite testing platform. This is the case for AmiBroker and TradeStation. AmiBroker's Monte Carlo analysis is so simple all you have to do is flip a switch. Click the Settings button in an Analysis window and hit the Monte Carlo tab (see Figure 8.9). You have seen this dialog before but this is the first time we have discussed the Monte Carlo settings. The default values are the most popular. The position sizing parameters offers four different options: (1) keep the sizing the same as the initial test, (2) use a fixed size of contracts or shares, (3) use a fixed dollar value for size computation, and (4) use a percentage of equity in fixed fractional approach. The fourth option can introduce serial dependency into the Monte Carlo simulation due to the fact that the size of the current trade is dependent upon the success of all of the prior trades. Utilizing this option might muddy the waters a bit when trying to determine algorithm robustness. Before we move on let's discuss the idea of serial correlation among the trades of a trading algorithm. This concept basically implies there is a relationship or connection between a trade and the subsequent trade or trades. Critics of Monte Carlo simulation on actual

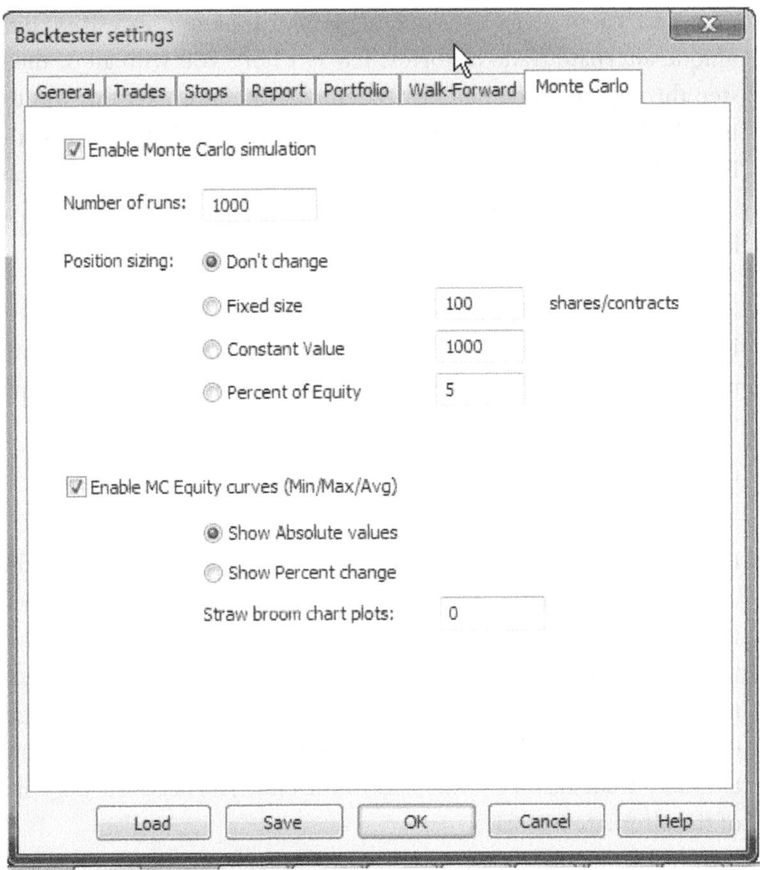

FIGURE 8.9 AmiBroker Monte Carlo settings dialog.

trades suggest this important correlation is ignored when trades are jumbled. If you think about it, it sort of makes sense when dealing with a trend-following algorithm. Trend-following trades can follow a cyclical pattern—one large winner due to a trend, followed by a series of small losers that occur in the absence of a trend. You can see that the small losers are a consequence of the dissipation of the trend. This series of trades, big winner, small losers demonstrates a level of trade interdependency. The Turtles felt like a loser might follow a winner and therefore utilized the *Last Trade Was a Loser* filter. There has been much research on this topic and the consensus has been that if serial correlation existed, it only applied to the first subsequent trade. All other trades were independent events. If serial correlation is a concern, a Monte Carlo simulation on equity curve segments would be a solution. Each segment would contain the same series of trades and therefore maintain the correlation. Since we are dealing with a large majority of alternate paths I don't necessarily think you need to concern yourself with serial correlation. So just go

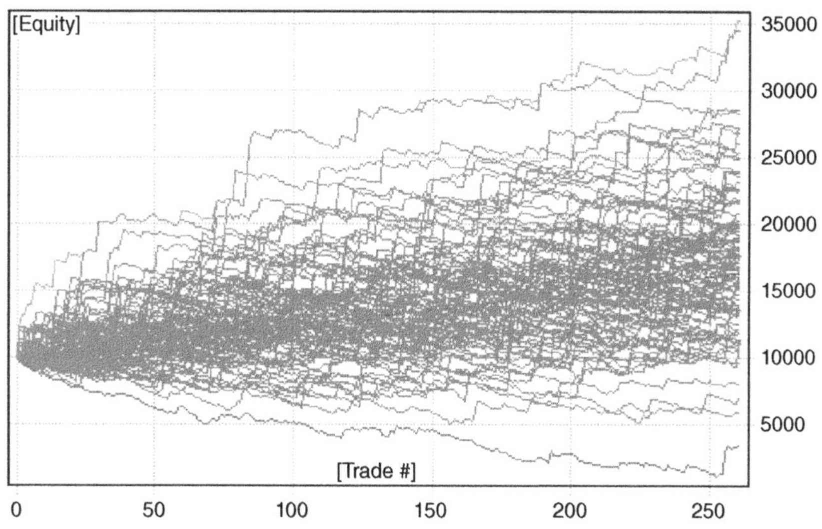

FIGURE 8.10 Monte Carlo Straw Broom chart of multiple randomized equity curves.

ahead and accept the default settings and click OK. AmiBroker creates a couple of charts/reports that will illustrate the usefulness of this form of simulation. The first chart is called a Straw Broom chart because of the way it looks (see Figure 8.10).

This is a representation of all of the alternate trade histories that were created by using the random number generator. As you can see, most of the histories end at different equity values and this is due to sampling with replacement. Had we not allowed replacement, then all of the equity curves would end at the exact same spot. The accumulation of all of the trades, irrespective of order, follows the commutative law. You can easily see the boundary (top and bottom) histories that represent the best and worst performance. The rest of the histories congregate in the middle and create a cloud. This cloud is what you want to see from your own algorithm simulation; many of the random histories created similar outcomes. AmiBroker also creates the following table that provides the statistics derived from the distribution of the simulation results (Table 8.8).

The first column shows the percentile level that certain observations fell. In the first row 1% of all observations had profit levels below \$5,706 and maximum drawdowns below \$1,302. These two events, based off of their probabilities, are unlikely to happen again. Fifty percent of the time you could expect profits to be less than or equal to \$16,174 and maximum drawdown to be less than or equal to \$2,747. Ninety-nine percent of the time you could expect drawdowns below \$7,685. Keep in mind what we expect and what really happens doesn't always jive. We are basing all of our expectations on historical results, results that have a certain level of built-in hindsight bias.

TABLE 8.8 Distribution Statistics from Monte Carlo Simulations

	Final Equity	Annual Return	Max. Drawdown $	Max. Drawdown %	Lowest Eq.
1%	5706	−7.37%	1302	7.23%	3618
5%	7987	−3.02%	1549	9.76%	5853
10%	9706	**−0.41%**	1726	11.32%	6690
25%	12851	3.48%	2136	14.38%	8107
50%	16174	6.78%	2747	19.77%	9135
75%	19632	9.64%	3563	27.63%	9640
90%	23258	12.21%	4626	**38.48%**	9922
95%	25269	13.48%	5292	45.47%	10000
99%	29139	15.71%	7685	**63.82%**	10000

Start Trade Drawdown

The maximum drawdown metric that is derived from backtesting is a key component used to help a trader judge the capitalization requirements of a particular trading algorithm. If an algorithm suffers a $50,000 drawdown, it logically follows that this event could occur again in the future. And accordingly the trader should allocate at least $50,000 to his trading account. What if the algorithm is very good and this one event doesn't cast it in a good light? What if the drawdown follows a large runup? In this case, the drawdown is somewhat a function of the system's success. Another drawdown metric, start trade drawdown, can help shed light on an algorithm's drawdown structure. A trader is most sensitive to drawdown when she initially starts to trade a new algorithm. A $50,000 drawdown that decimates a trader's account right off the bat is completely different than a $50,000 drawdown that occurs after a $200,000 runup. Wouldn't it be nice to know the probability of having a huge drawdown at the beginning of trading? Also wouldn't it be nice to know the probability of the maximum drawdown occurring again in the future for capitalization purposes? This concept of Start Trade drawdown can be attributed to Keith Fitschen. He describes it on his website, www.keithstrading.com, and in his book, *Building Reliable Trading Systems* (Wiley, 2013, New Jersey). Let's assume you have a trading algorithm that trades 100 times. Would a trader starting at trade #1 have a different drawdown than a trader starting at trade #50? This is a very good question and I guess Mr. Fitschen asked himself this exact same question. You could simply analyze the drawdowns that occur after trade #1 and the drawdowns that occur after trade #50 and answer the question. What if there was an analysis that could provide the probabilities of different drawdown magnitudes derived from the historical results of a trading algorithm? This could definitely help a person decide if a system is worth the risk, and at the same time know how much capital would be required to fund it. Well, thanks to Keith Fitschen, we have this analysis.

Calculating Start Trade Drawdown With the use of a computer, the process of this calculation is easily accomplished. This calculation is somewhat similar to the Monte Carlo simulation in that you are recreating multiple histories of a trading algorithm. However, this time an RNG is not utilized. The first trade history is the trade history that contains all of the historic trades. Subsequent trade histories start at the subsequent trade in the original history. For example, the second trade history starts at the beginning of trade #2 and the next trade history starts at beginning of trade #3, and so on. An original trade history containing 100 trades will spawn 100 histories starting at different trade numbers. Once all of the histories are created then all one needs to do is flow through each history and keep track of cumulative profit and maximum drawdown.

After creating and analyzing the 100 trade histories a cumulative frequency distribution table (CFDT) must be created. A CFDT is created by distributing the 100 drawdowns into different bins. The bins are the same size but have different boundaries. Assume the 100 drawdowns range from $5,000 to $25,000 and you want to store the different drawdown in 20 bins. The range is equal to $20,000 ($25,000 – $5,000) so each bin would have to be $1,000 wide ($20,000/20). Bin #1 would contain the drawdowns that ranged from $5,000.00 to $5,999.99, bin #2 would contain the drawdowns that ranged from $6,000 to $6,999.99, bin #3 would contain the drawdowns that ranged from $7,000 to $7,999.99, and so on. See how the bins are the same size but have different low and high boundaries?

Once the drawdowns are distributed into the different bins you can easily create a cumulative frequency by summing up the number of drawdowns in each bin. Once you have the cumulative frequency it is simple to calculate the probability of occurrence for each bin. With 100 different trade histories starting at different trade numbers, it is not uncommon to have less than 100 distinct max drawdown values. In some cases, the same max drawdown value will be observed when the starting point of each history is in close proximity. I wouldn't be surprised if the max drawdown was the same starting at trade #2 versus starting at trade #3. The fact is you will have 100 max drawdown values but they won't all be distinct. The bins will contain multiple duplicate drawdown values. Each bin will contain N number of values and the probability of the occurrence of that bin's max value and below will be the sum of N up to that bin/Total N. Let's say bin #1 [$5,000 – $5,999] contains 5 values and bin #2 [$6,000 – $6,999] contains 3 values. The probability of a drawdown less than $6,999 would be 8/100 or 8%. This type of information can be very beneficial at the beginning stage of trading a new algorithm.

Implementation of Start Trade Drawdown Simulation Using Python Simulation of the different trade histories depends on the actual number of trades generated by the algorithm. This simulation requires a nested for-loop where the outside loop loops from trade #1 to the last trade. The interior loop loops from the current trade number to the last trade.

```
# start trade draw down analysis - utilizing the tradeTuple
  tupleLen = len(tradeTuple)
  tradeTuple = sorted(tradeTuple,key=itemgetter(0))
  for x in range(0,tupleLen):
    cumStartTradeEquity = 0
    maxStartTradeDD = -99999999
    maxCumEquity = 0
    for y in range(x,tupleLen):
      cumStartTradeEquity += tradeTuple[y][1]
      maxCumEquity = max(maxCumEquity,cumStartTradeEquity)
      maxStartTradeDD = max(maxStartTradeDD,maxCumEquity -
                            cumStartTradeEquity)
    startTradeTuple += ((x,cumStartTradeEquity,
                          maxStartTradeDD),)
```

The outer loop indexed by **x** controls the number of trade histories. The inner loop indexed by **y** flows through the different trade histories and keeps track of each history's cumulative equity and maximum drawdown. At the beginning of each trade history, these two values are zeroed out. Each trade's P/L is stored as the second element in the tuple **tradeTuple**. This value is extracted through each **y** iteration and used to calculate the two performance metrics. Once an individual history is created it is then stored in a list of tuples named **startTradeTuple**. The first element in this tuple is x (the trade history number). The second element **cumStartTradeEquity** stores the cumulative equity of the history and the third element **maxStartTradeDD** stores the max drawdown of the history.

Once the trade histories are compiled, the bins that hold the different max drawdowns must be constructed. The first step in the construction process is to calculate the largest and smallest historic drawdown values.

```
  minDD = 99999999
  maxDD = 0
  for y in range(0,len(startTradeTuple)):
    print(startTradeTuple[y][0],'  ',startTradeTuple[y][1],
       '  ',startTradeTuple[y][2])
    if startTradeTuple[y][2] < minDD: minDD =
          startTradeTuple[y][2]
    if startTradeTuple[y][2] > maxDD: maxDD =
          startTradeTuple[y][2]
```

A loop is used to flow through each trade history and keep track of the maximum and minimum values stored in the third element of the startTradeTuple (max drawdown of each history).

Twenty bins will be used in this example to store the individual drawdown values. The bin size is calculated by dividing the range of drawdowns by 20. The size of the bin is stored in the variable **binInc** (bin increment). Each bin is constructed by storing each bin's boundary values in a list of tuples named **binTuple**. Each binTuple contains three elements: binNumber, binBottom, and binTop. The boundary values are calculated by starting at the smallest max drawdown of the histories (bottom of the first bin) and adding the bin size to get the top of the first bin. The next bin's bottom boundary becomes the prior bin's top and its top is calculated by adding the **binInc**. This process is repeated until all 20 bin tuples are filled up with the correct values.

```
numBins = 20
binTuple = list()
binInc = (maxDD - minDD)/20.0
binBot = minDD
for y in range(0,numBins):
    binTop = binBot + binInc
    binTuple += ((y,binBot,binTop),)
    print(binTuple[y][1],' ',binTuple[y][2])
    binBot = binTop + y
```

Once the bins are constructed all the different histories' max drawdowns are distributed into them. This is accomplished by comparing the max drawdown with each bin's top and bottom boundaries. If the drawdown value falls between the two boundaries, it is then placed into that bin. A blank list of bins is initially created.

```
bins = list()
bins[:] = []
for x in range(0,numBins):
    bins.append(0)
```

The different histories are looped through and are placed into the different bins. Well, not really, just the frequencies of the drawdowns are stored.

```
for x in range(0,len(startTradeTuple)):
    for y in range(0,numBins):
        tempDD = startTradeTuple[x][2]
        tempBot = binTuple[y][1]
        tempTop = binTuple[y][2]
        if (tempDD >= binTuple[y][1] and tempDD <
                binTuple[y][2]):
            bins[y] += 1
```

Once the frequency of each drawdown is stored in each bin the total number of drawdown occurrences must be calculated.

```
freqSum = sum(bins)
```

Python has a cool list method **sum**. This method sums up all of the values in the list in one fell swoop. This is the beauty of an object-oriented language. Once the total is calculated, the cumulative probabilities is just a loop away.

```
binProb = list()
for y in range(0,numBins):
    if y == 0:
        binProb.append(bins[y]/freqSum)
    else:
        binProb.append(bins[y]/freqSum + binProb[y-1])
```

The probability of bin #1 is simply the number of drawdowns in that bin divided by the total number of max drawdowns. The subsequent bin's probabilities are the probability of the current bin plus the prior bin's probability. This process accumulates the frequencies of the drawdowns. Here is a printout of a probability distribution of an algorithm trading different markets.


```
Probability of DD <   1547 is 0.060
Probability of DD <   3094 is 0.080
Probability of DD <   4643 is 0.080
Probability of DD <   6192 is 0.280
Probability of DD <   7743 is 0.320
Probability of DD <   9294 is 0.400
Probability of DD <  10847 is 0.400
Probability of DD <  12400 is 0.420
Probability of DD <  13955 is 0.640
Probability of DD <  15510 is 0.660
Probability of DD <  17067 is 0.680
Probability of DD <  18624 is 0.820
Probability of DD <  20183 is 0.880
Probability of DD <  21742 is 0.880
Probability of DD <  23303 is 0.900
Probability of DD <  24864 is 0.920
Probability of DD <  26427 is 0.940
Probability of DD <  27990 is 0.960
Probability of DD <  29555 is 0.980
Probability of DD <  31120 is 1.000
```

The maximum drawdown of this algorithm was around $30,000. The probability of this event occurring again is less than 2%. The probability of having a drawdown greater than $20,000 is less than 12%. These drawdowns only include closed trade drawdowns—the amount of drawdown after the trade was closed out, not while it was open. Open trade drawdown will always be greater than or equal to closed trade drawdown. The loss isn't realized until the trade is closed out. Again, keep in mind we are dealing with hypothetical performance metrics with an inherent hindsight bias. Stating that a drawdown has less than a 2% chance of occurring again cannot be said with a straight face. However, historic performance is all we have to hang our hat on.

Summary

The purpose of this chapter was to be a guide and explain concepts that on the cover seem to be beyond the reach of a typical algorithmic system developer/trader. Genetic optimization is just a very smart way to get to a solution quickly. Walk-Forward Optimization, Monte Carlo simulation, and Start Trade drawdown are tools that can provide the necessary evidence that a trading algorithm might have a chance of performing in the future. Python code was peppered throughout the text pertaining to Monte Carlo simulation and Start Trade drawdown to demonstrate how simple the processes are that carry out these particular forms of analysis. None of these tools will provide the "Holy Grail," but in this author's opinion, they will help the user develop a trading solution that best fits his or her own trading style.

CHAPTER 9

An Introduction to Portfolio Maestro, Money Management, and Portfolio Analysis

It has been mentioned in many trading circles through the years that money management is as important as the algorithm that generates the trade entries. The position size is paramount when it comes to utilizing capital in the most efficient manner. Thus far, we have simply tested on a one-contract basis, and that in of itself is a money management scheme. The one contract per market scheme was utilized, because the primary focus was on developing a trade entry-and-exit algorithm. Now that we have spent a sufficient amount of time on algorithm development, this guide would not be complete without a chapter on money management and portfolio analysis. This time we will lean on TradeStation to carry out our analysis—this platform has the toolset necessary to apply both portfolio and money management schemes to a trading algorithm.

Fixed Fractional

Fixed Fractional is by far the most popular form of money management in the world of futures trading. This approach allocates the same amount of capital to each market. Perceived risk is usually defined as a function of a market's average true range calculated over the last N days. Dividing the amount of capital by market risk gives the position size for the next trade. This form of money management normalizes the markets by maintaining the same amount of perceived risk across all markets in the portfolio. Here is the formula:

$$\text{Position size} = (\text{Account capital in dollars} \times \text{Risk per trade in percent}) / \text{ATR}(N) \text{ in dollars}$$

Assume you have a \$100,000 capital allocation, and you want to risk at most 1 percent on any given trade. Assume the 10-day ATR in Treasury notes is \$500. How many contracts should be initiated on the next trade? Plugging into the formula we get:

$$\text{Position size} = (100,000 \times 0.01) / 500$$

$$\text{Position size} = 1000 / 500 = 2$$

So two contracts of T-notes will fit our 1 percent risk criteria. Now assume you want to trade Eurodollars as well and need to know that position size. Let's say the 10-day ATR in Eurodollars is \$125. Plugging into the formula again, we get:

$$\text{Position size} = (100,000) \times 0.01\ ) / 125$$

$$\text{Position size} = 1000 / 125 = 8$$

Eight contracts of Eurodollars provides the same risk as two contracts of T-notes. See how the different markets are normalized to provide the same amount of risk? Utilizing a Donchian 55-day breakout with a trailing 20-day liquidation and a fixed dollar stop, let's see how this money management formula works in practice.

Portfolio Maestro

Portfolio Maestro (PM) is an add-on to TradeStation and requires an additional monthly fee. If you have it you might want to follow along with this tutorial. If you don't, then read on and see if it might be something you may want to investigate. From TradeStation you can launch PM by clicking on the Trading Apps tab, and then selecting Portfolio Maestro. PM will launch and you will be presented with the window shown in Figure 9.1.

Once you get used to the interface, building and testing portfolios will become old hat. However, the first few analyses may take multiple attempts to get everything the way you want. Hopefully, this tutorial will help along the way.

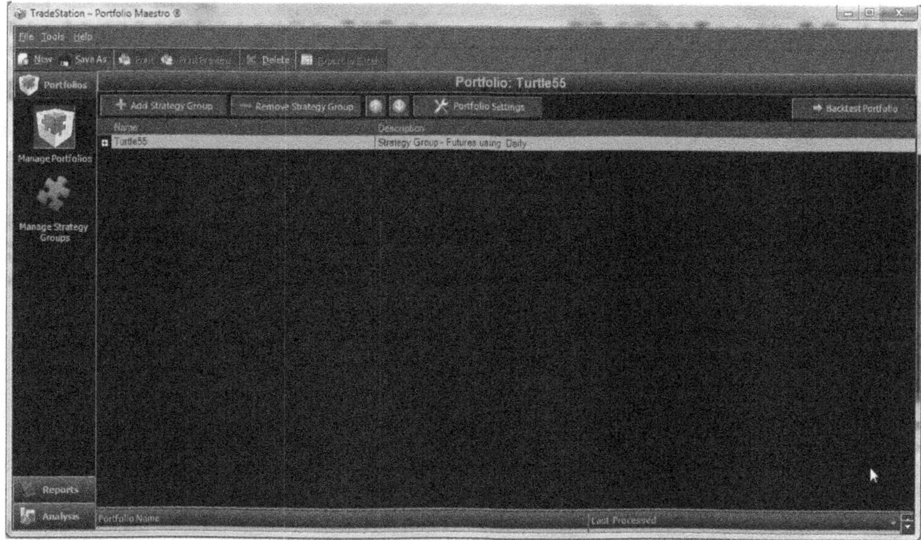

FIGURE 9.1 TradeStation's Portfolio Maestro (PM) launch window.

PM works around the concepts of a **Strategy Group** and a **Portfolio** of **Strategy Groups**. Before you can do anything you must build a **Strategy Group**. The Strategy Group that we will be using is one that incorporates our Turtle-like 55-day Donchian breakout. If you haven't imported the ELDs from the website, this would be a great time to do so.

Strategy Group

In PM, a **Strategy Group** consists of a trading algorithm and the portfolio of markets to which that algorithm will be applied. With the PM window in front of you click on the **File** menu, select **New**, and then select **Strategy Group**. Where it asks for Name type in **MyFirstStrategyGroup** and then select **Futures** as the asset class.

You will then be sent back to the PM main window. Click on the **Strategies** tab and then click on the **Add Strategy** button. Another window will open and list all of the strategies that are in your strategies library (see Figure 9.2).

Scroll down the list until you come to **Turtle 55**. If you don't see it, then you might need to reimport the ELD files from this book's companion website (www.wiley.com/go/ultimatealgotoolbox). If it's there, click on the name and highlight it. Then click OK. The PM window will now show **Turtle 55** in the **Strategies** window (see Figure 9.3).

We now have a strategy, but now we need to tell PM to apply it to a list or portfolio of markets. Click on the **Symbol Lists** tab right beside the **Strategies** tab. A window will appear similar to Figure 9.4.

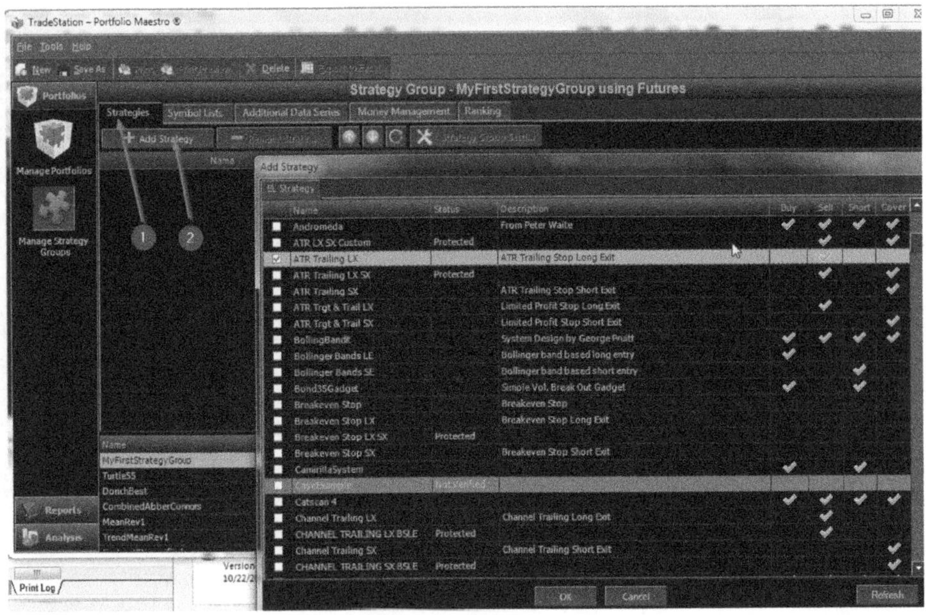

FIGURE 9.2 Add a strategy to your strategy group.

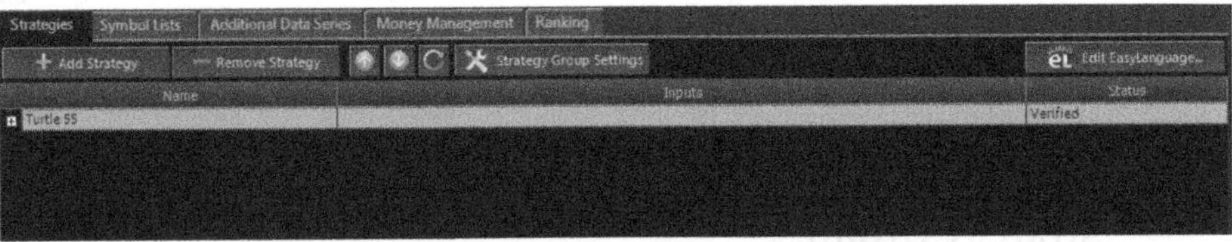

FIGURE 9.3 The Turtle 55 strategy is now in your strategies window.

PM asks you to select a preexisting list of markets. I've created a custom list for this book, labeled **UGTATS**, and it includes the following markets:

UGTATS Market List

Australian Dollar	Cotton	Gold
Beans	Crude	Heating Oil
British Pound	Dollar Index	Kansas City Wheat
Cocoa	Euro FX Currency	Lean Hog
Coffee	Euro Dollar	Live Cattle
Copper	Feeder Cattle	Mini-Russell
Corn	Five-Year Notes	Mini-SP400

Mini-SP500	Platinum	Treasury Bonds (30-Year)
Natural Gas	Silver	Unleaded
Orange Juice	Treasury Notes (2-Year, 5-Year, and 10-Year)	Wheat

If you need help creating a **Symbol List**, there is a short tutorial at www.georgepruitt.com. After selecting the **UGTATS** list your **Symbol List** window should look something like this (see Figure 9.5).

If you click on the plus sign beside the **UGTATS Symbol List**, the symbols of the markets included in the list will be shown (see Figure 9.6).

Now that we have created a complete strategy group (Strategy and Symbol List), it is now time to create a portfolio. Go back under the **File** menu, select **New**, and

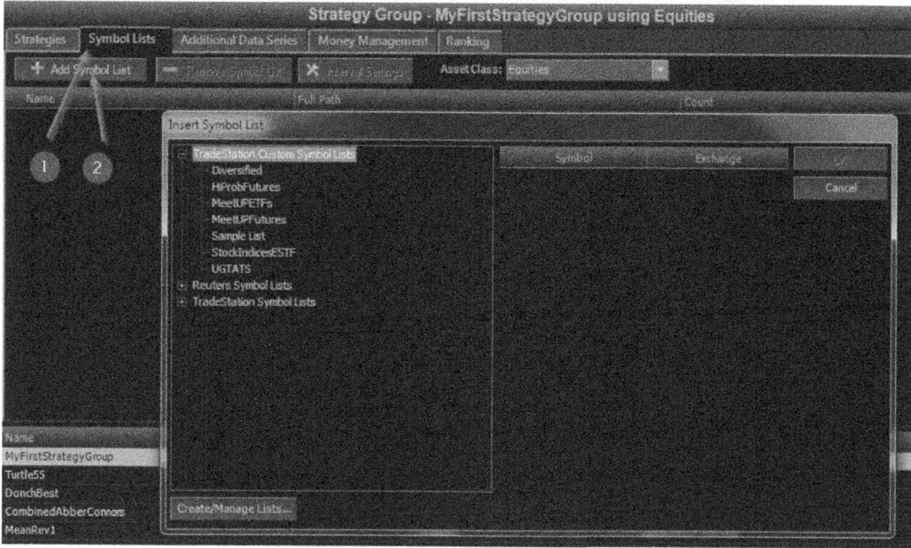

FIGURE 9.4 Add a symbol by clicking the Symbol Lists tab (indicated by Arrow 1), then clicking on Add Symbol List (shown with Arrow 2).

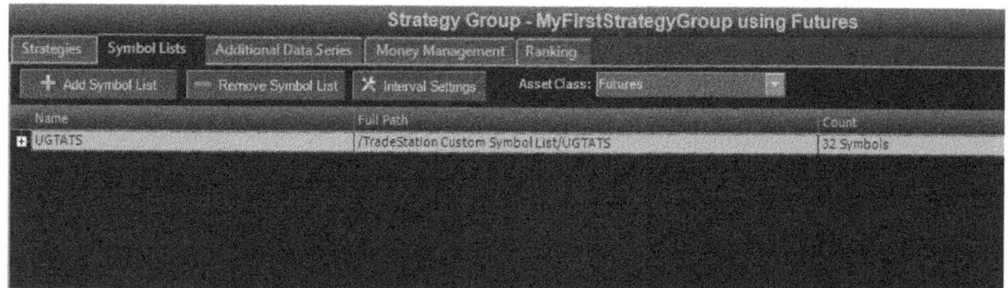

FIGURE 9.5 After selecting the UGTATS list, it will appear in your symbol list window.

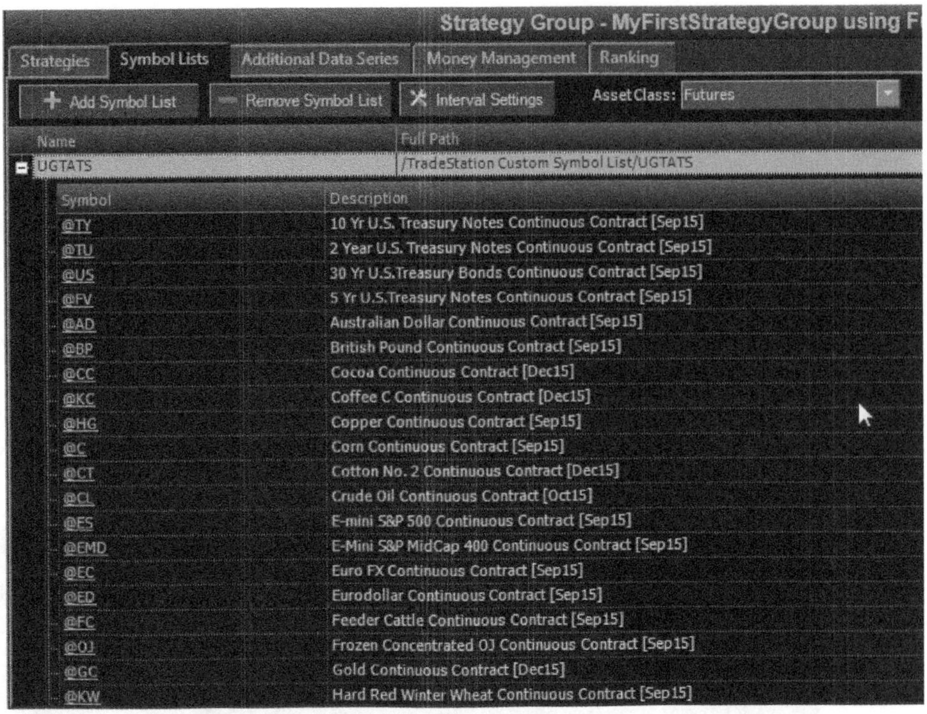

Strategy Group - MyFirstStrategyGroup using F

Strategies | Symbol Lists | Additional Data Series | Money Management | Ranking

Add Symbol List | Remove Symbol List | Interval Settings | Asset Class: Futures

Name	Full Path
UGTATS	/TradeStation Custom Symbol List/UGTATS

Symbol	Description
@TY	10 Yr U.S. Treasury Notes Continuous Contract [Sep15]
@TU	2 Year U.S. Treasury Notes Continuous Contract [Sep15]
@US	30 Yr U.S.Treasury Bonds Continuous Contract [Sep15]
@FV	5 Yr U.S.Treasury Notes Continuous Contract [Sep15]
@AD	Australian Dollar Continuous Contract [Sep15]
@BP	British Pound Continuous Contract [Sep15]
@CC	Cocoa Continuous Contract [Dec15]
@KC	Coffee C Continuous Contract [Dec15]
@HG	Copper Continuous Contract [Sep15]
@C	Corn Continuous Contract [Sep15]
@CT	Cotton No. 2 Continuous Contract [Dec15]
@CL	Crude Oil Continuous Contract [Oct15]
@ES	E-mini S&P 500 Continuous Contract [Sep15]
@EMD	E-Mini S&P MidCap 400 Continuous Contract [Sep15]
@EC	Euro FX Continuous Contract [Sep15]
@ED	Eurodollar Continuous Contract [Sep15]
@FC	Feeder Cattle Continuous Contract [Sep15]
@OJ	Frozen Concentrated OJ Continuous Contract [Sep15]
@GC	Gold Continuous Contract [Dec15]
@KW	Hard Red Winter Wheat Continuous Contract [Sep15]

FIGURE 9.6 The UGTATS markets and their corresponding symbols.

then select **Portfolio**. A dialog box similar to the one we used to create a New Strategy Group will pop up. In the **Name** field, type **MyFirstPortfolio** and then click OK. After clicking OK a blank portfolio window will appear. The message in the window ("This portfolio does not have any strategy groups … ") is informing you that you have not yet selected a strategy group. We can remedy this very quickly by clicking on the **Add Strategy Group** button. A list of strategy groups will be presented (see Figure 9.7). Select **MyFirstStrategyGroup** and it will be inserted into **MyFirstPortfolio** (see Figure 9.8).

You might need to expand the boxes to see the **Turtle 55** strategy and the **UGTATS** Symbol List. The **Portfolio** window shows the different strategy groups inside the **Portfolio**. You can have multiple **Strategy Groups** trading different **Strategies** on different **Symbol Lists**. This is a very powerful tool—the ability to merge multiple **Strategies** across multiple **Symbol Lists**. We touched on this exact subject of Multiple Algorithmic Strategies (MAS) in Chapter 3.

Before we backtest the portfolio, let's change the **Strategy Group** settings by going back to the **Strategy Group**. Click on the **Manage Strategy Group**

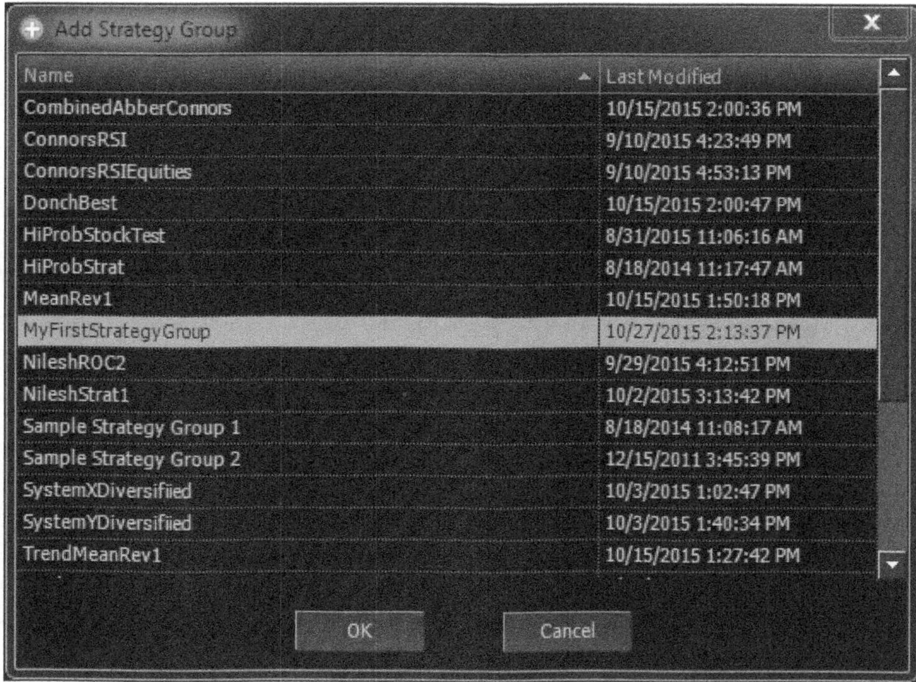

FIGURE 9.7 A list of available strategy groups, including MyFirstStrategyGroup, which we are using for this exercise.

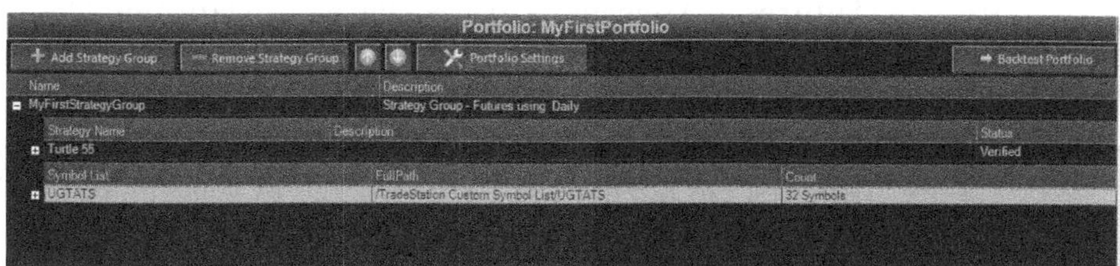

FIGURE 9.8 After selecting MyFirstStrategyGroup, you will see it in MyFirstPortfolio. In the expanded view, you can see the strategies and symbols that are part of your group.

(puzzle piece) button, and then click on the **Strategy Group Settings** button. The settings dialog box will open and should look similar to Figure 9.9.

From this dialog, we can change the commission and slippage and various other strategy-dependent parameters. You can even change the **Strategy Inputs** by clicking the **Strategy Inputs** tab. Go ahead and change the **Commission** and **Slippage** to $12.50 for each on a **Per Contract** basis. Click **OK**, and then, to be on the safe side, click on the **Symbol List** tab again and make sure the **Asset Class** is

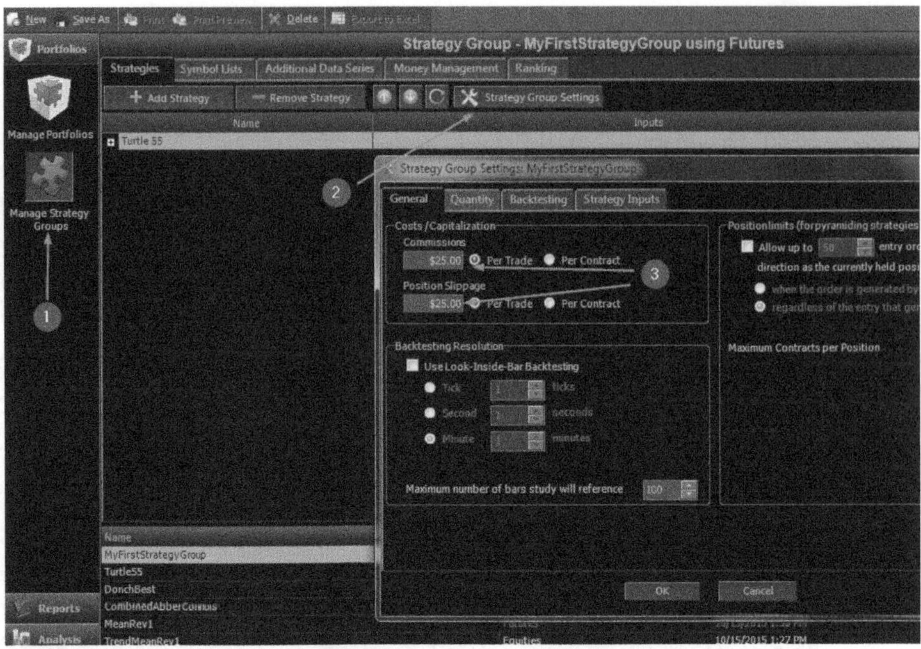

FIGURE 9.9 How to adjust the settings for a strategy group. Arrow 1 indicates the Manage Strategy Group button. Arrow 2 highlights the Strategy Group Settings button. Arrow 3 points to the controls that change the commission and slippage inputs.

still set to **Futures**. PM sometimes switches this back to **Equities**. Once you check this, click the **Manage Portfolios** button and finally click **Backtest Portfolio**. Another dialog window will appear that lets you change the test period, **Initial Capital**, the **Backtest Type** (standard or optimization), and the **Report Name** (Figure 9.10). You can also deselect certain markets by going to the **Symbols** tab. Change the test period to start 10 **Years Back**.

If everything looks OK, then click **Perform Backtest**. The test might take a few minutes if you have a large **Symbol List**. TradeStation first pulls the data from their data servers and then applies the strategy to each market. I have a feeling TradeStation will make this process much quicker by caching the data on the hard drive in the future.

Once the test is complete, PM will ask if you would like to view the report now or later. Go ahead and click **Now**. A window like the one in Figure 9.11 will open, and show you the portfolio performance of your **MyFirstPortfolio**. Remember this portfolio consists of two components, a strategy and a portfolio.

Figure 9.11 illustrates a portion of the performance metrics that are included in the **Summary** report. This portfolio actually did pretty well over the past 10 years: $739,684 in profits with an average trade of $426. You can scroll down and see a

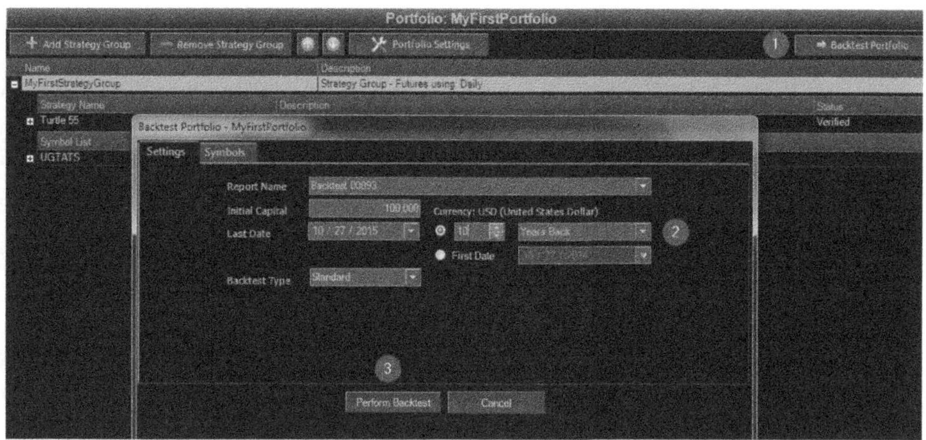

FIGURE 9.10 As you prepare to backtest your portfolio, ensure the settings are correct. Begin by clicking the Backtest Portfolio button (marked 1 in the figure). Then, check the initial capital, test period, and backtest type in the appropriate fields (marked with 2). When everything looks good, click the Perform Backtest button (number 3 in the figure).

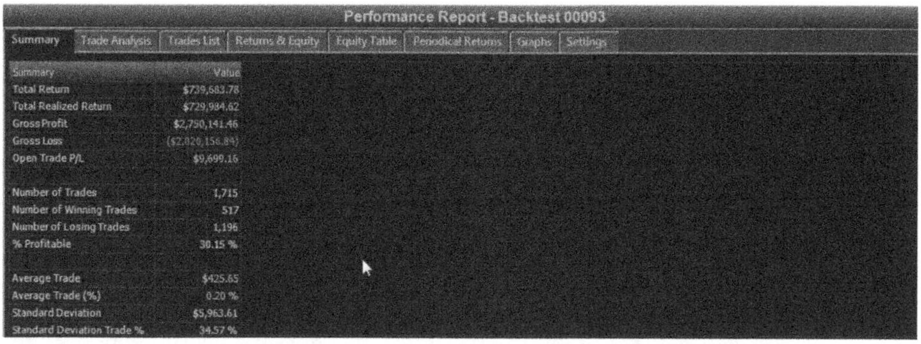

Performance Report - Backtest 00093

Summary | Trade Analysis | Trades List | Returns & Equity | Equity Table | Periodical Returns | Graphs | Settings

Summary	Value
Total Return	$739,683.78
Total Realized Return	$729,984.62
Gross Profit	$2,750,141.46
Gross Loss	($2,020,156.84)
Open Trade P/L	$9,699.16
Number of Trades	1,715
Number of Winning Trades	517
Number of Losing Trades	1,196
% Profitable	30.15 %
Average Trade	$425.65
Average Trade (%)	0.20 %
Standard Deviation	$5,963.61
Standard Deviation Trade %	34.57 %

FIGURE 9.11 A backtest performance report.

plethora of performance metrics. The one thing I would like PM to show in this report is the maximum drawdown. The maximum drawdown is shown but you have to hunt for it. Click on the **Trade Analysis** tab. The **Trade Analysis** drills down and proffers up even more performance metrics. If you are a statistician, then you will think you have died and gone to Heaven. The neatest feature in this tab is located at the bottom right and is labeled **View/Hide Symbols**. If you hit this button, then every market that was traded and their associated performance metrics will be added to the **Trade Analysis** window (see Figure 9.12).

Scroll around and make yourself comfortable with the report. I could write an entire book just on these neat reports and bore you to death. However, I will leave the exploration of all of the different report tabs up to you. But if you indulge me a

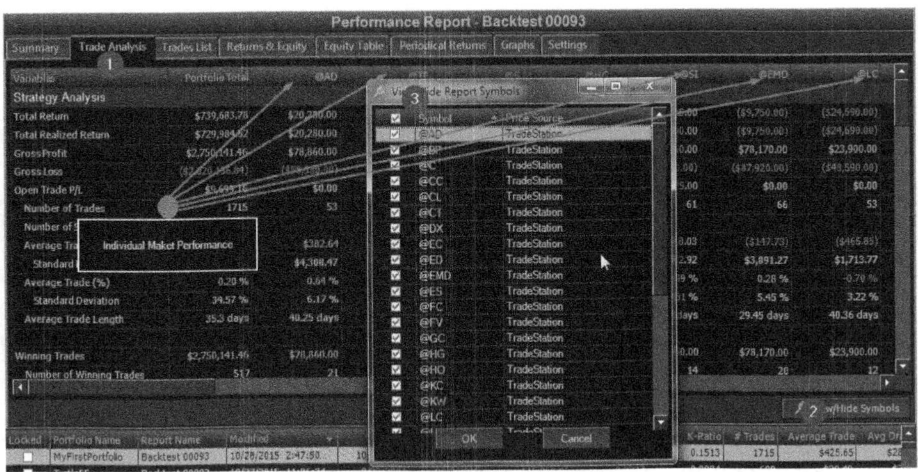

FIGURE 9.12 The Trade Analysis window displays trading statistics. To get to this screen, click the Trade Analysis tab (marked 1). The View/Hide Symbols button (marked 2) reveals the performance metric for every market in your portfolio (item 3).

little bit more, I will show two very interesting charts that PM generates that show the location of the maximum drawdown. Click on the **Graphs** tab and the equity curve for the portfolio will be plotted and look similar to the one in Figure 9.13.

If you want to see the contribution of each individual market to the portfolio, this is done by selecting Total P/L by symbol (Figure 9.14). This chart is a histogram of each market's contribution to the grand total. If you want to know the maximum drawdown of the portfolio, you will find this under the **Returns and Equity**

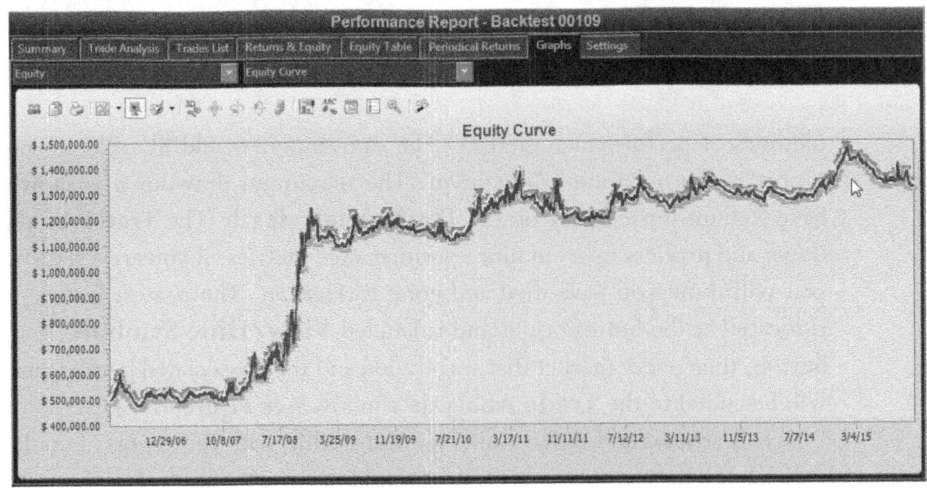

FIGURE 9.13 An equity curve chart that shows the maximum drawdown.

Source: TradeStation

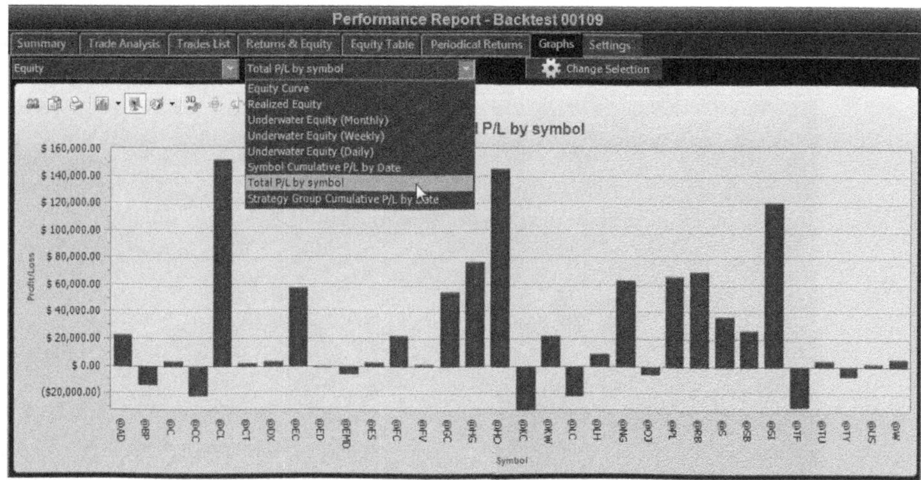

FIGURE 9.14 The Total P/L option displays individual profit and loss data for every market in the portfolio.

Source: TradeStation

tab about halfway down (Figure 9.15). This Turtle-like algorithm produced over $700K in profit but had a $201K drawdown. Not too bad, considering the size of the portfolio. The energy sector packed most of the punch, as you can see from the histogram.

This ability to merge the different equity curves together has not always been available in TradeStation. The lack of portfolio analysis was the major criticism of TradeStation over the years, but with the advent of PM, the critics have a lot less to complain about.

Fixed Fractional Money Management Overlay

Now that we know how to create a **Strategy Group** and a **Portfolio**, we can now apply a money management overlay and test it. With PM still on your screen, click the **Manage Strategy Groups** button and then the **Money Management** tab. In the **Money Management** window you will find a dropdown menu labeled **Method**. Click the down arrow and select **Fixed Fractional with ATR Risk**.

The resulting dialog box gives you the opportunity to change the parameters built into the Fixed Fractional formula. You can change these parameters:

- **Percent Risk**—The amount of capital to risk on each and every trade. Set this to 1 percent.
- **ATR Multiplier**—The number of times you want to multiply the ATR to estimate perceived market risk. The larger this number the riskier you perceive the market to be. Set this to two.

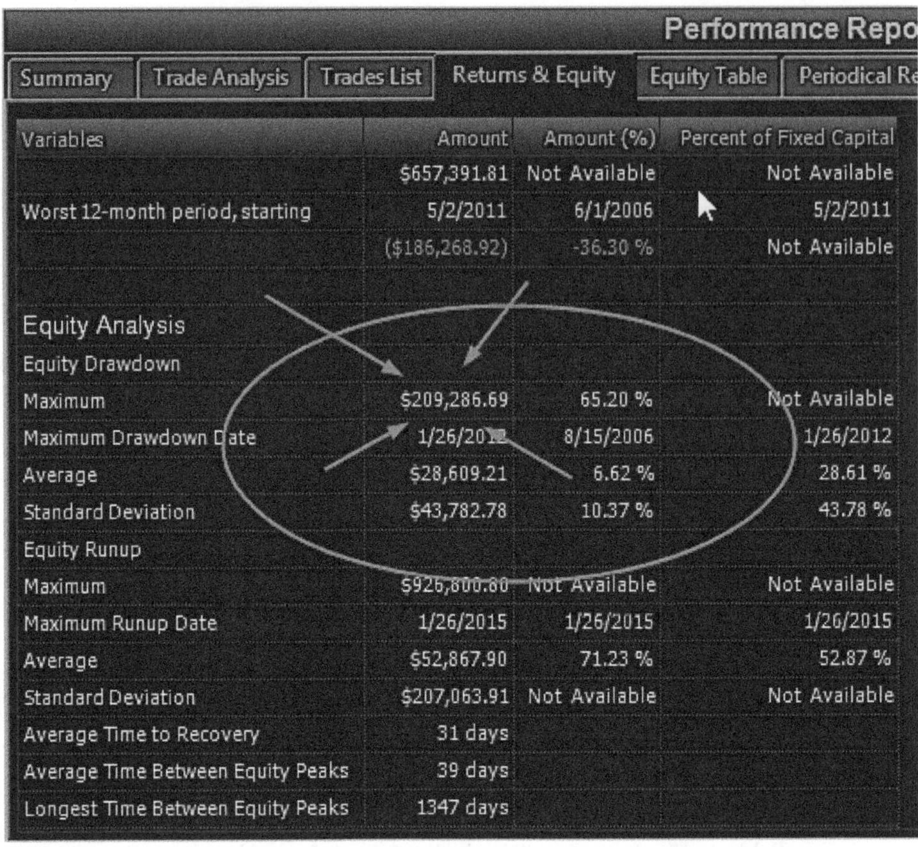

Performance Report

Summary | Trade Analysis | Trades List | Returns & Equity | Equity Table | Periodical Re

Variables	Amount	Amount (%)	Percent of Fixed Capital
	$657,391.81	Not Available	Not Available
Worst 12-month period, starting	5/2/2011	6/1/2006	5/2/2011
	($186,268.92)	-36.30 %	Not Available
Equity Analysis			
Equity Drawdown			
Maximum	$209,286.69	65.20 %	Not Available
Maximum Drawdown Date	1/26/2012	8/15/2006	1/26/2012
Average	$28,609.21	6.62 %	28.61 %
Standard Deviation	$43,782.78	10.37 %	43.78 %
Equity Runup			
Maximum	$926,800.80	Not Available	Not Available
Maximum Runup Date	1/26/2015	1/26/2015	1/26/2015
Average	$52,867.90	71.23 %	52.87 %
Standard Deviation	$207,063.91	Not Available	Not Available
Average Time to Recovery	31 days		
Average Time Between Equity Peaks	39 days		
Longest Time Between Equity Peaks	1347 days		

FIGURE 9.15 The Returns and Equity tab displays the portfolio's maximum drawdown in this case.

- **ATR Lookback**—How many days in the ATR calculation. The shorter lookback gives recent history more weight.
- **Maximum Quantity**—The largest position size that will be allowed on any given trade. Eurodollars are notorious for generating large position sizes. Since execution costs cut into the bottom line you probably should limit this to 10.
- **Round Quantity**—You cannot trade a fractional part of a futures contract, so always set this to one.

Look at Figure 9.16 and make your changes accordingly.

Now click on the **Manage Portfolios** button. You will notice that *Money Management: Fixed Fractional with ATR Risk* has been added directly under **Turtle 55** in the strategy portion of the dialog window. The description of the Money Management strategy is included as well:

Buy 2 times ATR over 10 bars lookback, but no more than 10. Risk no more than 1.00 percent of Equity.

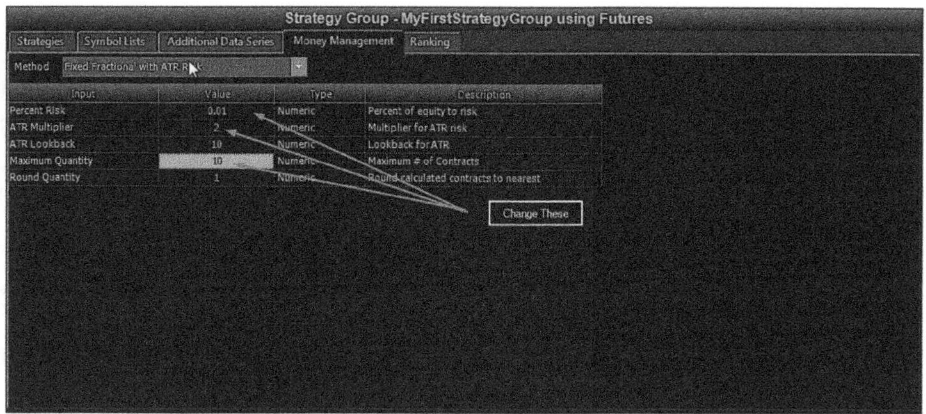

FIGURE 9.16 The arrows indicate the parameters that you can change from the Money Management window. For now, keep the ATR lookback set to 10 and the round quantity set to 1.

This overlay will calculate two times the 10-day ATR and use it as the denominator in our **Fixed Fractional** formula. The numerator will be 1 percent of the total portfolio balance. Both numerator and denominator will rise and fall. The denominator will replicate market volatility and the numerator will reflect 1 percent of the account as it grows or shrinks. Click on the **Backtest Portfolio** button and change the **Initial Capital** to 500,000. This test will apply the **Turtle 55** algorithm to the **UGTATS Symbol List** all the while overlaying a **Fixed Fractional** money management scheme. Sounds like a lot to carry out, so let's see what happens by clicking the **Perform Backtest** button (make sure you are going 10 **Years Back**). Figure 9.17 shows the equity curve of the backtest, and yes, you are seeing close to a million-dollar profit.

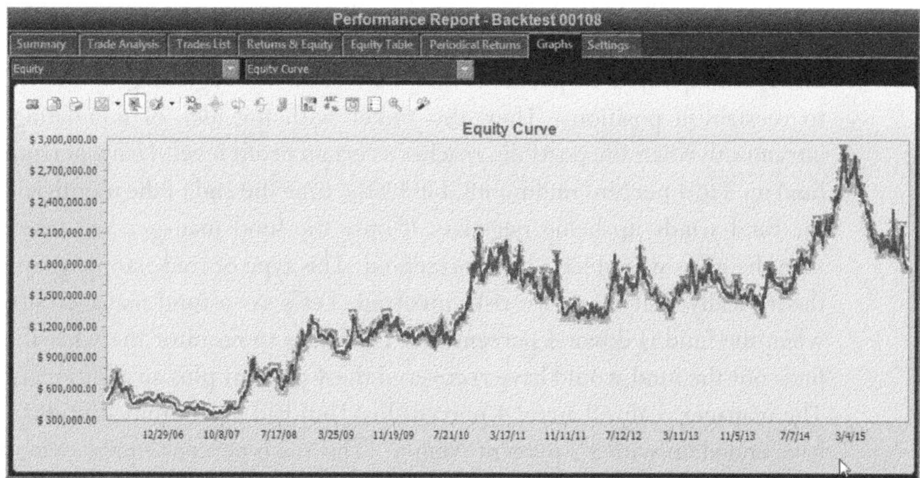

FIGURE 9.17 The equity curve of the backtest reveals a profit of nearly $1 million.

Source: TradeStation

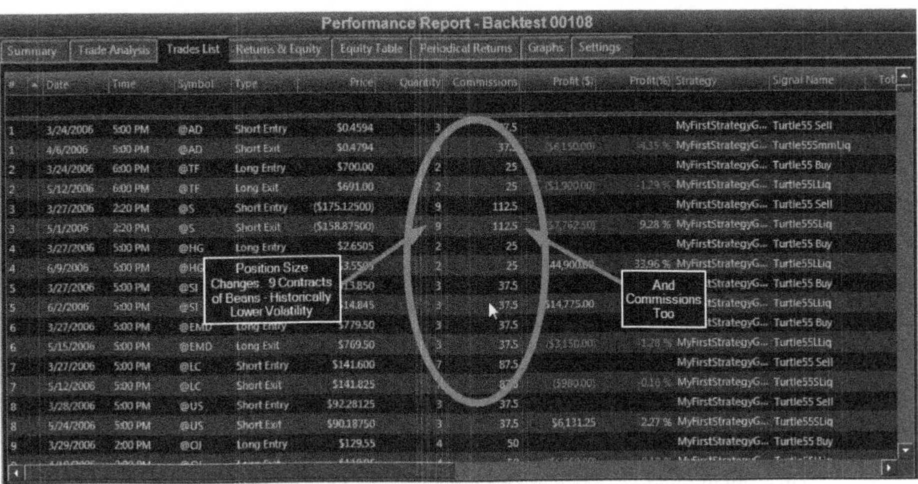

FIGURE 9.18 Profit and drawdown are directly proportional to position size. As your position size changes, so do your commissions and profits and losses.

The profit is spectacular but so is the drawdown—and not in a good way. This is how **Fixed Fractional** works—as the account grows so does the position size. And we all know profit or loss and drawdown are directly proportional to position size. Take a look at Figure 9.18 to see how the position size changes for the different markets in the portfolio.

Portfolio Analysis

Not only does PM allow you to overlay money management, but it also allows you to control portfolio management from a macroscopic perspective. Professional portfolio managers often tinker with the idea of placing a global portfolio stop after a big losing month. Let's say the portfolio is down 4 percent by midmonth; some managers liquidate all positions and wait until the beginning of the next month to reestablish positions. They also tinker with the idea of liquidating positions intramonth when the portfolio reaches a certain profit level. I have personally seen a fund up 3 to 4 percent midmonth, but by the time the end of the month rolls around, the fund winds up being negative. If only the fund manager had taken a profit, then the gains would have been preserved. This type of trade stoppage sounds great theoretically, but there are risks involved. Let's say a fund manager stops trading when the fund is down 4 percent, but continues to monitor the what-if trades and finds out the fund would have recovered the 4 percent plus an additional 2 percent. The manager realized a real 4 percent loss, but had he continued trading he would have ended up with a 2 percent winner. This is a 6 percent equity swing and could be the difference between holding on to some clients and losing them. The same risk occurs when flattening a fund because of what is perceived to be a "sizable" profit. Many times, a plus 4 percent month turns into a plus 8 percent. There is never a black-or-white answer to anything dealing with trading. This is why ideas are converted into diagrams, diagrams into pseudocode, pseudocode into an actual programming language and then tested, and tested, and tested.

Speaking of testing, let's go back to PM and test the ideas of trade stoppage once the portfolio, on an intramonth basis, digs itself into a 4 percent hole, or when the portfolio achieves a 4 percent profit. Trading will cease until the beginning of the following month. PM enables this type of testing with just a few keystrokes. Go back to PM and click on the **Manage Portfolio** button, then click on **Portfolio Settings**, then on **Portfolio Stops** (Figure 9.19).

The first parameter that needs to be set is the **Portfolio Stop Loss**. Click on the dropdown menu and select **Portfolio Stop Loss** and set the parameters as shown in Figure 9.20. Set the **Loss As Percent** to True, **Loss Target** to 4, and **Period** to 1. Click the **Set Stop** button and the **Portfolio Stop Loss** will be applied to the portfolio strategies.

Now let's set the **Portfolio Profit Target** by setting **Period** to 1, **PrftAsPercent** to True, and **PrftTarget** to 4 (Figure 9.21).

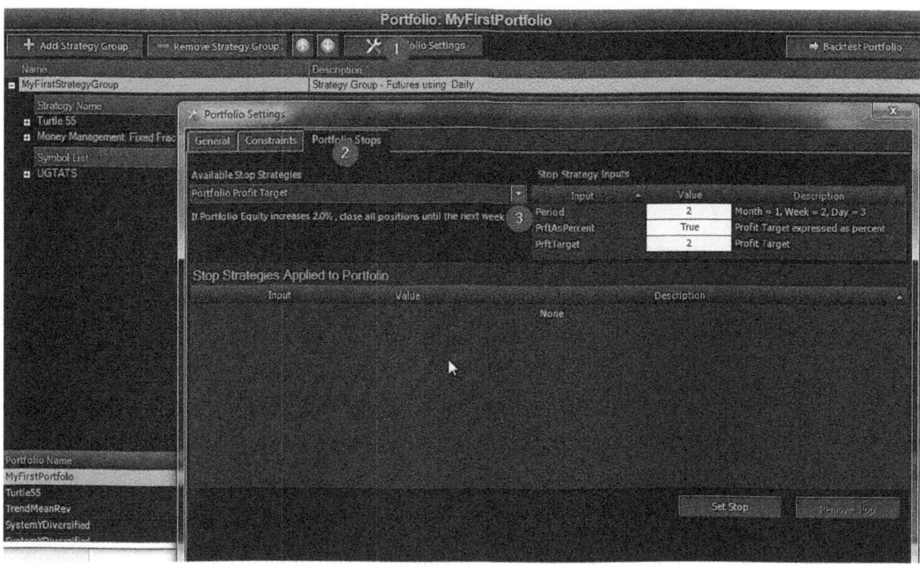

FIGURE 9.19 Under Portfolio Settings (marked as 1), go to the Portfolio Stops tab (marked as 2) and set the stop strategy of your choosing. Under the dropdown menu, there is a description of how the selected strategy will impact your portfolio (marked as 3).

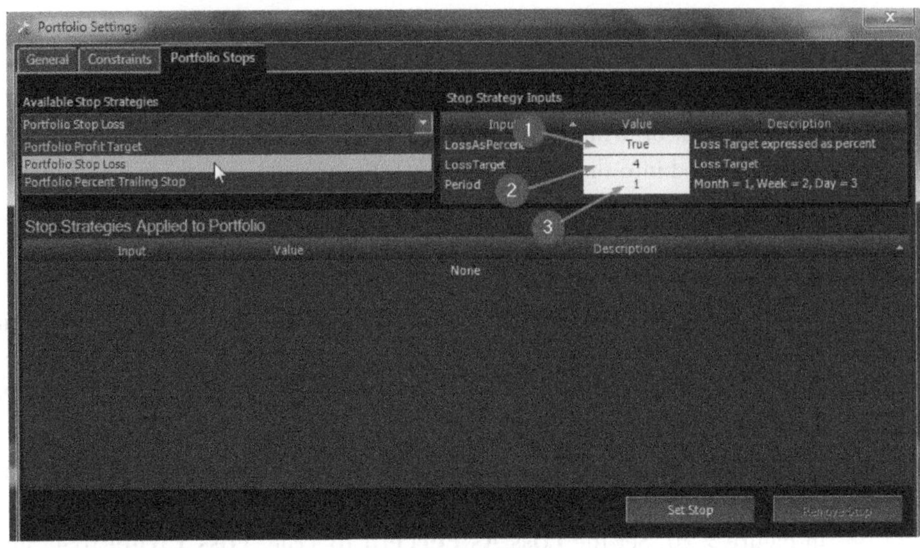

FIGURE 9.20 To set the portfolio stop loss, you can adjust the loss target percentage (marked as 1), loss target (marked as 2), and period (marked as 3).

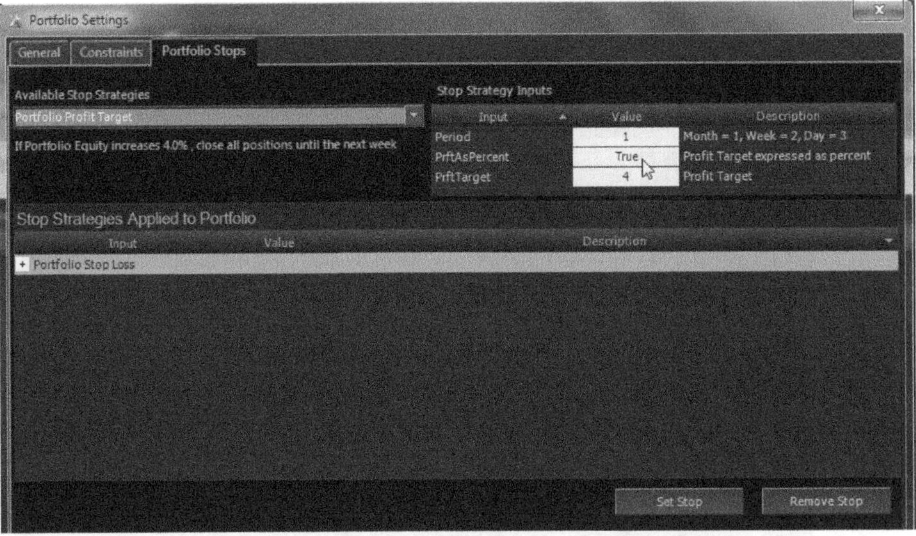

FIGURE 9.21 To set the portfolio profit target, you can adjust the period, profit target percentage, and profit target. These options align with those in the stop loss tab.

Stop Strategies Applied to Portfolio

Input	Value	Description
Portfolio Profit Target		
Period	1	Month = 1, Week = 2, Day = 3
PrftTarget	4	Profit Target
PrftAsPercent	True	Profit Target expressed as percent
Portfolio Stop Loss		
LossTarget	4	Loss Target
LossAsPercent	True	Loss Target expressed as percent
Period	1	Month = 1, Week = 2, Day = 3

Set Stop | Remove Stop

FIGURE 9.22 The portfolio profit target and stop loss now appear as strategies in your portfolio.

Go ahead and click **Set Stop** and you will see the **Portfolio Profit Target** will be added to the Strategies. Before we click OK, let's review both portfolio stops to make sure we have the parameters properly set. Expand the **Portfolio Profit Target** and the **Portfolio Stop Loss** strategies. The settings should look exactly like the ones in Figure 9.22.

Just to review, the **Portfolio Profit Target** will cause the portfolio to cease trading once the portfolio achieves a 4 percent profit level and the **Portfolio Stop Loss** will cease trading if the portfolio loses 4 percent. Once stopped, the portfolio will start trading automatically at the beginning of the next month. Go ahead and click **OK** and you will be returned to the **MyFirstPortfolio** window. You will notice another item has been added to the list, **Portfolio Stop**. Take a quick look at Figure 9.23.

If you see that **Portfolio Stop** has been added, then click **Backtest Portfolio.** All other parameters that were used in the prior Portfolio Analysis should still be set: 500,000 for **Initial Capital** and 10 **Years Back** for the test period. After the test finishes click OK to view the report now. First off, click on the **Graphs** tab to see if

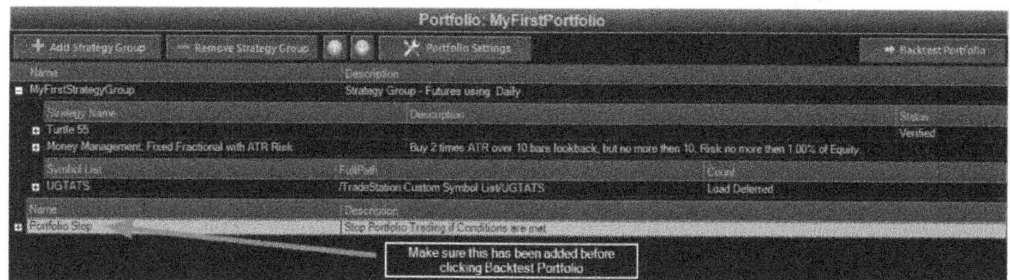

FIGURE 9.23 At the bottom of your screen, you should see the portfolio stop option.

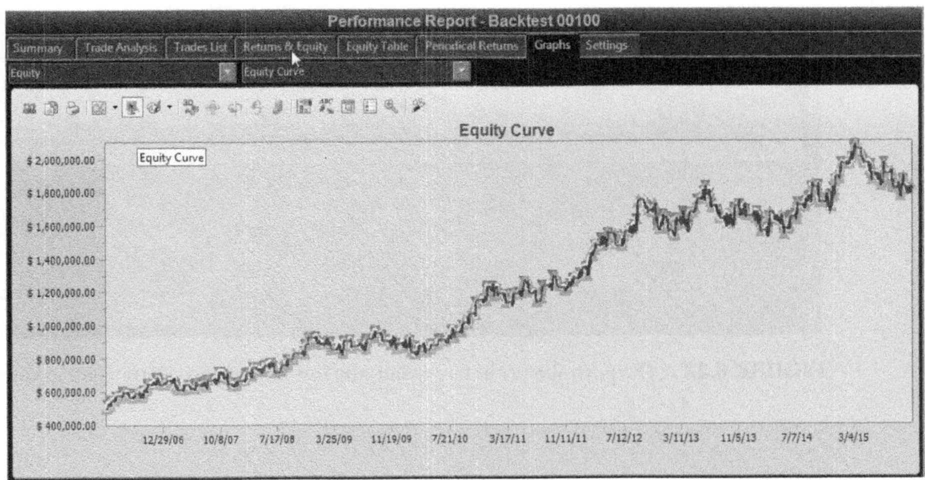

FIGURE 9.24 The equity curve of the portfolio once the stops have been added.

Source: TradeStation

the equity curve looks any better utilizing the **Portfolio Stops**. Figure 9.24 shows the equity curve of **MyFirstPortfolio** using the prescribed stop trading schemes.

A quick look reveals a smoother equity curve than the one from the prior portfolio analysis. Now click on the **Summary** tab and let's look at the results in a tabular form. Here are the differences between the first test and this test, which used portfolio stops:

Test 1:

Total Return: $1,307,354

Number of Trades: 1685

% Profitable: 30.92%

Average Trade: $724.27

Maximum Drawdown: $1,115,228.36

Test 2:

Total Return: $848,197

Number of Trades: 1940

% Profitable: 46.96%

Average Trade: $425.63

Maximum Drawdown: $350,500.34

TABLE 9.1 Portfolio Trades without Stops

No Portfolio Stops

Date	Mkt	Entry/Exit	Price	Quant	$P/L	Entry/Exit Name
3/24/06	@AD	Short Entry	0.4594	3		Turtle55 Sell
4/6/06	@AD	Short Exit	0.4794	3	($6,100.00)	Turtle55SmmLiq
4/26/06	@AD	Long Entry	0.4959	3		Turtle55 Buy
6/1/06	@AD	Long Exit	0.4933	3	($880.00)	Turtle55LLiq
8/10/06	@AD	Long Entry	0.5162	3		Turtle55 Buy
8/25/06	@AD	Long Exit	0.5042	3	($3,700.00)	Turtle55LLiq
9/5/06	@AD	Long Entry	0.5196	4		Turtle55 Buy
9/8/06	@AD	Long Exit	0.503	4	($6,740.00)	Turtle55LLiq

TABLE 9.2 Portfolio Trades with Stops in Place

With Portfolio Stops

Date	Mkt	Entry/Exit	Price	Quant	$P/L	Entry/Exit Name	First New Signal
3/24/06	@AD	Short Entry	0.4594	3		Turtle55 Sell	
3/31/06	@AD	Short Exit	0.4611	3	($610.00)	Portfolio Stop Short	
Stopped Trading 3/31/2006; Resume 4/01/2006							
No Signal Before the Next Stoppage							
Stopped Trading 4/20/2006; Resume 5/01/2006							
5/3/06	@AD	Long Entry	0.5105	3		Turtle55 Buy	First New Signal in May
5/11/06	@AD	Long Exit	0.5211	3	$3,080.00	Portfolio Stop Long	
Stopped Trading 5/11/2005; Resume 6/01/2006							
8/10/06	@AD	Long Entry	0.5162	4		Turtle55 Buy	First New Signal in Aug.
8/17/06	@AD	Long Exit	0.5167	4	$100.00	Portfolio Stop Long	
Stopped Trading 8/17/2006; Resume 9/01/2006							
9/5/06	@AD	Long Entry	0.5196	5		Turtle55 Buy	First New Signal in Sept.
9/8/06	@AD	Long Exit	0.503	5	($8,400.00)	Turtle55LLiq	

Which test would you trade? Needless to say, the test with the portfolio stops was much better. In Test 2, **Total Return** dropped precipitously, but so did **Maximum DD**. It is interesting to see that **Number of Trades** increased in Test 2, which at first seems counterintuitive. If trading is turned off, then you would expect to have fewer trades. However, the more you think about it, a higher trade count makes sense; trades are turned off, and then turned back on, which creates an additional exit and entry. In Test 1, a trade could have stretched for several weeks, but in Test 2, if trades are turned off, then this particular trade would be liquidated and then reinitialized at the beginning of the next month—thus generating an additional trade. Take a look at Tables 9.1 and 9.2, which show trades without and with the portfolio stops.

Portfolio Maestro does exactly what it is supposed to do. Trades are immediately liquidated on or near the stoppage date, and new trades are initiated on fresh signals after the beginning of the next month.

It is also interesting to note that the original **Turtle 55** strategy without money management or portfolio stops actually performed the best from a profit-to-drawdown perspective.

Summary

This chapter highlighted the capabilities of Portfolio Maestro:

- *Portfolio level analysis*—PM can test multiple markets and present a portfolio level report of them combined together.
- *Money management*—the Fixed Fractional technique was introduced and applied to our large portfolio of 30+ markets using the **Turtle 55** algorithm. Money management offers a process that normalizes one market to another, and offers a method to allocate capital in an efficient manner.
- *Portfolio analysis*—PM offers several different ways to manage a portfolio's equity curve:
  - Portfolio profit target
  - Portfolio stop loss
  - Portfolio trailing stop

The first two methods were tested and reviewed.

In addition to introducing Portfolio Maestro, this chapter also discussed money management and portfolio analysis. The topics of all three were barely scratched. However, I think enough was provided to excite further research on all three subjects. Ideas such as money management and portfolio management can be hypothesized all day long, but until you put these ideas to the test, you won't know if they are truly valuable. Most beginning traders do not believe money management techniques can be applied to small accounts, and they are partially correct. However, the concept of risk is always universally applicable, and that is a big part of all money management techniques. All traders can learn from these techniques and apply them in one form or another to their own trading.

To trade or not to trade—that is the question. Traders know there are times when standing aside with a flat position is a good trading strategy. However, determining these times is as difficult as timing the market. Should trading stop when a trading account is down a certain percentage during the month, or is it a good time to stop when the account is up a certain percentage? With tools such as PM, traders no longer need to wonder; they can set up the test and see for themselves. PM has many different built-in criteria, but users are not limited to just those. Its users can also dream up their own what-if scenarios, and program them directly into PM. This chapter solely relied on PM to carry out the various tests, but many of these same tests can also be accomplished with AmiBroker or TradersStudio.

AmiBroker

Here is a brief list of token names (keywords and identifiers) that are used internally in AmiBroker.

Keywords

The following is a subset of keywords:

- **buy**—Defines "buy" (enter long position) trading rule.
- **sell**—Defines "sell" (close long position) trading rule.
- **short**—Defines "short" (enter short position – short sell) trading rule.
- **cover**—Defines "cover" (close short position – buy to cover) trading rule.
- **buyprice**—Defines buying price array (this array is filled in with the default values according to the Automatic Analyser settings).
- **sellprice**—Defines selling price array (this array is filled in with the default values according to the Automatic Analyser settings).
- **shortprice**—Defines short selling price array (this array is filled in with the default values according to the Automatic Analyser settings).
- **coverprice**—Defines buy to cover price array (this array is filled in with the default values according to the Automatic Analyser settings).
- **exclude**—If defined, a true (or 1) value of this variable excludes current symbol from scan/exploration/backtest. They are also not considered in buy-and-hold calculations. Useful when you want to narrow your analysis to certain set of symbols.

- **roundlotsize**—Defines round lot sizes used by backtester (see explanations below). Automatic Analysis (new in 4.10).
- **ticksize**—Defines tick size used to align prices generated by built-in stops (see explanations below). (Note: It does not affect entry/exit prices specified by **buyprice / sellprice / shortprice / coverprice**.)
- **pointvalue**—Allows to read and modify future contract point value (see backtesting futures). CAVEAT: this AFL variable is by default set to 1 (one) regardless of contents of Information window UNLESS you turn ON futures mode (SetOption("FuturesMode", True)).
- **margindeposit**—Allows to read and modify future contract margin (see backtesting futures).
- **positionsize**—Allows control dollar amount or percentage of portfolio that is invested into the trade (more information available in the "Tutorial: Backtesting Your Trading Ideas").
- **positionscore**—Defines the score of the position. (More details: "Tutorial: Portfolio Backtesting.") Automatic analysis.
- **numcolumns**—Exploration only: defines the number of your own columns (excluding predefined ticker and date columns) and assigns the column value to the variable.
- **filter**—Exploration only: controls which symbols/quotes are accepted. If "true" (or 1) is assigned to that variable for given symbol/quote, it will be displayed in the report. So, for example, the following formula will accept all symbols with closing prices greater than 50: **filter** = close > 50;.

Flow Control Structures

Here are some identifiers to help you control program flow:

Loops:

do (part of do-while statement)

while

for

Conditional execution / Flow control:

if (part of if-else statement)

else (part of if-else statement)

switch

break (part of the switch statement or for/while statements)

case (part of the switch statement)

continue (part of for/while statements)

default (part of switch statement)

Functions

The following programming constructs are available for the creation of subprograms:

function

procedure

return

local (variable scope)

global (variable scope)

Utilizing Exploration for Debugging

AmiBroker provides a very easy to use form of program output to help with analysis and as a tool for debugging. You have probably already seen the **Explore** button right beside the **Backtest** button. **Explore** allows you to output various values created by your **AFL** code in an easy to read spreadsheet format. This output is displayed in the **Results** tab—the same place where a backtest outputs its information. Here is an example of an exploration that prints out various indicator values:

```
/* Sample Exploration
   Print out some indicator values */

Filter= 1;

myMACD = MACD(12,26);
myRSI = RSI(14);
myStoch = StochD(14,3,3);
myMovAvg = MA(C,19);
myClose = C;
```

```
AddColumn(myRSI,"RSI");
AddColumn(myStoch,"StochD");
AddColumn(C,"Close");
AddColumn(C>myMovAvg,"C>MAV(19)");
AddColumn(C,"Close",format= 1.4);
```

The code snippet starts out by assigning MACD, RSI, StochD, and MAV values to four user-defined variables: myMACD, myRSI, myStoch, and myAvg. These variables are then used in the **AddColumn** function along with a descriptive name. **AddColumn** can take a variable number of parameters, but most of the time you will only need to pass two or three. The first parameter is the name of the array that you want to print and the second parameter is a string that will be printed as the column heading. The third and optional parameter is the format the array will be printed out in. Figure A.1 shows the printout of this particular exploration.

Notice how the first "Close" column only shows two decimal places, whereas the second "Close" column has been formatted to show four. The **AddColumn** capability is very powerful because it is so easy to print out the internal workings of your algorithm. This tool comes in really handy when a trading algorithm isn't performing the way you intended—just print out the values that make up the criteria of your **buy / sell / short / cover** logic. Remember to include Filter = 1 at the top of your code listing. This informs AmiBroker to go ahead and allow values to be printed out in a spreadsheet format in the **Results** window.

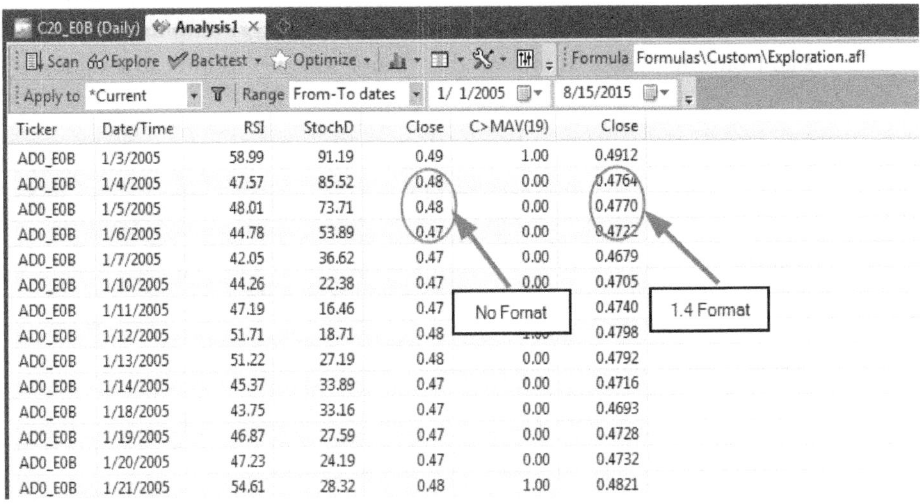

C20_E0B (Daily) Analysis1
Scan Explore Backtest Optimize Formula Formulas\Custom\Exploration.afl
Apply to *Current Range From-To dates 1/ 1/2005 8/15/2015

Ticker	Date/Time	RSI	StochD	Close	C>MAV(19)	Close
AD0_E0B	1/3/2005	58.99	91.19	0.49	1.00	0.4912
AD0_E0B	1/4/2005	47.57	85.52	0.48	0.00	0.4764
AD0_E0B	1/5/2005	48.01	73.71	0.48	0.00	0.4770
AD0_E0B	1/6/2005	44.78	53.89	0.47	0.00	0.4722
AD0_E0B	1/7/2005	42.05	36.62	0.47	0.00	0.4679
AD0_E0B	1/10/2005	44.26	22.38	0.47	0.00	0.4705
AD0_E0B	1/11/2005	47.19	16.46	0.47	[illegible]	0.4740
AD0_E0B	1/12/2005	51.71	18.71	0.48	[illegible]	0.4798
AD0_E0B	1/13/2005	51.22	27.19	0.48	0.00	0.4792
AD0_E0B	1/14/2005	45.37	33.89	0.47	0.00	0.4716
AD0_E0B	1/18/2005	43.75	33.16	0.47	0.00	0.4693
AD0_E0B	1/19/2005	46.87	27.59	0.47	0.00	0.4728
AD0_E0B	1/20/2005	47.23	24.19	0.47	0.00	0.4732
AD0_E0B	1/21/2005	54.61	28.32	0.48	1.00	0.4821

No Format

1.4 Format

FIGURE A.1 Results of an exploration with three parameters.

Here is the source code from Chapter 4 that included some interesting topics that is discussed here.

```
//Chapter 2 MACD utilizing AMIBROKERS
//Exploration Feature

Filter = 1;

PositionSize = MarginDeposit = 1;
```

Setting **Filter** = 1 turns on the **Exploration** tool. **PositionSize = MarginDeposit = 1** facilitates futures trading mode.

```
myMACD = MACD(fast=12,slow =26);
myMACDAvg = MA(myMACD,9);

myMACDDiff = myMACD - MYMACDAvg;

leftBar2 = Ref(myMACDDiff,-4);
leftBar1 = Ref(myMACDDiff,-3);
centerBar = Ref(myMACDDiff,-2);
rightBar1 = Ref(myMACDDiff,-1);
rightBar2 = Ref(myMACDDiff,0);
```

Call the **MACD** function and calculate the difference between it and its nine-period smoothing average. Utilize **Ref** to get historic values in the **myMACDDiff** array. Visualize the MACD difference plotted as a histogram. This bit of code is gathering information to determine if pivot point of the histogram has occurred. **CenterBar** is two bars back and leftBar1, leftBar2, rightBar1, and rightBar2 are self-explanatory.

```
COND3 = C > MA(C,100);

COND1 = centerBar < 0 AND centerBar < Min(leftBar2,
          leftBar1) AND centerBar < min(rightBar1,rightBar2);

COND2 = centerBar > 0 AND centerBar > Max(leftBar2,
          leftBar1) AND centerBar > Max(rightBar1,rightBar2);
```

COND3 is set to true when the close is above the 100-day moving average.
COND1 is set to true when the center bar forms a pivot low and is below 0.
COND2 is set to true when the center bar forms a pivot high and is above 0.

```
Buy = COND1 AND COND3;
Short = COND2 AND NOT(COND3);

BuyPrice = C;
ShortPrice = C;

longEntryPrice = ValueWhen(Buy,BuyPrice,1);
shortEntryPrice = ValueWhen(Short,ShortPrice,1);

Buy = ExRem(Buy,Short);
Short = ExRem(Short,Buy);
```

The **Buy** array is filled with 1's when a pivot low has formed below zero in the histogram and the current price is below the 100-day moving average. The **Short** array is filled with 1's when a pivot high has formed and the current price is below the 100-day moving average. The **longEntryPrice** is captured when **Buy** is set to 1. The **ValueWhen** function returns the second array value when the first array is set to 1. You must use the **ExRem** function to remove redundant Buys and Shorts. In other words, only turn subsequent Buys on or Shorts on when the existing long/short positions are either liquidated or reversed.


```
Sell = Cross(C, longEntryPrice - 3 * ATR(10));
Cover = Cross(ShortEntryPrice + 3 *ATR(10),C);

Buy = ExRem(Buy,Sell);
Short = ExRem(Short,Cover);

AddColumn(longEntryPrice,"BuyPrice");
AddColumn(longEntryPrice - 3 * ATR(10),"longStop");
AddColumn(Sell,"Sell ?");
```

Sell array (long liquidation) is turned on when the close crosses 3 ATR below the **longEntryPrice**.

Position Sizing in Futures Mode

Here is the exact formula used to apply an ATR Risk-Based Fixed Fractional money management scheme to a trading algorithm.

```
RiskPerContract = 2 * ATR(10);

PositionRisk = 1;
```

```
PctSize =  PositionRisk * MarginDeposit  / ( RiskPerContract
          * PointValue );

SetPositionSize( PctSize, spsPercentOfEquity );
```

At first, the formula might look confusing, but plugging in some values will help explain things. Assume you are working with the emini-SP and the **MarginDeposit** is \$5,600, **PointValue** is \$50, **InitialEquity** = \$500, 000, and **2 X ATR(10)** = 40.00.

$$\text{PctSize} = .01 \times \$5,600 \, / \, (40 \times \$50) = \$560/ \, \$2,000 = 0.028, \text{ or } 2.8\%$$

PctSize then can be used to calculate **PositionSize**:

$$\$500,000 \times 0.028/5600 = 2.5 \text{ contracts}$$

Compare this to the Fixed Fractional calculation without using the **margin-Deposit**:

$$\$500,000 \times 0.01 \, / \, (40 \times 50) = 2.5 \text{ contracts}$$

You get the exact same number of contracts, and since you can't have a partial contract, the number of contracts is rounded down to 2.

Excel System Backtester

The Excel System Backtester (ESB) utilizes Visual Basic for Applications and Excel spreadsheets to carry out the backtesting of your algorithms. There are several data arrays, keywords, and identifiers you will want to be aware of and not use as user-defined variables. This list will be updated regularly on www.georgepruitt.com. You can link to the page from this book's companion site.

The ESB source code is open source. Feel free to use it and modify it. A lengthy discussion on how the software works can be found at www.georgepruitt.com.

Data Arrays

myDate()
myHigh()
myLow()
myOpen()
myClose()
myRange()
myTrueRange()
myVol()
myOpInt()
equityStream()

Keywords

prevMarketPosition	symbol	orderTypeArr(10)
marketPosition	totProfit	sigNameArr(10)
entryPrice	maxDD	barsLong
executionCount	perCentWins	barsShort
entryBar	numTrades	tradeDays
intraDayTrdCnt	numWins	numRecords
multiDayOrders	numLosses	stp
Buy	commsn	lmt
Sell	equityPeak	mkt
ExitLong	dVal	moc
ExitShort	dSloVal	myTradeCollection
myTickValue	signalName	EquityClass
myMinTick	orderKindArr(10)	myEquityCollection
RampUp	trdPriceArr(10)	TradeInfo

Functions and Subroutines

Here is a list of available functions and subroutines in this current version of the ESB. Several of the indicators' functions are "Data Length Dependent," meaning that the current value of the indicator is dependent on when it was first applied to the data. This dependency does not have an impact if a large amount of data is used. The RSI on a six-week crude chart read 59.77, whereas it read 56.77 on a one-year chart. This dependency requires the last value to be carried over into the current indicator calculation, and this is no big deal unless you call the indicator function/subroutine multiple times on a single bar of data. Let's say you want an RSI(14) and an RSI(30) indicator calculated on the same bar; this requires a multiple function/subroutine call where the last values of the respective RSI calculations need to be carried over. Without the use of a class structure, the only way this can be handled is to pass values back and forth to the subroutine. Here is an example of how to handle a multiple subroutine call with different parameter values:

```
Call RSISub(myClose, 14, rsiVal1, upSumAvg1, dnSumAvg1, i, 1)
Call RSISub(myClose, 30, rsiVal2, upSumAvg2, dnSumAvg2, i, 1)
```

The first subroutine call holds the RSI value in **rsiVal1** and the **upSumAvg1** and **dnSumAvg1** values are held over until the next subroutine call. The second subroutine call stores its RSI value in **rsiVal2** and the up sum and down sum averages in **upSumAvg2** and **dnSumAvg2,** respectively. So keep in mind that if you want to call a subroutine more than once, then you will need to create separate parameter names so that the subroutine can keep track of the different lookback lengths and indicator values.

Function Highest(dataList, length, index, offset)

```
Function Highest(dataList, length, index, offset)
   Dim i As Integer
Dim tempHH As Integer

tempHH = 0
For i = (index - offffset) - (length - 1) To (index - offset)
         If (dataList(i) > tempHH) Then tempHH = myHigh(i)
Next i
Highest = tempHH
End Function
```

Sub RSISub(dataList, length, rsiVal, upSumAvg, dnSumAvg, index, offset)

```
Sub RSISub(dataList, length, rsiVal, upSumAvg, dnSumAvg, index, offset)

Dim i As Integer
Dim diff1, diff2, upSum, dnSum As Double


upSum = 0
dnSum = 0

If upSumAvg = 0 And dnSumAvg = 0 Then      'seed the original
  RSI Value
    For i = (index - offset) - (length - 1) To
              (index - offset)
        If dataList(i) > dataList(i - 1) Then
            diff1 = dataList(i) - dataList(i - 1)
            upSum = upSum + diff1
        End If
        If dataList(i) < dataList(i - 1) Then
            diff2 = dataList(i - 1) - dataList(i)
            dnSum = dnSum + diff2
        End If
    Next i
```

```
    upSumAvg = upSum / length
    dnSumAvg = dnSum / length
Else
    If dataList(index - offset) > dataList(index - 1 - offset) Then
        diff1 = dataList(index - offset) - dataList(index - 1 - offset)
        upSum = upSum + diff1
    End If
    If dataList(index - offset) < dataList(index - 1 - offset) Then
        diff2 = dataList(index - 1 - offset) - dataList(index - offset)
        dnSum = dnSum + diff2
    End If
    upSumAvg = (upSumAvg * (length - 1) + upSum) / length
    dnSumAvg = (dnSumAvg * (length - 1) + dnSum) / length
End If
If upSumAvg + dnSumAvg <> 0 Then
    rsiVal = (100 * (upSumAvg)) / (upSumAvg + dnSumAvg)
Else
    rsiVal = 0
End If
End Sub
```


Function RSI(dataList, length, index, offset)

```
Function RSI(dataList, length, index, offset)

Dim i As Integer
Dim diff1, diff2, upSum, dnSum As Double
Static upSumAvg, dnSumAvg As Double

upSum = 0
dnSum = 0

If upSumAvg = 0 And dnSumAvg = 0 Then
      'seed the original RSI Value
    For i = (index - offset) - (length - 1) To
            (index - offset)
        If dataList(i) > dataList(i - 1) Then
            diff1 = dataList(i) - dataList(i - 1)
            upSum = upSum + diff1
        End If
        If dataList(i) < dataList(i - 1) Then
            diff2 = dataList(i - 1) - dataList(i)
            dnSum = dnSum + diff2
```

```
        End If
    Next i
    upSumAvg = upSum / length
    dnSumAvg = dnSum / length
Else
    If dataList(index - offset) > dataList(index - 1 - offset) Then
        diff1 = dataList(index - offset) -
                    dataList(index - 1 - offset)
        upSum = upSum + diff1
    End If
    If dataList(index - offset) < dataList(index - 1 - offset) Then
        diff2 = dataList(index - 1 - offset) - dataList(index - offset)
        dnSum = dnSum + diff2
    End If
    upSumAvg = (upSumAvg * (length - 1) + upSum) / length
    dnSumAvg = (dnSumAvg * (length - 1) + dnSum) / length
End If
If upSumAvg + dnSumAvg <> 0 Then
    RSI = (100 * (upSumAvg)) / (upSumAvg + dnSumAvg)
Else
    RSI = 0
End If


End Function
```


Function Lowest(dataList, length, index, offset)

```
Function Lowest(dataList, length, index, offset)
Dim i As Integer
Dim tempLL As Double

    tempLL = 999999
    For i = (index - offset) - (length - 1) To (index - offset)
        If (dataList(i) < tempLL) Then tempLL = myLow(i)
    Next i
    Lowest = tempLL

End Function
```

Sub BollingerBand(dataList, length, numDevs, avg, upBand, dnBand, index, offset)

```
Sub BollingerBand(dataList, length, numDevs, avg, upBand,
  dnBand, index, offset)

Dim i As Integer
Dim sum, sum1, myDev As Double


For i = (index - offset) - (length - 1) To (index - offset)

    sum = sum + dataList(i)
    sum1 = sum1 + dataList(i) ^ 2

Next i

avg = sum / length

myDev = ((length * sum1 - sum ^ 2) / (length * (length - 1))) ^ 0.5

upBand = avg + myDev * numDevs
dnBand = avg - myDev * numDevs

End Sub
```

Function Average(dataList, length, index, offset)

```
Function Average(dataList, length, index, offset)
Dim i As Integer
Dim sum, sum1, myDev As Double


For i = (index - offset) - (length - 1) To index - offset

    sum = sum + dataList(i)

Next i

Average = sum / length


End Function
```

Function Xaverage(dataList, prevXavg, length, index, offset)

```
Function Xaverage(dataList, prevXavg, length, index, offset)

If prevXavg = 0 Then
    Xaverage = dataList(index - offset)
Else
    Xaverage = prevXavg + 2 / length * (dataList(index
                 - offset) - prevXavg)
End If

End Function
```

Sub MACD(dataList, shortLen, longLen, smooth, myMacd, mySmoothMacd, xMavg1, xMavg2, index, offset)

```
Sub MACD(dataList, shortLen, longLen, smooth, myMacd,
      mySmoothMacd, xMavg1, xMavg2, index, offset)

If xMavg1 = 0 And xMavg2 = 0 Then
    xMavg1 = dataList(index - offset)
    xMavg2 = dataList(index - offset)
    myMacd = 0
    mySmoothMacd = 0
Else
    xMavg1 = xMavg1 + 2 / shortLen * (dataList(index
               - offset) - xMavg1)
    xMavg2 = xMavg2 + 2 / longLen * (dataList(index
               - offset) - xMavg2)
    myMacd = xMavg1 - xMavg2
    mySmoothMacd = mySmoothMacd + 2 / smooth * (myMacd - mySmoothMacd)
End If

End Sub
```

Sub Stochastic(kLen, dLen, dSloLen, kVal, dVal, dSloVal, index, offset)

```
Sub Stochastic(kLen, dLen, dSloLen, kVal, dVal, dSloVal, index, offset)

Dim index1, index2, hh, ll, sum As Double
Dim i, j, k As Integer
Dim kSto(100) As Double
Dim dSto(100) As Double

indexPt = index - offset
index1 = kLen + dLen
index2 = dLen - 1
```

```
If (kVal + dVal + dSloVal = 0) Then
  'seed the original Sto Value
    For i = 1 To dLen + dSloLen - 1
        hh = 0
        ll = 999999
        For k = indexPt - (index1 - (i - 1)) To
                    indexPt - (index2 - (i - 1))
            If (myHigh(k) > hh) Then hh = myHigh(k)
            If (myLow(k) < ll) Then ll = myLow(k)
        Next k
        If (hh - ll = 0) Then hh = ll + 1
        kSto(i) = (myClose(indexPt - (index2 - (i - 1)))
                      - ll) / (hh - ll) * 100#
        kVal = kSto(i)
        If (i > dLen) Then
            sum = 0#
            For j = i - 2 To i
                sum = sum + kSto(j)
            Next j
            dSto(i) = sum / dLen
            dVal = dSto(i)
        End If
        If (i >= dLen + dSloLen - 1) Then
            sum = 0#
            For j = i - 2 To i
                sum = sum + dSto(j)
            Next j
            dSloVal = sum / dSloLen
        End If
    Next i
Else
    hh = 0
    ll = 999999
    For i = indexPt - (kLen - 1) To indexPt
        If (myHigh(i) > hh) Then hh = myHigh(i)
        If (myLow(i) < ll) Then ll = myLow(i)
    Next i
    kVal = (myClose(indexPt) - ll) / (hh - ll) * 100
    dVal = ((dVal * (dLen - 1)) + kVal) / dLen
    dSloVal = ((dSloVal * (dSloLen - 1)) + dVal) / dSloLen

End If

End Sub
```

APPENDIX C

Python System Backtester

The Python System Backtester (PSB) utilizes the Python programming language to carry out the backtesting of your algorithms. There are several data arrays, keywords, and identifiers you will want to be aware of and not use as user-defined variables. This list will be updated regularly on www.georgepruitt.com.

Data Arrays or Lists

listOfTrades
marketPosition
entryPrice
entryQuant
exitQuant
trueRanges

myDate
myTime
myOpen
myHigh
myLow
myClose
myVolume

myOpInt
dataClassList
systemMarketList
equityDataList
fileList
exitQuant

Keywords and Identifiers

currentPrice	numMarkets	totProfit
totComms	portfolio	todaysCTE
barsSinceEntry	commission	todaysOTE
numRuns	numBarsToGoBack	tradeName
myBPV	rampUp	mp
allowPyr	price	entryDate
curShares	trades	exitDate

Classes

equityClass

```
class equityClass(object):
    def __init__(self):
        self.equityDate = list()
        self.equityItm = list()
        self.clsTrdEquity = list()
        self.openTrdEquity = list()
        self.cumuClsEquity = 0
        self.dailyEquityVal = list()
        self.peakEquity = 0
        self.minEquity = 0
        self.maxDD = 0
    def setEquityInfo(self,equityDate,equityItm,clsTrdEquity,
           openTrdEquity):
        self.equityDate.append(equityDate)
        self.equityItm.append(equityItm)
        self.cumuClsEquity += clsTrdEquity
        tempEqu =self.cumuClsEquity+openTrdEquity
        self.dailyEquityVal.append(tempEqu)
        self.peakEquity = max(self.peakEquity,tempEqu)
        maxEqu = self.peakEquity
        self.minEquity = min(self.minEquity,tempEqu)
        minEqu = self.minEquity
        self.maxDD = max(self.maxDD,maxEqu-tempEqu)
        maxDD = self.maxDD
        maxDD = maxDD
```

marketDataClass

```
class marketDataClass(object):
    def __init__(self):
        self.symbol = ""
        self.minMove = 0
        self.bigPtVal = 0
        self.seed = 0
        self.date = list()
        self.open = list()
        self.high = list()
        self.low = list()
        self.close = list()
        self.volume = list()
        self.opInt = list()
        self.dataPoints = 0
    def setDataAttributes(self,symbol,bigPtVal,minMove):
        self.symbol = symbol
        self.minMove = minMove
        self.bigPtVal = bigPtVal
    def readData(self,date,open,high,low,close,volume,opInt):
        self.date.append(date)
        self.open.append(open)
        self.high.append(high)
        self.low.append(low)
        self.close.append(close)
        self.volume.append(volume)
        self.opInt.append(opInt)
        self.dataPoints += 1
```

tradeInfoClass

```
class tradeInfo(object):
    def __init__(self,tradeOrder,tradeDate,tradeName,
            tradePrice,quant,entryOrExit):
        self.tradeOrder = tradeOrder
        self.tradeDate = tradeDate
        self.tradeName = tradeName
        self.tradePrice = tradePrice
        self.quant = quant
        self.tradeProfit = 0
        self.cumuProfit = 0
        self.entryOrExit = entryOrExit
#        print("populating info: ",self.tradeName,' ',
#            self.tradePrice)
```

```
    def calcTradeProfit(self,order,curPos,entryPrice,
            exitPrice,entryQuant,numShares):
        profit = 0
        totEntryQuant = 0
        tempNumShares = numShares
        numEntriesLookBack = 0
        for numEntries in range(0,len(entryPrice)):
##              totEntryQuant += entryQuant[numEntries]
            if tempNumShares >= entryQuant[numEntries]:
                tempNumShares -= entryQuant[numEntries]
                numEntriesLookBack += 1
        if tempNumShares > 0 : numEntriesLookBack += 1
        tempNumShares = numShares
        for numEntries in range(0,numEntriesLookBack):
            if numEntries < 0:
                numEntries = 1
            if entryQuant[numEntries] < tempNumShares:
                peelAmt = entryQuant[numEntries]
                tempNumShares = tempNumShares - peelAmt
            if entryQuant[numEntries] >= tempNumShares:
                peelAmt = tempNumShares
            if order == 'buy':
                if curPos < 0:
                    profit = profit + (entryPrice[numEntries]
                                - exitPrice) * peelAmt
            elif order == 'sell':
                if curPos > 0:
                    profit = profit + (exitPrice
                                - entryPrice[numEntries])
                                * peelAmt
            elif order == 'liqLong':
                if curPos > 0:
                    profit = profit + (exitPrice
                                - entryPrice[numEntries])
                                * peelAmt
            elif order == 'liqShort':
                if curPos < 0:
                    profit = profit + (entryPrice[numEntries]
                                - exitPrice) * peelAmt
            if entryQuant[numEntries] == peelAmt :
                entryPrice.pop(numEntries)
                entryQuant.pop(numEntries)
```

```
            elif entryQuant[numEntries] > peelAmt:
                entryQuant[numEntries]
                            = entryQuant[numEntries] - peelAmt
        return profit

    def printTrade(self):
        print( '%8.0f %10s %2.0d %8.4f %10.2f %10.2f'
            % (self.tradeDate, self.tradeName, self.quant,
            self.tradePrice,self.tradeProfit, self.cumuProfit))
```

portfolioClass

```
from systemMarket import systemMarketClass

class portfolioClass(object):
    def __init__(self):
        self.portfolioName = ""
        self.systemMarkets = list()
        self.portEquityDate = list()
        self.portEquityVal = list()
        self.portclsTrdEquity = list()
        self.portDailyEquityVal = list()
        self.portPeakEquity = 0
        self.portMinEquity = 0
        self.portMaxDD = 0
        tempEqu = 0
        cumEqu = 0
        maxEqu = -999999999
        minEqu = 999999999
        maxDD = 0

    def setPortfolioInfo(self,name,systemMarket):
        self.portfolioName = name
        self.systemMarkets = list(systemMarket)
        masterDateList = list()
        monthList = list()
        monthEquity = list()
        combinedEquity = list()
        self.portPeakEquity = -999999999999
        self.portMinEquity = -999999999999

        for i in range(0,len(self.systemMarkets)):
            masterDateList += self.systemMarkets[i].equity.equityDate
            sysName = self.systemMarkets[i].systemName
            market = self.systemMarkets[i].symbol
            avgWin = self.systemMarkets[i].avgWin
```

```
            sysMark =self.systemMarkets[i]
            avgLoss = sysMark.avgLoss
            totProf = sysMark.profitLoss
            totTrades = sysMark.numTrades
            maxD = sysMark.maxxDD
            perWins = sysMark.perWins
            tempStr =""
            if len(sysName) - 9 > 0:
                for j in range(0,len(sysName)-8):
                    tempStr = tempStr + ' '
            if i == 0: print('SysName',tempStr,'Market TotProfit
                   MaxDD AvgWin AvgLoss PerWins TotTrades')
            print('%s %s %12d %6d  %5d   %5d    %3.2f
                   %4d' % (sysName,market,totProf,maxD,
                   avgWin,avgLoss,perWins,totTrades))

        masterDateList = removeDuplicates(masterDateList)
        masterDateList = sorted(masterDateList)
#        print(masterDateList)
        self.portEquityDate = masterDateList
        monthList = createMonthList(masterDateList)
        for i in range(0,len(masterDateList)):
            cumuVal = 0
            for j in range(0,len(self.systemMarkets)):
                skipDay = 0
                try:
                    idx = self.systemMarkets[j]
                          .equity.equityDate.index(masterDateList[i])
                except ValueError:
                    skipDay = 1
                if skipDay == 0:
                    cumuVal += self.systemMarkets[j]
                               .equity.dailyEquityVal[idx]
            combinedEquity.append(cumuVal)
            self.portEquityVal.append(cumuVal)
            if cumuVal > self.portPeakEquity: self
                      .portPeakEquity = cumuVal
            self.portMinEquity = max(self.portMinEquity,
                                 self.portPeakEquity - cumuVal)
            self.portMaxDD = self.portMinEquity

        print("Combined Equity: ",self.portEquityVal[-1])
        print("Combined MaxDD: ",self.portMaxDD)
```

```
        print("Combined Monthly Return")
        for j in range(0,len(monthList)):
            idx = masterDateList.index(monthList[j])
            if j == 0:
                monthEquity.append(combinedEquity[idx])
                prevCombinedDailyEquity = monthEquity[-1]
            else:
                combinedDailyEquity = combinedEquity[idx]
                monthEquity.append(combinedDailyEquity
                   -  prevCombinedDailyEquity)
                prevCombinedDailyEquity = combinedDailyEquity
            print('%8d %10.0f %10.0f ' % (monthList[j],
                monthEquity[j],combinedEquity[idx]))

def removeDuplicates(li):
    my_set = set()
    res = []
    for e in li:
        if e not in my_set:
            res.append(e)
            my_set.add(e)
    return res

def createMonthList(li):
    myMonthList = list()
    for i in range(0,len(li)):
        if i != 0:
            tempa = int(li[i]/100)
            pMonth = int(li[i-1]/100) % 100
            month = int(li[i]/100) % 100
            if pMonth != month:
                myMonthList.append(li[i-1])
            if i == len(li)-1:
                myMonthList.append(li[i])
    return myMonthList
```


Indicator Classes and Functions

Some indicators are programmed as classes due to their "data length dependence." Each indicator class can be instantiated multiple times, so the same indicator can be calculated multiple times on the same data bar.

class stochClass(object):

```
class stochClass(object):

    def __init__(self):
        self.fastK = 0
        self.fastD = 0
        self.slowD = 0
        self.seed = 0
    def calcStochastic(self,kLen,dLen,dSloLen,hPrices,
           lPrices,cPrices,curBar,offset):
        curBarLookBack = curBar - offset
        testSeed = self.seed
        if self.seed == 0:
            self.seed = 1
            stoKList =[]
            stoDList = []
            index1 = kLen - 1 + dLen - 1 + dSloLen -1
            index2 = dLen - 1 + dSloLen -1
            loopCnt = 0
            for i in range(0,index2+1):
                loopCnt = loopCnt + 1
                hh = 0
                ll = 9999999
                lowRngBound = curBarLookBack - (index1 - i)
                highRngBound =lowRngBound + 3
                for k in range(lowRngBound,highRngBound):
                    if hPrices[k] > hh:
                        hh = hPrices[k]
                    if lPrices[k] < ll:
                        ll = lPrices[k]
                if hh - ll == 0.0:
                    hh = ll + 1
                whichClose = curBarLookBack - (index2 -i)
                stoKList.append((cPrices[whichClose] - ll) /
                   (hh - ll) *100)
                lenOfStoKList = len(stoKList)
                self.fastK = stoKList[len(stoKList)-1]
                if (i >= dLen-1):
                    tempSum = 0
                    lowRngBound = len(stoKList)-dLen
                    highRngBound = lowRngBound + dLen
                    for j in range(lowRngBound,highRngBound):
                        tempSum += stoKList[j]
```

```
                stoDList.append(tempSum/dLen)
                self.fastD = stoDList[len(stoDList)-1]
            if (i == index2):
                tempSum = 0
                lowRngBound = len(stoDList) - dSloLen
                highRngBound = lowRngBound + dSloLen
                for j in range(lowRngBound,highRngBound):
                    tempSum += stoDList[j]
                self.slowD = tempSum / dSloLen
    else:
        hh = 0
        ll = 999999
        lowRngBound = curBarLookBack - (kLen - 1)
        highRngBound = lowRngBound + 3
        for i in range(lowRngBound, highRngBound):
            if hPrices[i] > hh:
                hh = hPrices[i]
            if lPrices[i] < ll:
                ll = lPrices[i]
        self.fastK = (cPrices[curBarLookBack] - ll )/
                        (hh - ll) * 100
        self.fastD = (self.fastD * (dLen - 1) +
                        self.fastK) / dLen
        self.slowD = ((self.slowD * (dSloLen - 1))
                        + self.fastD) / dSloLen

    return(self.fastK,self.fastD,self.slowD)
```

class rsiClass(object):

```
class rsiClass(object):


    oldDelta1 = 0
    def __init__(self):
        self.delta1 = 0
        self.delta2 = 0
        self.rsi = 0
        self.seed = 0
    def calcRsi(self,prices,lookBack,curBar,offset):
        upSum = 0.0
        dnSum = 0.0
        if self.seed == 0:
            self.seed = 1
```

```
        for i in range((curBar - offset) - (lookBack-1),
              curBar - offset +1):
            if prices[i] > prices[i-1]:
                diff1 = prices[i] - prices[i-1]
                upSum += diff1
            if prices[i] < prices[i-1]:
                diff2 = prices[i-1] - prices[i]
                dnSum += diff2
            self.delta1 = upSum/lookBack
            self.delta2 = dnSum/lookBack
    else:
        if prices[curBar - offset] > prices[curBar - 1
              - offset]:
            diff1 = prices[curBar - offset] -
                        prices[curBar - 1 - offset]
            upSum += diff1
        if prices[curBar - offset] < prices[curBar - 1
              - offset]:
            diff2 = prices[curBar - 1 - offset]
                        - prices[curBar - offset]
            dnSum += diff2
        self.delta1 = (self.delta1 * (lookBack -1)
                          + upSum) / lookBack
        self.delta2 = (self.delta2 * (lookBack -1)
                          + dnSum) / lookBack
    if self.delta1 + self.delta2 != 0:
        self.rsi = (100.0 * self.delta1) / (self.delta1
                        + self.delta2)
    else:
        self.rsi = 0.0
    return (self.rsi)
```


Highest Function/Module

```
def highest(prices,lookBack,curBar,offset):
    result = 0.0
    maxVal = 0.00
    for index in range((curBar - offset) - (lookBack-1),
          curBar - offset +1):
        if prices[index] > maxVal:
            maxVal = prices[index]
    result = maxVal
    return result
```

Lowest Function/Module

```
def lowest(prices,lookBack,curBar,offset):
    result = 0.0
    minVal = 9999999.0
    for index in range((curBar - offset) - (lookBack-1),
            curBar - offset +1):
        if prices[index] < minVal:
            minVal = prices[index]
    result = minVal
    return result
```

Simple Average Function/Module

```
def sAverage(prices,lookBack,curBar,offset):
    result = 0.0
    for index in range((curBar - offset) - (lookBack-1),
            curBar - offset +1):
        result = result + prices[index]
    result = result/float(lookBack)
    return result
```

Bollinger Bands Function/Module

```
def bollingerBands(dates,prices,lookBack,numDevs,
 curBar,offset):

    sum1 = 0.0
    sum2 = 0.0
    startPt = (curBar - offset)- (lookBack-1)
    endPt = curBar - offset + 1
    for index in range(startPt,endPt):
        tempDate = dates[index]
        sum1 = sum1 + prices[index]
        sum2 = sum2 + prices[index]**2

    mean = sum1 / float(lookBack)

    stdDev = ((lookBack * sum2 - sum1**2) / (lookBack
                * (lookBack -1)))**0.5
    upBand = mean + numDevs*stdDev
    dnBand = mean - numDevs*stdDev
#    print(mean," ",stdDev," ",upBand," ",dnBand)
    return upBand, dnBand, mean
```

Python-Specific Keywords

and	except	not
as	exec	or
assert	finally	pass
break	for	print
class	from	raise
continue	global	return
def	if	try
del	import	while
elif	in	with
else	is	yield
	lambda	

Monte Carlo and Start Trade Drawdown Source Code

Start Trade Drawdown section


```
# start trade draw down analysis - utilizing the tradeTuple
    tupleLen = len(tradeTuple)
    tradeTuple = sorted(tradeTuple,key=itemgetter(0))
    for x in range(0,tupleLen):
        cumStartTradeEquity = 0
        maxStartTradeDD = -99999999
        maxCumEquity = 0
        for y in range(x,tupleLen):
#            print("Trade Tuple ",tradeTuple[y][0]," ",
#               tradeTuple[y][1]);
            cumStartTradeEquity += tradeTuple[y][1]
            maxCumEquity = max(maxCumEquity,
                              cumStartTradeEquity)
            maxStartTradeDD = max(maxStartTradeDD,maxCumEquity
                                 - cumStartTradeEquity)
        startTradeTuple += ((x,cumStartTradeEquity,
                              maxStartTradeDD),)
    minDD = 99999999
    maxDD = 0
```

```
    for y in range(0,len(startTradeTuple)):
        print(startTradeTuple[y][0],' ',startTradeTuple[y][1],
            ' ',startTradeTuple[y][2])
        if startTradeTuple[y][2] < minDD: minDD =
              startTradeTuple[y][2]
        if startTradeTuple[y][2] > maxDD: maxDD =
              startTradeTuple[y][2]
    numBins = 20
    binTuple = list()
    binMin = minDD
    binMax = maxDD
    binInc = (maxDD - minDD)/20.0
    binBot = binMin
    for y in range(0,numBins):
        binTop = binBot + binInc
        binTuple += ((y,binBot,binTop),)
        print(binTuple[y][1],' ',binTuple[y][2])
        binBot = binTop + y
    bins = list()
    bins[:] = []
    for x in range(0,numBins):
        bins.append(0)
    for x in range(0,len(startTradeTuple)):
        for y in range(0,numBins):
            tempDD = startTradeTuple[x][2]
            tempBot = binTuple[y][1]
            tempTop = binTuple[y][2]
            if (tempDD >= binTuple[y][1] and tempDD
                  < binTuple[y][2]):
#                 tempVal = bins(y) + 1
#                 bins.insert(y,tempVal)
                bins[y] += 1
    freqSum = sum(bins)
    binProb = list()
    for y in range(0,numBins):
        if y == 0:
            binProb.append(bins[y]/freqSum)
        else:
            binProb.append(bins[y]/freqSum + binProb[y-1])
    for y in range(0,numBins):
        print("Probability of DD < %7d is %4.3f\n"
           % (binTuple[y][2], binProb[y]))
```

Monte Carlo Analysis

```
# Monte Carlo Analysis

    mcTradeTuple = list()
    for x in range(0,5): # number of alternate histories
        for y in range(0,len(tradeTuple)):
            randomTradeNum = random.randint(0,
                                    len(tradeTuple)-1)
            mcTradeTuple += ((x,y,
                                tradeTuple[randomTradeNum][1],
                                tradeTuple[randomTradeNum][0]),)
    mcTradeResultsTuple = list()
    whichAlt = -1
    for x in range(0,len(mcTradeTuple)):
        if mcTradeTuple[x][1]==0:
            print('New Alternate History Generated')
            cumEquity = 0
            maxTradeDD = -99999999
            maxCumEquity = 0
        cumEquity += mcTradeTuple[x][2]
        print('Randomized trade listing : ',
           mcTradeTuple[x][3],' ',mcTradeTuple[x][2])
        maxCumEquity = max(maxCumEquity,cumEquity)
        maxTradeDD = max(maxTradeDD,maxCumEquity - cumEquity)
        if mcTradeTuple[x][1] == len(tradeTuple)-1 :
            mcTradeResultsTuple += ((cumEquity,maxTradeDD,
                                    cumEquity/len(tradeTuple)),)
    for x in range(0,len(mcTradeResultsTuple)):
        mcCumEquity = mcTradeResultsTuple[x][0]
        mcMaxDD = mcTradeResultsTuple[x][1]
        mcAvgTrd = mcTradeResultsTuple[x][2]
        print('Alt history %5d Profit: %10d MaxDD:
           %10d Avg Trade %6d\n' % (x,mcCumEquity,
           mcMaxDD,mcAvgTrd))
```

TradeStation and EasyLanguage

Importing ELD file from Book Website

If you need help installing the EasyLanguage code from the book website, just follow these instructions.

Download **UATSTB.eld** from website and save to your Desktop. Launch the **TradeStation Development Environment** and go under the **File** menu. Select **Import/Export** and a dialog similar to the one in Figure D.1 should appear on your screen.

Select the **Import ELD, ELS, or ELA** Wizard and then click **Next**. Another dialog will appear and look like Figure D.2.

Navigate to the location of your **UATSTB.eld** file. If you saved it to your Desktop, it should be there. If not, then you will need to browse to it. Select the **UATSTB.eld** file and click **Open**. Once the ELD file is open it will list the **Analysis Types** that are included (see Figure D.3). The current, hot-off-the-press, **UATSTB.eld** file may contain more types than those listed in the figure. They all should be selected already, but if they are not, then click the box beside **Select All** and then click **Next**.

The final dialog will now open and all of the Analysis Techniques included in the ELD file will be listed (see Figure D.4). If you click **Finish**, they will all be imported into your own library. Once this process has completed then you will be able to follow along in the book.

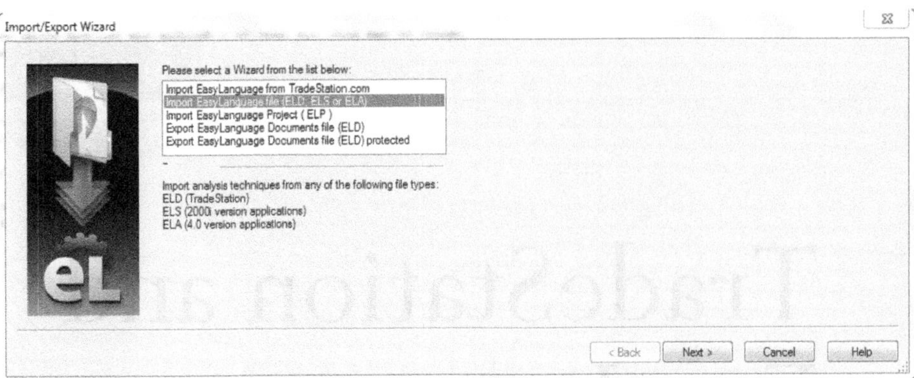

FIGURE D.1

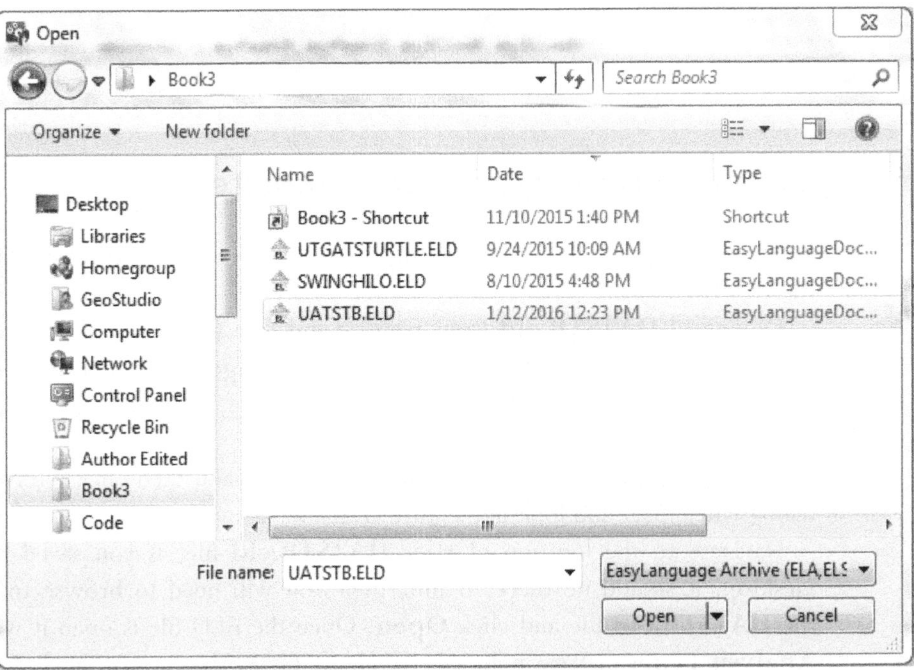

FIGURE D.2

Keywords and Functions

The number of reserved words, skip words, and functions are too numerous to include in an appendix. Here is a link to a TradeStation website that provides a complete and concise list: http://help.tradestation.com/08_08/tsdevhelp/mergedprojects/elword/elword.htm.

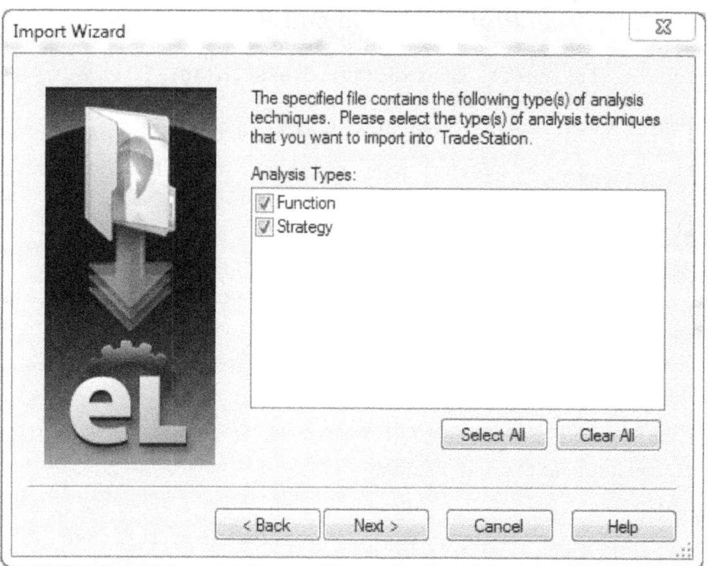

FIGURE D.3

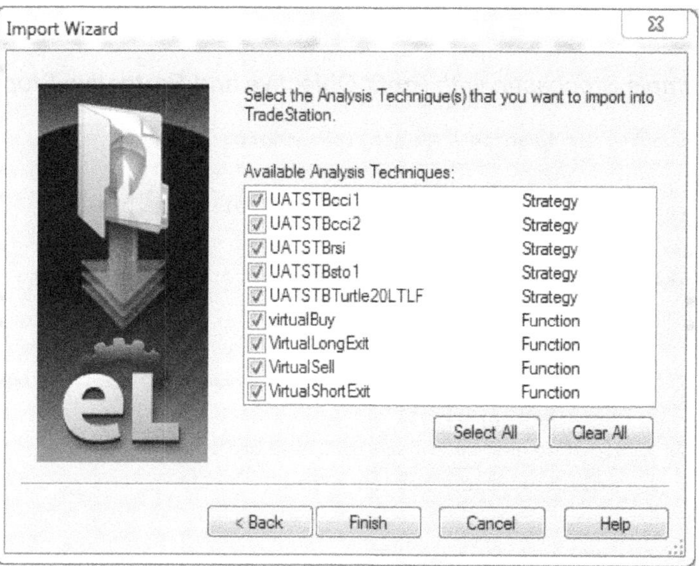

FIGURE D.4

Sample Algorithm Codes

All code presented in the book is available as a download on the companion website. This code includes all the necessary functions as well. Expanded research utilizing TradeStation, EasyLanguage, and Portfolio Maestro will also be included at www.georgepruitt.com.

Simple RSI with Profit Objective and Protective Stop

```
inputs: rsiLen(14),overBot(70),overSold(30);

If rsi(c,14) < overSold then buy this bar on close;
If rsi(c,14) > overBot then sellShort this bar on close;

If marketPosition = 1 then
begin
       If c > entryPrice + 3* avgTrueRange(10) then sell
             this bar on close;
       if c < entryPrice - 1* avgTrueRange(10) then sell
             this bar on close;
end;
If marketPosition = 1 then
begin
       If c < entryPrice - 3* avgTrueRange(10) then
             buyToCover this bar on close;
       if c > entryPrice + 1* avgTrueRange(10) then
             buyToCover this bar on close;
end;
```


Simple Stochastic with Profit Objective and Protective Stop

```
inputs: rawKlen(14),smooth1(3),smooth2(3);

vars: myFastK(0),myFastD(0),mySlowK(0),mySlowD(0);

Value1 = stochastic(h,l,c,rawKLen,smooth1,smooth2,1,myFastK,
            myFastD,mySlowK,mySlowD);

If mySlowK cross above mySlowD and mySlowD < 20 then buy
      this bar on close;
If mySlowK cross below mySlowD and mySlowD > 80 then
      sellShort this bar on close;

If marketPosition = 1 then
begin
       If c > entryPrice + 3* avgTrueRange(10) then sell
             this bar on close;
       if c < entryPrice - 1* avgTrueRange(10) then sell
             this bar on close;
end;
```

```
If marketPosition =-1 then
begin
        If c < entryPrice - 3* avgTrueRange(10) then
              buyToCover this bar on close;
        if c > entryPrice + 1* avgTrueRange(10) then
              buyToCover this bar on close;
end;
```

Simple CCI with Profit Objective and Protective Stop

```
inputs: cciLen(20),smooth(9);

vars: myCCIVal(0);

myCCIVal = average(cci(cciLen),smooth);

If myCCIVal crosses above -100  then buy this bar on close;
If myCCIVal crosses below 100 then sellShort this bar on
      close;

If marketPosition = 1 then
begin
        If c > entryPrice + 3* avgTrueRange(10) then sell
              this bar on close;
        if c < entryPrice - 1* avgTrueRange(10) then sell
              this bar on close;
end;
If marketPosition =-1 then
begin
        If c < entryPrice - 3* avgTrueRange(10) then
              buyToCover this bar on close;
        if c > entryPrice + 1* avgTrueRange(10) then
              buyToCover this bar on close;
end;
```

Connors / Alvarez with Time-Based Exit

```
inputs: mavlen(200),rsiLen(2),rsiBuyVal(20),rsiSellVal(80),
           holdPeriod(5);

Condition1 = c > average(c,mavLen);

Condition2 = rsi(c,rsiLen) < rsiBuyVal;

Condition3 = rsi(c,rsiLen) > rsiSellVal;
```

```
If condition1 and condition2 then buy this bar on close;
If not(condition1) and condition3 then sellShort this bar on close;

If barsSinceEntry = holdPeriod then
Begin
	if marketPosition = 1 then sell this bar on close;
	if marketPosition =-1 then buytocover this bar on close;
end;
```

Turtle with LTL Filter, Pyramiding and Position Sizing

```
inputs: absEntryChanLen(55),entryChanlen(20),exitChanLen(10),
	lastTradeLoserFilter(TRUE),accountSize(100000),
	   riskPerTradePer(.01),numPyraMids(1);

vars:lastTradeLoser(true),mp(0),virtmp(0),tradeProfit(0),
	virtBuyPrice(0),virtSellPrice(0),
	virtLongLiqPrice(0),virtShortLiqPrice(0),
	virtLongLoss(0),virtShortLoss(0),
	myFillPrice(0),N(0),N$(0),dollarRisk(0),lotSize(0),
	stopLoss(0),buyPrice(0),sellPrice(0),
	hh20(0),hh55(0),ll20(0),ll55(0),iCnt(0),initPrice(0),
	   stopLossPts(0),debug(TRUE);

mp = marketPosition;

if mp = 0 then
begin
	N = AvgTrueRange(20);
	N$ = N*BigPointValue;
	dollarRisk = AccountSize * riskPerTradePer;
	lotSize = IntPortion(DollarRisk/N$);
	if lotSize < 1 then lotSize = 1;
	lotSize = 1;
	StopLoss = 2 * N$ * lotSize;
	StopLossPts = 2 * N * lotSize;
	StopLossPts = 2000/bigPointValue;
	hh20 = highest(high,entryChanLen);
	hh55 = highest(high,absEntryChanLen);
	ll20 = lowest(low,entryChanLen);
	ll55 = lowest(low,absEntryChanLen);
end;
```

```
If mp <> 1 and mp[1] = 1 then
Begin
       tradeProfit = ExitPrice(1) - EntryPrice(1);
       lastTradeLoser = true;
       If tradeProfit > 0 then lastTradeLoser = false;
       if debug then
              print(date," Long Trader ",tradeProfit
                 *bigPointValue," ",lastTradeLoser,
              " ExitPrice ",ExitPrice(1):6:6," entryPrice ",
                   entryPrice(1):6:6);
end;
If mp <> -1 and mp[1] = -1 then
Begin
       tradeProfit = EntryPrice(1) - ExitPrice(1);
       lastTradeLoser = true;
       If tradeProfit > 0 then lastTradeLoser = false;
       if debug then
              print(date," **** Short Trader ",tradeProfit
                 *bigPointValue," ",lastTradeLoser,
              " mp ",mp," ",mp[1]);
end;

If lastTradeLoserFilter = False then lastTradeLoser = True;

If lastTradeLoser = False then
Begin
       if debug then
              print(date," In Virtual Section And VirtTmp = ",virTmp);
       If(virtmp = 1) then
       Begin
           virtLongLiqPrice = maxList(lowest(low[1],
              exitChanLen),virtLongLoss);
              if(virtualLongExit(virtLongLiqPrice,1,
                   myFillPrice) =1) then
              Begin
                     tradeProfit = myFillPrice - virtBuyPrice;
                     If tradeProfit < 0 then lastTradeLoser
                           = true;
                     virtmp = 0;
                     if debug then print(" Long Exit @ ",
                           myFillPrice);
              end;
       end;
```

```
If(virtmp = -1) then
Begin
        virtShortLiqPrice = minList(highest(high[1],
           exitChanLen),virtShortLoss);
        if(virtualShortExit(virtShortLiqPrice,1,
              myFillPrice) =1) then
        Begin
                tradeProfit = virtSellPrice
                   - myFillPrice;
                If tradeProfit < 0 then lastTradeLoser
                      = true;
                virtmp = 0;
                if debug then print(" ShortExit @ ", myFillPrice);
        end;
end;
if(virtualBuy(highest(high[1],entryChanLen),1,
      myFillPrice) = 1) then
Begin
        if virtmp <> 1 then
        begin
                virtBuyPrice = myFillPrice;
                virtLongLoss = myFillPrice
                   - stopLossPts;
                virtmp = 1;
                tradeProfit = 0;
                If virtmp[1] = -1 then tradeProfit
                      = virtSellPrice - virtBuyPrice;
                If tradeProfit < 0 then lastTradeLoser = true;
                if debug then print(" Long @ ",
                      myFillPrice);
        end;
end;
if(virtualSell(lowest(low[1],entryChanLen),1,
      myFillPrice) = 1) then
Begin
        if virtmp <> -1 then
        begin
                virtsellPrice = myFillPrice;
                virtShortLoss = myFillPrice
                   + stopLossPts;
                virtmp = -1;
                tradeProfit = 0;
```

```
                If virtmp[1] = 1 then tradeProfit
                    =  virtBuyPrice - virtSellPrice;
                If tradeProfit < 0 then lastTradeLoser
                    = true;
                if debug then print(" Short @ ",
                    myFillPrice, " trade Profit" , tradeProfit);
            end;
        end;
        if debug then print("End of Virtual Module : virTmp
            = ",virTmp," ",lastTradeLoser);
end;

for iCnt = 0 to numPyraMids-1
begin
        if lastTradeLoser then
        begin
            if mp <> -1 and currentContracts = iCnt
                * lotSize then
            begin
                buyPrice = hh20 + iCnt * N/2;
            end;
            if mp <> 1 and currentContracts = iCnt
                * lotSize then
            begin
                sellPrice = ll20 - iCnt * N/2;
            end;
            virTmp = 0;
        end;

        if lastTradeLoser = false then
            begin
            if mp <> -1 and currentContracts = iCnt * lotSize then
            begin
                buyPrice = hh55 + iCnt * N/2;
            end;
            if mp <> 1 and currentContracts = iCnt * lotSize then
            begin
                sellPrice = ll55 - iCnt * N/2;
            end;
            virTmp = 0;
        end;
end;
```

```
if lastTradeLoser then
begin
       if currentContracts < numPyraMids * lotsize then
             Buy ("Turtle20Buy") lotSize contracts next
             bar at buyPrice stop;
       if currentContracts < numPyraMids * lotsize then
             Sellshort ("Turtle20Sell") lotsize contracts
             next bar at sellPrice stop;
       if currentContracts < 4 * lotsize and debug then
             print(date," 20sellPrice ",sellPrice:6:6," ",
             currentContracts);
end;

if lastTradeLoser = false then
begin
       if currentContracts < numPyraMids * lotsize then
             Buy ("Turtle55Buy") lotSize contracts next bar
             at buyPrice stop;
       if currentContracts < numPyraMids * lotsize then
             Sellshort ("Turtle55Sell") lotsize contracts
             next bar at sellPrice stop;
       if debug then print(date," ",iCnt," 55sellPrice ",
             sellPrice:6:6);
end;

If mp = 1 then Sell ("TurtleSys1LExit") from
      entry("Turtle20Buy") next bar at
      lowest(low,exitChanLen) stop;
If mp = -1 then BuyToCover("TurtleSys1SExit")from
      entry("Turtle20Sell")  next bar at
      highest(high,exitChanLen) stop;

If mp = 1 then Sell ("TurtleSys2LExit") from
      entry("Turtle55Buy") next bar at lowest(low,20) stop;
If mp = -1 then BuyToCover("TurtleSys2SExit")from
      entry("Turtle55Sell")  next bar at
      highest(high,20) stop;

If mp = 1 then Sell ("TurtleLExit2N") next bar at
      entryPrice - stopLossPts stop;
If mp = -1 then BuyToCover("TurtleSExit2N") next bar at
      entryPrice + stopLossPts stop;
```

EasyLanguage Code for TA1

```
inputs:
cmiLen(20),cmiSmooth(9),markCondIndicVal(50),chopBuyPer(.5),
   chopSellPer(.5),trendBBOLen(9),trendSBOLen(9);

inputs: volLen(20)

value1 = choppyMarketIndex(cmiLen);
value2 = xaverage(value1,cmiSmooth);

if value2 < markCondIndicVal then
begin
       buy("ChopBuy")next bar at highest(h,trendBBOLen) stop;
       sellshort("ChopSell") next bar at lowest(l,
          trendSBOLen) stop;
end;

if value2 >= markCondIndicVal then
begin
       buy("TrendBuy") next bar at c + xaverage(range,
          volLen)*volPer stop;
       sellShort("TrendSell") next bar at c
          - xaverage(range,volLen)*volPer stop;
end;
```

EasyLanguage Code for TA2

```
Inputs: buyLen(40),sellLen(40),longLiqLen(20),sellliqLen(20);

Buy next bar at highest(h[1],buyLen) stop;
Sellshort next bar at lowest(l[1],sellLen) stop;

If Marketposition = 1 then sell next bar at lowest(low[1],
      longLiqLen) stop;
If Marketposition = -1 then buytocover next bar at
      highest(high[1],sellLiqLen) stop;
```

EasyLanguage Code for TA3

```
inputs:movAvgLen(50),pivotHiLookBack(10),pivotHiStrength(2),
   pivotLowLookBack(10),
pivotLowStrength(2);
inputs: LprofitObj(500),LstopLoss(500),longExitDays(10),
   SprofitObj(500),
SstopLoss(500),shortExitDays(10);
```

```
Value1 = swingHighBar(1,h,pivotHiStrength,pivotHiLookBack);
Value2 = swingLowBar(1,l,pivotLowStrength,pivotLowLookBack);
If c > average(c,movAvgLen) then
Begin
     If Value2 > -1 and marketPosition <> 1 then buy this
          bar on close;
end;

If c < average(c,movAvgLen) then
Begin
     If Value1 > -1 and marketPosition <> -1 then sellshort
          this bar on close;
end;
If Marketposition = 1 then
Begin
     sell("L-profitObj") next bar at entryPrice
        + LprofitObj/Bigpointvalue limit;
     sell("L-protStop") next bar at entryPrice
        - LstopLoss/Bigpointvalue stop;
     If Barssinceentry >= longExitDays then sell this bar
          on close;
end;
If Marketposition = -1 then
Begin
     Buytocover("S-profitObj") next bar at entryPrice
         - SprofitObj/Bigpointvalue limit;
     BuyToCover("S-protStop") next bar at entryPrice
         + SstopLoss/Bigpointvalue stop;
     If Barssinceentry >= shortExitDays then sell this
          bar on close;
end;
```

APPENDIX E

A list of George's favorite books on Algorithmic Trading:

Oldies

- **Computer Analysis of the Futures Market** by LeBeau and Lucas
- **New Concepts in Technical Trading Systems** by Welles Wilder
- **The Elements of Successful Trading** by Robert Rotella
- **Portfolio Management Formulas** by Ralph Vince
- **Trading Systems and Methods** (any edition) by Perry Kaufman
- **Trading Systems That Work** by Thomas Stridsman
- **Money Management Strategies for Futures Traders** by Nauzer Balsara
- **Street Smarts: High Probability Short-Term Trading Strategies** by Linda Bradford Raschke and Laurence A. Connors
- **New Market Timing Techniques** by Tom DeMark
- **How I Made One Million Dollars Last Year Trading Commodities** by Larry Williams
- **Trading for a Living** by Alexander Elder
- **How to Make Money in Commodities** by Chester Keltner

Newbies

- **Quantitative Technical Analysis** by Dr. Howard Bandy
- **Modeling Trading System Performance** by Dr. Howard Bandy
- **Evidenced-Based Technical Analysis** by David Aronson

- **Statistically Sound Machine Learning for Algorithmic Trading of Financial Instruments** by David Aronson and Timothy Masters
- **The Evaluation and Optimization of Trading Strategies** by Bob Pardo
- **Building Winning Algorithmic Trading Systems** by Kevin Davey
- **Trading Systems: A New Approach to System Development and Portfolio Optimization** by Emilio Tomasini
- **Algorithmic Trading** by Ernie Chan
- **Building Reliable Trading System** by Keith Fitschen
- **Using EasyLanguage 9.X** by Murray Ruggiero

Programming Books

- **Python Programming** by John Zelle
- **Genetic Algorithms and Investment Strategies** by Richard Bauer
- **Mastering VBA for Microsoft Office** by Richard Mansfield
- **Python for Finance** by Yves Hilpisch

ABOUT THE COMPANION WEBSITE

All of the source code for the trading algorithms, data, and testing platforms is included on the Wiley website.

In addition, the website www.georgepruitt.com will provide updates to the trading algorithms, data, and testing platforms. You will also find more tools to add to your toolbox that weren't mentioned in the book. Questions can be directed to George using his george.p.pruitt@gmail.com email address.

INDEX

Note: Page references followed by f, t, and b indicate an illustrated figure, table, and box respectively.

A

Absolute price oscillator (APO), 57
ACCEPT state, 16–18, 20–21
Adaptation in Natural and Artificial Systems (Holland), 230
ADX. *See* Average Directional Movement Index
ADXR, 29
AFL. *See* AmiBroker Function Language
Algorithm
  backtesting
    Excel, usage, 145
    Python, usage, 167
  CCI algorithm, trades (generation), 50f
  codes. *See* EasyLanguage; TradeStation.
  criteria, 1–2
  defining, 1
  development, 1
  flowchart (FC), stochastic oscillator crossover (entry signal usage), 45f
  genetic algorithms, identification, 228–230
  mean reversion algorithm, equity curve, 108f
  parameters
    comparison, 94t
    results, 245t
    sets, 96t–97t
  pseudocode, example, 6
  ramp-up data, insufficiency, 158f
  RSI algorithm, performance, 38t
  stochastic algorithm, performance, 47t
  trading algorithm, example, 7b–8b
Algorithmic traders, programmer ability, 2
Algorithmic trading, books (source), 335–336
Algo Testing Software, example, 3b
AmiBroker, 293
  debugging, Exploration (usage), 295–298
  Exploration, results, 296f
  functions, 295
  keywords, 293–294
  loop programming, 139–140
    code, sample, 140f
  Monte Carlo settings dialog, 262f
  Monte Carlo simulation, 261–264
  position sizing, futures mode, 298–299
  walk-forward optimizer, usage, 107f
AmiBroker Function Language (AFL), 113
  array programming, 120–129
  Automatic Analysis dialog box, 138f
  backtest, parameters (setting), 126f
  broker integration (feature), 114
  Check icon, 125f
  code samples, 141–143
  Code Wizard
    Add item, 134f
    button, 133f
    Edit Rule dropdown list, 135f
    window, 133f
  data, 114
    algorithm, application, 126f
    types, 115–116

AmiBroker Function Language (AFL) (*Continued*)
Editor, 114
auto-completion tool, 124f
function helper, 124f
launching, 122f
window, example, 123f
Edit Rule pane, parameters (change), 136f
error warning, 125f
expressions, 116–117
results, 117–118
features, 113–114
initiation, 113–118
integrated development environment (IDE), 114
knowledge, programmer requirements, 115–118
operators, 116–117
precedence, 117–118
parameters, setting, 126f
portfolio results, 128
power (feature), 114
price (feature), 113
request (sending), exclamation point (clicking), 137f
Send to Analysis window icon, 126f
Set Futures mode, 127f
simple moving average crossover, 120
speed (feature), 114
syntax, 129–133
3-D optimization chart, 130f
trade-by-trade report, 128f
usage, 227–230
variable naming, 116
variables, 115–116
names, restrictions, 115
Wizard, 133–139
(AmiBroker keyword)
flow control structures, 294–295
Analysis phase, 125
Analysis window, 129, 131
Annual return, performance metric, 91
APO. *See* Absolute price oscillator
Appels, Gerald, 53, 56b
ApplyStop function, 132
Arguments, usage, 161f
Arithmetic expressions, 116
ASCII
database (futures prices), 121
data importer, 114
ATR. *See* Average true range
Auto-generated formula, 135, 137
Average (VBA function), 160–161
Average Directional Index (ADX), 29
Average Directional Movement Index (ADX), 26–32
14-day ADX, calculation, 28–29
length, 28
trend detector function, 29f
Averages, 24
Average true range (ATR), 11b, 272
ATR Sell MOC, 35b, 46b, 49b, 52b, 56b
BuyToCover MOC, 40b, 46b, 49b, 52b, 56b
5X ATR profit objective, usage, 165–166
lookback, parameter (change), 282
multiplier, parameter (change), 281
3X ATR stop, usage, 164, 165–166
2 ATR, usage, 69
usage, 70–71
Averaging methods, performances, 59, 62
avgLen, default value, 124
avgMP, 119
AvgTrueRange, 208

B

Backtest
equity curve, profit (display), 283f
parameters, setting, 126f
performance report, 279f
Backtest button, 129
Backtester settings, example, 262f
Backtesting
Excel, usage, 145
software structure, 149–154
flowchart, 150f
Bandy, Howard, 114
Bars held, performance metric, 91
BASIC. *See* Beginner's All-purpose Symbolic Instruction Code
BBandBot, 124
BBandTop, 124
Beginner's All-purpose Symbolic Instruction Code (BASIC), 145, 154
Berkely, George, 243
Berlinski, David, 1
bin increment (binInc) variable, 267
binTuple, 267
Bollinger algorithm
benchmark, 73
optimization, 104t
Bollinger Bands, 62–68
algorithm
best parameter sets, 74t
version 1 (performance), 65t
version 2 (performance), 68t
breakout, 93t

calculation
2 standard deviations, usage, 63
60 days standard deviation, usage, 63
data, Keltner Channel data (comparison), 71f
example, 90b
function, 196
Function Module, 319
optimization, 72f
routine, defining, 148f
60-day, two-SD Bollinger Band, example, 63f
subroutine, 160–161
system, example, 9b–10b
trend algorithm, 64
trend follower function, 63b–64b
BollingerBand subroutine, 147
Bollinger Benchmark, Keltner Challengers (contrast), 74t
Bollinger, John, 62
Bollinger performance, three-dimensional contour chart, 98f
Boolean expression, 116
Boolean flags, usage, 15b
BOTTOM failure, 39
bottoming out, term (removal), 6
Building Reliable Trading Systems (Fitschen), 264
buy (AmiBroker keyword), 293
Buy-and-hold mentality, 26
BUY order, 121
buyprice (AmiBroker keyword), 293
buy (keyword), recognition, 4

C

CCI. *See* Commodity Channel Index
CFDT. *See* Cumulative frequency distribution table
change (keyword), recognition, 4
Choppy Market Indicator (CMI), 243–244
Chromosomes
crossing, VBA Excel (usage), 238–240
dartboard
creation, VBA Excel (usage), 236
example, 236
dart-throwing blindfolded monkey (simulation), VBA Excel (usage), 236–237
finding moms and pops, VBA Excel (usage), 238–240
fitness of chromosomes (testing), VBA Excel (usage), 232–233
genes allocation process, VBA Excel (usage), 240
genes passage, 240f
initial population setup, VBA Excel (usage), 232
mutation, 240–243
VBA Excel, usage, 242–243
population, 231
probability of being hit by dart calculation, VBA Excel (usage), 235
replacement function, VBA Excel (usage), 237–238
reproduction, 238–240
selection, 233–238
slice size, 234
fitness conversion, VBA Excel (usage), 235
class (object), 176
ClassicShell, 169
class rsiClass(object):, 317–318
class stochClass(object):, 316–317
Cluster analysis. *See* Walk-forward optimization
CMI. *See* Choppy Market Indicator
Code, arguments (presence), 161f
Code Wizard. *See* AmiBroker Function Language
Coincident indicator performance, 54t
Combination lock (workings), finite statement machine modeling, 17f
Comment text, usage, 157f
Commitment of Traders Report (COT), 111
commName, 183
Commodity Channel Index (CCI), 48–53
algorithm
coincident indicator performance, 54t
example, 221–222
performance, 51t
trades, generation, 50f
OB/OS system description, 49b–50b
profit objective, usage, 327
protective stop, usage, 327
system, usage, 53f
trend following system, 52b
p-code, 52b
20-day CCI, calculation, 48
Computer language, syntax (understanding), 2
Conditional execution, 294–295
Connors/Alvarez, time-based exit (usage), 327–328
Consecutive bar exact sequence paradigm, 12, 21
Consecutive bar sequence, 21–23
COT. *See* Commitment of Traders Report
cover (AmiBroker keyword), 293
Cover arrays, 121–122
coverprice (AmiBroker keyword), 293
Crossover rate, 247
Crude oil, 60-day, two-SD Bollinger Band (example), 63f
Cumulative daily equity/drawdown, plotting (example), 153f

Cumulative frequency distribution table (CFDT), 265
curBar (sAverage function parameter), 172
Curve fitting, 227
  prevention, 247–249
Customize Ribbon, 154

D

Daily bars (pivot high points), strength differences (examples), 13
Dartboard
  creation, VBA Excel (usage), 236
  example, 236f
Dart-throwing blindfolded monkey (simulation), VBA Excel (usage), 236–237
Data arrays (ESB), 301
Data arrays (PSB), 309
DataMaster worksheet, usage (example). *See* Excel System Backtester
DC. *See* Donchian Channels
Definiteness (algorithm criteria), 1
Dependencies, nesting, 221f
Developer tab option, example, 155f
Directional movement (DM), 26–29
  algorithm, 31f
    performance, 33t
  concept, introduction, 26
  examples, 27f
  system description, 30b–31b
Directional Movement Index (DX), 29
DM. *See* Directional movement
DMA. *See* Double simple moving average
dnSum (variable), 177
Donchian algorithms, results, 103t, 105t
Donchian Channels (DC), 90b
  breakout, 93t
Donchian lengths, Donchian Channel breakout (usage), 93t
Double simple moving average (DMA) algorithm, 95
Double simple moving average (DMA) crossover, 89b
  algorithm, 92t
downward, term (removal), 6
Draw down. *See* Trade draw down
DX. *See* Directional Movement Index

E

EasyLanguage, 203, 204, 323
  abbreviations, 212t
  algorithm codes, 325–334
  chart, strategy application, 213f
  codes, usage, 333–334
  comments, 209
  Connors/Alvarez, time-based exit (usage), 327–328
  editor, 206f
    line number display, 219f
  editor, usage, 208f
  functions, 324–325
  inputs, change (process), 215f
  keywords, 212t, 324–325
  mean reversion strategy (change), input variables (usage), 215f
  profit objective, usage, 326–327
  project
    creation, 220f
    strategy, addition, 220f
  protective stop, usage, 326–327
  remarks, 209
  reversion analysis strategy, 214f
  samples, 221–224
  SKIP words, 209
  strategy
    adjustment process, 215f
    algorithm, dependencies/functions (nesting), 221f
  syntax, 209–221
  Turtle, LTL filter/pyramiding/position sizing (usage), 328–332
Editor. *See* AmiBroker Function Language
  line number display (EasyLanguage), 219f
Edit (keyword), recognition, 4
Effectiveness (algorithm criteria), 2
ELD files
  importing, 323–324
  reimporting, 273
EMA. *See* Exponential moving average
End Of Day (EOD)
  data feeds, 114
  historic database, 151
Entry logic, 7b
Entry rules, template (example), 9b–10b
EOD. *See* End Of Day
equityClass, 188, 310–311
Equity curve
  chart, maximum drawdown (display), 280f
  creation, 247
  example, 107f
  mean reversion algorithm, 108f
  multiple randomized equity curves, chart, 263f
  pattern system, 109f
  profit, display, 283f
  stops, addition, 288f
EquityStream worksheet, macro (launch), 153f

ES. *See* Exhaustive search
ESB. *See* Excel System Backtester
Eurocurrency downturn, CCI system detection, 53f
Excel
data, 148–149
worksheet, example, 151f
ribbon, customization, 155f
usage, 145. *See also* Visual Basic for Applications.
Visual Basic Editor, example, 156f
ExcelSystemBackTester, 152
Excel System Backtester (ESB), 145, 301
components, 149, 151
data arrays, 301
DataMaster worksheet, usage (example), 152
EquityStream worksheet, macro (launch), 153f
functions, 302–308
keywords, 302
programming environment, 154–163
Results worksheet, trades/performance metrics listing, 153f
source code, 147
subroutines, 302–308
VBA code, 155–163
ExcelSystemTester, functions/subroutines, 148
exclude (AmiBroker keyword), 293
Exhaustive search (ES)
algorithm, parameters (results), 245t
Exhaustive search (ES) optimization engines, 228
Exit
procedure, 162
rules, template (example), 10b–11b
Exit logic, 7b–8b
exitPos function, 180
Exploration
results, 296f
usage, 295–298
Exponential moving average (EMA), 58–62
Expressions
AmiBroker Function Language (AFL), 116–117
arithmetic expressions, 116
logical expressions, 116
results, 117–118

F

Failure swing algorithm, performance, 43t
Failure swing system description. *See* Relative Strength Index
Fast %D, 42
Fast %K, 42
filter (AmiBroker keyword), 294
filterTrade variable, 67
Finding moms and pops, VBA Excel (usage), 238–240
Finiteness (algorithm criteria), 1
Finite state machine (FSM), 16, 24
code, example, 224–226
diagram, 17–18
modeling, 17f, 18f
Fitness conversion, VBA Excel (usage), 235
Fitness of chromosomes (testing), VBA Excel (usage), 232–233
Fitschen, Keith, 264
5X ATR profit objective, usage, 165–166
Fixed Fractional, 272
formula, 283
money management overlay, 281–284
parameters, change, 281–282
Flowchart (FC), 21, 24
example, 22f
usage, example, 23f
Flow control structures, 294–295
for loop, 139, 184, 186
for-loop, 174
FORTRAN, 168
14-day ADX, calculation, 28–29
14-day RSI, calculation, 32, 34
14-day stochastic (FAST), calculation, 42
FSM. *See* Finite state machine
Functions
definition, colon (usage), 172
Functions, nesting, 221f
Future leak, advantage, 148
Futures mode option, 127
Futures prices, ASCII database, 121

G

Garbage in garbage out (GIGO), 152
Generation, 231
concepts, 230
Genes allocation process, VBA Excel (usage), 240
Genetic algorithms (GAs)
concepts, 230
crossover rate, 247
curve fitting, prevention, 247–249
generations, 246
identification, 228–230
mutation rate, 246
population size, 246
usage, 243–247
Genetic optimization (GO), 95, 227
getData(), 182
GetData (ESB component), 149
Graphical user interface (GUI), 168

H

head (variable), 185
Helper functions (PSB), 180–181
Hermawanto, Denny, 228, 230
Highest Function/Module, 318
Hindsight, usage, 253f
Histogram pivot points, usage, 55f
Histogram system. *See* Moving Average Convergence Divergence
Holland, John, 230
How to Make Money in Commodities (Keltner), 69

I

IDE. *See* Integrated development environment
Identifiers (PSB), 310
IDLE. *See* Integrated DeveLopment Environment
Indicator.py, 171–179
Indicators
  categories, 25
  classes/functions (PSB), 315–319
input (algorithm criteria), 1
InSampleBarsPerRun, 253
In-sample (IS) testing, 250–251
In-sample (IS) time period
  Bollinger algorithm, optimization, 104t
  Donchian algorithm, results, 103t
  portfolio, parameters, 104t
Instruction ste, variability, 14–15
Integrated development environment (IDE), 114
Integrated DeveLopment Environment (IDLE), usage, 169–170
IS. *See* In-sample
Iteration growth rate, parameters (example), 229f

J

Janeczko, Tomasz, 114

K

Kaufman, Perry, 86
Keltner Challengers, Bollinger Benchmark (contrast), 74t
Keltner Channel, 69–75
  algorithm, best parameter sets, 75t
  calculation
    2 ATR, usage, 69
    60 days, usage, 69
  data, Bollinger Bands data (comparison), 71f
  optimization, 73f
  trend follower function, 69b–70b
Keltner, Chester, 69
Keywords (EasyLanguage), 212t

L

Lagging indicator, 25
Lambert, Donald, 48
Lane, George C., 42
LastBarOfMonth (LBM) pattern, 110b
Last trade was a loser filter (LTLF), 79, 262
  absence, 80
    examples, 81t, 82t
  engagement, 86
  inclusion, examples, 83t, 85t
  usage, 328–332
LBM. *See* LastBarOfMonth
Limit (lmt) order, 161
Lists, initiation (PSB), 181–182
load (keyword), recognition, 4
Logical expressions, 116
Long division procedure, example, 4–5
Long entries, 9b–10b
Long entry signal description, 13–14
  usage, 14f
LONG position, establishment, 16
Long position exit instruction (TradeStation), 218
lookback (sAverage function parameter), 172
Loops, 294
  programming. *See* AmiBroker loop programming.
Lowest Function/Module, 319
LTLF. *See* Last trade was a loser filter

M

MACD. *See* Moving Average Convergence Divergence
Macro, ESB launching, 153f
MarginDeposit, 123
margindeposit (AmiBroker keyword), 294
marketDataClass, 187, 311
  objects, 186–187
marketDataClass() method, 185
Market on Close (moc), 21
  order, 162
Market (mkt) order, 162
Markets To Test, opening, 171
marketSystemClass, 188
MAS. *See* Multi-algorithm strategy
maxContractPoints, 223
maxContractProfit, 223
Maximum drawdown, display, 280f, 282f
Maximum quantity, parameter (change), 282
Mean reversion (MR), 109b
  algorithm, equity curve (usage), 108f
  strategy (change), input variables (usage), 215f
MeanReversion (name), 220

Mini Russell day trading system, narrow range day (usage), 110f
mmStop defaults, 132
MOC. *See* Time-based market order
moc. *See* Market on Close
Money management, 271
  Fixed Fractional money management overlay, 281–284
  stop, exit procedure, 162
Money Management window, 281
  parameters, change, 283f
Monte Carlo analysis, 227, 258–264, 322
Monte Carlo settings, AmiBroker Monte Carlo settings dialog, 262f
Monte Carlo simulation
  AmiBroker Monte Carlo simulation, 261–264
  distribution statistics, 264t
  implementation, Python (usage), 259–261, 265–269
Monte Carlo source code, 320–322
Monte Carlo straw broom chart, 263f
Moving Average Convergence Divergence (MACD), 53–58
  calculation, 12-day/26-day moving averages (usage), 55
  histogram system, 56b–57b
Moving averages
  crossover algorithm, 88
  double simple moving average (DMA) crossover, 89b
    algorithm, 92t
  exponential moving averages, 58–62
  simple moving averages, 58–62
  single simple moving average (SMA) crossover, 89b
    algorithm, 91t
  triple simple moving average (TMA) crossover, 89b–90b
    algorithm, 92t
  20-day moving averages, examples, 59f
  200-day moving average, 5
  weighted moving averages, 58–62
MR. *See* Mean reversion
Multi-algorithm strategy (MAS), 108–111
Multiple randomized equity curves, chart, 263f
Mutation, 240–243
  concepts, 230
  occurrence, 240–241
  rate, 246
  VBA Excel, usage, 242–243
myAvg, 115
myCondition, variable (initiation), 210
myDayCount, 158
MyFirstPortfolio, 277f, 288
MyFirstStrategyGroup
  list, 277f
  selection, result, 277f
myProfitTarg, 158
MySecondAlgoWizard, 137
mySum, 115
myTickValue, 163
myTrueRange, 148
myValue, 130–131

N

Narrow range day, usage, 110f
Net profit, performance metric, 90
New Concepts In Technical Trading Systems (Wilder), 26
New Trading Systems and Methods (Kaufman), 86
Number of trades, performance metric, 91
numcolumns (AmiBroker keyword), 294

O

OB/OS system description. *See* Commodity Channel Index
offset (sAverage function parameter), 172
OOS. *See* Out-of-sample
Operators
  AmiBroker Function Language (AFL), 116–117
  precedence, 117–118
Optimization
  genetic optimization, 227
  parameter sets, 98t
  3-D optimization chart, 130f
Optimize button, 129
Orders, types, 161–162
Oscillators, 25, 26
  crossover, entry signal usage. *See* Stochastics.
Outlining, 206
Out-of-sample (OOS)
  in-sample (IS), ratio, 102
  number of bars, 253
  percentage, 256
  report, 257t
  testing, 251–252
    example, 252t
  time period, Donchian algorithm results, 103t, 105t
  timespan, 104–105
OutOfSampleBarsPerRun, 253
output (algorithm criteria), 1

P

Paintbar, 206
Paradigms, example, 12–23
Parameters
  Bollinger performance, three-dimensional contour chart, 98f
  change, 136f
  comparison, 94t
  sets, 96t–97t
    optimization usage, 98t
    robust parameter sets, presence, 247f
  setting, 126f
  stress, 248
Partner matching probability, 238
Pattern system, equity curve, 109f
p-code, 36b, 46b
Percentage price oscillator (PPO), 57
Percent Risk, parameter (change), 281
Performance metrics, 90–91
  example, 153f
Peters, Tim, 170
Pivot bar, strength (basis), 13
Pivot high points, strength differences (examples), 13f
Pivot point entry algorithm, example, 19b
Pivot-point long-entry algorithm, FSM modeling, 18f
PM. *See* Portfolio Maestro
pointvalue (AmiBroker keyword), 294
Population, 231
  concepts, 230
  initial population setup, VBA Excel (usage), 232
  size, 246
Portfolio
  AFL results, 128f
  algorithm, usage (decision), 101–108
  analysis, 271, 284–290
  backtesting, preparation, 279
  composition, 100–108
  correlation matrix, portion, 100f
  equity curve, stops (addition), 288f
  parameters, 104t
  profit targets, examples, 286f, 287f
  sample, Turtle system 2 (example), 85t
  Settings, 285f
  setup, PSB (usage), 182–193
  stop loss
    appearance, 287f
    setting, 286f
  stop option, 287f
  trades, stops
    exclusion, 289t
    inclusion, 289t
portfolioClass, 187–188, 313–315
Portfolio Maestro (PM), 203, 271, 272–290
  backtest performance report, 279f
  equity curve chart, maximum drawdown (display), 280f
  fixed fractional money management overlay, 281–284
  launch window, 273f
  Manage Strategy Group button, indication, 278f
  Money Management window, parameters (change), 283f
  MyFirstPortfolio, 277f
  MyFirstStrategyGroup, selection, 277f
  portfolio
    analysis, 284–290
    backtesting, preparation, 279f
    equity curve, stops (addition), 288f
    profit targets, examples, 286f, 287f
    stop loss, appearance, 287f
    stop option, 287f
  Portfolio Settings, 285f
  position size, profit/drawdown (correlation), 284f
  Returns and Equity tab, maximum drawdown (display), 282f
  strategy group, 273–274
    list, 277f
    settings, adjustment, 278f
    strategy, addition, 274f
  Strategy Group settings button, 278f
  symbol, addition, 275f
  Total P/L option, 281f
  Trade Analysis window, trading statistics display, 280f
  Turtle 55 strategy, appearance, 274f
  UGTATS list, selection, 275f
  UGTATS Market List, 274–281
  UGTATS markets, symbols, 276f
Portfolio Profit Target, impact, 287
Portfolio sample, Turtle system 1
  last trade was a loser filter (LTLF)
    absence, 81t, 82t
    inclusion, examples, 83t, 85t
positionscore (AmiBroker keyword), 294
PositionSize, 123
positionsize (AmiBroker keyword), 294
Position size, profit/drawdown (correlation), 284f
Position sizing, 99–100
  futures mode (AmiBroker), 298–299
  usage, 328–332

PPO. *See* Percentage price oscillator
Predictive indicator, 25
Price bar interface, 118–120
  reserved words, 118
Price-based indicators, 25, 58
prices (sAverage function parameter), 172
Probability of being hit by dart (calculation), VBA Excel (usage), 235
Problem solving, 230–231
Profit factor, performance metric, 91
Profit/loss, performance metric, 91
Profit objective, usage, 326–327
Programming environment, 154–163
Protective stop, usage, 326–327
PSB. *See* Python System Backtester
PSBBollinger, opening, 170
Pseudocode, 5–6
  algorithm pseudocde, 6
  conversion process, 12
Pyramiding, usage, 80, 328–332
Python
  code, example, 6
  dynamic typing, 168–169
  installation, 169
  interpreted language, 168
  shell, presence, 168
  usage, 167, 259–261, 265–269
    reasons, 167–169
  user's group, presence, 169
Python Monte Carlo simulation, 261
Python Programming (Zelle), 168
Python System Backtester (PSB), 168, 309
  Bollinger Bands Function Module, 319
  classes, 310–315
  class rsiClass(object):, 317–318
  class stochClass(object):, 316–317
  configuration, 182–193
  data arrays, 309
  data import, 182–193
  equityClass, 310
  helper functions, 180–181
  Highest Function/Module, 318
  identifiers, 310
  IDLE, usage, 169–170
  import section, 179–193
  indicator classes/functions, 315–319
  indicator.py, 171–179
  installation, 169–170
  keywords, 310, 320–322
  lists, 309
    initiation, 181–182
  Lowest Function/Module, 319
  marketDataClass, 311
  Monte Carlo
    analysis, 322
    source code, 320–322
  portfolioClass, 313–315
  portfolio setup, 182–193
  rsiClass, 174–178
  sAverage, 172–174
    function, parameters, 172
  Simple Average Function/Module, 319
  Start Trade Drawdown
    section, 320–321
    source code, 320–322
  structure, 171–193
  SystemTester.py, 178–179
  tradeInfoClass, 311–313
  usage, 193–202
  variables, initiation, 181–182

Q

Quantitative Trading Systems (Bandy), 114

R

rampUp, 157
Ramp-up data, insufficiency, 158f
Random number generator (RNG), 231, 239
  tool, 258–259
  usage, 260
Range
  function, 174
  10-day average, calculation, 111b
Real Time data feeds, 114
Relative strength (RS), 34–35
Relative Strength Index (RSI), 5, 24, 32–42
  algorithm, performance, 38t
  divergence, example, 39f
  failure swing algorithm, performance, 43t
  failure swing system description, 39b–41b
  14-day RSI, calculation, 32, 34
  pivots, value, 41
  profit objective, usage, 326
  protective stop, usage, 326
  system
    description, 35b–36b
    p-code, 36b
  trading algorithm, flowchart (FC) diagram, 37f
  usage, example, 35f
  VBA function, 161
removeDuplicates, 192
Replacement function, VBA Excel (usage), 237–238
Reproduction, 238–240
  concepts, 230

Reserved words, 118
Results worksheet. *See* Excel System Backtester
Reversal, algorithm exit procedure, 162
Reversion analysis strategy (EasyLanguage), 214f
Risk aversion, 64, 66
Risk of ruin (RoR)
  calculation, 88
  competitors, examples, 89b–90b
  impact, 87–88
RNG. *See* Random number generator
Robust parameter sets, presence, 247f
RoR. *See* Risk of ruin
roundlotsize (AmiBroker keyword), 294
Round quantity, parameter (change), 282
RSI. *See* Relative Strength Index
rsiClass, 174–178
Ruin, risk
  calculation, 88
  impact, 87–88
Run menu, 199
run (keyword), recognition, 4

S

sAverage, 172–174
  function, parameters, 172
save (keyword), recognition, 4
Selection (chromosomes), 233–238
Selection of the fittest, concepts, 230
sell (AmiBroker keyword), 293
Sell arrays, 120–121
SELL order, 121
sellprice (AmiBroker keyword), 293
Send To Analysis, 125
setSysMarkInfo, 190
Sharpe ratio, performance metric, 91
short (AmiBroker keyword), 293
Short entries, 9b–10b
shortprice (AmiBroker keyword), 293
short (keyword), recognition, 4
Simple Average Function/Module, 319
Simple moving average crossover algorithm, 88
Simple moving average crossover system
  AFL usage, 120
  3X ATR stop, usage, 164
Simple moving averages, 58–62
Single simple moving average (SMA) crossover, 89b
  algorithm, example, 91t
SKIP words, 209
Slow %D, 42
Slow %K, 42
Slow stochastic system description, 46b
SMA. *See* Single simple moving average
Source code, initiation, 157f
Standard deviation (SD) Bollinger Band, 62
START state, 16–18, 20–21
Start Trade Drawdown, 264–269
  analysis, 90–91
  calculation, 265
  source code, 320–322
Stochastic (STO), 25, 42–47
  algorithm, performance, 47t
  14-day stochastic (FAST), calculation, 42
  oscillator crossover, entry signal usage, 45f
  profit objective, usage, 326–327
  protective stop, usage, 326–327
  slow stochastic system
    description, 46b
    p-code, 46b
  trading algorithm, flowchart (FC) diagram, 44f
  usage, examples, 41f, 60t–61t
  VBA function, 161
Stop loss, setting, 286f
Stop (stp) order, 161
Strategy Group
  concepts, 273
  creation, 281
Straw broom chart, 263f
Subroutines. *See* Visual Basic
  returns, 161
  values, 161
Symbol List, creation, 275
Syntax
  AmiBroker Function Language (AFL), 129–133
  EasyLanguage, 209–221
  errors, list (TradeStation), 219f
Sys Drawdown, performance metric, 90–91
systemMarket, 191
systemMarketClass, 189
System TA2, WFO default settings (usage), 252–254
SystemTester module, 155
SystemTester.py, 178–179

T

TA. *See* Trading algorithm
TDE. *See* TradeStation Development Environment
10-day average, calculation, 111b
TestSystem (ESB component), 149, 151
3D Optimization chart, 129
3D Optimization chart, 130f
3X ATR stop, usage, 164
ticksize (AmiBroker keyword), 294

Time-based market order (MOC), exit procedure, 162
TMA. *See* Triple simple moving average
TOP failure swing, occurrence, 39
TotalBarsPerRun, 253
Total P/L option, 281f
Total transaction costs, performance metric, 91
TP. *See* Typical price
Trade Analysis
  tab, 279
  window, trading statistics display, 280f
Trade-by-trade report, 128f
Trade draw down, initiation, 264–269
tradeInfoClass, 311–313
Trades
  example (generation), RSI (usage), 35f
  generation (example), stochastics (usage), 41f, 60t–61t
  signals (initiation), histogram pivot points (usage), 55f
  skipping, 149
TradeStation, 113, 323
  algorithm codes, 325–334
  Connors/Alvarez, time-based exit (usage), 327–328
  dates/times, storage, 212
  functions, 324–325
  keywords, 324–325
  long position exit instruction, 218
  Portfolio Maestro (PM) launch window, 273f
  profit objective, usage, 326–327
  protective stop, usage, 326–327
  syntax errors, list, 219f
  Turtle, LTL filter/pyramiding/position sizing (usage), 328–332
  usage, 227–230
TradeStation Development Environment (TDE), 203, 204
  algorithm, 208f
  code verification/recalculation, confirming message, 218f
  EasyLanguage editor, 206f
  initial screen, 205f
TradeStation IDE, 204–209
  home screen, 204f
  trading apps, 205f
tradeTuple, 261, 266
Trading
  idea, pseudocode conversion process, 12
  statistics, display, 280f
  system development, genetic algorithms (usage), 243–247
Trading algorithm 1 (TA1), EasyLanguage Code (usage), 333
Trading algorithm 2 (TA2)
  EasyLanguage code, usage, 333
  WFA report, 254t
Trading algorithm 3 (TA3)
  EasyLanguage code, usage, 333–334
  WFO report card TA3, 257t
Trading algorithms, 77
  describing/programming, 12
  example, 7b–8b
  flowchart (FC)
    example, 78f
    usage, example, 23
  programming, Boolean flags (usage), 15b
  RSI trading algorithm, flowchart (FC) diagram, 37f
  stochastic trading algorithm, flowchart (FC) diagram, 44f
Trading Blox testing platform, 82, 84
Trend
  detector, function, 29f
  follower, 63b
  following system. *See* Commodity Channel Index.
  trading, 86–100
Trend follower function
  Bollinger Bands, 63b–64b
  Keltner Channel, 69b–70b
Trigger, incorporation, 44
Triple simple moving average (TMA) crossover, 89b–90b
  algorithm, 92t
True range (TR), 28
Turtle 55 strategy, appearance, 274f
Turtle, LTL filter/pyramiding/position sizing (usage), 328–332
Turtle system
  examples, 79b
  LTLF
    absence, examples, 81t, 82t
    inclusion, examples, 83t, 85t
  trading algorithm flowchart, example, 78f
12-day moving averages, usage, 55
20-day CCI, calculation, 48
20-day moving averages, examples, 59f
26-day moving averages, usage, 55
Typical price (TP), 48, 69

V

Variable bar liberal sequence paradigm, 12, 21
Variable bar sequence, 13–21
  depiction, long entry signal description, 14f

Variables, 115–116
initiation (PSB), 181–182
names, restrictions, 115
Vars statement, 210
VBE. *See* Visual Basic Editor
Visual Basic Editor (VBE), 154
example, 156f
Visual Basic for Applications (VBA)
average, function, 160–161
code. *See* Excel System Backtester.
code, comment text (usage), 157f
comments, ending, 157f
error message, example, 158f
Excel, usage, 232–240
functions/subroutines, 147–148
RSI function, 161
source code, initiation, 157f
stochastic function, 161
usage, 113
Volatility
cycle, function, 84
usage, 64

W

Walk forward, 227
Walk-forward analysis (WFA), 250
forward roll, graphic representation, 251f
report, 254t
Walk-forward efficiency (WFE), 254
Walk-forward optimization (WFO), 106, 228
cluster analysis, 256–258
cluster results matrix, 256f
default settings, usage, 252–254
entries/exits code, 255
examples, 249–258
in-sample testing, 250–251
TA2, example, 251t
out-of-sample (OOS)
report, 257t
testing, 251–252
example, 252t
report card TA3, 257t
Walk-forward optimizer
usage, 107f
value, 249–258
Walk-forward performance, equity curve (example), 107f
Walk-forward testing
backtest, usage, 106f
out-of-sample (OOS) time period, 105t
steps, 105
Weighted moving averages, 58–62
WFA. *See* Walk-forward analysis
WFE. *See* Walk-forward efficiency
WFO. *See* Walk-forward optimization
Wilder, J. Welles, 26, 30, 32, 35

Z

Zelle, John, 168

d by CPI Group (UK) Ltd, Croydon, CR0 4YY
23/04/2025
0004